LINKAGE INC.'S BEST PRACTICES IN LEADERSHIP DEVELOPMENT HANDBOOK

Second Edition

LINKAGE INC.'S BEST PRACTICES IN LEADERSHIP DEVELOPMENT HANDBOOK

Second Edition

Case Studies • Instruments • Training

EDITORS

David Giber
Sam Lam
Marshall Goldsmith
Justin Bourke

Foreword by Warren Bennis

Pfeiffer
A Wiley Imprint
www.pfeiffer.com

Linkage
Unleash your full potential.

Published by Pfeiffer
An Imprint of Wiley
989 Market Street, San Francisco, CA 94103-1741
www.pfeiffer.com

For additional copies/bulk purchases of this book in the U.S. please contact 800-274-4434.

Pfeiffer books and products are available through most bookstores. To contact Pfeiffer directly call our Customer Care Department within the U.S. at 800-274-4434, outside the U.S. at 317-572-3985, fax 317-572-4002, or visit www.pfeiffer.com.

Pfeiffer also publishes its books in a variety of electronic formats. Some content that appears in print may not be available in electronic books.

Acquiring Editor: Matthew Davis
Marketing Manager: Brian Grimm
Production Editor: Mary Garrett/Susan Geraghty
Editorial Assistant: Lindsay Morton
Manufacturing Supervisor: Becky Morgan

Library of Congress Cataloging-in-Publication Data
    Linkage Inc.'s best practices in leadership development handbook: case studies, instruments, training / David Giber . . . [et al.], editors. — 2nd ed.
      p. cm.
   Includes bibliographical references and index.
   ISBN 978-0-470-19567-3 (cloth)
    1. Leadership—Case studies. 2. Strategic planning—Case studies. I. Giber, David J. II. Linkage Inc. III. Title: Best practices in leadership development handbook.
   HD57.7.L564 2009
   658.4'092—dc22
                                    2008041910

Printed in the United States of America
SECOND EDITION
HB Printing 10 9 8 7 6 5 4 3 2 1

CONTENTS

FIGURES, TABLES, AND EXHIBITS

Figures

Tables

Exhibits

FOREWORD

Warren Bennis

Developing leaders is an important activity, but it is elusive and difficult to pull off. In almost every aspect of the social sciences, "development" is always the most challenging area, whether it is economic, human, political, or psychological. Development means that things are always moving and evolving. We've come so far in leadership development, but there is still much to learn and so many possibilities. When I was coming up in this field, I remember my mentor, Douglas MacGregor, would say that organizations are transitive. His point was that one job would prepare you for the transition to the next. I believe that these wise remarks were well placed at the time, but perhaps not so anymore in the current structure of more complex organizations and niche roles.

Today, being in job A may not only fail to prepare you for job B but may eventually lead to stagnancy and possible regression in the less specific, more universal leadership competencies. In today's world, real leadership is getting you ready for anything. The fundamental challenge of leadership development at this time is how to create adaptive capacity. How do you teach people to be ready for anything? I believe that the leadership curriculum of the future needs to help people develop some broad generalist capabilities. Leaders may be anchored in one area they know really well, but they have to be able to integrate multiple perspectives. Here's a simple example: I have worked with the great department store Nordstrom, which has been around for over a hundred years and realizes that its winning capability is customer service. But in that organization today, understanding service is not enough. It needs leaders who can integrate customer service with merchandising and an understanding of how to create the products it offers. Being great at one part of the business is not enough. Many of the outstanding programs described in this book are trying to tackle this challenge of creating adaptive, integrative leaders.

Leadership development thinkers like George Hollenbeck and Morgan McCall have said that strategy has to drive the leadership qualities or competencies that an organization needs. I recognize that strategy may have to precede competencies so that the organization begins to recognize and reward leadership behavior aligned to its strategy. All of the programs in this book are strategic in this sense. But great leadership development still must be anchored in understanding individuals and the crucibles they encounter at work and in life. I am impressed with the work that I see from leadership practitioners in trying to address fundamental individual human elements like the need for self-understanding, judgment, or confident decision making. How do leaders, and indeed all of us, understand our talents, and not only what we are good at but what we love doing? This is the most basic formula for leadership success, and when this is achieved, one finds that as the great baseball athlete Nolan Ryan said, "Even on your bad days, you win." Helping people and organizations unlock their strengths is the most exciting part of our field. Understanding the ingredients of core human activities and strengths such as how to foster adaptive capacity, judgment, and decision making is where leadership development has room to grow.

For all of us in this field, it is a balance. On the one hand, we need to recognize the limitations of our leadership development practices in terms of all the variables and complexity we cannot control. On the other hand, we need to keep our aspirations high. At the University of Southern California, where I teach, we have followed more than five hundred people from my honors course over the past thirteen years. Our data show that this one course helped people by influencing their worldview, it helped determine their choices and decisions, and for some, it affected their career trajectory. The multifaceted programs examined in this book are ones that can and do make a difference, though we may have to track people over the long term to see what affected them and why. They provide great examples of how far we have come and set the challenge of how far we have to go.

◆ ◆ ◆

Warren Bennis is a distinguished professor of business administration and founding chairman of the Leadership Institute at the University of Southern California. He has authored numerous books in the field of leadership development, most recently *Judgment: How Winning Leaders Make Great Calls* with Noel Tichy, and *Transparency* with Danny Goleman and James O'Toole.

INTRODUCTION

David Giber

In 2000 Louis Carter, Marshall Goldsmith, and I organized the case studies for the first edition of *Linkage Inc.'s Best Practices in Leadership Development Handbook*. It is useful to reflect on what we found then as we reviewed the outstanding case studies and research captured in that book. First, we found that the most significant differences between those examples could be derived from a general preference for one of the following: the individual, the team, or the organization and its strategy.

Analyzing the programs in this new edition, we found that many more of them had incorporated common program ingredients that have been proven widely and continuously since 2000. Many were using at least one or more element (for example, assessment or coaching) to have an impact on the individual, while at the same time using other elements (action learning, simulations) to have an effect on teamwork. Most leadership programs seem to include many, if not all, of the elements of assessment, coaching or mentoring, action learning (even if it is more individually based), use of internal leaders as faculty, and a global perspective. The elements are used systematically and more fluidly. The ubiquitous nature of these elements meant we had to dig deeper to find programs that we felt were unique and had high impact. We looked for programs that quite often contained all of the core components gleaned from best practices but also emphasized at least one major element particularly well. We took a different tack in this edition by including overall studies of such critical areas as assessment, developing women leaders, and global leadership. In addition, we have found that many programs have more focus on such areas as improving processes to drive change and innovation and to build networks.

The challenge to practitioners today that we believe this edition's contributors have answered for their organizations is: How do I create a unique and memorable impact on individuals, teams, and eventually the organization? How can I take one avenue or aspect of experience and infuse it with something that creates learning and behavioral change?

This is what I call *creating a signature experience*. The experience has an impact on both the heart and the mind; it challenges and alters thinking and embeds itself in the memory and behavioral repertoire of the participant. This edition presents outstanding examples of such signature experiences. The socialization process at Bank of America is an outstanding example of an organization that has built a unique, multifaceted approach to the challenge of on-boarding executives and accelerating their transition to key roles. The chapter from Dell not only provides a multileveled approach to leadership development, but includes a description of an in-depth coaching program that was global and long-term in scope. The strategic team process at McKesson combines both leaders teaching leaders and a team-based, action learning process into a dynamic, high-impact combination. From a government perspective, the case study of the Victoria Department of Treasury and Finance provides a thoughtful approach to connecting leaders to their mission and strategy through a well-structured process for team building and process improvement. The Executive Quality Leadership Development program of Johnson & Johnson, Action Learning Forums of Cisco Systems, and the cascading Real World Work process at Humana build depth in these organizations' strategic, quality, and problem solving, aiming at nothing less than transformational change. The Land O'Lake's example contains not only an excellent use of action learning, but an innovative approach called the Leadership Edge, where participants grapple with a series of customer and market challenges. Yahoo!'s program incorporates most key best practices while focusing on reinforcing the corporate culture and keeping the unique values of Yahoo! alive. The Macy's chapter shows a unique take on tailoring the design and implementation of various leadership development programs for different levels and functions in the organization and how these programs can tie in to create a high-performing system. Finally, the chapter from PricewaterhouseCoopers shows how a well-designed and effective leadership development experience can elicit steadfast engagement and commitment from all levels of the organization.

The depth of these programs reflects the increasing demand on leadership development practitioners to create impact and link leadership development to business results. In Chapter One, Rich Rosier identifies the processes, mental models, and business considerations that weigh into the design of a leadership development system and shows the individual steps to creating a leadership development strategy that fully aligns with the organization's values and objectives. And to take it to the next step, Chapter Two by Marshall Goldsmith and Kelly Goldsmith on helping people achieve their goals shows how to execute a leadership development strategy by making it easier for leaders to stay committed and tenacious in reaching their development goals.

To achieve lasting impact, the connection to succession and talent systems must be strong. In Chapter Three, Stephen Miles provides a comprehensive overview of the state of the assessment field and the potential for connecting it to longer-term leadership bench strength issues.

These challenges are magnified on the global level. In Chapter Six, Mick Yates's brilliant and provocative discourse on leadership in a global world provides practical examples of leadership development in global organizations while connecting them to larger questions of the qualities that leaders need to develop and foster in others. Yates raises the issue that leadership programs need to encourage innovation, engagement, and what he terms "networks of trust." Today's leadership development practitioner needs not only to develop high-impact experiences, but also to determine how to use the organization's internal and external networks to share best practices across disciplines and geographies. More important, these networks need to be, according to Yates, "actionable, searchable, and trustworthy." Responding to pressures of this sort, Humana uses a consortium model to share learning, tools, and services. Chapter Five by Scott Anthony, Kevin Bolen, and associates from Innosight points out the measurable value of such networks in fostering innovation. This challenge of how to network learning so that the impact is multiplied is one we have only begun to address in this volume.

In addition to globalization comes an increase in diversity. This represents a strong advantage for growing organizations, but also one that is strongly dependent on the ability of a leadership development system to meet the unique development needs of different demographics. Chapter Seven, by Maya Hu-Chan, Patricia Wheeler, and Tracey Wik, on investing in women, shows how different groups face different challenges and how these challenges can be addressed, resulting in personal empowerment and greater value for the organization.

Back in 2000, we had defined a six-phase approach to leadership development:

1. Business diagnosis
2. Assessment
3. Program design
4. Implementation
5. On-the-job support
6. Evaluation

Although this approach is still relevant, we find much greater emphasis and innovation today in the areas of assessment, creating interactive and highly challenging program designs, and making more means available for follow-up support and evaluation of impact. In Chapter Four, Robert Fulmer and Jared Bleak provide support for these and other trends. They emphasize the focus of top companies on aligning their leadership development programs with succession management and on holding line management responsible for the results.

We hope that this second edition expands and extends the perspective that many readers found useful in our first collection. It is rewarding to see that in some way, books such as these have spread the best practices of leadership development around the world. We thank all our contributors for sharing their learning and experience and for their willingness to be part of this global leadership development practitioner's network.

LINKAGE INC.'S BEST PRACTICES IN LEADERSHIP DEVELOPMENT HANDBOOK

Second Edition

PART ONE

DEFINING LEADERSHIP DEVELOPMENT

CHAPTER ONE

CONTEXT, CULTURE, AND COMPLEXITIES

Best Practices Versus Best Fit

This chapter outlines the most proven approaches to leadership development and shows how to maximize the use of these approaches by identifying the future needs of the organization and its leaders and leveraging this context to create an overall strategy that is "best-fit," not just "best-practice."

When it comes to developing the leaders within an organization, the stakes are high, and the potential payoff is enormous. This chapter focuses on the creation of a systemic approach to leadership development that is aligned with an organization's strategy, culture, and the critical initiatives required for future competitiveness.

An effective leadership development system is crucial to the long-term success of any organization. It can build sustainable competitive advantage for organizations that take the time and make the effort to design and implement the system.

Since developing leaders takes years, the leadership development system needs to be built around the future leadership needs of the organization and appropriately adjusted to reflect changes in strategy. At the macrolevel, a systemic approach to leadership development is based on four strategic questions:

1. What capabilities will our leaders need to have in three to five years?
2. What capabilities do our leaders currently have? What gaps do we need to fill between our current capabilities and those required in the future?
3. What do we need to do to develop our leaders?
4. How do the components and processes of our overall human resource (HR) system need to be aligned with our leadership development system for maximum return on investment?

Based on these questions, those who are designing a leadership development system need to:

1. Identify future leadership requirements
2. Assess current leadership capabilities to identify the gaps
3. Build and reconfigure the tools, activities, and processes of leadership development, talent management, and performance and succession management in order to develop the necessary leadership capability for the future

Figure 1.1 illustrates the step-by-step process for designing leadership development as well as the key HR processes that need to be aligned with the leadership development system.

FIGURE 1.1.   ALIGNING LEADERSHIP DEVELOPMENT WITH STRATEGIC HR COMPONENTS

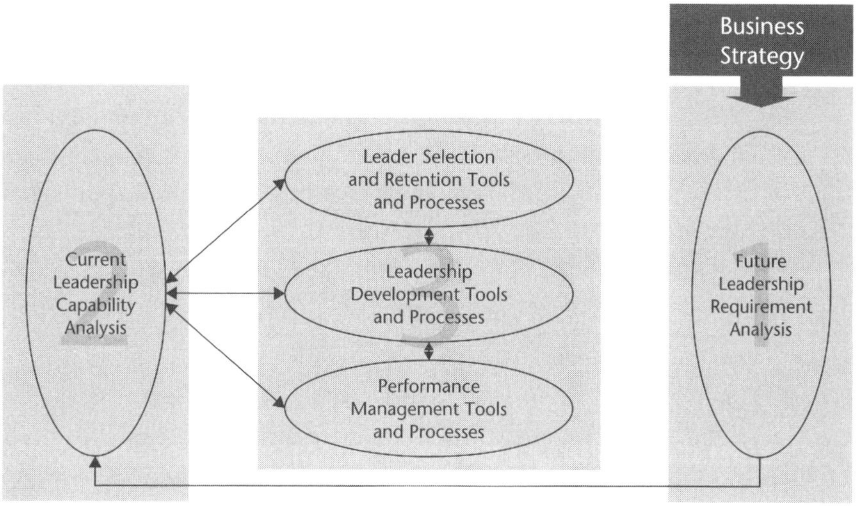

Business Strategy

The design of a best practice leadership development system must begin with an assembly of the "right people" who are critical stakeholders in the overall architecture of the system. In best practice organizations, this "leadership development council" is typically made up of key members of the executive team, business unit and functional staff leaders, members of the board of directors, and in some instances key customer or supplier representatives. By involving these key stakeholders from the beginning, these organizations face fewer difficulties with issues of "buy-in" and senior leader support that can plague organizations. In addition, involvement at this level leads to much easier adoption of another leadership development best practice: leaders teaching leaders.

The first job of the leadership development council is to conduct a thorough review (if it already exists) or lead the construction (if it does not exist) of the organization's future strategy. Although this chapter does not go into the details of creating a well-crafted strategy, the leadership development council should address the following questions in analyzing the organization's future "business strategy":

- What is the organization's most desirable future state? (vision)
- Why does the organization exist? (mission)
- What will the organization do better than any other organization in the world? (strategy)
- How will the organization achieve its strategy? (business and operating plans)
- What future expectations exist among key stakeholders? (goals)
- What common factors guide all employees of the organization as they execute their work? (values)

Once there is clarity and agreement among the key stakeholders with respect to these questions, the leadership development council is ready to proceed to the next step in the process.

Future Leadership Requirement Analysis

The future leadership requirement analysis determines the critical capabilities required of leaders to deliver on the organization's future strategy. Once these leadership capabilities are identified, they serve as the foundation for the relevant HR processes that must be aligned with the leadership development tools and processes in order to deliver the leaders required to execute future strategy. Only if the analysis of the future leadership requirements is accurate will the rest of the leadership development system be built effectively and contribute to the future success of the organization.

The involvement of the leadership development council is critical in the future leadership requirement analysis. Research has shown that top-performing organizations are 35 to 50 percent more likely to have CEO and board-level involvement than average-performing companies.

The work of conducting the future leadership requirement analysis can be summarized in three steps:

Step 1: Identify organizational opportunities and challenges based on a thorough review of the future strategy.

Step 2: Identify the future outputs that leaders will need to produce in order to capitalize on the opportunities and overcome the challenges.

Step 3: Identify the future leadership competencies and capabilities required to produce these outputs at the highest quality levels.

In today's best practice organizations, the identification of critical leadership outputs and competencies is always oriented toward future business strategy rather than backward to the outputs and competencies that distinguished superior leaders in the past.

Depending on the amount of time and resources, both personnel and financial, that the organization can allocate to the identification of the outputs and competencies, there will be a continuum of options to choose from. On the relatively inexpensive end of the continuum, you can facilitate a deductive process using a card deck or generic output dictionary to efficiently and effectively identify the core outputs the leaders will need to produce to execute the business strategy. On the other end of the continuum, you can assemble a team of industrial/organizational psychologists or other skilled professionals to use a combination of interviews, observation, surveys, external benchmarking, and other data-gathering tools to produce the required outputs. There are numerous examples of best practice organizations that have used the full continuum of options to generate the list of their leader's future outputs.

The same continuum of options is available to build the leadership competency model. Again, we have identified best practice organizations that achieved their success using any of the various approaches. Nevertheless, all had a leadership competency model as the foundation of their leadership development system. If you choose to develop a leadership model internally, we recommend using an experienced and effective facilitator, members of the leadership development council, and a competency dictionary or card deck (which represents a number of common competencies) as a starting point. The process typically unfolds as follows:

Step 1: Based on the previous identification of the leader's future outputs, whittle the complete card deck or competency list (through a card sorting process) down to the core seven to ten competencies that the team concludes are the most critical in enabling leaders to deliver these outputs.

Step 2: Define the organization-specific knowledge, skills, and behaviors associated with each competency. This step ensures that the accompanying competency definitions and descriptors accurately capture how a superior performer exhibits that competency in the organization.

Step 3: Create a rating scale for each competency that distinguishes the various proficiency levels in which the competency is observed. The key in this step is to develop clear, specific, reliable, and one-dimensional behavior anchors to describe each point on the rating scale.

Step 4: Create a matrix worksheet. List the outputs (one output per row) in the far-left column and the competencies (one competency per column) across the top.

Step 5: Starting with the first competency, discuss with the team how critical this competency is to producing each of the outputs. Rate its criticality on a scale of 1 to 5, with (1 = unnecessary and 5 = critical). Repeat this process for each of the competencies identified.

Step 6: When the matrix is completed, each column should contain at least one 5, and each row should contain at least one 5. (If not, review the selected outputs or competencies and reconsider those choices.)

Step 7: Once you are confident that you have identified the competencies that are most critical to delivering the superior quality outputs required to execute the future business strategy, the final step is to graphically depict the competencies in a model that will be shared throughout the organization.

The future business strategy has been clarified and the corresponding leadership outputs and competencies that are required to successfully execute that strategy have now been identified. Next is conducting an accurate assessment of the organization's current leadership capabilities.

Current Leadership Capability Analysis

The current leadership capability analysis evaluates the capabilities of the organization's leaders against the identified future leadership requirements. The resulting assessment is used to identify the strengths and development opportunities that exist between the current leadership capabilities and those required in the future.

Typically organizations tend to focus their leadership assessment work at the level of individual leaders. They do this by designing or purchasing assessment tools that in the best practice organizations tie directly to the leadership competency model. Among the many individual leadership capability assessments are these:

- Multirater leadership assessments or 360-degree feedback assessments
- Personality, style, and motive assessments
- Specialized inventories (e.g., decision-making assessments, IQ/EQ tests, potential derailers)
- Assessment center data
- Internal observations and interviews with peers, managers, subordinates, customers, and relevant others
- Past performance reviews and appraisals

Although individual leadership competency assessments are an important component of the current leadership capability analysis, they should not be the only focus. A systemic approach to leadership development requires an analysis of leadership capability and performance from both an individual and an organizational perspective.

Best practice organizations use a variety of tools to analyze current organizational performance to inform their assessment of current leadership capability—for example:

- Culture assessments
- Employee satisfaction surveys
- Customer surveys
- Employee turnover and exit interview analysis
- Financial analysis of actual performance versus goals

- Aggregate utilization rates of development opportunities
- Impact analysis of developmental experiences versus results

A thorough and objective analysis of current leadership capability allows the leadership development council not only to identify the critical gaps that need to be closed through a well-integrated leadership development system, but also to highlight the shortfalls, if any, that the previous developmental experiences have produced in terms of improved results. The best practice organizations are constantly monitoring the return on investment of their leadership development tools and processes and the results that leaders produce. In addition, they work extremely hard to ensure that the other critical HR processes are aligned so that they are successful in accomplishing their overall objective of increasing the quantity and quality of existing and future leaders.

Leader Selection and Retention Tools and Processes

In order to efficiently and effectively develop the quantity and quality of the organization's leadership cadre, best practice organizations ensure that their leader selection and retention tools and processes are fully aligned with their leadership development, performance, and succession management tools and processes.

The first step in this phase of the design is to identify which leadership competencies are easier and more cost effective to hire than to develop. Practitioners with experience in this domain recognize that although it is debatable as to whether certain competencies are innate and therefore cannot be developed, few (if any) would debate that those same competencies are acquired fastest and cheapest by hiring leaders who are already highly proficient. As a colleague once said, "You might be able to train a turkey to climb a tree, but why not just hire a squirrel?"

Although the distinctions made in the first step are important, the next step is to ensure that all key stakeholders in the hiring process are aware of the newly created or revised leadership competency model. This also implies that there must be a coordinated approach to support all stakeholders involved in the assessment of leader candidates against that competency model. To save time and money, we recommend using the same tools and processes that were developed or tailored in the assessment of the current leadership capability to inform leader selection decisions.

In addition to the organization's own work on leader selection, the quantity and quality of the leadership bench are determined by the number of great leaders the organization already has. Through our research at Linkage, we have found that the best practice organizations maximize their retention of great leaders by focusing on six satisfiers:

1. *Work, role, and objectives.* Do the job functions, outputs, and responsibilities fit my needs and expectations?
2. *Salary and benefits.* Does the remuneration match my needs and expectations—and what the marketplace will pay?
3. *Career development.* Does the level of learning and growth meet my needs and expectations?
4. *Team.* Do I fit with and relate to the team and my manager?
5. *Culture.* Do the values, operating principles, and beliefs of the organization fit mine?
6. *Work/life balance.* Does the job permit me to strike an acceptable balance between work and personal life?

Finally, the leader selection and retention tools and processes provide the organization with the ability to predict leadership turnover percentages and to set an ideal mix of internally developed and externally acquired leadership talent in accordance with the future leadership requirement analysis. When properly aligned, the leader selection retention tools and processes will enable the organization to:

- Recruit and select on the basis of the critical leadership capabilities.
- Balance short-term and long-term recruiting. Strategic recruiting and hiring are needed to build capacity for future.
- Identify targets for internal promotion and external recruitment for all levels of management.
- Identify those with high potential on the basis of evidence that they possess the critical leadership capabilities.

- Predict leadership turnover percentages for all levels.
- Ensure that leaders who are hired have the tools and knowledge to become effective and successful as quickly as possible.

In parallel with the work to align and implement leader selection and retention tools and processes that are tied to business strategy, future leadership requirements, and current leadership capability, best practice organizations are working on aligning and implementing their leadership development tools and processes.

Leadership Development Tools and Processes

The goal of leadership development tools and processes is to maximize the internal leadership talent available within the organization. Best practice organizations use the model in Figure 1.2 to guide their design and implementation of their work in this phase:

◆ ◆ ◆

- *Individual leadership capability assessment.* This assessment is the process of evaluation and assessment of individual leaders' capabilities to meet the current and future needs of the organization.
- *Individual development planning.* This aligns the individual's development activities and learning with capabilities the organization has determined he or she will require for success as a leader currently and in the future.
- *Individual career pathing.* This process provides a map defining the expectations to be met by an individual in order to move up in the organization. Career pathing identifies specific job assignments and projects that can provide the individual with the sequential steps of experience, skill, and capability building needed to attain specific career goals.
- *Comprehensive set of leadership development experiences.* An effective leadership development system needs to provide flexibility of choice through a range of learning experiences designed to meet the needs of a variety of users of the system based on their current competency level and their level of experience as a leader. That range of activities

FIGURE 1.2. LEADERSHIP DEVELOPMENT TOOLS AND PROCESSES

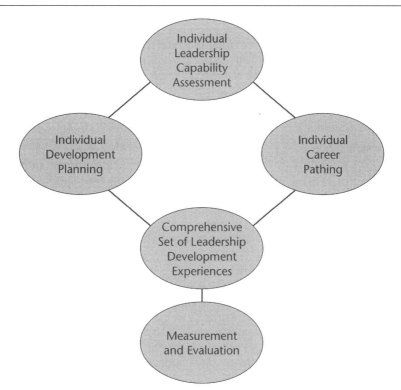

needs to include those shown in Table 1.1. Best practice organizations often create a leadership development resource guide that provides an overview of the development experiences available for each of the key leadership competencies by individual development goal and level. A list of development options from which the individual leader can choose is provided for each competency or capability.

- *Measurement and evaluation.* A well-functioning leadership development system contains measurement and evaluation of key elements. This measurement and evaluation are normally focused on changes in leadership behavior resulting from the leadership development system. However, measurement and evaluation also need to include elements of organizational performance considered indicative of critical elements of leadership by the executive sponsors of the leadership development system.

TABLE 1.1.   LEARNING EXPERIENCES FOR LEADERSHIP DEVELOPMENT

Development Activities	Characteristics
On-the-job activities	Focused on learning by doing
	Include specific practices that people can apply to their day-to-day activities (for example, people who need to develop their ability to focus can track the amount of time they spend doing planned versus unplanned activities)
	Designed and selected for that person to develop a specific competency (example: international assignment)
Project assignments	Focused equally on output and learning
	Offer the individual the opportunity to become part of a project team to practice new competencies or further develop current competencies
	Example: A variation of a project assignment is an action learning project
Competency-specific training courses	Designed as an internal or external course
	Provide participants the opportunity to develop specific competencies
	Example: Linkage "Advanced Consulting Skills" workshop
Leadership development programs[a]	Designed to provide leaders at various levels of the organization with a common learning experience, a common vocabulary for leadership, and an opportunity to make contact with people across the organization
	Provide high-performing leaders three to ten days of intensive training
Coaching	Designed to provide leaders one-on-one feedback to enhance their existing capabilities
	Focused strictly on the needs of an individual
	Used for very senior people because it is expensive
Mentoring	Focused often as much on the social aspect (such as networking) as on the development of competency
	Provides process through which a mentor helps the individual to enhance his or her overall potential in the context of the organization

[a]This is the one that most people jump to when thinking about developing leaders.

Performance Management Tools and Processes

The performance management tools and processes focus on the delivery of outcomes required for the current and future success of the organization. They encourage and reward leaders at all levels to develop their own capabilities and those of their team members in alignment with the future capabilities identified in the future leadership requirement analysis.

The following factors are critical for the alignment of performance management tools and processes:

- The goals being set include key business results and reinforce the critical leadership capabilities.
- Successful completion of the individual development plan is a critical element in the performance management process.
- Individuals who focus on their own development are rewarded by the compensation system.
- Managers are accountable to developing leaders at all levels of the organization.
- Managers who spend time helping develop their people are recognized and rewarded for doing so.

The performance management tools and processes provide an evaluation of the extent to which the individual leader embodies the critical leadership capabilities in his or her annual performance.

We have included the quick assessment in Tables 1.2, 1.3, and 1.4 for monitoring the extent to which key HR processes that make up an overall leadership development system are kept in alignment and are working in concert to achieve the desired overall objective of increasing the quantity and quality of your leadership cadre.

Directions

Step 1: Read the questions in Tables 1.2, 1.3, and 1.4, and rate each question on the scale provided by circling what best represents your organization.

Step 2: Total the scores for each of the three areas, and identify the area with the lowest score.

Conclusion

Conventional knowledge stipulates that a combination of the methods set out in this chapter represents the most effective way to develop leaders in an organizationwide context. It is important to realize, though,

TABLE 1.2. RATING TALENT MANAGEMENT TOOLS AND PROCESSES

How Aligned Are Your Talent Management Tools and Processes?	Certainly	Probably	Not Sure	Probably Not	Certainly Not
Do you recruit and select on the basis of critical leadership capabilities?	5	4	3	2	1
Do you balance short-term and long-term recruiting?	5	4	3	2	1
Have you identified targets for internal promotion and external recruitment for all levels of management?	5	4	3	2	1
Do you identify those with high potential on the basis of evidence that they possess the critical leadership capabilities?	5	4	3	2	1
Does your organization predict turnover percentages for all levels?	5	4	3	2	1
Do you ensure that newly hired leaders have the tools and knowledge to become effective and successful as quickly as possible?	5	4	3	2	1
Total					

that this does not imply that all leadership development programs should be the same.

Designing and operating a leadership development system that works is much more than simply implementing a smattering of "best practice" methods identified by thought leaders in the field. A number of variables should be carefully considered based on the unique aspects of each organization, of which there are certainly many. Should facilitators be primarily external experts or internal executives? If external, how should they be selected? And if internal, what is the best way to ensure that facilitators possess teaching expertise to match their knowledge of the relevant content? Should leadership development programs be handled internally

TABLE 1.3. RATING LEADERSHIP DEVELOPMENT TOOLS AND ACTIVITIES

How Aligned Are Your Leadership Development Tools and Activities?	Certainly	Probably	Not Sure	Probably Not	Certainly Not
Are managers at all levels provided with feedback regarding their performance against the critical leadership capabilities?	5	4	3	2	1
Are you using an appropriate range of assessment tools, including 360-degree assessments, personality and style assessments, performance appraisals, managers' assessments, and interviews?	5	4	3	2	1
Does everyone at all levels have a recent individual development plan? Are the critical capabilities integrated into the development planning process?	5	4	3	2	1
Do career paths provide leaders with an opportunity to develop and apply the critical leadership capabilities?	5	4	3	2	1
Do leadership development activities provide leaders with a variety of opportunities to strengthen those critical leadership capabilities?	5	4	3	2	1
Do you identify and manage candidates for succession on the basis of their possession of the critical leadership capabilities?	5	4	3	2	1
Total					

or externally, and if external, which vendors offer the best choices for the organization? Which leaders should be targeted with these initiatives? How can accountability be incorporated into the system? These are just some of the questions that all leadership development practitioners must ask.

Designing a leadership development system is first and foremost dependent on a deep knowledge of the ideal leadership qualities in the organization and the current status of the talent around those qualities. Next comes

TABLE 1.4.   RATING PERFORMANCE MANAGEMENT TOOLS AND
PROCESSES

How Aligned Are Your Performance Management Tools and Processes?	Certainly	Probably	Not Sure	Probably Not	Certainly Not
Do the goals include key business results and reinforce the critical leadership capabilities?	5	4	3	2	1
Is the successful completion of the individual development plan a critical element in the performance management process?	5	4	3	2	1
Are individuals who focus on their own development rewarded by the compensation system?	5	4	3	2	1
Are managers held accountable for developing leaders at all levels of the organization?	5	4	3	2	1
Are managers who spend time developing their staff recognized and rewarded for doing so?	5	4	3	2	1
Do the performance management tools and processes provide data regarding the extent to which individual leaders embody the critical leadership capabilities?	5	4	3	2	1
Total					

an understanding that a leadership development system is more than just the sum of its parts. Rather than having a series of mutually exclusive programs, everything must be completely aligned and fit together like puzzle pieces. The most important lessons from this chapter are as follows:

◆ ◆ ◆

- *The key to an effective leadership development infrastructure is variety.* There must be a number of learning methods and interventions incorporated into the system to account for several factors. First, no two learning styles are the same. Second, some approaches may be better for top senior leaders (such as coaching), while others may be more appropriate for those with high potential (such as leadership development programs or peer mentoring). Finally, having a variety of options for participants will likely increase the chances of positive engagement.

- *Leadership development should be a continuous process, not a series of "episodes."* It is easy to lose sight of a development plan or career path. Learning should be ongoing so that it is constantly at the front of the leaders' priorities and perhaps even incorporated into their work. This also ties in with variety: having a wide range of leadership development initiatives will likely allow practitioners to design ongoing systems that avoid becoming redundant.

- *Leadership development does not exist in a vacuum.* All efforts around leadership development should be tied in with other parts of the business. First, the system as a whole should be aligned with the objectives of the organization. If the company is going through change or is predicted to enter into a state of large-scale change over the next three to five years, then change leadership should be a top priority. Similarly, if improving innovation is a highly prioritized challenge, then at least some aspect of the leadership development system should be focused on building a culture of innovation. Second, it should be integrated into other processes of the organization. Leadership development is most effective when results are tied to both real performance and compensation or rewards. This ensures that leaders are able to see the results of their learning and that managers are held accountable for the development of their own leaders. Also, competency models and current gap analyses should be used in conjunction with talent management efforts, influencing the hiring of external candidates as well as the promotion of internal talent.

- *Leadership development must constantly be reviewed, measured, and scrutinized to ensure relevance.* Organizations change quickly, which means values and high-level strategies do too. At the same time, derailment, recruitment, and role changes cause leadership tiers to change as well. Leadership development is very much a dynamic process, and that requires careful attention to which systems work and which are becoming outdated. Measurement of leadership development efforts is also important for individual practitioners, who often must satisfy the expectations of various stakeholders who wish to see monetary results from the organization's investment.

About the Contributor

Rich Rosier is a principal consultant and senior vice president of Linkage. In this capacity, he has leadership and profit-and-loss responsibility for the educational programs business unit.

During his fifteen years in the leadership and organizational development industry, he has worked closely with renowned thought leaders, including Peter Drucker, Warren Bennis, Marshall Goldsmith, and Dave Ulrich. This, combined with his work with global best practice organizations, gives him a unique and authoritative expertise in the learning and development field.

He continues to serve as a core member of Linkage's executive team, under whose leadership Linkage has twice been named to the Inc. 500, a list of the fastest-growing private companies in the United States. He launched and led Linkage's international events business, founded Linkage Educational Resources and Linkage Press, coauthored with Warren Bennis a *Sloan Management Review* article entitled "Leading in Unnerving Times," and edited four volumes of the highly acclaimed *Competency Model Handbook*.

He is currently the moderator of the internationally subscribed Excellence in Management and Leadership Series featuring business and thought leaders such as Michael Porter, Rudy Giuliani, Jack Welch, Malcolm Gladwell, and Thomas Friedman.

CHAPTER TWO

HELPING PEOPLE ACHIEVE THEIR GOALS

This chapter outlines some of the common reasons that goals don't reach completion and gives practical advice for setting goals, both for yourself and for others, in a way that improves long-term engagement and increases the chances of successful execution.

In today's competitive world, top executives increasingly understand that sustaining peak performance requires a commitment to developing leaders throughout the organization. Leaders need to develop other leaders. An important part of this development process includes helping people set—and achieve—meaningful goals for personal change. All too often, however, goals are not set in a way that helps ensure the follow-through needed to turn great plans into successful outcomes.

Our research on goal setting and our experience in coaching have helped us better understand the dynamics of what is required to actually produce positive, long-term change in behavior. We believe that the lessons executive coaches have learned in helping their clients set goals apply to leadership development in a wide variety of settings. Whether you are a professional coach, a leader coaching your direct reports, a mentor advising a younger colleague—or just working on your own development—a better understanding of the dynamics of goal setting and the challenges of goal achievement may help you understand why people often set great goals yet lose the motivation to achieve them. This understanding can help ensure that the people you are coaching stick with the plan and ultimately reach their desired targets.

In this chapter, we focus primarily on behavioral goals, such as becoming a better listener or more effective at involving team members in decisions. Much of the published research in the field of goal setting involves health-related goals, such as losing weight. We show how many of the challenges that occur when changing behavior that is related to great health (such as more exercise) are similar to challenges that occur in changing behavior that is related to great leadership (such as more listening)!

Why do goal setters frequently give up in their quest for personal improvement? Most of us understand that New Year's resolutions seldom last through January—much less for the entire year. What goes wrong?

Six primary reasons explain why people give up on goals. Understanding these roadblocks to goal achievement can help you apply a little preventive medicine as you help others set goals—so ultimately they will be more likely to achieve their objectives for change.

Ownership

> I wasn't sure this idea for changing behavior would work in the first
> place. I tried it out—it didn't seem to do that much good. As I guessed,
> this was kind of a waste of time.

One of the most common mistakes in all leadership development is
the rollout of programs and initiatives that promise, "This will make you
better." A classic example is the performance appraisal process. Many
companies change their performance appraisal forms on a regular basis
with the promise that the "new and improved" form will lead to more
effective feedback. How much good effect do these changes usually have?
None! The new appraisal forms usually just confuse leaders and are seen
as annual exercises in futility. What companies don't want to face is the
real problem with the appraisal process—it is almost never the form.
The real problem is the managers who lack either the courage or the discipline required to deliver effective feedback.

The problem with "this will make you better" is that the emphasis
is usually on the "this" and not the "you." Leaders who want to help
their people develop as leaders need to communicate a clear message:
ultimately, only you can make you better.

Successful people tend to have a high need for self-determination.
In other words, the more leaders commit to coaching and behavioral
change because they believe in the value of the process, the more likely
the process is to work. The more they feel that the change is being
imposed on them—or that they are just trying it out—the less likely the
coaching process is to work.

In goal setting, you need to ensure that the change objectives come
from inside the person you are coaching—and are not just externally
imposed with no clear internal commitment. As executive coaches, we
have learned that our clients need to understand that they are ultimately
responsible for their own behavior. Leaders, who are also coaches, need
to communicate the same clear message.

Time

I had no idea this process would take so long. I am not sure it is worth it.

We all have a natural tendency to underestimate the time needed to reach targets. Everything seems to take longer than we think it should! When the time elapsed in achieving our goals starts exceeding our expectations, we are tempted just to give up on the goal. Busy, impatient professionals can be even more time-sensitive than the general population.

While the "optimism bias" about time is true of goal setters in general, it can be even more of a factor for leaders who are trying to change while the perceptions of coworkers seem to ignore their new behavior. We all tend to see people in a manner that is consistent with our previous stereotype—and we look for behavior that proves our stereotype is correct. Coworkers are no different from anyone else. Research reported in the Fall 2004 issue of *Strategy + Business* shows that the long-term follow-up and involvement of coworkers tend to be highly correlated with positive change in the perceived effectiveness of leaders. This positive change in perception does not occur overnight. Harried executives want to "check the box" and assume that once they understand what to do—and communicate this understanding to others—their problems are solved. If only the real world were that simple!

In helping others set goals, it is important for them to be realistic about the time required to produce a positive, long-term change in behavior. Habits that have taken forty years to develop will not go away in a week. Help them understand that others' perceptions may seem unfair and that—as they change their behavior—others may not recognize this change for months. If you help them establish realistic expectations in the goal-setting process, people will not feel there is something wrong with them or their coworkers when they face a time challenge. They will realize that this is a normal part of the change process. Ultimately, as the research shows, changed leadership behavior will lead to changed perceptions and more effective relationships with coworkers.

Difficulty

> This is a lot harder than I thought it would be. It sounded so simple when we were starting out.

The optimism bias of goal setters applies to difficulty as well as time. Not only do most achievements take longer than expected—they also require more hard work! Managers often confuse two terms that appear to be synonymous but are actually quite different: *simple* and *easy*. We want to believe that once we understand a simple concept, it will be easy to execute a plan and achieve results. If this were true, everyone who understood that they should eat a healthy diet and exercise regularly would be in shape. Diet and exercise books are almost always at the top of the best-seller lists. Our challenge for getting in shape—as well as changing leadership behavior—is not understanding; it is doing!

Long-term change in leadership effectiveness requires real effort. For example, it can be challenging for busy, opinionated leaders to have the discipline to stop, breathe, and listen patiently while others say things they do not want to hear. While leaders may understand the need to change—and even have a great desire to change—it is still hard to have the discipline to change.

It is critical to help goal setters understand that real change requires real work. Trying to get buy-in with statements like "this will be easy" or "this will be no problem for you" can make goal setters feel good in the short term but can backfire in the long term—when they finally realize that change is not that easy and begin to face trade-offs and challenges in their journey toward improvement. Helping goal setters understand the price for success in the beginning of the change process will help prevent the demoralization that can occur when challenges arise later in the change process.

Distractions

> I would really like to work toward my goal, but my company is facing a unique challenge right now. It might be better if I just stopped and worked on this goal at a time when things aren't so crazy!

Goal setters have a tendency to underestimate the distractions and competing goals that will invariably appear throughout the year. One good counsel you can give to the person you are coaching is, "I am not sure what crisis will emerge in the next year—but I am almost positive that some crisis will emerge!"

In some cases, the distraction or crisis may come from a problem; in other cases, it may result from an opportunity. For example, mad cow disease was a crisis for leaders in the meat-packing industry. It is hard to focus on long-term leadership development when the company is facing a short-term financial crisis! On the positive side, when Cabbage Patch Kids became a craze, the company started selling more dolls than anyone could ever imagine. It is hard to focus on long-term leadership development when your company has a once-in-a-lifetime short-term profit opportunity.

In planning for the future, coaches need to help goal setters assume that unexpected distractions and competing goals will occur. Leaders should expect the unexpected and build in time to deal with it. By planning for distractions and competing goals in advance, leaders will be far less likely to give up on the change process when either special problems or special opportunities appear.

Rewards

Why am I working so hard at becoming a more effective leader? After all my effort—we still aren't making any more money!

People tend to become disappointed when the achievement of one goal doesn't immediately translate into the achievement of other goals. For example, dieters who lose weight may give up on their weight loss efforts when prospective dates don't immediately become more attracted to them.

Hewitt Associates has done some fascinating research (summarized in *Leading the Way* by Robert Gandossy and Marc Effron) that documents the positive, long-term relationship between a company's investment in leadership development and its long-term financial success. By contrast, no research shows that investment in developing leaders produces greater short-term profits.

Increasing leadership effectiveness is only one factor in determining an organization's overall success. For example, a company may have the wrong strategy or be selling the wrong product. If a company is going down the wrong road, increasing people management skills will only help it get there faster.

Managers need to personally buy in to the value of a long-term investment in their own development. If they mistakenly believe that improving leadership skills will quickly lead to short-term profits, promotions, or recognition, they may become disappointed and give up when these benefits don't immediately occur. If they see personal change as a long-term investment in their own development—a process that will help them become more effective over the course of their careers—they will be much more likely to pay the short-term price needed for long-term gain.

Maintenance

I think I did actually get better when I was being coached, but I have let it slide since then. What am I supposed to do: work on this stuff for the rest of my life?

Once a goal setter has put in all the effort needed to achieve a goal, the reality of the work required to maintain changed behavior can be tough to face. One of the first reactions of many dieters on reaching their weight reduction goal is to think, "This is great! Now I can start eating again. Let's celebrate with some pizza and beer!" Of course this mind-set leads to future weight gain and the yo-yo effect that is unfortunately so common in dieters.

Leaders need to understand that leadership is a process, not a state. Leaders can never "get there." Leaders are always "getting there." The only way exercise helps people stay in shape is when they face reality: "I do have to work on this stuff for the rest of my life!" Leaders need to accept that their leadership development is an ongoing process that will never stop. Leadership involves relationships—when people change, relationships change—and maintaining any positive relationship requires ongoing effort over a long period of time. Relationships don't remain great because someone "got better" and stayed in this state of "betterness" forever—with no additional work.

Real Change Requires Real Effort

Leaders can help people set goals that increase their probability of lasting change—or they can help them set goals that may feel good in the short term but lead to disillusionment and giving up in the long term.

The typical advertisement or infomercial designed to help people get in shape provides a great example of what not to do in goal setting. The message is almost always the same: "For an incredibly small amount of money, you can buy a revolutionary product that is amazingly easy and fun to use. This product will produce fantastic results in almost no time, and you will have the body that you always wanted." Most infomercials imply that you will not have to continue exercising and dieting for years— that you will continue to look young—and that you will be a magnet for members of the opposite sex for the rest of your life!

In reality there is no easy answer. Real change requires real effort. The quick fix is seldom the meaningful fix. Distractions and competing responses are going to happen. The higher the level of the leader, the more likely it is that these things will happen. Improving leadership skills, like getting in shape, won't solve all of life's problems. And finally, great leadership is not a game that can be won in a year—it is a process that requires the commitment of a lifetime!

One of our great teachers, Paul Hersey, always said, "Leadership is not a popularity contest." An important component of leadership is coaching. Coaching should never become a popularity contest either. Coaches, whether inside the company or external, need to have the courage to tell the truth up front. By challenging people in the goal-setting process and helping goal setters face the difficult realities of lasting change, good coaches can go a long way toward ensuring that behavioral change becomes a reality and that goals don't become more New Year's resolutions that feel good for a few days but then disappear over time. This message may sound tough but at least it is real.

Successful people are not afraid of challenging goals; they just need to understand the true commitment that will be required to reach these goals. In fact, clear and specific goals that produce a lot of challenge—when coupled with a realistic assessment of the roadblocks to overcome in achieving these goals—can produce consistently strong long-term results.

The benefits of well-thought-out goal setting are clear. Honest, challenging coaches can help people make a real difference in both their organizations and the lives of the people they help.

Reference

Gandossy, R., and Effron, M. *Leading the Way.* Hoboken, N.J.: Wiley, 2003.

About the Contributors

Marshall Goldsmith has recently been named by the American Management Association as one of the fifty great thinkers and leaders in the field of management over the past eighty years. He has been featured in the *Wall Street Journal*, the *New Yorker, Forbes,* and the *Economist.* He is author or coeditor of eighteen books, including the best-seller *The Leader of the Future.* A modified version of this chapter appears in *Coaching for Leadership: The Practice of Leadership Coaching from the World's Greatest Coaches,* Second Edition (2005).

Kelly Goldsmith is a Ph.D. candidate in behavioral marketing at the Yale University School of Management. She is also conducting research for Yale's Center for Consumer Insights. Kelly is an honors graduate of Duke University. She has been a participant in *Survivor: Africa* and has worked as a casting associate for both *Survivor* and *The Amazing Race.*

CHAPTER THREE

ASSESSING THE LEADER

This chapter outlines and answers four key questions that identify how executive assessments can play a powerful impact for the leader and the organization when used properly in a comprehensive leadership development system.

Thanks to Michael Krot, associate principal of Heidrick & Struggles Leadership Consulting, for his work in handling the research, introduction, and review of this chapter.

This chapter is organized around four key questions. Through answering each, it becomes possible to develop an appreciation of the role a best practices approach to executive assessment plays in creating value for companies. First, *Why perform assessments?* Answering this question involves describing the different ways assessment can be used to improve the effectiveness of an executive—and in aggregate the effectiveness of a company. Second, *How do you identify what to assess?* Answering this question outlines how decisions are best made as to the capabilities, personality characteristics, and experiences an assessment process is designed to gauge, so that companies can be certain they are focusing on what matters. Third, *How do you measure what matters?* Knowing what might improve executive effectiveness is just half the battle, of course. If those precursors of high performance cannot be measured in a reliable and valid manner, the battle will be lost in the end. Answering this question provides guidance in regard to the steps necessary to ensure reliable and valid results. Finally, *How do you develop what matters?* Whereas the specific goals of executive assessment may vary from company to company and executive to executive, one common denominator is the opportunity to use the results to develop executive talent further. Answering this question gives rise to ideas for how best to leverage the assessment opportunity for developmental purposes.

As is true for many things, the best place to start is with a clear definition of *executive assessment,* a phrase loosely used to refer to a range of activities performed by companies, retained search firms, leadership consulting firms, executive coaches, and others. Executive assessment is a systematic process that should not be confused with the tools it uses. For example, performance appraisal systems, psychological and psychometric instruments, 360-degree feedback, and self-assessment instruments can be useful in conducting assessments, but each is simply a tool. Considered from a best practice perspective, executive assessment is a deliberate process through which data describing a candidate or a team are collected from multiple sources, analyzed using rigorous techniques, interpreted by experienced professionals, and finally used to reach a conclusion about the candidate's capabilities and potential and develop actionable recommendations to help realize the candidate's full potential.

The emphasis on assessment as a deliberate process cannot be understated. The single greatest distinction between a best practices approach and what is too often the approach adopted is the degree of scientific rigor deployed. Assessments are best thought of as research projects that must be conducted with rigor in order to deliver reliable and valid results to decision makers. Without rigor, the data collected may be incomplete or unreliable, the interpretation of the data may be biased or uninformed, and the resulting recommendations about capabilities and development are now fruit of the poisoned tree.

This chapter illustrates the importance of three elements that must be at the core of a best practices approach to assessment. First, the approach should be strategic in regard to the methodologies and tools chosen for data collection. Second, emphasis should be placed on identifying capable and experienced assessors, whether from inside the company or retained from another, to analyze, interpret, and then consult on the data. When understood this way, it becomes clear that assessment as defined here is typically reserved for top and high-potential executives due to the associated direct and indirect costs. Companies are willing to pay these costs because they recognize assessment is not simply an aid in their decisions around succession planning. Instead, the expense is an investment that is expected to yield a return. For this to happen, the third critical element of a best practices approach needs to be present: proper engagement from company management. This engagement is necessary because accurate assessments must be informed by a deep understanding of the company, its industry, and its strategy. Certainly this knowledge should be a criterion considered when selecting the right individuals to lead assessment, but even the most experienced assessor who brings increased objectivity to the process may not have the same depth of knowledge around these issues as fellow executives would.

Background

This review of what has been written about executive assessment as a process uncovered three useful treatments toward my purpose in this chapter. In the *2008 Pfeiffer Annual Leadership Development*, Adam Ortiz (2008) defined *executive assessment* as "a process that establishes criteria for an executive's success, measures those criteria on an individual-by-individual basis, and then provides input to help executives and their managers make decisions and form plans to enhance individual and organizational performance." Ortiz later suggests that simply administering the Myers-Briggs Type Indicator or 360-degree feedback is not an executive assessment. He emphasizes the importance of an assessor's bringing together sources such as behavioral interviews, personality and cognitive ability testing, simulations, and interview feedback and then identifying themes based on the many sources of information in combination. Ortiz described what he considers to be the constants of the executive assessment process: define what is to be measured through the assessment, ensure that people know what to expect, use the right tools to obtain the right information (behavioral interview, observations, tests and inventories), bring it all together, share the results, and make the most of the assessment investment.

Much of what has been written about executive coaching and leadership development considers assessment tools a necessary part of a best practice approach to developing leaders. For example, in *Coaching for Leadership*, Goldsmith and Lyons advise coaches to collect feedback as part of the coaching for behavioral change program, and they recommend interviewing key stakeholders for senior leaders and acknowledge that traditional 360-degree feedback is suitable for lower-level managers. However, there has been little systematic investigation of executive assessment as a process in this stream of research.

In the classic *Passing the Baton: Managing the Process of CEO Succession* (1987), Harvard professor Richard Vancil described a process for assessing internal candidates that is undertaken by CEOs with board oversight. The process entailed a series of conversations and challenges CEOs posed to the candidates over several years. This approach leverages the intuition and judgment of the incumbent CEO. It would be a stretch to characterize this approach to assessment of the potential of CEO successors as a formal executive assessment in the way I have defined them because it is not a systematic research process.

Over time I have seen the movement from intuition to process. Researching and writing twenty years later, Harvard researcher Joseph Bower describes best practices in CEO succession differently. In *The CEO Within: Why Inside Outsiders Are the Key to Succession Planning* (2007), Bower makes several observations about executive assessments as part of a CEO succession planning process: "Even companies that have great processes for the development and selection of talent find that they make mistakes that search firms or search consultants may help them avoid. Search firms can sometimes surface great Inside Outsiders simply because they themselves are outsiders." He goes on to add, "A search firm may be able to smoke out such potential leaders. Also, many companies are not sure that their internal candidates are right, and they therefore want to see what the outside candidates look like." In Bower's view, a best practices approach to succession planning leverages the CEO's nuanced view about the internal candidates, the board's vision about where the company and the industry are going in the next decade, and external executive assessment and benchmarking.

Writing about succession planning more generally, Sobol, Harkins, and Conley, the editors of Linkage Inc.'s *Best Practices in Succession Planning* (2007), state that the first essential event in the succession planning process is assessment. They scope out two aspects of assessment as part of succession: assessing the succession candidates and assessing the talent requirements of the organization. They state, "There are a variety of strategic choices that can be made as to how that assessment is structured, what instruments or processes are used, and how the information is shared with the candidate. Assessment must be based on a review of the capabilities needed to drive the organization toward the future, determining the balance of personal, business, and other characteristics that need to be assessed" (p. 201).

Why Perform Assessments of Senior Executives?

There are a number of reasons for performing assessments of senior executives. Speaking broadly, assessments of performance and potential constitute the core of a company's talent management processes. Assessments are performed on candidates during searches to fill open positions. Assessment can also be an important tool in identifying talent during a company's succession planning efforts. It can be used as a development tool to identify areas where, through training or coaching, improvements in individual performance might be recognized. Next, assessments can be used in efforts to build and deploy a top management team best. Finally, assessments are often used as part of a merger or acquisition to assist management of the new company in their efforts to institute a process that is seen as fair and just when making decisions about how best to allocate executives—many of whom are unfamiliar to them. Of course, these reasons for assessment are not mutually exclusive. In all, assessments are not ends themselves but rather means to achieving organizational ends.

Assessment as a Selection Tool

Executive assessment is most familiar as a selection tool that a company's management team uses to evaluate potential candidates for an open position. In this context, most companies have relied on it as a way to vet external candidates. Internal candidates have traditionally not been subjected to formal assessment; management teams often view them as known quantities. Recently, however, more companies have been designing systems where internal candidates are subjected to formal assessment just as outside candidates are. This is an encouraging trend because it means management teams will have more truly comparable data on each of the candidates for the position. Without this practice in place, internal candidates are not as easily objectively viewed. While this could result in either an over- or an underconfidence in the suitability of internal candidates, our experience indicates that in fact, internal candidates often suffer relative to candidates from the outside. On the one hand, some internal candidates may undeservedly wear a halo as someone's golden child. On the other hand, sometimes internal candidates suffer from a bias rooted in a belief that external candidates somehow bring more excitement to the table. Stated in a slightly different way, there are instances where there is a bias toward the devil you do not know, and internal candidates may undeservedly suffer from their reputations where external candidates may appear better than they are. In addition, because external candidates lack tacit appreciation for the company, they represent a greater transition risk that is often underestimated during the assessment process.

Assessment in Succession Planning

External executive assessment should be a central component of a company's succession planning. A best practice approach to succession planning begins with a comprehensive competency-based assessment of the key internal talent. Outside consultants can be an important resource here because of their ability to provide an independent perspective, benchmark against industry norms, and provide insights regarding the broader marketplace for talent. Commonly these assessments are performed on the direct reports to the CEO.

Another emerging and encouraging trend is to be more inclusive in this process by including an additional level or two (depending on the company's size) on the organizational chart. This approach offers deeper visibility into the company's talent pipeline and as a result is valuable in planning several succession moves ahead. Often the assessment team interviews the board members to better understand the strategic challenges facing the company in the next ten years and the leadership characteristics that are most important for the future leader.

Companies must resist the temptation of doing succession planning in the rearview mirror. Just because the departing executive was effective in the role does not mean a capability clone will be the answer for the future. Companies that are seriously committed to best practices succession planning will conduct assessments like this periodically because executive capabilities change, as do the needs of the company. Ongoing assessment is critical to maintaining alignment between what the company needs and what the executives can deliver.

Assessment as a Developmental Tool

Assessment should always be framed as an opportunity to help executives develop. If the exercise is instead viewed as a way merely to reveal an executive's Achilles' heel, its biggest potential upside will be missed. This is a reason that companies that invest in regular assessments have better success with the tool. If assessment is not part of the organizational routine and instead is employed only when a vacancy needs to be filled, the purpose of the assessment is transparent because it is precisely about including or excluding individuals from opportunities. When done regularly, assessment can honestly be presented as a development tool that allows the organization to manage its talent pipeline.

For that reason, assessments should first be focused on finding what is right with each executive and reinforcing those strengths. Next, the process should clearly focus on one to three things the executive should do to become more effective in his or her current role. The best approach here is to be as concrete as possible in describing behaviors and tools that have worked for other executives and by providing examples. Finally, the assessment should look into potential next roles for the executive to identify possible experiential and behavioral gaps and then make recommendations about how to bridge them. For example, an executive may be missing international exposure, experience in a functional area, or knowledge of a product line. These are easily remedied shortcomings.

One challenge to realizing the developmental value of executive assessment has its roots in the stigma that some hold about having weaknesses exposed. Overcoming this stigma is yet another reason that routine assessment is beneficial. And it means that the way the process is framed is also important. Most will quickly recognize that even individuals at the top of their game, like golfer Tiger Woods, continually invest in coaching to gain insight into the way they play the game. Without that objective outsider input, bad habits develop and performance eventually suffers. Moreover, moving to the next level of performance often requires the executive to learn new behaviors and leadership tools, just as Tiger Woods has invested in efforts to rebuild his swing.

Assessment to Develop a High-Performance Top Management Team

There is an increasing awareness that is critical to the development of a high-performance top management team and has come to be known as complementarity. Complementarity refers to a complex multidimensional fit of the members of a team. Simply put, some teams are made up of members with redundant capabilities; others are missing critical capabilities for high performance. Through assessment practices, boards and CEOs can develop a sense of how well a team presents itself in a complementary manner, and as turnover occurs, they acquire a clearer sense of the particular capabilities that need replenishing (or development among remaining team members).

Assessment in the Context of a Merger or Acquisition

Mergers and acquisitions represent unique challenges for companies and their leadership teams. Whereas the specific circumstances can vary widely, what is common is the challenge of sorting through gaps and redundancies in the capabilities of the combined executive team. Assessment can play a valuable role in sorting through this, and such a practice is increasingly being deployed by, for example, larger firms as they make bids for smaller companies. Similarly, the purchasers of these assessments include private equity firms as they become owners of a previously publicly held company.

What Should You Measure in Executive Assessment?

Assessment has predictive value only when what is measured meets two tests: reliability and validity. In an assessment context, two types of reliability are important. *Test-retest reliability* means that the method of gauging an underlying dimension is stable over time. That is, an assessment performed on one day would yield results similar to those from an assessment performed another day; only a true change would be reflected in the results. *Interrater reliability* means that the results are not subject to bias from the person conducting the rating. In an assessment context, it means that an executive's result would be the same regardless of which member of the assessment team conducted the process—or that fellow executives would rate the target executive similarly (that is, differences in their evaluations would reflect only a true score difference in what each saw in the target). Clearly both kinds of reliability are important in ensuring the company that the results obtained from the process are a function of the true capabilities of the executive, not a function of when or by whom the process was performed. *Validity* in this context means that the results of the assessment are predictive of performance: individuals suggested by the results to be high performers are in fact high performers. An assessment protocol that lacks validity is simply not useful for any of the purposes described here. In choosing what to measure, companies need to narrow their focus to what can be measured in a reliable and valid way.

There have been many attempts to describe the most important characteristics of executives, which focuses our attention on what is important to assess in executives. Instead of focusing on the specific characteristics, I offer several principles and maps of the territory of the vast leadership literature.

Past Behavior as a Predictor of Future Behavior

Most writing on leadership, assessments, leadership development, executive coaching, and succession planning is grounded in the widespread belief that the best predictor of future behavior is past behavior. Kouzes and Posner's *The Leadership Challenge* (2002) provides a good example of this view. These authors offer a behavioral model of leadership built on five major practices: modeling the way, inspiring a shared vision, innovating and leading change, enabling others to act, and recognizing and celebrating the contributions of others.

Contingency theory and the situational leadership model provide perspectives to assess the relevance of past behavior to predict future behavior and success. Contingency theory suggests that leadership style and organizational structure are influenced by environmental factors, and situational leadership proposes that different leadership styles are better in different situations. The presence or absence of these factors is a contingency that determines executive behavior in some part. An understanding of how past contingencies or situational factors influenced past executive behavior and the likelihood in the future of the executive navigating similar challenges and situations provides a more nuanced assessment than relying on behavior alone.

Mutually Exclusive, Collectively Exhaustive Categorizations

One way to review measures in executive assessment is to identify categorizations of specific characteristics. Whereas the number of categories and the specific content of each category are open to debate, a best practice scheme should be collectively exhaustive, and the categories should be mutually exclusive. In other words, the categories should cover the universe, and no category should overlap any other category. This allows more efficient data gathering, tighter analysis and coding of data collected, and clearer recommendations.

For example, "bucket 1" could be the qualifications (degrees, certifications), years and kinds of experience, language facility, knowledge (general and specific awareness), and skills (the ability to use one's knowledge effectively). These are the facts—the quick qualifiers. Executives either have them or they do not, and if they have them, they can be scaled in terms of how much they have them and for how long they have had them. This category also includes functional competencies, which are different from leadership and management behavioral competencies.

Bucket 2 could be leadership and management behavioral competencies. Assessments of leadership and management behavioral competencies examine what executives do and how they do it. Good leadership and managerial behaviors are required to effectively perform the current or future role in the organization and help the business meet its strategic and operating objectives. Often assessors develop competency rating scales in which each number is associated with a description of the behavior. These scales range from three to seven (or more) items per scale.

Bucket 3 could be termed personal characteristics. Assessment of personal characteristics includes personality traits, motivation, values, personal style, and other personal characteristics. Many executives firmly believe that personal characteristics are an important element of fit in an organization, but they are often the most difficult to measure in a reliable and valid manner.

Developmental Leadership Models

Identifying and categorizing interrelated leadership characteristics that are a best fit for the challenges of a certain leadership level is a growing area of research. Research on CEO succession planning, such as Bower's *The CEO Within* (2007), and CEO derailment factors, such as David Dotlich and Peter Cairo's *Why CEOs Fail* (2003) and Patrick Lencioni's *The Five Temptations of a* CEO (1998), focus on the unique challenges of enterprise leadership. Nathan Bennett and Stephen Miles's *Riding Shotgun: The Role of the COO* (2006) focuses on the additional role requirement of the chief operating officer. Each expands on a notion of effective leadership by noticing the nuances of the specific leadership role.

More generally, in *Leadership Without Easy Answers* (1994), Ronald Heifetz suggests that leaders face technical challenges, which have a right or wrong answer that can be solved with the prevailing paradigm, or adaptive challenges, which require a change in values, beliefs, or behavior. Typically, the higher the level of leadership, the more the focus is on dealing with adaptive rather than technical challenges. For example, an assessment might suggest that one executive is particularly capable at managing the technical challenges of the finance function, but may not have developed the adaptive abilities necessary to lead change as a business unit head with profit-and-loss responsibility.

In *Good to Great* (2001), Jim Collins offers a developmental leadership model consisting of five stages, each building on the next, beginning with the Highly Capable Individual stage and culminating in the Level 5 Leader stage. Collins's research revealed that the most effective enterprise leaders possessed a paradoxical mixture of personal humility and professional willpower, which he named the Level 5 Leader. In his model, Level 5 Leaders possess the characteristics of each of the five layers of his scheme.

Three contributions to the research on leadership build on this idea of situational characteristics of leading and present a developmental view of leadership across levels. In *The Leadership Pipeline: How to Build the Leadership Powered Company* (2001), Ram Charan, Stephen Drotter, and James Noel describe the six passages of leaders from an individual contributor role to an enterprise leadership role. They persuasively argue that each passage requires additional skills, which are the additional capabilities necessary to execute new responsibilities; expanded time horizons, which refer to the widening perspective on longer-term implications of leadership; and work values, which are the things that executives consider important and focus their attention.

In their April 2005 *Harvard Business Review* article, "Seven Transformations of Leadership," David Rooke and William Torbert present a related notion about what develops in leaders. They have applied research findings from constructive-developmental psychology to better understand the abilities of leaders to cope with the complexity of their roles. They propose that each leader possess an action-logic, which is a description of the deeper structure of his or her worldview. Certain action-logics are a better fit for increasing complexities and time horizons of executive leadership and are associated with certain values orientations. For example, a leader at the achiever action-logic stage would be less effective leading organizational change than a leader at a later stage such as the strategist action-logic. Center for Creative Leadership researchers Wilfred Drath and Chuck Palus offer a similar perspective in *Making Common Sense: Leadership as Meaning-Making in a Community of Practice* (1994), as do Harvard psychologists Robert Kegan and Lisa Lahey in *Adult Leadership and Adult Development* (1984).

Head, Heart, and Guts

Daniel Goleman, in *Working with Emotional Intelligence* (1998), suggests that emotional intelligence is more important to leadership effectiveness than IQ. Goleman offers a leadership competency model based on emotional intelligence that groups twenty-five behavioral competencies into five categories: self-awareness, self-regulation, motivation, empathy, and social skills. While aspects of emotional intelligence do seem essential for effective executive leadership, empirical research has not demonstrated that emotional intelligence is the main factor predicting future success for executives.

In *Head, Heart, and Guts: How the World's Best Companies Develop Complete Leaders* (2006), David Dotlich, Peter Cairo, and Stephen Rhinesmith offer a perspective that tries to accommodate both the executive intelligence and emotional intelligence perspectives on leadership capability. They suggest that what matters most is a balanced combination of head leadership, heart leadership, and guts leadership. Head leadership is about intelligence. Heart leadership includes much of what Goleman considers in his emotional intelligence model. Guts leadership is about the drive to achieve results and includes risk taking, perseverance, and integrity and is similar to Collins's fierce resolve and humility characteristics.

How Do You Collect Your Data?

Each of the choices in regard to data collection varies in terms of time and cost and familiar trade-offs with regard to reliability and validity.

Business Context and Leadership Requirements Interviews

A best practices executive assessment process is grounded in an understanding of the business context and the leadership requirements. Often assessors conduct formal or informal interviews to better understand the industry dynamics, the strategic imperatives, and the leadership requirements. Sometimes these findings are documented and shared with the CEO and top management team, while at other times, the findings are simply applied in the assessment process.

In-Depth Executive Interviews

An assessor conducts structured in-depth interviews to review an executive's career history. During this interview, the assessor typically probes for situations that provide the executive with an opportunity to describe specific situations, actions, and results for critical leadership competencies. These so-called behavioral event or competency-based interviews provide a structure for the assessor to evaluate an executive. The key notion here is that the executive provides example after example of things he or she actually did versus trying to game the interview by giving the assessor the "right" answer.

In-Depth 360-Degree Reference Interviews

Assessors often interview up, across, and downward references in order to better understand the executive's strengths, development areas, specific results, and competency-based behaviors. In addition to improving the accuracy of the assessment, these confidential, nonattributed reference interviews provide valuable feedback for the executive.

360-Degree Surveys

An assessor collects questionnaire feedback from an executive's up, across, and downward relationships to collect information about performance and potential against key leadership competencies. These surveys differ from 360-degree feedback tools because the assessors analyze and synthesize the 360-degree data with the rest of the assessment sources of information to form a holistic perspective about the executive that is contextually relevant.

External Benchmarking

External benchmarking involves comparing the assessed executive against an external peer reference group. The comparison is made for the executive's current role or potential role, or both. One benefit is that the organization develops an understanding of how a key executive stacks up against the competition. Another benefit is the valuable information learned about how attractive a competitor might find the executive. Armed with this information, the organization can take action to ensure that star executives and those with high potential choose to remain in the organization.

Assessment Centers and Simulation

Developed at AT&T, assessment centers are often used as input in an executive assessment. Although they were originally designed to assess candidates for first-line supervisory positions, assessment centers have been used for higher levels of management. In this approach, assessors use job-related simulations to observe how an executive handles challenges for the next job level.

Group Evaluation Methodology

The group evaluation methodology is an approach to collecting information in an executive assessment that uses a group discussion format with the executive's peers. In this approach, the assessor poses questions to the group and facilitates the discussion. Multiple perspectives about the same question are surfaced, and the assessor explores differing perspectives and consensus to glean deeper meaning. This approach typically focuses on a description of the individual's leadership behavior, prediction of future performance in the same or different roles, and generation of areas for development.

Psychological and Psychometric Tools

On occasion, assessors use psychological instruments to study the personality or cognitive abilities of an executive. These instruments are best used as complementary with interview findings and understood within the context of the executive in the business environment. A review of these instruments is beyond the scope of this chapter.

How Do You Develop an Executive Where There Are Gaps?

The perfect executive is a fiction. Furthermore, leadership jobs are not getting any easier. Global competition, challenging economic conditions, increasing public scrutiny over a company's financial or environmental performance, and difficulties in getting and keeping talented employees are just a few of the many reasons that this situation persists. Consequently, the case for ongoing executive development is easy to make, and clearly that process begins with assessment. Understanding each executive's strengths and weaknesses, as well as the challenges that loom on the company's horizon, provides a basis for the development of an executive coaching plan. Coaching should focus on the critical few: at any time, an executive should be working on one, two, or at most three ways to improve his or her effectiveness in the job today or readiness for the job of tomorrow.

In a best practice arrangement, one of the work products would be a development plan, which typically expands on development areas. To make the most of the investment, the assessment team works with the executive to put together a plan. Suggested behaviors to start, stop, or continue are identified for each of the development areas. Often a best practice development plan describes potential benefits to the individual or organization if the behavior change is successfully made.

Once the development plan has been created, the organization and executive have a range of developmental options. Executive coaching is an increasingly used option to support behavior change. Typically the coach helps the executive effect measurable behavioral change in a few key areas based on the executive assessment. External executive coaching can be highly valuable to executives, especially those who are most senior in a company, because they often have few people they can truly confide in on issues. Seeing a coach has become less stigmatized; in fact, if an executive is not using a coach, others will perceive that something is wrong. At lower levels in the organization, formal or informal mentoring programs are an excellent way to offer coaching to developing leaders.

Developmental assignments are often used to immerse the executive in a business situation that is different from his or her experience. If a new assignment is not possible, an in-role action learning project is often a good choice. Here, the executive is assigned a project designed to provide challenge in a specific area. In some cases, the assignment of a mentor is sufficient to help address a developmental area. Executive education and corporate training are traditional choices. Finally, accelerated leadership development programs that combine action learning, executive coaching, and a transformational learning curriculum have become popular, especially in addressing the developmental needs of high-potential leaders and accelerating succession readiness. Regardless of the developmental option selected, a best practice executive assessment is the foundation of subsequent development.

A Best Practice Approach to Executive Assessment

A best practice approach to executive assessment can be described in four discrete steps: (1) preassessment activities, (2) assessment design and implementation, (3) reporting results, (4) postassessment activities, and follow-up refresh.

Preassessment Activities

The central preassessment activities are directed toward developing a deep understanding of the critical success factors for each focal position, as well as a similarly deep appreciation for the company, its culture, its current competitive position, and its foreseeable future challenges. Through this process, a likeness of the strongest incumbent for each position will emerge.

The challenge in getting commitment to this critical exercise is a tendency for those involved to think the answer for the company's future is simply to get younger versions of their current team. But typically this is not a winning strategy. In only the rarest cases will the challenges ahead require the same skills that worked in the past. GE is a good example. The current and two previous CEOs—Reg Jones, Jack Welch, and Jeff Immelt—are starkly different people. In its CEO succession, GE has done a good job of looking "through the windshield" rather than "in the rearview mirror" in order to understand what the next CEO needs to bring as a leader.

In summary, the key to preassessment work lies in developing an understanding of the business environment, the organizational context and positioning, the future requirements of the role, strategy, and so on. In addition, it is important to establish the key leadership and technical competencies required to be successful against the above conditions. The preassessment phase is often done by engaging a number of key people inside the client company: CEO, human resources, or key functional or business leaders with specific knowledge.

Assessment Design and Implementation

The second part of the assessment process addresses project management and project execution. When an outside firm is engaged to conduct assessments, it is important to ensure that it has a key contact placed at a high level in the company so that access to the necessary individuals and information is unfettered. Agreements also need to be reached with regard to the number and types of individuals to include in the assessment—and for each of those individuals, the right number and types of references or 360-degree appraisal participants. During this stage, decisions around the use of any preexisting psychometric tests and internal performance data are made.

The biggest decisions in this part of the process concern the methodology used to collect assessment data. As is true in many other situations, companies are faced with a series of trade-offs. At one extreme, rich data are available using expensive methods that are time-consuming for everyone. At the other extreme, affordable and easily administered protocols are available off the shelf. These tools are by design fairly generic in nature and produce a much less rich set of data from which to draw conclusions.

Assessment experts are in agreement that the best practice technique for conducting senior-level executive assessments is the behavioral event or competency-based interview. The key to competency-based interviewing is to look for examples of life experiences from the individual that reveal capabilities. Through consideration of sets of experiences, patterns begin to be revealed that are telling as to the focal executive's capabilities. Our experience working with the most senior teams at the Fortune 500 is that very few senior executives have truly been assessed and as a result can be uncomfortable with the process. Recognizing this from the outset allows the assessor to begin interviews in nonthreatening but still robust ways. As the executive builds comfort through a discussion of uncontroversial aspects of his or her career, some rapport develops that then allows the assessor to move on to less comfortable but important areas.

Heidrick & Struggles has developed a model that serves as an organizing framework for the competencies experience reveals as critical to executive success. Of course, the exact nature of the way the framework is deployed may vary as a function of preassessment work with the client. Generally, however, evaluation of executives uses the LEEED model. LEEED is an acronym that represents the model, which assesses five dimensions:

1. *Learning,* the degree to which an executive, through education and experience, has and can expand an honest and complete awareness of the industry, best practices therein, customer preferences, and competitor strategies
2. *Envisioning,* to indicate the executive has the ability to create excitement around a vision of what the company could be and can build buy-in from those whose efforts are necessary to achieve it
3. *Engaging,* which focuses the assessment on the executive's ability to effectively lead a team, including communication skills, and the abilities to develop and empower subordinates
4. *Executing,* the most intuitive of these five, which assesses the individual's track record and capabilities to decisively and persistently drive results
5. *Deducing,* the label given to the set of competencies that help the executive analyze large volumes of data—some quantitative and some qualitative—in rigorous and creative ways to make good business decisions

The assessment process looks different at different levels in the organizational hierarchy. Typically, at the lower levels of an organization, an assessor is able to use more leverage in the forms of psychometric tests and online tools combined with simulations like an in-box or business case simulation. These methodologies tend to be lower touch and less personalized, which means the process can run a lot more people at a reasonable cost. There are specialized firms such as DDI, PDI, and

Corporate Insights, among many others, that specialize in these highly leveraged approaches to executive assessment. These approaches are often psychologically driven, and those doing the assessment work often have a doctorate in psychology. For junior executives, this approach works well because a company can affordably assess fairly large numbers of early-career executives to get a view of their potential. The downside is that these more standardized approaches may not be taking into account important nuances. There is a trade-off between how many people can be assessed and how customized the process is.

Reporting Results

The best way to report results depends on the choices made regarding the type and volume of data collected. The central consideration here is to be certain the reporting is clear in terms of three things. First, does the report clearly explain executive strengths and weaknesses? The best reports provide concrete examples of events or behaviors that exemplify each. This feedback is much more actionable because it points to specifics the executive can implement. Second, does the report provide benchmarking to help the company and the executive understand this individual's capabilities relative to the appropriate comparison group? Finally, does the reporting of results provide a solid foundation for the development plan that should accompany the assessment process?

In addition to the form and content of the report, it should be made clear at the outset of the assessment process who will be privy to the results and in what manner they will be rolled out. The process creates consternation on the part of executives when individuals they did not think would see results do and when results are shared so that individuals hear about their results from others before their own debriefing.

Depending on the nature of the assessment project, it may be appropriate for the assessor to provide anything between a broad overview and a very deep look into results to the top management team. This presentation includes benchmarking, talent mapping of assessed executives as a group into different talent segments, strengths and limitations as a team of a group of assessed individuals, and risk assessments of internal candidates for successor roles.

Postassessment Activities and Refreshment

The strong likelihood is that everyone involved in the assessment project will be presented with areas where they can raise their game. A best practices approach to assessment includes from its initiation a plan to provide the necessary support to executives—whether it is something the company does (such as job rotation or international assignment) or simply provides (such as education or training or executive coaching). The importance of this element of the plan cannot be overstated: an assessment that ends by pointing out a deficiency and then leaving it in the lap of the executive to attend to will not be well received. The quality of facilitation of the developmental feedback to the executive often determines much of the overall value of the process. The best researched and written report is useless unless the assessor builds enough trust and credibility to help the executive take in not only positive feedback but also constructive recommendations. Organizations often sponsor refresh assessments with some light 360-degree referencing to determine progress against the prior developmental recommendations and identification of emerging issues. These refresh assessments are often invaluable because the process can help references see the progress of a motivated-to-change executive that their biases may have blocked them from noticing. It also creates a huge motivation for these executives to engage personally with their feedback and actively work on their key developmental areas because they know they will be measured again in the future.

Conclusion

This chapter began by posing four questions critical to understanding the role executive assessment can play in talent management. To best recognize a return on this sort of investment, thoughtful answers to each of the four questions should be developed early in the process. First, decision makers should make sure there is a consensus regarding why the investment is being made. As in other contexts, investor goals may differ. Because the process itself needs to be tailored to the desired outcomes, agreement a priori on what success looks like is important. Second, an ever-widening swath of executive competencies is replete with candidates for measurement. Because the responsibilities and, consequently, the needed knowledge, skills, and abilities vary from position to position, decision makers are cautioned to think carefully about what to measure. The most important consideration here is the best possible forecast about the way each focal position will evolve over the next few years. Third, it is important to work with assessment tools that are established and appropriate. The last key point is a strong admonition that assessment should represent a beginning, not an ending. If the process ends without a deliberate plan in place to help individuals remediate areas of relative weakness, then both the assessed executives and the company have been shortchanged.

Done well, executive assessment is a powerful tool that serves companies and executives. Companies glean a deep understanding of their talent pipeline, and executives benefit from detailed coaching plans. The investment that assessment represents signals executives as to their value to the company; assessments may in fact serve some value as a retention vehicle. It is truly becoming a best practice that some of the world's most admired corporations use.

It is indisputable that boards of directors will continue to seek more information about their company's leadership pipeline. The benefit of choosing an external provider to lead the process is that provider's ability to provide an independent and market-calibrated view of the client's talent pipeline. And an external executive assessment can be a tremendous complementary tool used in partnership with a company's internal talent processes. Finally, few executives are either truly comfortable with or particularly good at providing developmental coaching. An externally driven assessment process coupled with a detailed coaching and development plan can provide the vehicle for more productive conversations between managers because the process is robust and depersonalized. As a result, both parties find it easier to focus on the developmental opportunities. In the end, that is where each individual's greatest benefit lies.

References

Bennett, N., and Miles, S. *Riding Shotgun: The Role of the COO.* Stanford: Stanford University Press, 2006.

Bower, J. *The CEO Within: Why Inside Outsiders Are the Key to Succession Planning.* Boston: Harvard Business School Press, 2007.

Charan, R., Drotter, S., and Noel, J. *The Leadership Pipeline: How to Build the Leadership Powered Company.* San Francisco: Jossey-Bass, 2001.

Collins, J. *Good to Great: Why Some Companies Make the Leap and Others Don't.* New York: HarperCollins, 2001.

Dotlich, D., and Cairo, P. *Why CEOs Fail: The Eleven Behaviors That Can Derail Your Climb to the Top—and How to Manage Them.* San Francisco: Jossey-Bass, 2003.

Dotlich, D., Cairo, P., and Rhinesmith, S. *Head, Heart, and Guts: How the World's Best Companies Develop Complete Leaders.* San Francisco: Jossey-Bass, 2006.

Drath, W., and Palus, C. *Making Common Sense: Leadership as Meaning-Making in a Community of Practice.* Greensboro, N.C.: Center for Creative Leadership, 1994.

Goldsmith, M., and Lyons, L. *Coaching for Leadership: The Practices of Leadership Coaching from the World's Greatest Coaches.* San Francisco: Jossey-Bass, 2006.

Goleman, D. *Working with Emotional Intelligence.* New York: Bantam Books, 1998.

Heifetz, R. *Leadership Without Easy Answers.* Cambridge, Mass.: Belknap Press of Harvard University Press, 1994.

Kegan, R., and Lahey, L. "Adult Leadership and Adult Development: A Constructivist View." In B. Kellerman (ed.), *Leadership: Multidisciplinary Perspectives.* Upper Saddle River, N.J.: Prentice Hall, 1983.

Kouzes, J., and Posner, B. *The Leadership Challenge.* San Francisco: Jossey-Bass, 2002.

Lencioni, P. *The Five Temptations of a CEO.* San Francisco: Jossey-Bass, 1998.

Menkes, J. *Executive Intelligence: What All Great Leaders Have.* New York: HarperCollins, 2005.

Ortiz, A. "Executive Assessment for Succession Planning and Development: A Sequenced Process and a Few Helpful Hints." In J. Noel and D. Dotlich (eds.), *The 2008 Pfeiffer Annual Leadership Development.* San Francisco: Jossey-Bass/Pfeiffer, 2008.

Rooke, D., and Torbert, W. "Seven Transformations of Leadership." Harvard Business Review, Apr. 2005, pp. 1–11.

Smart, B. *Topgrading: How Leading Companies Win by Hiring, Coaching, and Keeping the Best People.* New York: Penguin Group, 2005.

Sobol, M., Harkins, P., and Conley, T. *Linkage Inc.'s Best Practices in Succession Planning: Case Studies, Research, Models, Tools.* San Francisco: Jossey-Bass, 2007.

Vancil, R. *Passing the Baton: Managing the Process of CEO Succession.* Boston: Harvard Business School Press, 1987.

About the Contributor

Stephen Miles is the managing partner Americas within Heidrick & Struggles's Leadership Consulting Practice and oversees the worldwide executive assessment and succession planning practice. He is a key member of Heidrick & Struggles's CEO and board practice. With over thirteen years of experience in assessment, succession planning, organizational effectiveness, and strategy consulting, Miles focuses on CEO succession and has partnered with numerous boards of global Fortune 500 companies to ensure that successful leadership selection and transition occur. He is a recognized expert on the role of the chief operating officer (COO) and has consulted to numerous companies on the establishment and the effectiveness of the position.

He also coaches a small number of very senior global executives at the CEO and COO level. He focuses on high-performance coaching with a heavy emphasis on the business and cultural contexts. Miles works internationally extensively, and his clients cut across all industry sectors.

CHAPTER FOUR

LEADERSHIP DEVELOPMENT AND ORGANIZATIONAL STRATEGY

This chapter outlines key elements for aligning leadership development with the broader organization and offers approaches for leveraging leadership development to create and communicate the organization's strategy and improve competitiveness.

For more on the case studies presented in this chapter see R. M. Fulmer and J. A. Conger, *Growing Your Company's Leaders: How Great Organizations Use Succession Management to Sustain Competitive Advantage* (New York: AMACOM, 2004).

Perhaps the most critical change facing senior executives in global organizations is preparing a new generation of leaders who will continue and extend the strategic reach of the organizations they currently head. Being built to last requires constant renewal, and this renewal is typically based on leaders' continuing to develop themselves and their successors.

Leadership and learning play a critical role in enabling organizational growth and transformation—and ultimately strategic success. Good strategy identifies an organization's current reality as well as its desired destination—what it needs to develop and how it needs to change in order to successfully compete and achieve its business objectives. The gap between current reality and desired destination can be filled by increasing individual competency as well as building organizational capability. A complete and well-developed competitive strategy includes direction on the steps to be taken to develop leaders and the skills and the behaviors these leaders need in order to fill the gap and propel the organization to its desired future destination (Figure 4.1).

FIGURE 4.1. STRATEGY: MOVING FROM CURRENT REALITY TO DESIRED DESTINATION

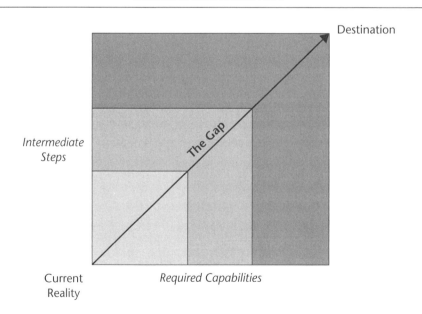

FIGURE 4.2. LEADERS AS STRATEGIC ARCHITECTS, TRANSLATORS, AND DOERS

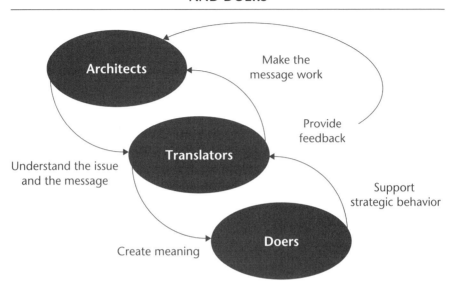

Realizing strategic direction requires organizational capability. It is increased capability ultimately that provides the bridge from current reality to the desired destination and is driven by individual competency. Focusing on increasing organizational capability requires developing the collective capabilities of various groups and teams in the organization.

Today's (and tomorrow's) leaders must be flexible, collaborative, able to leverage subject-matter expertise, and willing to continue learning. Learning organizations must be able to support leaders as they develop those characteristics. For an organization to be successful, its leaders must not only act as architects of the strategy, setting the best course for the company in the marketplace, but must also continually work to implement strategic directives while also acting as translators of the strategy to the rest of the organization: the leaders who will actually be the doers of the work (see Figure 4.2). Of course, this occurs at different leadership levels within the organization, but underscores the fact that leadership is needed throughout an organization for strategic and business success.

Astute line executives use leadership development as a powerful tool to create, translate, and communicate strategy. Carefully crafted leadership and learning strategies can assist in providing help to leaders in their roles of architect, translator, and doer. This is done by effectively communicating the reasons for and implications of corporate strategy in learning programs to managers, who will need to translate the strategy for employees throughout the organization so they understand their role in making it happen.

Various studies have concluded that 60 to 70 percent of all strategies fail to be successfully implemented. Top leadership development companies seem to have discovered that one way to beat these odds is to ensure that everyone in the organization understands the strategy, the reasons for it, and their role in making it happen. These companies also understand that effective developmental activities can be a means of sharing the information and providing some of the tools for successful implementation.

How to Achieve Excellent Organizational Results

Research has shown that when leadership development is considered a strategic objective and when development is tied closely to the strategy and needs of the business, excellent organizational results follow. We review this research in laying out a set of strategic leadership development principles.

Tie Leadership Development to Business Strategy

Leadership development should begin and end with the business's strategy and objectives in mind. Hewitt found that the top twenty companies in the United States in leader development closely linked development strategies with business strategies (Salob and Greenslade, 2005). This was done even over the temptation to build development practices that were composed of best practices from other companies or heralded in benchmark studies or training magazines. Indeed, alignment with business strategy and priorities was seen to win out over a hodgepodge of benchmark programs.

The pressure and need to organize development activities and initiatives into an integrated strategy is perhaps the most important, overarching trend in leadership development. In a 2004 study, 69 percent of respondents noted that the "creation of an integrated strategy and system for all executive development" was the leading priority of their learning and development organizations (Bolt, 2004). These results replicated an earlier study as well (Bolt, 2000).

Many corporate learning and development organizations see leadership development as a set of puzzle pieces representing initiatives and programs that should somehow fit together but never seem to come together in the right way. These pieces include competency models, 360-degree and other assessments, developmental job rotations, experiential and action learning, talent management, succession planning, rewards and recognition, and coaching and mentoring. A leadership development architecture can bring these often disjointed elements together into a whole that has a greater chance of delivering real results. This architecture must be integrated and linked to the strategy and needs of the business in order to increase the potential for real impact and then communicated widely to engender support (Bolt, 2004).

The best companies for leaders consistently execute the strategies that lead to good leadership development. They create enterprisewide standards, practices, and metrics for leadership; cascade programs and processes down through the organization to improve impact and drive cultural change; include flexibility in centralized leader development programs in order to address specific business needs; and customize developmental solutions for business units in order to better ensure senior management support and engagement (Council, 2004; Fulmer, 2005; Salob and Greenslade, 2005; Saslow, 2004a).

Don't Forget About High Potentials

An important leverage point in leadership development efforts is the high-potential leader population within companies. Accelerating the development of these people was listed as a key objective by 62 percent of learning and development professionals (Bolt, 2004). However, even with this objective in mind, 46 percent of companies have no systemic process for identifying and developing candidates for key leadership positions, including high potentials. And 37 percent of companies see their inability to identify leadership potential as a serious weakness (Bernthal and Wellins, 2004). Among the top companies in leader development, 95 percent identify high potentials as compared to 77 percent of other companies. In addition, 68 percent then inform those high potentials of their status, and 72 percent track their progress and turnover systematically (Salob and Greenslade, 2005).

Even greater differentiation in the development of high-potential leaders can be seen in the techniques and methods used. Ninety-five percent of top companies provided increased access to senior leaders for their high-potential leaders as compared to 45 percent of other companies. Similarly, top companies provided internal training (90 percent versus 51 percent), developmental assignments (89 percent versus 43 percent) and mentoring and coaching (58 percent versus 24 percent) at a much higher rate than did companies not considered benchmarks for leadership development (Salob and Greenslade, 2005).

Even when a good high-potential development program is in place, these efforts can end in frustration without an equally effective succession management strategy and process. Overall, half of internal candidates selected for leadership positions fail when no succession management system is in place (Bernthal and Wellins, 2004). And if they had the opportunity, organizations would rehire only 62 percent of their executives (Rioux and Bernthal, 2006). To increase the odds of success, an effective succession management process should include visible support by senior management and line leaders who are involved in identifying and developing succession candidates, a time frame for achieving planned development actions, flexibility to change in response to strategic needs or competitive pressures, and the sharing of information with candidates (Fulmer and Conger, 2004).

Hold Leaders and the Organization Accountable for Results

Holding people and the organization accountable for the success of strategic leadership developmental efforts is a trend that continues to gain momentum, especially in an increasingly competitive environment where any investment or outlay is carefully considered and monitored for a return. In fact, 52 percent of learning and development professionals planned to use systematic measurement and evaluation to measure the impact of their efforts (Bolt, 2004).

Best practice firms anchor their leadership development efforts with lean competency models that are tied to performance and reward systems (Salob and Greenslade, 2005) and ultimately address the skills, behaviors, and mind-sets needed to meet strategic goals. A clear, lean set of competencies was heralded as top companies in leadership development integrate their competencies into succession planning (100 percent of top companies versus 78 percent of others) and make the competencies a baseline for identifying and then developing high-potential employees as part of succession planning. In the top quartile of leadership development companies identified by Hewitt, metrics were integrated with succession planning 71 percent of the time versus only 45 percent of the time in companies in the bottom quartile. These companies also more fully integrated competency measures into formulas for base pay (60 percent versus 30 percent), annual incentives (60 percent versus 31 percent), and long-term incentives (65 percent versus 23 percent) (Salob and Greenslade, 2005).

Even with these results, many companies do not measure results in learning and development as they should. In a study that looked specifically at European-based multinationals, 63 percent reported never measuring return on investment in learning and development (Saslow, 2004b), even though these same firms reported that the importance of learning and development was higher than ever before. There is clearly more work to be done in holding people and organizations accountable for learning and development results, even when strategy depends on these results.

Broad Themes in Strategic Leadership Development

With these three principles in mind, we can take a closer look at best practices and explore some of the practical implications and methods for developing leaders strategically and developing strategic leaders.

The following lessons were taken from our own experience in working with many different corporations over the years and as part of the work of Duke Corporate Education, but also from a recent study where we looked closely at five best practice leadership development companies: Caterpillar, Cisco Systems, PepsiCo, PricewaterhouseCoopers, and Washington Group International. We selected these companies because of their success in four areas:

1. Tying leadership culture, values, practices, and development to business strategy
2. Creating strategically relevant collective learning opportunities
3. Integrating a leadership development architecture with various development initiatives for maximum impact
4. Using leadership development to support the execution of business strategy and long-term needs to develop individual competencies while also building immediately needed organizational capability to address business challenges

We discuss four broad themes in strategic leadership development:

1. Developing leadership strategy
2. Creating an integrated architecture for strategic leadership development
3. Implementing strategic leadership development
4. Evaluating success

Under the umbrella of these themes, we have articulated several key concepts in more specific messages.

Developing Leadership Strategy

For a leadership development system to be successful, there must be a clear strategy to guide its implementation and maximize its impact for the leaders and the organization. The three key elements to this strategy are to ensure that it is grounded in a consistent set of competencies, that it aligns with the organization, and that development resources are given to the right people at the right time.

Look for the Organization's Teachable Moment. Much has been written about the importance of providing developmental opportunities for individuals at the appropriate teachable moment. The evidence is ample that managers benefit more from educational experiences that are just in time for them to use them rather than just in case they eventually need a new set of skills. These moments often occur when individuals have just been asked to change their identities: become managers rather than individual contributors, managers of managers, or general managers with overall operational responsibility for a business unit.

Similarly, organizations seem to have moments when the development and articulation of a leadership strategy are especially appropriate. In our research, it appears that these opportunities generally occur when there is a new CEO who wishes to align the organization around a new strategy, when two organizations have merged, or when there is a significant organizational crisis.

For example, when Jim Owens became CEO of Caterpillar in 2004, one of his early decisions was to empower the Leadership College of Caterpillar University to create the Leadership Quest program for the firm's high-potential leaders. This program built on an earlier initiative that created the firm's leadership framework, or competency model, and was intended, according to Owens, to "give our next generation of leaders an infusion of 'yellow blood.'"

After the merger of Pricewaterhouse and Coopers and Lybrand, a significant teachable moment occurred. Differing cultures needed to be reconciled, and leader behaviors and mind-sets needed to shift. PricewaterhouseCoopers (PwC) used this event as the starting point for leadership development and overall firm strategy.

In 2002, Washington Group International, an engineering, construction, and management solutions firm, emerged from Chapter 11 with a four-person "office of the chairman" headed by Stephen Hanks as CEO and a new threefold mission statement that identified people and their development, as well as profitability and performance, as top priorities.

According to Hanks, "The company that develops talent the fastest will take the hill."

Each benchmark company used a key organizational transition, the teachable moment, to develop, articulate, and align a new leadership strategy with the strategic direction of the firm and formed crucial starting points for achieving excellence in leader development.

Tie Leadership Development to Corporate Strategy. Having a direct link between a leadership development strategy and corporate strategy provides great benefit to an organization and its employees, and is a key concept for successful leadership development. Organizations that realize this establish a leader development philosophy that permeates the organization and is meaningful to all employees, tying leadership development to corporate planning as well as the business strategy to create alignment and leverage.

At Caterpillar, alignment is achieved by receiving input from the executive office, business units, and process owners of the critical success factors. To embed leadership development into the business strategy, metrics were established to connect leadership to the business. PwC links development activities to its strategy to become a "distinctive firm." Leadership development programs are designed to reinforce corporate strategy, thus ensuring linkage and success. PepsiCo's leadership development strategy is grounded in the belief that strong leaders are needed for success in the marketplace.

Identify a Lean Competency Model to Serve as the Foundation of the Leadership Development System. A simple leadership model with a concise statement of values serves as an important point of focus in leadership development. The benchmark companies in our research kept their values and competencies simple and straightforward, understanding that competencies should be observable, managers should be able to give real-time feedback on them, and they should apply at all levels within an organization—and lead directly to better performance.

Creating an Integrated Architecture for Strategic Leadership Development

For a leadership development effort to succeed, it must be fully integrated into the organizational architecture and built for lasting success. A leadership system is highly dependent on consistent buy-in from the organization as a whole and the leaders targeted for development. By structurally building in support from other business functions and designing the initiative to create a lasting engagement from the participants, a development effort can be better suited to reach its desired outcome.

Develop a Partnership Between Senior Executives and Multiple Human Resource Systems. Support from senior executives, usually starting with the CEO, is critical for successful leadership development. Yet even the most effective CEO cannot ensure success without involving the entire human resource (HR) system. Conversely, training and education professionals will not be successful unless they reach out and collaborate with their colleagues in line positions and other HR specialties.

Within Cisco's HR function, for example, the organization's Worldwide Leadership Education group works with leaders to identify candidates for its leadership development programs. Executives then help design the programs, ensuring that they meet business needs and align with strategy. Each Cisco program has an established cross-functional steering committee that ensures linkage between the program and the business. The business leaders on the steering committees help drive the design of the programs and recruit appropriate executives into the classrooms. During the design phase of the program, the steering committees meet often, approximately once a month. In addition, the programs employ the role of executive faculty—people who bring participants a strategic perspective.

A board of governors for Caterpillar University includes the CEO and senior executives who approve learning budgets and priorities as well as determine policy. An advisory board for each college includes senior leaders from business or user groups. This group has a geographical and subject matter mix and membership from most of Caterpillar's business units.

At Washington Group International, corporate leadership and the business units share responsibility for leadership development. The development and strategy office is responsible for the design, development, implementation, and maintenance of the programs, while the office of the chairman reviews, approves, and provides feedback on moving forward with development. The fourteen-member senior executive leadership team meets regularly to discuss leadership development.

Similarly, organizations that are committed to leadership development understand its relationship with other talent management systems and practices, such as performance reviews, management development, and succession planning. Washington Group International, for example, integrates leadership development with every aspect of talent management. This process begins with establishing a vision of what positions will need to be filled and then forecasting, identifying, and preparing candidates. Subsequently, employee development plans are carefully crafted for each employee. An overall employee development strategic plan is then created and fed into the succession planning process, which is used in the leadership development program.

Cisco uses executive coaches to accelerate development as part of its high-potential program. In this program, those with high potential are paired with an external executive coach for a year, and although the coach is an external resource, he or she is fully trained in "the Cisco way" prior to the assignment.

Aim for a Multiplier Effect for Strategic High-Potential Programs.
Substantial organizational impact can be gained by involving small numbers of people with high potential who will return to their regular jobs and translate their learning for others. These "translators" of both strategy and learning serve a valuable place in any organization.

Although PwC designed its PwC University experience for two thousand U.S. partners and Caterpillar involved all managers in its 2005 strategy rollout, we have found that most key corporate initiatives are focused on those with high potential. For example, Caterpillar's Leadership Quest involves approximately fifty key midlevel leaders each year. PepsiCo's CEO program involves approximately forty high potentials each year. Washington Group International's Leadership Excellence and Performance project began in 2002 and had graduated forty-eight participants by mid-2006. Cisco's Executive Leader Program focuses on the company's strategic intent and serves approximately forty top leaders annually. This program was designed for employees who are newly promoted to the vice-presidential level or are filling a vice-presidential role.

Implementing Successful Development Strategies

In the development of leaders who will both create and implement strategy, the central question is how to maximize their strategic capabilities—how to get them as thinkers and doers to be more strategic. This question is at the heart of leadership development and is one that every company should consider carefully. Success often depends on a leader's ability not only to envision the future strategically, but also to act on a daily basis in order to make this vision a reality.

The connection between thought and behavior is important. Although it seems logical that behavior follows thought, this connection often works in the other direction. In fact, at Duke Corporate Education, where we have developed many successful programs focusing on changing both behavior and thought or mind-set, we believe that leaders often must change behavior first in order to change their thinking. In other words, we cannot ask leaders to think their way to acting differently. We have to ask them to act first, and then they will start thinking differently. In this way, leadership development, especially to develop more strategic thinkers, is more about helping a leader see herself acting differently and then a change in her beliefs will follow.

Consider the set of practices that follow when working to develop a leader's ability to think and act strategically.

Use Metaphor. Duke Corporate Education has pioneered the use of metaphor in helping leaders learn to think and act strategically and in changing a leader's mind-set and behavior for increased success. Its metaphoric experience learning method takes a leader out of her familiar environment, using role-playing to force her to experiment with new behaviors, skills, and perspectives in an unfamiliar but compelling context. For example, auditors at a public accountancy have become doctors engaged in medical diagnosis, marketers at a software company have become political consultants conducting polling, and executives at a global energy corporation have become tobacco executives facing a congressional subcommittee.

The power of using metaphor in development is found in the ability to reach leaders at a deeper level, with more impact. Metaphoric experiences put leaders in a context and position to think very differently about their work while still allowing them to draw important lessons. They are memorable, change the frame on problems leaders face so they can be seen in a new way, and lead to consideration of new behaviors and mind-sets that would never have been possible through a traditional classroom experience. However, these experiences will be nothing more than an entertaining diversion if they are not carefully designed to meet the expected business outcomes of the company and learning needs of the participants. After the experience, it is essential that the metaphor and experience be tied back to the business and learning outcomes. A rigorous debriefing that explores implications, challenges, and insights is crucial to this method.

Play Games. Playing games at work is becoming more accepted as a serious developmental activity. Learning through games, particularly multiplayer video games, is now seen as an important avenue for leadership development and is becoming part of many organizations' leadership development strategies.

These games, both multiplayer and individual, provide leaders and learners a practice field where risk taking is encouraged and different behaviors and strategies can be employed. Multiplayer games can help prepare leaders to function better in a corporate world of virtual teams where influence and authority operate differently. In games, leaders are forced to make decisions quickly and operate at a different speed—an environment more akin to the increasingly fast-paced, competitive environment of most industries. In addition, games provide leaders the chance to gain experience more quickly and in a different time frame—to finish whole projects and live an entire life in the game environment.

They give leaders the chance to experience leadership and make mistakes in a place where the consequences are mild and easy to recover from.

Will games work to develop better leadership skills in everyone? The answer has to be no, but for many, this is the new frontier for leadership development breakthroughs.

Make It Ongoing. Learning and development should be seen and constructed as a process rather than a set of isolated events. The best organizations for leadership development strive to cultivate and maintain a legacy of teaching and learning throughout the organization, supported by both formal education (programs) and informal learning (team-based learning, on-the-job teaching, and coaching). These organizations see learning and knowledge development as central to their competitive advantage and business strategy.

To remain successful, these companies employ a wide range of learning methods driven by a clear focus on intended business outcomes. Informal learning opportunities are more highly developed in these firms. Most have deliberate routines that bring learning closer to work (for example, after-action reviews and rounds), create opportunities for practice that are oriented to the needs of individuals, and employ techniques such as shadowing as an investment in staff development.

Change the Nature of the Classroom. Stretching leaders in the classroom is essential to any development strategy, especially if the goal is to make leaders more strategic thinkers and doers. Changing the traditional lecture to an environment that involves, stretches, and challenges will develop leaders faster and change them from passive bystanders in learning to active participants.

Using debates, simulations, group activities and projects, facilitated discussions, and other pedagogical techniques expands the impact of the classroom and increases the challenge for developmental impact and learning. We have had firefighters and ballerinas in the classroom to help participants feel and experience leadership in a new way and from a new perspective. We have used naturally occurring problems and challenges leaders face in their everyday work as the teaching material in the classroom in order to create appropriate context and make the learning real and helpful. These methods stretch and engage to a greater extent than lecture does, demanding participants to think and behave differently than they typically do.

Of course, using these and the other techniques may move learning away from the safe environment that is often spoken of, but safety is not in fact the goal; rather, it is development. Changing the nature of the classroom and using different teaching methods will help learning move from being safe to being developmental.

Make Leaders Teachers. A growing trend among senior executives is the practice of leading by teaching. There are important opportunities for synergies between the current generation of top executives and the leaders who will succeed them. While leveraging development programs to achieve their own objectives, leaders can also contribute to the development of the next generation. By serving as teachers and role models, top executives provide direction and insights into their strategic intent and help to ensure that the firm's leadership strategy and developmental programs support the strategic needs of the business, today and tomorrow.

At PepsiCo, senior leaders speak of "the magic of leaders developing leaders." According to one executive, "People learn best when they get to learn from someone they really want to learn from! At PepsiCo, the 'teachers' our executives want to learn from are our own senior leaders. They are world class, widely respected and have proven that they can do it HERE!" Senior executives are asked to share their personal perspectives and then build participants' confidence and skills while demonstrating support for their growth. Of equal importance, senior leaders get greater teamwork from participants and get to know key young leaders, while developing more loyalty, motivation, productivity, and better alignment around vision and key strategic initiatives. PepsiCo leaders are encouraged to think of learning as an important "arrow in their quiver" for helping to drive strategic change. At PepsiCo, leadership development and learning become something to live, not just another thing to endorse.

Evaluating Success

Maintaining organizational commitment to leadership development requires rigorous processes for proving its effectiveness. The companies that are able to most accurately measure the impact of development are those that learn to evaluate their leadership programs using both quantitative and qualitative metrics and focus on both the participants and the organization.

Developing People: A Growing Measure of Executive Success. Best-in-class learning organizations take the development of their people very seriously. They believe that financial results are a lagging indicator of organizational success, while people development is a leading indicator. Consequently, people development is becoming an important part of the assessment of executive performance.

PepsiCo has historically allocated one-third of incentive compensation for developing people, with the remainder for results. In 2007, the company moved to an equal allocation of incentive compensation for people development and results. Pepsi also uses the results from its semi-annual climate survey and 360-degree feedback as part of the performance review process.

Caterpillar found that managers were superb at the execution portion of their leadership framework and satisfactory in the vision category, but they needed more attention to the legacy (developmental) set of behaviors. Consequently, it has begun to focus on this theme in learning programs and in performance assessment.

Corporate Success: The Ultimate Measure of Success in Leadership Development. All five companies we studied in depth were familiar with the Kirkpatrick and Phillips models of evaluation (Kirkpatrick, 2005; Phillips, 2003). However, Caterpillar was perhaps the most rigorous in attempting to measure the return on its learning investment.

That Caterpillar University was established during a recession may have forced its leaders to develop the value proposition for learning early in its history. As part of this, Caterpillar University created a document, "Business of Learning," where each college developed a value proposition for key initiatives based on net benefits, return on investment (ROI), and other standards. This evolved into the enterprise learning plan: a 161-page document that discussed the state of learning at Caterpillar, articulated the value proposition for learning, and estimated the ROI for Caterpillar University at 50 percent for 2003. This was then followed by seven detailed ROI studies. These leveraged focus groups, surveys, and in-depth discussion with participants and identified the benefits, dollar benefits, costs, net benefits, and ROI. Having established the value proposition, Caterpillar has not repeated this process for all subsequent iterations of a program and is beginning to speak about return on learning rather than the more formalized process for ROI.

PepsiCo does not attempt to measure the value created by a program, but the CEO attends each of the major high-potential programs and is the primary facilitator. Since she is intensely involved with program design and delivery, ratings are less of an issue. At the end of each program, participants are asked to send the CEO an e-mail indicating what they will be doing differently as a result of attending the session. Six months later, they are asked to send the CEO another e-mail reporting on how well they have done in meeting their commitment.

Cisco collects both quantitative and qualitative measures. Worldwide Leadership Education has a formal system for measuring the outcomes of leadership development strategy. Examples of metrics include "price range for a one-week course," "customer satisfaction scores," "percentage of class graduates who have used learnings in their jobs and had a positive impact," and "percentage of learners who stay with the company." The team concentrates on metrics showing the application of learning to jobs and changes in business results. An example is the retention percentage for employees going through the programs compared to the general employee population, which has turned out to be quite favorable for Cisco: approximately 93 percent across the organization.

Moving from Events to Process. In the past, corporate educational programs were a disconnected series of independent events. Today they are typically part of an integrated career development plan tied to strategic objectives with specific, actionable objectives. They are seldom one-week discrete events and often include team or individual applications.

The Cisco Leadership Series operates in a three-phase structure that facilitates the employee's ability to put learning into action. It is an events-to-process model. Employees who participate in the various programs progress through each phase: preparation, program, and application on the job. Although the face-to-face portion of Cisco's programs may be only five days, the process for the participants extends over eight to ten months.

Caterpillar's core leadership programs leverage key transition points in its leaders' careers and build on one another in a building-block fashion. Underlying all of its programs is its foundational Making Great Leaders program. These transitions take place as individuals move from supervisor (frontline leader), to manager (leader of leaders), to department head, and finally to executive. A person's movement through these programs and transitions is all part of the developmental journey at Caterpillar.

Conclusion

No business or strategy is good enough to succeed without strong leadership. And this strong leadership has been shown to be at the essence of exceptional organizational performance. Leadership development and learning can play a critical role in helping a company move from its current reality to a desired future destination. Part of closing the gap between these two places is developing leaders who are flexible, collaborative, able to learn and adapt to changing circumstances, and willing to continue their learning journey to becoming better strategic thinkers and doers. When leadership development is seen as a strategic imperative and then tied closely to the strategy and needs of the business, excellent organizational results follow.

Best-in-class strategic leadership development companies have understood these principles well and created best-in-class leadership development strategies, practices, and measures that have contributed to their overall financial and strategic success. They know that great leaders develop great strategies and then deliver on these visions as architects, implementers, and doers.

References

Bernthal, P., and Wellins, R. S. *Leadership Forecast: 2003–2004.* Bridgeville, Pa.: Development Dimensions International, 2004.

Bolt, J. *Executive Development Trends 2000.* Kansas City, Mo.: Executive Development Associates, 2000.

Bolt, J. *Executive Development Trends 2004: Filling the Talent Gap.* Kansas City, Mo.: Executive Development Associates, 2004.

Council, C. L. *Driving Performance and Retention Through Employee Engagement.* Washington, D.C.: Corporate Leadership Council/Corporate Executive Board, 2004.

Fulmer, R. M. *Next Generation HR Practices.* Houston, Tex.: APQC, 2005.

Fulmer, R. M., and Conger, J. A. *Growing Your Company's Leaders: How Great Organizations Use Succession Management to Sustain Competitive Advantage.* New York: AMACOM, 2004.

Kirkpatrick, D. L. *Evaluating Training Programs: The Four Levels.* (3rd ed.) San Francisco: Berrett-Koehler, 2005.

Phillips, J. J. *Return on Investment in Training and Performance Improvement Programs.* (2nd ed.) Burlington, Mass.: Butterworth-Heinemann, 2003.

Rioux, S. M., and Bernthal, P. *Succession Management Practices.* Bridgeville, Pa.: Development Dimensions International, 2006.

Salob, M., and Greenslade, S. *How the Top Twenty Companies Grow Great Leaders.* Lincolnshire, Ill.: Hewitt Associates, 2005.

Saslow, S. *Current Challenges in Leadership Development.* Palo Alto, Calif.: Institute of Executive Development, 2004a.

Saslow, S. *Leadership Development in European Organisations: Challenges and Best Practices.* Palo Alto, Calif.: Danish Leadership Institute and Institute of Executive Development, 2004b.

About the Contributors

Robert M. Fulmer is an academic director at Duke Corporate Education and a Distinguished Visiting Professor at Pepperdine University. A world expert in leadership development, he has designed and delivered executive seminars in twenty-three countries and on six continents. His research and writing have focused on future challenges of management, implementation of strategy, and leadership development as a lever for strategic change. He was named one of the top fifty executive coaches in *The 2004 Handbook of Best Practices in Executive Coaching.*

Fulmer was previously the W. Brooks George Professor of Management at the College of William and Mary and a visiting scholar at the Center for Organizational Learning at MIT. He also taught organization and management at Columbia University's Graduate Business School. For six years, he was director of executive education at Emory University, where he directed the Executive M.B.A. program as well as public and customized programs for general and functional managers.

He earned his M.B.A. from the University of Florida and his Ph.D. from the University of California at Los Angeles.

◆ ◆ ◆

Jared L. Bleak is an executive director at Duke Corporate Education, where he designs and delivers educational programs that meet clients' strategic challenges. He holds an Ed.D. from Harvard University and has taught across the United States, Europe, Africa, and Asia with clients such as Siemens, PricewaterhouseCoopers, Lehman Brothers, Rio Tinto, and Lafarge. His research focuses on leadership development, organizational culture, and executive learning, and he is currently leading a research effort aimed at improving the learning environment in corporations by translating the methods and culture of top-rated teaching hospitals to the corporate environment. He is the author of *The Leadership Advantage: How the Best Companies Are Developing Their Talent to Pave the Way for Future Success* and *When For-Profit Meets Nonprofit: Educating Through the Market,* and has published several other book chapters and articles.

CHAPTER FIVE

DEVELOPING THE INNOVATIVE LEADER

This chapter outlines how leadership development principles can be applied to the creation of innovation teams to provide a strong platform for development and drive disruptive innovation throughout the organization.

The content of this chapter is derived from both *The Innovator's Guide to Growth* by Scott Anthony and Associates and *Mastering Transformation*, a white paper from Innosight. See www.innovatorsguidetogrowth.com and www.innosight.com for further information on these resources.

Innovation. The word oozes with potential: shed the skin of the old; embrace the new; and emerge better, stronger, and more powerful.

Companies are increasingly recognizing that mastering innovation is becoming a competitive imperative. As formerly isolated markets collide and competitors from emerging markets hone disruptive approaches, product life cycles are shrinking and competitive advantage is dissipating more rapidly than ever before. The average length of time a company spends on the Standard & Poor 500 list has shrunk from thirty years to about ten. Long-term survivors underperform market indexes. Companies are accumulating hoards of cash, making massive acquisitions, and buying back stock because they cannot create organic growth. A managing director at Credit Suisse said, "Corporate America is the growth stock that can't grow."

Case studies of sweeping organizational transformation show that success is possible: Nokia moved from rubber boots to mobile phones, Kimberly Clark shifted from a paper provider to a consumer packaged goods leader, Apple sextupled its stock in five years after a decade of stagnation, Google moved from a technology company to an advertising powerhouse, and Procter & Gamble hopped from soaps, to laundry, to skin care, to health care. But the breathless hype behind these stories obscures a brutal reality: most efforts at innovation fail miserably. Just about every manager has lived through an innovation effort that starts brimming with unbridled hope and ends in crashing disappointment.

This unnerving and frustrating reality should not be a surprise. After years of pervasive "continuous improvement" programs, executives are reaping what they have sown. Their organizations, from executives down through to the rank and file, have been motivated and compensated to focus on incremental improvement. These improvements are measured quarterly and annually along competitive performance parameters established years before. To expect this system to create the breakthrough innovations that power transformation is simply unrealistic. Years of continuous improvement training have caused corporate innovation muscles to atrophy.

Institutionalizing Innovation: Developing Deep Organizational Capabilities

This reluctance to focus on innovation is not surprising. Innovation is a punishing game. Follow the right process, introduce a winning model, and competitors flood in. Race to move up-market, and run the risk of running smack dab into the innovator's dilemma, first described by Clayton Christensen in 1997 in the best-selling book by the same name, where yesterday's winning formula not only stops producing meaningful results but conceals great growth opportunities.

Many of the case studies of established companies that have successfully created new growth businesses detail a single success. The companies that have gotten it right once or a handful of times—such as ING's creation of its rapidly growing ING Direct offering, Motorola catching the mobile phone market off guard with its ultra-thin RAZR phone, and Procter & Gamble creating new categories with products such as Swiffer, Febreze, and Crest WhiteStrips—surely demand respect and admiration. Managers of the success stories know all too well how hard it is to fend off the forces that make the creation of innovation-driven growth businesses tricky for market-leading incumbents.

Success, then, requires going beyond winning once to developing deep capabilities that allow a company to repeatedly disarm disruptive threats and seize new growth opportunities. To achieve this goal, companies need to organize in ways that maximize their ability and churn out successful growth businesses year after year.

This chapter examines three key focus areas to make the pursuit of growth through innovation more systematic:

- Defining innovation structure
- Building and empowering growth teams
- Providing additional environmental support

Working through each of these areas and tailoring the design to fit their own circumstances will afford leaders the greatest opportunity for success and repeatable, predictable growth.

Defining Innovation Structure

Organizing to innovate is no small task. It goes beyond providing one team with resources and autonomy to pursue a specific idea. It is about creating an environment in which carefully chosen resources can reliably examine, prioritize, and develop an array of new growth opportunities.

It is also important to note that organizing to innovate is different from organizing for research and development. Innovation goes beyond research and development. A properly structured innovation engine considers new business models, creative financing approaches, and unique partnership strategies, along with more traditional technology levers.

Our belief is that there is no one-size-fits-all way to organize for innovation. Rather, companies need to assess the strategic goals of their innovation structure and the degree to which active management is required to achieve those goals to pick the most appropriate structure (or structures).

Picking a Strategic Goal

The mission of an innovation unit may encompass all or only a piece of the overall innovation activity in a company. Some units simply enhance the innovative mind-set of an organization. Others seed the broader organization with good ideas. Still others drive the organization's growth and profitability. In essence, however, senior management can choose to pursue one of four fundamental goals:

1. *Stimulate innovation* by broadening awareness and building skills. Companies that choose this path typically believe that their organization has the right basic infrastructure to support innovation. However, they believe that managers and teams need help solving practical innovation problems, developing new mind-sets, or gaining exposure to important external developments.
2. *Shepherd innovation* by championing innovation efforts and removing obstacles that would otherwise limit the potential for innovative ideas to succeed. This is a more hands-on approach that helps to nurture

and safeguard innovative efforts, but still relies on the rank and file to drive individual initiatives.

3. *Spearhead innovation* by providing the resources and environment to take ideas from concept to commercialization. This more resource-intensive approach seeks to build new growth initiatives. Companies that follow this approach generally believe that following business as usual will not allow them to meet their innovation objectives.

4. *Source innovation* by borrowing, acquiring, or participating in innovative efforts outside the organization. Companies that choose this path do so because they wish to participate in innovative efforts well outside their core, see little promise of internal innovation, or are looking for ways to augment internal efforts without distracting the core.

Determining the Degree to Which Active Management Is Required

After determining the strategic intent of innovation structure, assess the degree to which these innovation efforts require active management by asking a handful of straightforward questions that cover the external and internal environments:

External Environment

• Is your industry nascent or mature (McGahan and Silverman, 2001; Klepper and Grady, 1990; Gort and Klepper, 1982)?[1] Generally innovation comes more naturally to companies in nascent industries, although companies like CEMEX in cement and Dow Corning in silicones show how innovation can thrive in seemingly mature businesses.

• Is the pace of innovation in your industry slow or fast? If innovation happens slowly, you can afford less active management. If innovation happens rapidly and you are behind the curve, your organizational structure will need to have reasonable impact quickly.

• Is asset intensity low or high? Industries that have high asset intensity often require more active management because the risk in any particular effort is high.

Internal Environment

- Can innovation be isolated to particular departments or groups (an individual manager can "do it alone"), or does it require careful coordination across multiple parts of the organization? The more that innovation efforts are dispersed throughout the company, the more active coordination is required.
- Is the culture open to innovation or myopic in its view of innovation? The less naturally innovation comes to the organization, the more active management is required.
- Are there a high number of innovative-minded managers in the organization, or are the innovators few and far between?

Although clearly these questions simplify complex situations, they provide a helpful way to provide direction on the selection of an appropriate innovation engine architecture.

Picking the Approach

Combining the two areas discussed above suggests eight ways to organize to innovate, set out in Table 5.1.

Building Successful Decision-Making Bodies

Many of the approaches described in Table 5.1 feature a small group of senior managers who review ideas and allocate resources. Whether the group is called a board, a council, or a fund management committee, some general principles can ensure success:

- *Make it easy to get a hearing.* Do not make it difficult for people to suggest ideas, or they never will. If you believe (as we do) that the first cut of a new strategy is wrong anyway, design an approach that promotes the submission of rough ideas that the board can help shape.
- *Stage investment.* Do not flood ideas with capital. Instead, give teams a small amount of money to test key assumptions. Step up investment

TABLE 5.1. EIGHT WAYS TO ORGANIZE TO INNOVATE

Strategic Choice	Degree of Active Management Required	
	Low	High
Stimulate	*Training unit* Helps to build disruption-specific skills and culture Methodically builds the skills and changes the mind-set of core personnel to fuel internal innovation	*Advisory board* Helps serve as vehicle to expand the organization's innovation perspective Fewer than ten people May have outsiders such as academics, consultants, customers, suppliers, thought leaders, and a handful of key internal representatives Interacts with companies in a relatively unstructured way, enabling idea sharing and open dialogue
Shepherd	*Growth council* Brings together a subset of senior leaders from across the company to develop a unified view of the innovation priorities for the organization Identifies areas of strategic interest to the company, vets and prioritizes all early-stage ideas, and actively shepherds disruptive ideas through the innovation process	*Intrapreneur fund* Plays a more active role than growth councils, doling out money and providing support to disruptive projects Teams within the organization propose ideas that do not fit within standard operating procedure
Spearhead	*Incubator* Cross-functional, fully dedicated teams that take a rough idea and spend a brief period of time (four to eight weeks) turning it into something bigger, better, cheaper, and faster Once disruptive ideas have received a focused push, they can be reabsorbed into core innovation processes Teams often have significant flexibility in how they test a concept, but tend to pursue a consistent approach Output of their effort is a systematic plan to test and learn about key assumptions	*Growth group* The next logical step beyond incubators Strategic mission is to commercialize new growth initiatives Role involves both proactive identification and development of noncore business concepts as well as responsive efforts to explore concepts deemed interesting but outside the comfort zone of the core
Source	*Venture capital* Looks externally Seeks ideas, intellectual property, or growth opportunities that do not or could not emerge within the confines of the core Experts agree that the best approach is seeking opportunities that promise both strategic and financial returns	*Acquisitions unit* Seeks opportunities to purchase companies in high-potential markets Examines acquisition targets using a rigorous set of criteria and prioritizes targets based on the core organization's overall growth objectives and risk tolerance Has a mandate from senior management, and works closely with a company's leadership

as they learn more and reshape their strategy to increase their chances of success. Remember the curse of too much capital: overinvestment can allow teams to run fast and hard in the wrong direction.

- *Involve outsiders.* Innovation almost always comes at the intersections, where people look at ideas from different perspectives. Outsiders can help shape ideas in unanticipated ways. Consider bringing in outside industry experts like professors, venture capitalists, or entrepreneurs whose experience helps them identify successful growth strategies.

- *Know what you are looking for.* It is critical to build broad consensus about what a good idea is and communicate that broadly. Some groups use short gut checklists; others use sophisticated screening tools. Regardless of the question list, make sure the decision-making body is looking at everything in the same way and that idea submitters know the evaluation criteria.

- *Make it a pleasant experience.* Funding boards should not seek to tear apart ideas or the managers who submitted them. They should give constructive feedback to even the seemingly worst ideas because it is entirely possible that there is a nugget of brilliance in one of them that can be reshaped into a powerful growth business.

Building and Empowering Growth Teams

The art of team formation and management is seemingly fraught with even more unpredictability than even the knottiest technological problems. Consider this dichotomy: Six Sigma principles suggest that a company should tolerate an error rate of less than 3.5 defects per million in its manufacturing processes. Yet most managers will admit that one in four hiring decisions ends up being a mistake. Teams that hum along merrily in the core business can struggle to master disruptive growth. And teams that start brimming with disruptive potential can slowly and subtly wander off the disruptive path. In short, forming and managing teams is a critical invisible barrier that makes it difficult for even the best-run incumbents to realize their innovation potential.

Setting Objectives and Degrees of Freedom

Teams chartered with creating new growth strategies need guidance about their objectives and degrees of freedom. Left to their own devices, teams often assume they can do things that they cannot, layering on risks that the company is not willing to consider. Even worse, they can assume they cannot do things they actually can. Teams that fall into this trap end up creating close-to-the-core, unexciting growth strategies. This lack of clarity can leave teams paralyzed or can result in their spending a lot of time analyzing an issue that is unimportant.

To address this problem, we suggest creating a team charter: a one-page document that helps the team set off in the right direction. Start that charter with the team's objectives. You might not know what the ultimate successful growth strategy will be, but the odds are high that your first strategy is wrong in some meaningful way. However, you should have a good sense of your overall strategic objectives. Perhaps it is to develop a new growth opportunity in an identified adjacent market. Maybe you are seeking to find a way to leverage a particular technology in a new way. Regardless of the objective, we have found it helpful to summarize the team's strategic objective in one sentence.

Following that sentence should be a description of what the team can unquestionably do, what it can consider doing, and what is off the table. Build off your corporate goals and boundaries to provide guidance to the team about dimensions such as the target customer and geography, distribution channel, steady-state revenue and margin target, type of offering, brand, and tactics.

The key is identifying what is desirable (what you want), what is discussable (what you will consider), and what is unthinkable (what is out of bounds). Making these parameters clear at the start and being willing to consider changing them as new information comes in can help ensure that teams focus on the right activities.

Staffing for Success

Beyond creating a clear charter, senior managers need to staff the team appropriately. The challenge in getting the team right should be familiar to anyone inside a large organization. Sometimes companies try to assemble the "best and brightest." But the best and brightest are typically vital cogs of the core engine that powers the company. Although there might be good bench strength and significant processes to ensure the core keeps humming, losing a key line manager can cause the core to stumble in a damaging way. In addition, the people who are best at running the core business can be the worst at running new ventures.

At other times, companies staff new growth initiatives with the diamonds in the rough. Innovation requires doing things differently, the argument goes, so getting people who think differently may seem like a good idea. In fact, assembling together the land of the misfit toys is unlikely to be the vehicle that drives growth either. These teams can lack the required discipline to move ideas forward and the appropriate organizational gravitas to influence internal resources.

When pursuing disruptive innovations, it is best to select team members who have attended schools of experience where they wrestled with challenges you can predict the team will encounter. To use the schools of experience model, ask two simple questions:

- What problems do we know we will encounter?
- Who, in or out of the organization, has encountered this problem?

It is quite likely that the managers who have addressed identified challenges are not the typical names that bubble up to the top of the list for high-profile ventures. Disruptive pursuits almost always require very different experiences from what a manager faces in the core business. In fact, many of those schools of experience might have come from experiences that managers had in other parts of their career.

Although the challenges teams will encounter often are idiosyncratic, there are some schools of experience that are generally helpful for managers staffed on disruptive projects:

- *Dealt with ambiguity.* Ambiguity typifies disruptive projects. Managers who have worked in highly ambiguous situations are often well prepared for disruptive projects; those who have worked in roles where they have had to ruthlessly remove or minimize ambiguity can be ill suited for disruptive circumstances.

- *Confidently made decisions based on pattern recognition and judgment.* Disruption requires intuition, judgment, and the ability to recognize patterns. Many core roles require managers to dispassionately make decisions based on the numbers or fixed rules.

- *Experimented and found unanticipated customers for a product or service.* In some companies, identification of market opportunities requires meticulous planning and research. Approaches that appropriately hone in on core opportunities can completely miss disruptive opportunities. Managers must be comfortable following novel approaches to understand customer or end consumer needs. They have experience working with the raw data, not delegating research to junior team members or market research firms.

- *Used a deep network to overcome a barrier or solve a problem.* In some organizations, success requires playing by organizational rules such as sticking to the chain of command or avoiding seeking answers externally. Solving disruptive challenges requires the ability to network to overcome a barrier, smartly bend rules, or look outside the company for the answer.

- *Operated in constrained environments.* Managers who have operated in resource-rich environments have the luxury of patiently following a predetermined course and carefully analyzing key unknowns. In constrained environments, managers must scramble and fumble to find success. There are more ways to obtain this school of experience than working at a cash-strapped start-up company. Managers who have experience in developing economies often have to find creative ways to solve problems.

- *Demonstrated a bias for action.* Many managers carefully and cautiously analyze important decisions and seek to build deep consensus before taking action. This approach is valuable for critical decisions that affect core operations, but it can paralyze disruptive ideas. Remember that the first strategy is almost always going to be wrong. Seek managers who moved forward even if the idea later required adjustment.

Identifying critical schools of experience gaps on the team can help inform internal staffing decisions. In addition, it can highlight the need to pull in outsiders who have had a greater chance of addressing the issue than the internal manager.

Case Study: Pandesic

Pandesic was a joint venture established by technology titans Intel and SAP in 1997. Its mission was to develop and sell a simpler, less-expensive version of SAP's enterprise resource planning (ERP) software to small and medium-sized businesses. At its heart, Pandesic was a highly disruptive idea. Historically, SAP targeted its products at huge enterprises and sold its products through established channel partners such as Accenture.

Intel and SAP staffed the Pandesic team with some of their best managers—leaders who had successfully led initiatives within the core SAP and Intel businesses. Pandesic ramped up to a hundred employees in eight months and quickly established offices in Europe and Asia.

Pandesic's managers decided to take their lower-priced, easier-to-implement ERP package to market through the same channel partners it used for SAP's large company systems. The product, initially intended to be a simple ERP solution delivered to small businesses over the Internet, evolved into a completely automated end-to-end solution.

The outcome was predictable. The channel was not motivated to sell Pandesic's simpler, cheaper product that did not need implementation support, when it could make substantial money on the large-scale traditional SAP products. And so Pandesic ended up failing miserably. It sold very few systems and shut its doors in February 2001, after having spent more than $100 million.

What might have happened if SAP and Intel had sought managers who had had different schools of experience? Those managers could have realized that trying to sell the Pandesic product through the same channel as SAP's core products was a huge mistake. This would have been obvious if they had wrestled with a problem like this before in a "school" they had previously attended.

The leaders of Pandesic were not incompetent; they did what made the most sense to them based on their own schools of experience. But they did not have the right schools to know the right questions to ask with a new disruptive venture.

Pandesic made a common mistake. Many companies rely on employees from the core organization to staff new ventures. Using these employees is tempting: they are close to the issues, and hiring managers usually have some previous experience working with them. However, they are grounded in work processes and decision-making patterns that may be dysfunctional in the new environment. Their thinking is also likely to remain focused on the core market, even if they are physically or financially separated from the parent organization.

Similarly, companies can make a mistake when bringing in senior leaders. One of the cases taught in Harvard Business School's entre-preneurial management department describes key lessons learned from a venture capital firm, ONSET Ventures (Roberts and Tempest, 1998). ONSET studied all of its investments that were a success and all of its investments that had failed. One key success factor was hiring a CEO only after a successful business model had emerged. If the business model was not clear, hiring a CEO too soon could be a mistake, because the CEO would default to using a business model that had worked in the past for that person. Once the business model was clear, the search for a CEO became much easier.

Other Supporting Structures and Systems

Even the best innovation structures can fail to drive innovation if they are not supported by other structures and systems. Companies that suc-cessfully generate this environment develop tools that are appropriate for innovative businesses, share a common language of innovation, draw on substantial external input, and create policies and incentives that encourage people to take managed risks on the path to innovative growth.

Appropriate Tools

Companies that are excellent at running their core business often find that tools designed to manage core innovations can stand in the way of suc-cessfully creating new growth initiatives. The problem is as much use and interpretation as it is the tool itself. After all, the intent of most tools in core operations is to manage allocation of resources and gain internal alignment. Precise tools help companies make sure they move the right projects forward, manage their supply chain appropriately, allocate internal resources at the right rate, and develop a winning relationship with key channel partners.

True innovation is necessarily imprecise, particularly in the early days. Tools that force precision too soon can cut off great opportunities or force innovators to move in more sustaining directions to make the numbers.

Typically the very theory of how to use a tool needs to change. When a company is working on a close-to-the-core initiative, tools typically are used to validate hypotheses. If the data do not conform to a predetermined hypothesis, the default behavior is to use the tool again. For disruptive initiatives, tools need to be used for discovery. If data do not conform to a predetermined hypothesis, the team needs to examine the hypothesis. This distinction becomes particularly critical if the tool being used asks the wrong question for a disruptive project.

Companies that find that their existing tool kit is inadequate for disruptive growth have two choices. One is to change the tools they use. Instead of feeding results from a large-scale survey into a ten-year forecast, use qualitative data to estimate how passionate customers are about an idea. Alternatively, existing tools can be used in different ways. For example, instead of producing a point estimate of volume and net present value, companies can develop scenarios or create ranges for alternative scenarios. This approach can be difficult for senior managers who are trained in looking for the number, but it is a more realistic estimate of an idea's potential.

A Common Language of Innovation

Succeeding with disruptive innovation requires taking action that may be at best unfamiliar and at worst antithetical to many corporate managers. Innosight's experience suggests that a common language helps companies avoid some of the many mind-set traps that make the pursuit of disruption difficult, such as pursuing perfection when "good enough" would be sufficient, overestimating knowledge of new markets, and planting big bets when a small start is more appropriate.

It is important that senior managers and middle managers alike break these mind-sets. After all, many of the most important resource allocation decisions are the incremental choices made by project teams. Middle managers who do what they have always done can destroy the best intentions of senior managers; senior managers who still subscribe to these harmful mind-set traps can derail a middle manager's well-designed approach. Companies need to have a common language related to innovation that allows them to work together in new ways.

External Insight

In the past few years, companies have begun to realize the real power of what Hank Chesbrough (2003) calls "Open Innovation." Procter & Gamble is an instructive example. Historically the company had a reputation for being highly insular, yet several years ago, CEO A. G. Lafley set out a stark challenge: by 2010, at least 50 percent of the company's innovations should involve some form of outside connection. Procter & Gamble has augmented its research and development capability with the ability to connect and develop. As Huston and Sakkab (2006) noted in a *Harvard Business Review* article, the company is shifting its "attitude from resistance to innovations 'not invented here' to enthusiasm for those 'proudly found elsewhere.'"

Generally companies should involve external perspectives deeply in the innovation process. They should have well-defined ways to routinely and repeatedly interact with their core customers, learn from noncustomers, monitor ongoing industry experiments, scan for emerging technologies, and learn from other industries. Setting up regular ways to draw on these kinds of external stimuli, including some of the mechanisms described here, can expose previously invisible opportunities for innovation.

Enabling Human Resource Policies

Finally, companies must consider rearchitecting their policies, incentives, and development paths to make them innovation friendly. Instead of looking for managers who have succeeded in core assignments, companies need to seek those who have attended the right "schools of experience" that will help them spot and nurture new-growth businesses. For many companies, finding the right managers might require an external search because even the most capable internal managers have not wrestled with challenges related to creating new growth businesses.

Getting incentives for innovation right is clearly a large hurdle for an established company. A start-up company can issue equity that allows managers to share in a venture's upside potential. Following the same approach inside an established company requires some creativity. Companies need to find a way to link managed risk taking with pay structures, bonuses, or career progression, or some combination of these. It is unlikely that intrapreneurs will have the pure upside of entrepreneurs, but that is appropriate because they also have significantly lower downside risk. Despite the attention showered on the success stories, the vast majority of new ventures fail. If an internal venture fails, managers can easily move to another position instead of having to search for an entirely new job.

Finally, consider creating development paths that make it attractive for high-potential employees to spend time working on promising growth initiatives. Working on risky ventures can be an effective proving ground for emerging leaders because many of the challenges the venture will face will be general management issues.

As you develop human resource structures that will enable your organization to achieve its innovation goals, consider the incentive and learning value offered by rotation programs. Creating the possibility for high-potential employees or business unit members with relevant knowledge to participate in innovative growth initiatives can provide them with exposure to new ways of problem solving and new decision-making challenges. At a minimum, their experience working on such initiatives will provide them with rich learning to bring back to their core area after their participation. At the extreme, you might create the leaders of your next new core business.

Conclusion

Innovation is not easy for companies struggling to balance the need to grow in new areas against the need to maintain their competitive position in current markets. But it can be made more predictable by focusing on the structure, staffing, and support of the program. Structure must take into consideration the market conditions, internal environment, and growth imperative. Staffing must consider schools of experience to ensure that the appropriate level of leadership is provided at each evolutionary phase of a new offering. Support should empower the teams to succeed efficiently and can come from tools, techniques, language, and human resource practices.

Note

1. McGahan and Silverman (2001) have indicated that the rate of innovation and the emphasis placed on innovation (as measured by the number of new patents issued per year in an industry) do not change significantly in mature industries as classically defined. However, the skills and supporting organizational structure to operate and innovate in that industry certainly must. Furthermore, one could contend that the nature of innovations tends to shift from disruptive or radically sustaining to more incrementally sustaining over time, leaving the door open for a new disruption.

References

Anthony, S. D., Johnson, M. W., Sinfield, J. V., and Altman, E. J. *The Innovator's Guide to Growth: Putting Disruptive Innovation to Work.* Boston: Harvard Business School Press, 2008.

Chesbrough, H. *Open Innovation.* Boston: Harvard Business School Press, 2003.

Christensen, C. *The Innovator's Dilemma.* Boston.: Harvard Business School Press, 1997.

Gort, M., and Klepper, S. "Time Paths in the Diffusion of Product Innovations." *Economic Journal,* 1982, *92,* 630–653.

Huston, L., and Sakkab, N. "Connect and Develop: Inside Procter & Gamble's New Model for Innovation." *Harvard Business Review,* 2006, *84,* 58–66.

Innosight, LLC. *Mastering Transformation.* January 2008.

Klepper, S., and Grady, E. "The Evolution of New Industries and the Determinants of Market Structure." *Rand Journal of Economics,* 1990, *21*(1), 27–44.

McGahan, A. M., and Silverman, B. S. "How Does Innovative Activity Change as Industries Mature?" *International Journal of Industrial Organization,* 2001, *19*(7), 1141–1160.

Roberts, M. J., and Tempest, N. "ONSET Ventures." *Harvard Business School Case* 9–898–154, 1998.

About the Contributors

Scott Anthony is president of Innosight LLC and author of *The Innovator's Guide to Growth* (2008).

◆ ◆ ◆

Mark Johnson is chairman and cofounder of Innosight.

◆ ◆ ◆

Joe Sinfield is a senior partner of Innosight.

◆ ◆ ◆

Liz Altman is vice president of strategy and business development for Motorola's Mobile Devices unit.

◆ ◆ ◆

Kevin Bolen is a senior director with Innosight and author of *Mastering Transformation* with Scott Anthony (2008).

CHAPTER SIX

DEVELOPING LEADERS IN A GLOBAL LANDSCAPE

This chapter outlines the impact that globalization is having on leadership and the art of developing leaders and introduces the concept of "distributed leadership" as a means of optimizing leadership across global barriers.

My aim in this chapter is to explore how the impact of globalization is changing the nature of leadership. Yet that said, much about the leadership process has not really changed throughout history. It requires identifying and articulating a clear vision, an effective (and competitive) tool kit, appropriate organizational structure, and empowered and energized people. It has also become clearer over time that leaders and followers must share a common set of values and beliefs.

The literature shows that leadership is a multifaceted activity (a process), not an abstract concept. Effective leadership is all about change (Kotter, 1996), combining action, people, and organizational skills (Fiedler, 1967; Hosking and Morley, 1988). Leadership is a process, and it can be learned (Grint, 1997). Leaders and followers are inseparable (Burns, 1978), and leadership is a moral activity (Gardner, 1990).

Armed with this background, I have used my professional experience and subsequent research to build a simple leadership framework designed to analyze what leaders do and how they can all do better. This 4E's framework (envision, enable, empower, energize) is focused on actions in use rather than espoused competencies, individual styles, or personality types. It attempts to isolate common characteristics of leaders, rather than create a "super-set" of perfect leadership. I explore details later, but in short:

- *Envision:* Values-driven setting of goals and strategies
- *Enable:* Identification of appropriate tools, technologies, organization, and people
- *Empower:* Creation of trust and interdependence between leaders and followers
- *Energize:* Personal leadership motor to drive the entire system

The complexity organizations face today suggests that leadership must be distributed rather than focused on a small group of individuals (Gronn, 2002). Only then can organizations use the combined power of everyone in the enterprise to meet the challenge of the ever more complex range of issues they face. Distributed leadership as a concept was probably first suggested by Gibb (1954). But it is only relatively recently, with the growth of networks, virtual teams, and communities of practice, that it has been broadly studied. Gronn (2002) suggested that distributed leadership has two threads:

1. *Numerical or additive*, which refers to "the aggregated leadership behaviour of some, many or all of the members of an organisation or an organizational sub-unit." It means that leadership is "dispersed rather than concentrated."
2. *Concertive action*, in which distributed leadership is more than the sum of its parts. Distributed leadership is about the leadership that emerges from "multi-member organizational groupings" and is defined as "the demonstrated or presumed structuring influence attributable to organisation members acting in concert."

Building on this leadership base and to help us all grapple with the complexities of the global world, I have created a simple global leadership framework with four areas of focus:

1. *Distributed leadership:* Creating the environment and common value system and training to build and encourage leadership at all levels of the enterprise
2. *Loose-tight innovation:* Using clearly defined success models to roll out quickly and efficiently across the world, balanced with local innovation driven by customer needs and differences
3. *Networks of trust:* Creating communities of innovation across the enterprise that share ideas and expertise and help their members grow to trust each other and that learn from today's science of networks
4. *Strategic engagement:* Ensuring that everyone in the enterprise understands the strategy, shares its values, and is engaged in executing its plans

And I am suggesting that we use the 4E's—envision, enable, empower, and energize—to organize this framework.

Global Leadership

I want to be clear about my starting point: globalization is a positive force and it is irresistible. Having visited India, Russia, and China in the 1970s, it is clear to me that people in those countries are on average much better off today than they were thirty years ago. There are many challenges, many people still must escape poverty, and many need to be truly free. But the general sweep of human history is positive, and never more so since the end of World War II.

Globalization has always been a force in the world, from the expansion of ancient empires through to the age of discovery and then the era of colonialism. These gave way to major industrial shifts and today's drive for efficiency and lowest production costs from around the world. Add to this the interconnectedness of political and social concerns, unparalleled impact from computer and telecommunications technology, and the ubiquity of the Internet, and it is clear that globalization is here to stay.

What makes understanding leadership quite challenging today are several almost paradoxical pressures. There is an explosion of information and knowledge, and occasionally wisdom, from the burgeoning knowledge economy. This means that even the most efficient of today's organizations struggle to keep up with rapidly changing customer needs and competitive innovation. They require ever more specialized responses, yet also a broader contextual understanding of customers' issues. To compound things, there is a simultaneous convergence and divergence in science and technology. No one scientist can understand all science; specialization is essential. Yet there is much crossover, for example, from biological computing to the need to understand physical fluid dynamics in the practice of advanced surgery. And the multiplication of alliances, business networks, outsourcing, and the like, both internal and external to the enterprise, makes it hard to drive focus and simplification in delivering consistent results.

In the political and social arenas, we must also take account of the various views on terrorism and the ongoing tussle between developed and developing nations. And we have (it seems) more and more countries and nationalities to understand and contend with than ever before in history.

There are 101 definitions of *globalization*, although most of them seem to be economically based and are built around open markets in a borderless world. Globalization is an intense engagement in both economic and social openness, and today's leadership must reflect this. Held and McGrew (2002) called it "a widening, deepening and speeding up of interconnectedness in all aspects of contemporary social life from the cultural to the criminal, the financial to the spiritual." One of the better formal approaches to defining *globalization* is from the consultancy group KOF, which publishes annual indexes on how global countries are (Belgium is the current world champion). The index reflects economic globalization, characterized as long-distance flows of goods, capital, and services, as well as information and perceptions that accompany market exchanges; political globalization, characterized by a diffusion of government policies; and social globalization, expressed as the spread of ideas, information, images, and people.

So how should leaders think and act to embrace globalization and then manage it? I suggest that the economics side is now well-trodden territory, and although political policies need careful and systematic understanding, even these are getting to be manageable; witness the success of multinational companies and today's interconnected world of commerce.

I focus here on the social side of globalization because it remains challenging for leaders. And as I have studied the issue, one question that always arises is which of the historic truths of the leadership process can we hold onto and which need to be modified to reflect our own era.

Many macrosocial drivers are forcing us to think in new ways, starting with technology and economics. But I also contend that individual human aspirations (the microview) suggest that people want similar things from their leaders as they always have.

We start an exploration of what seems new in today's version of globalization and then examine how to lead in this world.

What's New About Globalization?

Let me start by telling a short story.

Learning from India. In the early 1990s, I was responsible for a business that was introducing a concentrated powder detergent into India. India at that time was not only the biggest market for detergents in the world, but most people used bar soap and took up to five hours to do the daily laundry. The new powder used world-class technology and even had the same name as its European cousin. It allowed soaking and less manual labor, and at least halved the entire washing time. The team had decided to sample the product using more affluent households because although the cost per wash was the same as before, the actual unit packet price was a lot more than bars of soap. The initial cost outlay for the consumer was quite high by Indian standards of the time.

After the launch, we were walking through Visakhapatnam, the town on the east coast of India where we were test marketing. I was stopped by a lady who walked out of a shanty. She was clearly not very well off, but asked me in understandable English if I would like tea. She explained that she had seen the TV advertisement for the new product.

She told me in no uncertain terms that we were not giving her a chance to try it because she had not received a sample, and she could not risk the amount of money needed to buy a whole packet. She was also very clear that sending her children to school in clean, white blouses was as important to her as to richer people. Needless to say, we gave her and her friends samples.

The Moral of the Story. When it comes to the most important things in life, people often want very similar things. In India, the marketing execution needed to be tailored, but not the product fundamentals or the value proposition to the customer. Eighty percent of what we were doing would apply to most markets of the world. The 20 percent tailoring made all the difference, but we were right to start with what was the same with the rest of the world rather than what was different.

Meeting the Indian woman taught me a lot about global common ground, the leapfrogging of technology in developing markets, and the

80:20 rule. Since then, my core operating principle has been that people are more the same than they are different. Of course, there are historical, cultural, and economic differences, but a good place to start any leadership dialogue is to figure out the common aspirations and needs.

The Indian woman wanted exactly the same as her European counterparts: the ability to choose for herself. She also had the same basic need: to get her laundry done as easily and cheaply as possible. Even the "meta need" (to send her children to school as smartly as possible) reflected the thoughts of parents the world over. She really did exemplify Pareto's 80:20 rule.

So how can leaders' get to grips with this 80:20 rule to isolate what is the same and then be able to understand and respond to unique local needs and characteristics? All over the world customers are continually upping their expectations of the products and services they use. And in the fastest-growing markets, consumers are leapfrogging traditional technologies. For example, China and India now have the world's biggest mobile phone user bases. So from a product and services point of view, it is usually best to use highest-common-denominator technology for the most competitive delivery of benefits.

But what about the organizational side of things? What is today's highest-common-denominator approach to global leadership and organization development? From a practical perspective, focusing on similarities allows us to build constructive discussion and move toward shared goals. But if you start by seeking out and highlighting differences, you will find it harder to create a shared understanding. Focusing on differences pushes us toward confrontation and a debate about who is right and who is wrong.

Can we therefore pick a few common-ground social drivers in today's version of globalization that will allow us to do a better job? I do not mean the technology or the economic changes, but rather some of the deeply rooted social changes that drive people's needs, ideas, and behaviors. As a filter, my premise is that leaders and their followers must develop congruent value systems for them to coexist and cooperate.

There are at least four major social trends to consider, and each has special leadership lessons:

1. The increasing democratization of decisions of all kinds
2. A desire to build our relationships, fueled by new technologies and the creation of networks going well beyond our immediate geographies
3. Increasing pressure on the globa-local paradox, where it seems we all want similar things yet all want more local choice
4. The need for more personal engagement in enterprises that is reflected on the macrostage and in our workplaces

Democratization of Decisions

We take democratization of decisions for granted, and when we do not have it, we want it. While in the West, we seem to vote less than we used to, we still demand the right to have a vote and to be heard. Of course, part of this is an increasing demand for transparency and good governance.

In the developing world, there are struggles for more democracy everywhere and a demand for the rule of law. As these countries move swiftly into the twenty-first century, they work hard to keep the best of their traditional culture with the most helpful aspects of the modern world. Democratization tends to be a fundamental plank of modernization.

Late in 2007, Hong Kong's chief executive announced that the Beijing government will allow the territory to directly elect its leader by 2017 and all its lawmakers by 2020. Although this is a long time in the future, it is an inevitable result of China's social and political evolution on the global stage.

At work, we also want to be heard and respected, and we want people to abide by collective rules. The best leaders have always reflected the needs of their followers, and in that sense, they have democratized decisions. But the days of one leader deciding for everyone are long gone. Yes, leaders point the way, but they must be ever more cognizant of the needs and desires of their constituencies and stakeholders or they will lose their jobs.

Witness what has happened to so many CEOs in the past five years, and the move off-stage of a seemingly impregnable politician such as Tony Blair underlines that no one is above public opinion. The desire we all have to know what is going on and to have a voice in matters is amplified by today's around-the-clock communications. Every leadership decision is scrutinized, from the highest level of political theater to the shop floor.

The Leadership Lesson: Distributed Leadership. No one individual can handle all of this democratization. Leadership is no longer positional or belongs to just a few people. Technology is too complex, democratization so widespread, and social interactions too diverse. Leadership must have a common purpose and shared values that allow it to move around fluidly depending on need, expertise, and the personal desire to lead in certain circumstances.

Hierarchy lost out to teams in the 1950s and 1960s, and matrices became trendy in the 1970s and 1980s. Networks are increasingly seen as the main metaphor of today's organization, and within them, ideas, concerns, actions, and emotions move around constantly. Leaders can spring up in unpredictable areas and in unexpected ways. But what if an enterprise can harness this power?

Distributed leadership is a concept that is coming into its time. We need to have leadership responsibility move around an organization depending on the need, expertise, and opportunity rather than have it positionally frozen in an organization chart.

Building Relationships

To one degree or another, we are all proud to be a national of our own country. Even people most noted for political cynicism defend the hard-won rights of their national laws, culture, and social system. And we often use this to define our place in the complexity of the globe.

But today we also want to be part of nongeographical communities, both real and virtual. Increased leisure time has led to a myriad of clubs, sporting complexes, and entertainment facilities across the world. And in the virtual space, the explosion of social network sites such as MySpace, LinkedIn, flickr, and Facebook demonstrate the need in all of us to qualify our lives in terms of relationships and not just geography. It appears we see these communities as ways of defining who and what we are. And we are learning how to pick and choose the positives and negatives from all of our affiliations. We value our friends, we block those we do not value, and we pride ourselves in choosing to be with like-minded groups. Empires today are increasingly built on shared values, ideas, and common interests, whatever one's geographical or ethnic origin. They are increasingly about personal relationships.

Once more let me tell a short story.

Learning from Thailand. In the mid-1990s, Johnson & Johnson (J&J) was figuring out how best to balance its very successful autonomous business unit approach with the need to share best practice and build regional cooperation. Other companies had adopted a global approach, pushing out common products and services everywhere as fast as possible, and some had stuck almost religiously to local independence. J&J wanted to find a balance better suited to the company's culture.

My role was company group chairman for the consumer business in Asia Pacific. Our management team had determined that we would create Asia-wide brand teams—maybe not a novelty since other companies started these in the 1980s in Europe, but certainly a change for J&J in Asia.

Early in the process I was having dinner with a group of marketing people from J&J's Thailand company. A young brand manager asked, "Tell me, what it will be like when we do what you say we are planning to do?"

I answered:

Today, when you have a problem you can't solve on your own, you ask your manager, and then if he can't help, he or she escalates the question up the hierarchy. At some point, it may reach me. This all takes time and is very bureaucratic. In the future, you will know a colleague in, for example, Australia, who may not know the answer but will be able to put you in touch with someone who can help.

You will take what they offer, modify it to your local needs, and armed with the answer, you tell your manager how you've resolved things. In this new world, you are in charge, not me.

You will balance the best practice from around the world with your local knowledge, and your personal network of contacts will help you succeed.

The Moral of the Story. Often before it globalizes an enterprise is built on strong geographical, functional, or service line structures and processes, which it has honed as it became successful. While it is obviously important to retain strong skill sets and competencies, this very strength can lead to a negative mentality.

People tend to trust what they know and are resistant to change. We all rely on existing relationships before we move to new ones. To change, we need to feel more comfortable with where we are going than where we have been. Leaders must build shared responsibility and trust, aiming to break down these silos at every level: enterprise, team, and individual.

Critical to trust is the sharing of values, clear roles and responsibilities in the new environment, and strong personal relationships within the group. Clear communication about what is expected in the future state is critical.

During a 2004 survey conducted by LeaderValues.com, a random group of leaders was asked what they believed were the critical components of trust. Each leader was only allowed to choose one answer, and the results were as follows.

What are the critical components of trust?

Common goals	3%
Common values	31%
Personal relationships	23%
Clear measurements	3%
Strong leadership	8%
"Trust but verify"	5%
Clear roles and responsibilities	23%

In the business world, Western enterprises tend to view the value of their business as the sum of its transactions. The measurement focus tends to be on shareholder value. There is a transactional bias, in that stakeholders get a return based on the specific activities of the business.

In Asia, shareholder return is also important, but the perceived value of a business also usually includes the sum of its relationships.

Effort is applied to building strong relationships with customers, suppliers, employees, investors, and even competitors. Witness the rise of Toyota, just-in-time manufacturing, and the Total Quality Movement as a whole, which all depend on excellent supplier relationships.

Today, Western companies are also working to improve their relationships with all of their stakeholders in what can only be described as a positive blurring of global paradigms. Tesco is a great example. It is one of the most successful retailers and, like many of its competitors, has a customer loyalty program. Tesco, however, says that the program is to allow it to be loyal to its customers, not the other way around. Leaders who want the loyalty of their followers would do well to remember this simple statement.

The Leadership Lesson: Networks of Trust. Our webs of relationships need to be formally recognized, analyzed, and acted on. The science of networks is still a young one, but it offers many clues for leaders who want to embrace the desire for ever more complex human relationships.

Leadership must clarify how these processes will work and offer a court of last resort to resolve issues if necessary. Sometimes a decision actually can build trust, not negate it.

Since the 1980s, most organizations, big and small, have created matrices and networks designed to balance functional and geographical activities, competencies, and learning. All matrices have flaws, yet generally the benefits are considered to outweigh these flaws. Matrices can be of many forms—for example, functionally focused, where employees remain full members of functional organizations; balanced between functions or geographies, service lines, or customer units; or project based, with movement between functions and geographies depending on need.

But all of these matrices lead to a high level of virtuality and multisite team dealings across functions and geographies. Experience suggests that some of the following get in the way of trust building:

- *Misaligned goals and strategies.* This can occur in all kinds of enterprises and organization structures.

- *Resistance to or misunderstanding of change.* Individuals react to change by embracing it, being overwhelmed by it, or simply remaining stuck in their old ways. An effective and defined multistep change process is essential in moving to a new matrix or team structure.

- *Unclear roles and responsibilities.* In the early days of a new team, individuals are uncertain of their role (inside the enterprise), their responsibilities (including in relationship to customers and the external world), and their own personal future development. Well-defined and well-executed measurement processes must build on clear roles. They must reflect not only an individual's specific responsibilities, but also that person's responsibilities to the organization as a whole in the team setting.

- *Ambiguous or unclear decision-making processes.* In traditional or start-up organizations, leadership is usually vested in specific individuals and often personified by them. While effective individual leadership is, if anything, even more important in virtual teams, the structure itself can create significant confusion. For example, some individuals may have direct authority by make decisions in certain areas, yet be only advisory or matrixed in others. This adds to the concerns and can create negative tensions, lack of motivation, and, in the worst case, internal sclerosis.

- *Silo-focused organizations and employees.* Successful enterprises are built on strong and well-honed functional or service-line structures and processes. Although it is obviously important to retain strong skill sets and competencies, this very strength can lead to a negative silo mentality. Instead, we must seek to build a sense of shared responsibility and risk. Different approaches can be used to break down these silo walls, working at the enterprise, team, and individual levels. And consideration of the power of communities of practice can be helpful here.

- *Insufficient attention to trust building.* This often reflects an imbalance between how best to deliver the goals of an enterprise and how best to both empower and trust employees to independently handle the tasks at hand. Clear roles and good personal relationships with shared values are key components to help build trust—once the goals, strategies, structures, and measurements are clearly defined.

- *Infrequent personal feedback and team celebration.* In many multisite teams, the only kind of individual feedback people get is infrequent and usually by e-mail or a telephone call. E-mail is notorious in being easy to misunderstand in such situations; it can be terse and lacking in context and nuance. At the end of the day, there is no substitute for some face-to-face contact, especially to discuss performance issues. Celebrations of team accomplishments can also be rare (other than the laudatory e-mail). I am not arguing for instituting "party time," but even virtual teams need to meet occasionally to celebrate success and failure.

Poor communication is at the root of many (if not all) trust problems with virtual and multisite teams. There is a need to systematically build communication into the day-to-day activities of teams:

- *Find ways to build face-to-face time.* It is important to have initial meetings with all team members to define the project or scope of activities. If all members of the team cannot physically get together, the team leadership must travel to meet the members, carrying consistent messages. And then they must meet face-to-face periodically throughout the life of the team, building project understanding and commitment and personal relationships.
- *Routinely give team members a sense of how things are going.* There are many ways to do this: e-mail, Web based, newsletters, conference calls, and others. The point is that the leadership must systematically define and then execute this.
- *Establish a day-to-day code of conduct.* Define and share how the team should take operate, and not just at the values level but in day-to-day operations. For example, decide how long it should take to answer phone calls and e-mails, and so help ensure that all members of the team keep their high- and lower-level promises and commitments to each other.
- *Do not let team members vanish.* For example, use work-group software to communicate members' calendars, set up routine project reporting mechanisms, and establish management mentoring of junior people.

- *Augment text-only communication.* A picture is worth a thousand words, and virtual team communication is no exception.

The Global-Local Paradox

On a global scale, we are ever more connected: an Asian currency crisis or a U.S. mortgage crunch directly affects shopping on the High Streets of England. A war anywhere is now always a world war, both on television and in reality. Yet in many countries, nationalism is on the rise and immigration is frowned on despite the economic need. Suffice it to say that just as things are getting more global (with living standards going up and people wanting similar things), so the desire for fragmentation into local communities gets stronger (we all want to have specific common interests and relationships).

The following story predates e-mail and other technology advantages but nevertheless illustrates some of these things and how to overcome them.

Learning from Europe. In the 1980s as a young general manager, I was involved with helping rebuild Procter & Gamble's Pampers business across Europe. The brand had been outmaneuvered by competition with better products and sharper pricing. So P&G needed a way of managing across geographical boundaries in Europe to get the business fixed, and fast. The job was to assemble, for the first time, a "Euro team" and make it work. And there was a catch: I did not have direct-line responsibility over the countries involved—a classic matrix.

The first thing to define was how to make our product better than the competition's. P&G's centralized R&D pulled this off. They looked around the world for the best possible products, whether P&G's or otherwise. Manufacturing then upgraded all production facilities to make the new products efficiently. This sounds easier than it was, as a series of massive and gutsy financial decisions was taken at the CEO level. But the principle of "Global Best in Class" was embraced by all.

However, marketing was quite tricky, as every country previously had autonomy. How should we market the new products? We applied similar rules: search out the best in class first. The most vital part of the Pampers business was in the Benelux, where the advertising and sampling mix had held market share in the face of major competitive challenges. But how could we get the Germans, the British, the French, and the Italians to accept what the Euro team wanted to do? In fact, that was easier than we had expected. First, everyone was desperate for a business fix. Second, the multicultural nature of the Euro team helped by making everyone feel part of the solution.

But we still did not want the Euro team to trample on national pride or responsibility. And we were paranoid about the need to encourage ever more innovation to stop disaster from happening to Pampers again. So we jointly struck a deal: copy the marketing success model from the Benelux, but when that was running in each country, the local teams were encouraged to test anything else to see if they could do better. The Euro team not only agreed to this but helped execute it with the local team.

It worked, and a good eighteen months ahead of schedule. Pampers remains the market leader in Europe today.

The Moral of the Story. First, look for the best available global or regional strategies, technologies, and executions in all aspects of defining a success model. Then encourage local innovation to beat it. In other words, deal with the global-local paradox by going after both ends of the spectrum at the same time, but in a measured, well-understood, and jointly agreed process.

The Leadership Lesson: Loose-Tight Innovation. From a leadership perspective, we must embrace the paradox and set a common course that is both mindful and respectful of differences yet has sufficient common ground that it is applicable to all. A great idea to spread best practice is the building of success models (discussed later in this chapter).

We need to create innovation processes that broaden the access to information and best practice and simultaneously drive down responsibility as far as we can in our enterprises. I call this "loose-tight innovation." We must also use networks of trust to create innovation from outside the defined boundaries of our enterprises, because no one business can invent everything itself.

Organizations such as Innocentive help connect inventors with companies needing their ideas, and many enterprises now use such networks to boost internal invention. Toyota has done this for years through the supplier network, and P&G uses the well-documented Connect and Develop approach.

The Need for Personal Engagement

Once more, a short story is instructive.

Learning from Japan. At another point in my Procter & Gamble career, I became responsible, as the president, for the newly acquired Max Factor business in Japan. By way of background, in Japan Max Factor is a competitor to Chanel and Shiseido, with beauty counselors in department stores and a flagship prestige product called SKII. It is not the supermarket brand seen in many other parts of the world.

In the first month of my stay in Japan, I visited the plant at Shiga, near Tokyo. It was meant to be a first look around, meeting people and starting to form opinions. I was accompanied by Nozaka-san, the president before the acquisition, and one of the architects of the company's success in Japan. At one point, I found myself speaking formally to fifty or so managers in the plant. During the question time, I was asked to describe the next ten years of Max Factor's future in Japan. I felt I was a pretty experienced speaker and manager, so, helped by my translator, Yasaki-san, I proceeded to do my best with the vision.

As I started to speak, everyone took out their notepads and started to write down verbatim what I was saying. I discovered later that the managers wanted to know not only the strategic vision but also what their role was in executing it. Talking "big picture" just would not cut it. No one would blindly accept the ideas, and everyone needed to know where they fit. And beyond understanding the plan, they also needed to get the measure of their new president: me.

The Moral of the Story. Be prepared, never wing it, and recognize that different cultures deal with the joining of strategy and execution in diverse ways. Leaders need to engage their organizations in the way they want to be engaged, not necessarily how the leaders think it should be.

Part of that engagement is strategic and relates to the personalization of the plan. And part of it is intensely personal, where the leader is constantly being measured, appraised, and either accepted or rejected by his or her followers.

The Leadership Lesson: Strategic Engagement. Leaders the world over tell stories that bring the strategy alive to make sense for the individual. Think of President Kennedy's soaring vision: "By the end of the decade, we will put a man on the moon and bring him home safely." This not only energized an entire scientific and industrial strategy, it brought alive what was being done to the man in the street. And the context (of getting to the moon before the Russians, having been beaten by *Sputnik*) became a source of national pride and energy.

Dave Hanna, a former colleague, once said that "every organization is perfectly designed to get the results it gets." Leaders must always start with a clear understanding of the strategic choices of the enterprise and their goals. But how they are communicated and how employees engage with these choices is critical to success.

Unfortunately, establishing clear goals and communicating them effectively are common challenges for many organizations. A 2004 LeaderValues.com survey asked the question of what most leaders find makes their work most difficult. Here is how they responded:

Technology	3%
Unclear goals and objectives	40%
Management of change	6%
Poor communications	35%
Our work processes	5%
Customer Needs	3%
Managing knowledge and ideas	5%

All employees want to feel valued for their contribution. A working definition of employee engagement might be "the measurable extent to which employees are aligned with and emotionally attuned to the values, goals, strategies, and tactics of their enterprise." This can be achieved only with what I call strategic engagement. The top-level strategic story must directly connect with everyone's understanding of the task and their unique part in it. On the global stage, when dealing with so many diverse views, relationships, and cultural impacts, this is mission critical.

Leadership and Culture

Now that I have established the four main leadership lessons—the need for distributed leadership, networks of trust, loose-tight innovation, and strategic engagement—we turn to one area that varies across the world, culture, and, following that, an area that seems to me to be consistent— the leadership process. I then pull this all together with the global leadership framework.

Cultural Considerations

Colonialism is dead, and businesses need to benefit from the economies of global scale while also meeting unique local needs. As we globalize, we need clear and well-communicated strategies with the same values in action all over the world. We cannot just use slogans. But if there is an 80:20 at work, what is the impact of culture? Is it an 80 or a 20? The answer, not completely helpful, is that it all depends on the issue at hand. When it comes to the technology of washing products, culture probably has little impact, and the 80 might even be close to 100. How the consumer used the product is, of course, the 20. But when it comes to motivation of employees, it gets trickier. Leaders must dig below obvious things (shared strategies, goals, action plans, and the like) and understand fundamental values. Perhaps cultural difference is indeed an 80.

Too many new expatriate managers focus on the wrong things. I get tired of hearing them say, "They just don't get it," "They need to be taught," or "It is so much easier at home." We must respect diversity, and we must see going global as a personal learning opportunity. My advice to new expatriate managers has always been the same. First, accept an assignment because you want to learn, not because you want to get promoted. Second, encourage your family to learn what they can about the people around them to feel more comfortable in their new home. And third, learn from the new culture around you to better understand yourself and the society you came from. In all of the years my family has been on the road, home has always been where we were stationed at that moment, not where we were born or where we had a vacation home.

I get equally annoyed with an overreliance on superficial "cultural training": how to use chopsticks, when not to sneeze, don't point your feet at people, and the like. This is all useful stuff (and often necessary), but it is not sufficient. Serious leaders need to make serious attempts to understand and respect the cultures they are dealing with.

Giles Amado noted, "The intention of understanding is a key issue—perceived on both sides—to create a positive climate. Respect for others is a common language: This overcomes many cultural and communication barriers, if it is honest and not manipulative." He also suggested, "Finding the Japanese in you is a way of respecting and working with other cultures," which implies that we should all operate at a human level with other humans rather than attempt to create some artificial constructs of understanding and interaction. But to operate at that human level, we must understand the other person—not just the facts and opinions being communicated, but the cultural and social context in which they are being offered.

Understanding Cultural Differences. The work of Geert Hofstede is, in my opinion, among the most useful on understanding the core cultural differences across the world. I have often found his insight into the way different nationalities think and behave as the most powerful advice I have received on cultural issues. Hofstede conducted one of the largest-scale social studies ever run. It was executed across forty countries with over one hundred thousand respondents in the late 1960s and early 1970s (China was missing, given its Maoist exclusion from world affairs at that time). The study was conducted inside one global corporation, IBM, which provided a standardized work environment and so allowed Hofstede to focus on isolating deeply rooted social differences. He identified four axes of similarity and difference across nationalities: masculinity/femininity, uncertainty avoidance, individualism/collectivism, and power distance.

The discussion that follows is based on Hofstede's *Culture's Consequences* (1980). He published follow-up studies in the 1990s and updated the classifications. Fons Trompenaars and Charles Hampden-Turner (2004) built on his work, but to my mind, nothing seriously challenged his original conclusions.

Hofstede (1980) defined culture as collective programming: "Culture is the collective programming of the human mind that distinguishes the members of one human group from those of another. Culture . . . is a system of collectively held values."

Masculinity/Femininity. On this axis, the dominant values in society are material success (money and things), which represent masculinity, versus caring for others and the quality of life, representing femininity. A nationality with high masculinity focuses on equity, competition, and performance, and managers are expected to be decisive and assertive. With a feminine culture, there is stress on equality, solidarity, and quality of work life. Managers use intuition and strive for consensus. Japan, Italy, the United Kingdom, Germany, and Mexico are more "masculine" than the United States. And France, India, and Brazil are more "feminine," with Scandinavia and the Netherlands ranking the most feminine in the world.

A leader cannot (and should not) attempt a personality shift when crossing cultures. You are what you are, and you must be authentic to yourself, or else no one will respect or trust you. But you can respect the needs of the people around you and how they want to be treated. That is the real lesson for a leader: that the combination of personal respect and broad cultural understanding is the key to mutual success.

Uncertainty Avoidance. This is the extent to which people feel threatened by ambiguous circumstances and have created beliefs and institutions to avoid such conditions. High uncertainty avoidance means many rules and low tolerance of deviant ideas, with much resistance to change. Low uncertainty avoidance suggests fewer rules and a high tolerance for deviant and innovative ideas.

Here, an observation is that the U.S.-U.K. special relationship comes to the fore, as the people of neither country like rules being applied to them. By contrast the French seem to really want to know where things stand, and most European countries seem to be in the middle. Interestingly, Japan, Mexico, Turkey, and Belgium were relatively high on avoiding uncertainty, and India, Hong Kong, and Singapore seem to thrive on it. This underpins the undoubted entrepreneurial spirit in all three countries.

The lesson is that leaders need to understand the basic innovation spirit in their people. But they must also be aware that great ideas come from everywhere and not just from the so-called low-uncertainty cultures. Their aim must be to get everyone more comfortable with uncertainty and ambiguity.

Individualism/Collectivism. Individualism applies to societies in which the ties between individuals are loose: everyone is expected to look after themselves and their immediate family. Identity is thus based on the individual, and task orientation prevails over relationships. "Collectivism" reflects societies in which people from birth onward are integrated into strong, cohesive groups that protect them in exchange for loyalty throughout their lives. Identity is based on social grouping, and relationships prevail over tasks.

Individualism is one thing Americans, British, Dutch, Australians, Italians, and the French share. No wonder we are all trying to pursue our own agendas. In fact, most of Europe is moderate or high on this count. Europe might have been the birthplace of socialism, but apparently everyone there still prefers to be individuals. It is in Asia and Latin America where things really move toward collectivism, including countries such as Singapore. India and Japan rank about in the middle.

A leader's role is, of course, to help everyone feel part of the collective endeavor. In that sense, it is a collective activity. Yet to become part of the whole, people need to feel free to be themselves. Helping people express themselves is often a way to get a shared sense of belonging.

Power Distance. This is the extent to which the less powerful expect and accept that power is distributed unequally. A low power distance means that the manager should be a resourceful democrat because having hierarchy in organizations is seen as exploitive. A high power distance allows the manager to be a benevolent autocrat, as hierarchy in organizations is believed by all to reflect natural differences.

Again, there is a lot of similarity between the United States, the United Kingdom, Italy, Netherlands, and Germany: all expect more democratic management. France and Belgium are at the other end of the scale, in the company of most Asian and Latin American countries.

Not surprisingly, I believe that the days of the benevolent dictator are just about numbered. Still, it is useful to point out to your team when you are in democratic mode and when you are making the decision. Leaders can do both as long as their teams know which is which.

Leadership Lesson. This macrolevel cultural understanding is very useful in modifying approaches in different countries. I offer two approaches to using it that can help in dealing with multicultural and multiethnic groups.

The first is facilitation. Leading across geographies and cultures needs actionable facilitation rather than directive hierarchy. The best leaders must learn and then teach facilitation skills. Although I am grossly oversimplifying cultural differences, Westerners tend to expose their ideas with words, while Asians tend to expose their values with actions. Bringing both out in discussion is fundamental to successful facilitation.

The other approach is action learning. The most effective people and programs are built around real business issues, not theories, that deliver measurable results. In my experience, there is no substitute for getting diverse teams to work together on common problems. For example, at

Johnson & Johnson in rolling out their Standards of Leadership initiative in the Asia-Pacific area, we used action workshops focused on actual business projects. This both encouraged learning about the leadership standards and drove results that could be used in the marketplace. We also grouped the workshops with a mixture of natural teammates and newcomers to the subject to encourage divergent thinking and innovation. It is often helpful to have teams that have no real experience of each other to tackle such problems, break down historic silos, and start to build trust.

The Leadership Process

What about the leadership process rises above both time and culture? What is essentially unchanged about leadership in this new global world?

Despite the massive changes in the world today, many aspects of the leadership process have not changed throughout history and seem to be independent of culture and country. There are many definitions of leadership, and I offer mine here: leadership is the energetic process of getting other people fully and willingly committed to a new course of action to meet commonly agreed objectives while holding commonly held values. (It is worth noting that this embraces leadership as a process, not as a position or an individual.)

Historically, leadership was defined by personal traits or "great man" theories, and transactional or output-based thinking tended to dominate. In the late 1960s to the 1980s, contingency and situational theories were advanced, and writers such as Chester Barnard (1935) and John W. Gardner (1990) infused leadership study with values considerations. In the 1990s, reengineering and innovation leadership were de rigueur, and today a range of approaches is on the table: visionary, charismatic, adaptive, transformational, and ethical. Time will tell what history will focus on.

As the literature has developed, several themes have appeared. Organizations have been designed specifically to achieve a certain task or set of tasks, and there is an increasing attempt to balance enterprise needs and human needs. There is a merging of leadership and organizational paradigms and methodologies, and a coevolution of thinking reflecting science and technology. The drive to be market focused has become ever more important, as has adaptation to meet the challenge of multinational and global operations.

But the fact is, whether they may be a politician, a soldier, a small business owner, a multinational leader, or president of the local PTA, all effective leaders require a clear vision, a useful (and competitive) tool kit, a sound organizational structure to meet the task at hand, and empowered and energized people within their organization.

So what appears to be common to all of these leaders?

Values Congruence Among All of the Players. Writers such as Barnard (1935), Burns (1978), Gardner (1990), and Heifetz (1998) infused leadership study with values considerations. Leaders must understand and then communicate their own value systems if they are to be trusted and followed.

Burns dismissed Machiavelli's (and Nietzsche's) theories of power as being amoral and favored what he considered moral leaders without the "will to power": "naked power-wielding can be neither transformational nor transactional; only leadership can be" (1978). In Burns's view, Hitler's death camps disqualify him as a leader, as does the gulag of Stalin's prisons. Thus, the amoral leader is neither transactional nor transformational; in fact, the term is an oxymoron. To be a moral leader, Burns believed, one must be sensitive to the needs and motives of potential followers. The purpose of the leader is fundamental, and the cult of personality is totally inappropriate.

Leadership comes from within us, in the sense that deeply held values and principles provide a road map for the way we lead and the way others respond. It is always the leader's personal value system that sustains him or her in the quest, whether this is a person of impeccable moral fiber or quite disreputable. This is as true for a modern leader as it was for Gandhi, Churchill, or Mohammed. Gardner (1990) added to this thought and wrote: "We want effective leadership; but Hitler was [unfortunately] effective. Criteria beyond effectiveness are needed. Ultimately, we judge our leaders in a Framework of Values [even though] the Framework differs from one culture to the next and from one era to the next." Gardner called for leaders who are able to renew values and can also train others—in essence, stating that such renewal is the true calling of all leaders.

Change and Innovation. John Kotter (1996) used the lens of change to drive a distinction between management and leadership:

> Management is a set of processes that can keep a complicated system of people and technology running smoothly. The most important aspects of management include planning, budgeting, organizing, staffing, controlling, and problem solving. Leadership is a set of processes that creates Organizations in the first place or adapts them to significantly changing circumstances. Leadership defines what the future should look like, aligns people with that vision, and inspires them to make it happen despite the obstacles.

In other words, leadership is all about setting a vision and an agenda for the future, driving a different future state, and aligning and inspiring people to meet that objective.

Interdependence Between Leaders and Followers. Leaders cannot do everything alone: they need the help of others. They find ways to create groups of followers, so they can change things together. There is thus symbiosis between leaders and followers: both need each other. Without followers, there are no leaders. Chester Barnard (1935) wrote: "Followers make the leaders, though the latter may also affect and must guide the Followers."

One can be a leader only insofar as one is recognized by others, argued Ralph Stacey (2001). He also defined leadership as a social process. Followers must follow willingly, or else the leader is a dictator. Coercion will not build interdependence, and trust between leaders and followers is essential.

Leaders can get other people to do only things that are latent within them. Paradoxically, therefore, the leader is also a follower, in the sense of reflecting the wishes of others. Leadership is indeed as much an art as a science, with the implication that it cannot be imposed, as the follower has a choice and will need to feel motivated and inspired.

Successfully Handling Complexity. Elliot Jaques (1986) suggested that leaders develop through levels of cognitive complexity, seeing how all the moving parts fit and then judging how best to nudge them in the right direction. This is an area that is both the same and different over time. Handling complex situations in a smart and effective way has always been a leadership characteristic, but it is getting harder given the interconnectedness of today's world, our technologies, and our multiple constituencies. Nearly all organizational dysfunction can be traced to poor structure and systems, not deficient employees. Jaques's helpful model of requisite organization explicitly includes matching personal capability to job complexity, the right number of organizational layers, management accountability, cross-functional working relationships, and compensation related to job complexity.

In a discussion of leadership and values, Jaques and Clement (1994) recognized that values congruence between leaders and followers is a key to handling complex organizations and situations: "If the CEO can establish over-arching corporate values and philosophies, which are nested within basic societal values, and which meet people's own generic values, he or she can get the whole organization working effectively in the same broad direction. . . . It is our values that move us, bind us together, push us apart, and generally make the world go round."

That said, I find that Jaques's notion of accountability rests too heavily on the manager's "getting it right" on behalf of the employees. Of course, this is partly true, but it does not allow the possibility of innovation, which breaks through traditional models of responsibility. Nor does it (in my view) do enough to encourage people at all levels of an organization to take accountability. Jaques also uses the hierarchy as the way of meeting customer needs. But in my experience, hierarchies are too concerned with the status quo to truly innovate on behalf of customers' new needs. And in the global context, Jaques does not define how to distribute leadership at all levels of the organization, across multiple sites and cultures. His work was also focused more on organization design than on operational strategy.

So is this yet another call for better understanding of distributed leadership?

Leadership as a Teachable Process. Warren Bennis (1989) offered that "the most dangerous leadership myth is that leaders are born—that there is a genetic factor to leadership. This myth asserts that people simply either have certain charismatic qualities or not. That's nonsense; in fact, the opposite is true. leaders are made rather than born."

With a process orientation to leadership, everyone can develop and hone their leadership skills. We cannot all aspire to be Churchill, Kennedy, or Gandhi, but we can always do a better leadership job. We can learn to be better mathematicians, although we may never be another Einstein. And we can all learn how to play or sing some form of music even if we will never compose as Mozart did.

And because we can train, the results can be measured. Studies by Marshall Goldsmith and others clearly indicate that by using 360-degree development tools and mapping the process steps of leadership, personal progress can be made. As the old adage states, "If you can measure it, you can improve it."

The 4E's Framework

Armed with this background, my professional experience, and subsequent research, I have developed a simple leadership framework. Its aim is to analyze what leaders do and how we can all do better.

This framework (envision, enable, empower, energize) is focused on actions in use rather than espoused competencies, individual styles, or personality types. It attempts to isolate common characteristics of leaders rather than create some kind of superset of perfect leadership. In short:

- *Envision:* values-driven setting of goals and strategies
- *Enable:* identification of appropriate tools, technologies, organizations, and people

- *Empower:* creation of trust and interdependence between leaders and followers
- *Energize:* personal leadership motor to drive the entire system

The 4E's framework has two axes (Figure 6.1). One deals with organizational issues (values, people, structure, rewards), and the other handles task or operational concerns (strategies, technology, tools). It is designed to include both strategic issues and leadership requirements. The first three E's are the collective "what" and "why," and the last E is the individual "what," for the leaders and the team.

Envision is about the values-driven setting of goals and strategies. A robust view of the external world drives the formation of the mission

FIGURE 6.1.   THE 4E'S FRAMEWORK

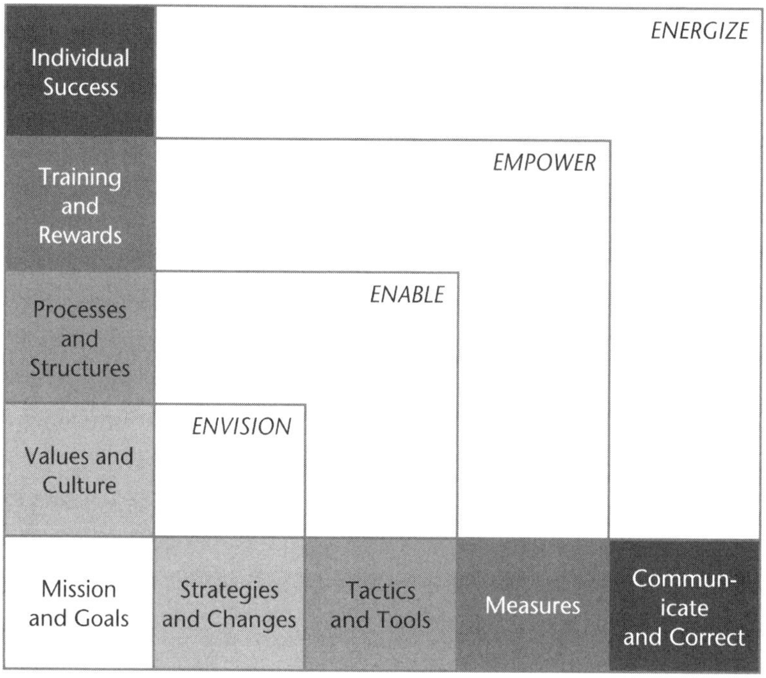

Source: © Mick Yates, 2004.

and builds clear goals. Coherent values will be shared by leaders and followers to provide a solid foundation. It is helpful to distinguish between verbal objectives (the mission) and numerical objectives (the goals) and between strategies (choices of what to do and what not to do) and tactics (the actions to take). Measurement against the tactics' progress is essential, as is being clear about the timing sequence.

Enable means that leaders must identify appropriate tools, technologies, organization structures, and people. On the operational axis, this includes tools, technologies, and business methodologies. "A better mouse trap" is a good mechanism to bring about change. The second set of enablers (on the organizational axis) includes processes and structure. It also requires ensuring that the right people and skill sets are in place to get the job done, building toward interdependence.

Empower refers to creating trust and interdependence between leaders and followers. The leader has a contract with his or her followers for mutual success and failure, reward and sanction, so the two are interdependent. Both sides are given mutual freedom yet are held mutually accountable. On the organizational axis, the team needs training to get the job done. Empowerment must also bring rewards and sanctions or challenges for improvement. On the operational axis, leaders and followers must measure progress, which encourages dialogue and continuous improvement.

Energize, on the organizational axis, means that the maximum energy will result from the combination of winning (in the marketplace) and achieving a sense of personal success and satisfaction. This requires clarity of purpose. The more energy the team generates, the more energy the leader has, in a virtuous circle of reinforcement. On the operational axis, continuous communication and course corrections are the key activities. This includes walking the talk and having a clear and persuasive story. The leader is a kind of motor for the change providing energy to the team.

This is a critical role of the leader, and team members are quite cognizant of the effect that leadership has on their collective performance. In the 2004 LeaderValues.com survey mentioned previously, test participants were asked to provide their input on how leaders best energize

FIGURE 6.2.   THE ROLE OF LEADERSHIP IN THE 4E'S FRAMEWORK

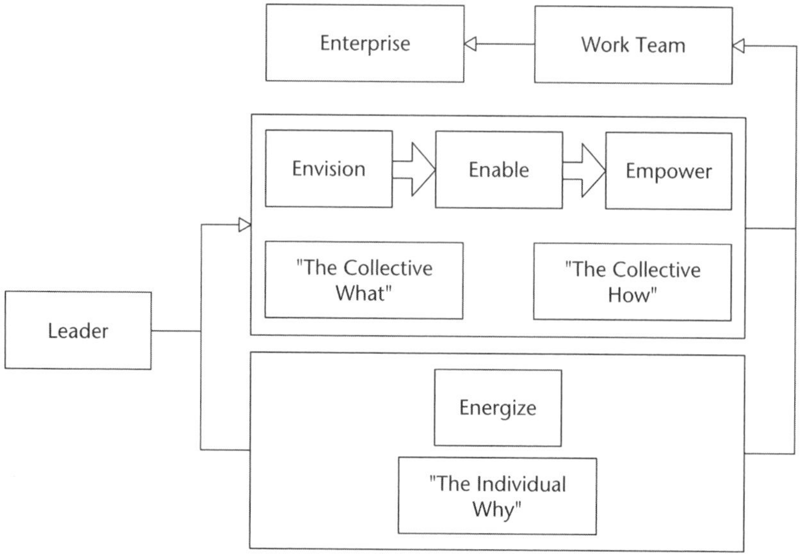

Source: © Mick Yates, 2004.

their teams. The table following shows the percentage of respondents who indicated each option:

Providing constructive criticism	5%
Making timely decisions	6%
Making complex situations simple	28%
Remaining optimistic	19%
Telling inspirational stories	8%
Helping deal with different opinions	3%
Appreciating the value of diversity	22%
Other	5%

The 4 E's framework is a contingent approach, in that its execution depends on the situation the leader is in. But it is different from both contingency theory of leadership and situational leadership.

Fiedler (1967) moved away from "great man" and traits, and also largely from behavioral analysis, to develop contingency theory.

This reflects the situations leaders find themselves in and is all about "directing and coordinating the work of group members." Fielder also was clear that the essence of a leader's personality will remain unchanged: you are what you are. He wrote, "The effectiveness of a group depends on two interacting factors: (a) the personality of the leader (leadership style), and (b) the degree to which the situation gives the leader control and influence, or, in somewhat different terms, the degree to which the situation is free of uncertainty for the leader."

Fiedler's theory states that leaders are either task motivated or relationship motivated, and they have power through their position. Contingency is well researched and a very helpful model: leadership depends on the situation at hand and the followers present. It is thus not a fixed individual characteristic, set of traits, or set of behaviors. Nevertheless, contingency theory misses the strategic and organizational dimension. Once one understands the situation, what framework is there for the leader to envision the future and understand and choose strategies and tools to enable success? And where is the focus on communicating with, empowering, and energizing others?

Blanchard and Hersey (1969) built on contingency and the Blake-Mouton grid. They measured behavior in different situations, using the complementary axes of task and relationship. Their proposition was that leaders can adapt their style depending on the situation they are in:

- High task, low relationship: Telling is every leader's first choice.
- High task, high relationship: This requires the leader to sell his or her position.
- Low task, high relationship: The leader needs participatory activity from others.
- Low task and low relationship: The leader must delegate the task.

This is a popular training (and consultancy) model, and it is clearly helpful to leaders to be able to identify in which kind of situation they find themselves and how they might respond.

Yet personal development across the broad palette of strategic and tactical skills once more is open to question. What does the model do to help leaders decide what they have to do as opposed to how? There are thus similar questions as with contingency theory. And are we to change a leader's behavior in a manipulative fashion depending on what we are trying to achieve? Finally, although there is a focus on degree of relationship, the model does little to help the leader authentically enter new relationships with followers.

Case Study

Save the Children is one of the world's best-known nongovernmental organizations and was founded in the United Kingdom in 1919 by Eglantyne Jebb. Jebb innovated in instituting modern scientific and management methods in charity work and stressed sustainable programs and self-help rather than handouts. She also was the architect of what was to become the United Nations Convention on the Rights of the Child, adopted by all nations on earth except one.

Save the Children has field operations in over 110 countries. Organizationally it is a decentralized alliance of twenty-seven independent, individual country members (Save the Children USA, Save the Children UK, Save the Children Japan, and so on). Different members sometimes adopt different programmatic focus areas. For example, some members are focused on child rights and advocacy focused, whereas other are more field driven.

A 2004 project with three pilot countries within the Save the Children organization started by tailoring the organization's leadership standards within a 4E's frame, and then moved through online self-assessments to team workshops and follow-up interventions. The 4E's were not used to score one organization against another, but instead formed a basis for internal benchmarking and action.

Two core findings emerged. First, the strengths of the organizations were very consistent across the globe, shown in the consistency of responses sorted by the top five answers, which included a focus on such things as values-driven activities, taking personal responsibility, and encouraging diversity. Second, relative weaknesses varied markedly, providing a fruitful basis for internal action planning. This allowed the 4E's to become central to the alliance's best practices in leadership, made available globally to all twenty-seven member countries.

Here is another short story, by coincidence related to Save the Children.

Learning from Cambodia. For some years, my family has been involved in helping a program building schools in Cambodia. Parts of the country got out from under the Khmer Rouge only in 1998, when Pol Pot died. There had been virtually no decent schooling for thousands of children for twenty years. When we first visited, we remember being told that the children had been taught to plant land mines by the Khmer Rouge teachers. In fact, the average Khmer Rouge soldier was just like every other Cambodian—a family man, wanting to live in peace and prosperity.

Early in 2000 we traveled to Trapeang Prasat, near the Thai border, an area that had been under Khmer Rouge control since the 1970s. We met a soldier's family: he and his wife had four children, one of whom seemed to have a leg problem. They were clearly poor but proud and explained through an interpreter that all they wanted was for their children to go to school. There was a new school nearby, so the program helped extend it.

Just over two years later, we visited the school, now serving over six hundred students of all grades. A woman approached us, wearing a smart pink silk suit and holding her young son's hand. It was the same woman we had met before. Now her son was in school and by all accounts doing well. Even more, she was deputy chair of the commune committee and heavily involved in school activities. All she and her family needed was to be offered an opportunity. The rest they took care of themselves.

The Moral of the Story. Empowerment is critical, and control is not a long-term strategy. Energize is the personal leadership motor to drive the entire system. On the organizational axis, the maximum energy will result from the combination of winning (against the shared goal) and achieving a sense of personal success and satisfaction. This requires clarity of purpose. The more energy the team generates, the more energy the leader has, in a virtuous circle of reinforcement. On the operational axis, continuous communication and course corrections are the key activities.

This includes walking the talk and having a clear and persuasive story. The leader is a motor for the change providing energy to the team.

◆ ◆ ◆

In summary, there are tectonic changes in the world, and nationalities have distinct macrocultural characteristics. Yet global leaders can also count on some of the fundamental truths of leadership that scholarly study and practical experience have handed down to us.

Now we are armed with enough insight to create the global leadership framework.

Global Leadership Framework

There are four areas of global focus: distributed leadership, loose-tight innovation, networks of trust, and strategic engagement, And I am suggesting that we use the 4E's leadership framework to highlight the leadership process. They are combined in Table 6.1.

Distributed Leadership

Senior managers of most enterprises seem to be preoccupied with two people development issues: how to reward and develop high-potential people and how to win the war for talent. Both are important. But both, if not thoughtfully considered, can have unexpected effects.

First, most organizations have a large group of middle-rank employees who keep the wheels turning. These same people could, if suitably encouraged, trained, and rewarded, be increasingly positive contributors to the collective success. By contrast, an overfocus on top performers can distract from encouraging this middle group. Having a few outstanding managers is powerful, but imagine the strength in getting an entire organization inspired and feeling well rewarded.

Second, winning the external war for talent is of course important in keeping an organization vital and energetic. But it often seems easier to hire a high-flying manager than it is to help large groups of existing

TABLE 6.1. THE GLOBAL LEADERSHIP FRAMEWORK

	Envision	Enable	Empower	Energize
Distributed leadership	Common values Common purpose Integrate paradoxes	Roles and responsibilities Decision processes	Training and development Delegation of authority	Action learning Minimum layering
Loose-tight innovation	Knowledge sharing Networks of innovation	Success models Local innovation	Reward innovation	Encourage change Technology
Networks of trust	Collective purpose	Searchability Member identities	Communities of excellence	Actionability
Strategic engagement	Global and local knowledge Customer understanding Technology impact	Common systems Common work culture Objectives, goals, strategies, tactics, and measurements	Integrated goal setting Feedback systems	Communication to all Facilitate Walk the talk

employees learn to do a better job, use their experience, and enjoy doing it.

It is my contention that the test of great leadership is to raise the standard across the entire organization, not focus on just a few key players—hence, the focus on distributed leadership. So the envisioning focus is on the creation of common values and creating common purpose. The aim is always to push responsibility out to wherever the decision can best be taken. Enabling demands that clear roles and decision processes be in place, and empowerment is about providing the necessary training and development throughout the enterprise. Cutting out nonessential organizational layers (note Elliot Jaques's work) and using action learning programs are among the energizing activities.

Loose-Tight Innovation

Knowledge must be shared yet local innovation encouraged. A success model defines the critical elements of a project and identifies which items of execution are not so critical. It must be remembered that successes all happen somewhere first; very few organizations go global on day one. So capturing the learning, course correcting, and improving are essential actions.

The subtlety is in defining what is globally common and what is locally different. A success model needs to address these elements:

- *Customer needs:* What exactly is being delivered that is of value to the buyer?
- *Product or service advantage:* What exactly is the sustainable advantage over competition?
- *Critical geographical differences:* What is locally needed and what is not (the 80:20)?

The leader's role is to encourage (and sometimes enforce) the use of the basic success model, but then to encourage and facilitate innovation at all levels of the enterprise.

Networks of Trust

We all use networks to communicate ideas and share knowledge. We have networks of friends, career advisors, coworkers, clubs, and teaching mentors, for example. And experience suggests that it is networks within an enterprise that get things done rather than simple reliance on the organization chart.

Dramatic progress is being made in understanding small worlds (we all may be within six degrees of separation of everyone else) and scale-free networks (represented by the Internet, the airline hub and spoke systems, gene expression pathways in the body, and so forth). These imply ways to make networks more robust and to speed up communication. Importantly, networks do not replace current structures but rather coevolve with them (Stephenson, 1998).

Experience suggests that there are certain characteristics of networks that must be built in if they are to be effective.

Purpose. Effective organizational networks have a human or organizational purpose that must be predefined; then its outputs can be measurable. This is not always the case with networks in the scientific literature. For example, while one can say we all use the Internet, it is hard to argue that the Internet itself has a purpose other than providing pathways over which information can flow. And how many of us belong to business networks that provide little value other than social interaction? We might enjoy the socialization, but it does not always further our business needs. Leaders must be clear about the purpose of the networks they create and ensure that all members of the network both agree with this and use it accordingly.

Member Identity. This is essentially an accessible catalogue of all of the skills, knowledge, motivations, problems, geographical locations, time linkages, goals, and beliefs of everyone in the network, and it is critical to how they interact. This goes beyond a list of roles in the network or a list of linkages. Publicizing these identities and connecting similar members will help form communities from which useful work will emerge. Over time, these communities will become collective experts on certain subjects—something I call communities of excellence—and be empowered to operate almost autonomously. Clarity on member identities will also help define where the leadership should be (and maybe already is) distributed in an organization, depending on the issue at hand.

Actionability. The links between members of the network must be actionable, meaning that they have practical value in real interactions. For example, I may be within one link of the prime minister of country X, having met him in an earlier role. Although it still may theoretically be possible to engage him in a discussion about his country's economics, the probability of a serious talk about photography is essentially zero. This link is nonactionable. As another example, we may know photographers from their exhibitions, so a future conversation will be extremely easy using these actionable links.

A prerequisite of actionability is that individuals must be able to engage in a useful conversation with other cluster members; there is little social distance. Recall the example I used of the Thai brand manager. She would need actionable links with her peers in Australia to be able to get her job done and probably needed to have been face-to-face with them at least once.

Searchability. This is critical in finding existing data, generating new knowledge, and thus delivering on the purpose of the network. Examples of the types of insight we may be seeking include these:

- *Informational:* "Where are all the good Thai restaurants in town?"
- *Intellectual:* "What can I learn from the local history?"
- *Actionable:* "How can I get better sales results in this country?"
- *Relational:* "How can I work better with my local fellow employees?"
- *Judgmental:* "How can I decide the real truth in the local politics?"
- *Contextual:* "How can I integrate the varied aspects of my life?"

It is not necessary to predict an exact search path through a small world network, just to start it on the right trajectory. Peter Dodds, Roby Muhamed, and Duncan Watts (2003) note that a successful search is conducted primarily through weaker links (for example, through a friend of a friend), does not require highly connected hubs to succeed, and disproportionately relies on professional relationships. Successful search paths must be captured, stored, and reused as appropriate by other network members.

Trustworthiness. How we can trust the information flowing through a network? I offer that the combination of the member identity of an authority (which is transparently available to all members with similar interests) and the actionability of the links contribute to a network's trustworthiness. I also suggest that defining an authority relates to his or her information flow: this person is most likely a net exporter of information. This will build trust over time.

❖ ❖ ❖

Most of these points are common sense, but it is amazing how often one hears that people want to network for networking's sake. Leaders who want to get things done must consider all five of these points in constructing a truly useful and productive network.

Strategic Engagement

Employee engagement is a combination of shared goals and shared values, aided by tools and organization structures that allow people to take appropriate action.

The process of engagement should start with an understanding of the changes facing the enterprise and work toward building a collective view of the future state. Choices define strategy, so development tends to be an interactive and iterative process to put the best ideas on the table and involve others in the solution early on.

A successful strategic deployment then ensures that all members of the enterprise understand and can contribute to the execution of the plan. A detailed plan should be built using objectives, goals, strategies, tactics, and measurements. This specific tool was pioneered in Procter & Gamble and is now used by many other enterprises. This not only details the plans, but also provides a way of tracking progress. It can be cascaded throughout the organization, with higher-level tactics becoming lower-level goals. This can align the entire organization around a common action plan and so help communication between all levels on what is working and what needs modification.

Adding to this, the RASCI definitions ensure that everyone knows who is responsible, who has to agree, who can support, who needs to be consulted, and who should be informed.

Conclusion

We are more the same than we are different, and the leadership process is much as it has always been. Leaders must have a great vision and strategy; find competitive tools, technology, and great people; train and empower everyone in the organization to do the job; and then energize and inspire them all. That all sounds so simple. Less simple is how to balance the forces of globalization, which are simultaneously pulling us all together and giving us the opportunity to go our own fragmented ways. And then how do we balance the macrocultural forces at work with the individual needs of our stakeholders?

There are no easy answers, but there are many clues. I hope that this chapter has posed the right questions and laid out ways to think about finding the answers.

References

Barnard, C. *Functions of the Executive.* Cambridge, Mass.: Harvard Business School Press, 1935.

Bennis, W. *On Becoming a Leader.* London: Arrow, 1989.

Blanchard, K., and Hersey, P. *Management of Organizational Behavior: Utilizing Human Resources.* Upper Saddle River, N.J.: Prentice-Hall, 1969.

Burns, J. M. *Leadership.* New York: HarperCollins, 1978.

Dodds, P., Muhamed, R., and Watts, D. "An Experimental Study of Search in Global Social Networks." *Science Magazine,* 2003, *301,* 827–829.

Fiedler, F. E. *A Theory of Leadership Effectiveness.* New York: McGraw-Hill, 1967.

Gardner, J. W. *On Leadership.* New York: Free Press, 1990.

Granovetter, M. "The Strength of Weak Ties." *American Journal of Sociology,* 1973, *78,* 1360–1380.

Gibb, C. A. "*Leadership.*" In G. Lindzey (Ed.), *Handbook of Social Psychology.* Reading, Mass.: Addison-Wesley, 1954, pp. 877–917.

Grint, K. *Leadership: Classical, Contemporary and Critical Approaches.* New York: Oxford University Press, 1997.

Gronn, P. "Distributed Leadership as a Unit of Analysis." *Leadership Quarterly,* 2002, *17,* 681.

Hanna, D. *Designing Organizations for High Performance.* Reading, Mass.: Addison-Wesley, 1992.

Heifetz, R. *Leadership Without Easy Answers.* Boston: Harvard University Press, 1998.

Held, D. and McGrew, A. *Globalization/Anti-Globalization.* Cambridge, Mass.: Polity Press, 2002.

Hofstede, G. *Culture's Consequences: International Differences in Work-Related Values.* Thousand Oaks, Calif.: Sage, 1980.

Hosking, D. M., and Morley, I. E. "The Skills of Leadership." In J. G. Hunt, R. Baliga, P. Dachler, and C. Schriesheim (Eds.), *Emerging Leadership Vistas.* Lexington, Mass.: Lexington Press, 1988.

Jaques, E. *Requisite Organization: The CEO's Guide.* London: Cason and Hall, 1986.

Jaques, E., and Clement, S. *Executive Leadership.* London: Cason and Hall, 1991.

Jaques, E., and Clement, S. D. *Executive Leadership: A Practical Guide to Managing Complexity.* Oxford, U.K.: Wiley-Blackwell, 1994.

Kotter, J. *Leading Change.* Boston: Harvard Business School Press, 1996.

Shaw, R. *Trust in the Balance.* San Francisco: Jossey-Bass, 1997.

Stacey, R. *Complex Responsive Processes in Organizations.* London: Routledge, 2001.

Stephenson, K. "What Knowledge Tears Apart, Networks Make Whole." *Internal Communication Focus,* 1998, *36.*

Stogdill, R. M. "Personal Factors Associated with Leadership: Survey of Literature." *Journal of Psychology,* 1948, *25,* 35–71.

Trompenaars, F. *Riding the Waves of Culture.* London: Nicholas Brealey, 1993.

Trompenaars, F., and Hampden-Turner, C. *Managing People Across Cultures.* Chichester, U.K.: Capstone, 2004.

Watts, D. *Six Degrees: The Science of a Connected Age.* New York: Vintage, 2004.
Yates, M. *The 4E's Leadership Framework (MSc).* Paris: HEC, 2004.

About the Contributor

Mick Yates is a globally experienced executive with a successful track record across Europe, Asia-Pacific, Australasia, and the United States. He has held leadership positions in both Fortune 50 and social development enterprises.

In 1997, he founded www.leader-values.com, a leadership development site that features Yates's own leadership framework, the subject of his master's degree thesis at Oxford University and HEC (Paris).

Until mid-2001, he was company group chairman of Johnson & Johnson's consumer business in Asia-Pacific, based in Singapore and responsible for all aspects of the region's operations. He was also a corporate officer and a member of the global operating committee. Prior to this, he spent twenty-two years at Procter & Gamble, latterly as regional vice president based in Hong Kong and then in Japan. In all, he has spent eleven years as a regional CEO of Asian businesses.

In 2001 he left Johnson & Johnson to engage in several new enterprises.

CHAPTER SEVEN

INVESTING IN WOMEN

Why It Is Critical for Companies in the Twenty-First Century

This chapter outlines the important role that women play in successful companies and shows how specific investment in women leaders can maximize their potential as contributors to the organization.

We gratefully acknowledge Alexcel member Susan Diamond, who facilitated our original teaming on this project. The names of women in our study have been changed for confidentiality.

Whether it's PepsiCo CEO Indra Nooyi smiling from the cover of *Fortune* magazine in February 2008, former Hewlett-Packard executive Carly Fiorina on the book covers at Borders, or German Chancellor Angela Merkel standing confidently among the G8 leaders, there is no shortage of women in power today. Is it time to close the discussion on equity at the executive level? Not yet. A look one step below the surface at the numbers of women executives will quickly show that although we have come a long way, we still have a long way to go in establishing an appropriate gender infrastructure for leadership development and advancement. Although women make up more than half of the managerial and professional labor pool, they still account for no more than 1 percent of all Fortune 500 chief executives (Eagly and Carli, 2007).

The question to ask as a practitioner charged with addressing the issue of advancing women in the workplace is: What accounts for the lack of women in key leadership roles when the business case for having them there is clear? If we look at the numbers, we will see that the facts are grim despite years of effort and investment. It would be easy as an internal practitioner to become cynical and resigned about these efforts. However, the numbers do not tell the whole story. The question becomes: What can you do inside your organization to advance women toward senior management?

There are methods that may be put into practice to help your organization. One of them is to build on the successes we find in industry. For example, according to Tom Vines, IBM's vice president for human resources, there was just one female executive in IBM's Asia Pacific region in 1996; there are one hundred today (interview, March 20, 2008).

In this chapter, we argue first that the case for investing in women can be built on solid business strategy and performance. This investment must be articulated clearly by senior management, and as the internal practitioner you are uniquely positioned to educate them on the difference between tolerance and inclusion. Rather than using a cookie-cutter version of the male approach to development, which often requires women to fit into the dominant leadership style of the organization, investment in women requires an understanding of women's unique contributions, building on skills, gender culture, and the latest research on brain science.

Second, barriers to advancement are alive and well in modern organizations, and sometimes the very people who are committed to removing the barriers are the ones who blindly keep them in place. It is difficult for senior management to see the disparity between their thoughts and their actions. It is your job to help senior leaders see how they may be unintentionally keeping obstacles in place that stand in the way of moving talented women forward.

Finally, creating a culture that values and, more important, includes women's leadership requires a variety of methods rather than a one-size-fits-all approach. We discuss some of these methods and emphasize coaching because we believe that the most effective means to increase women's representation at the top of organizations is the practice of coaching. Drawing on the methodology of Alexcel, the global coaching and consulting alliance formed in 1999, we discuss why it is so effective and what women learn from coaches that men may not.

The Case for Investing in Women: What the Research Says

In 1995, only 8.7 percent of Fortune 500 corporate officers were women; in 2002, the total was 15.7 percent (Wellington, Kropf, and Gerkovich, 2003). There is an increase in representation, but it is very small. In 2006, women represented only 6.7 percent among top earners. The wage gap between men and women is particularly wide in the United States, where women earn only 78 percent of the male wage. In France, women earn 81 percent, in Sweden 84 percent, and in Australia 88 percent. The situation of women executives is not improving dramatically either: in 2006, the number of women Fortune 500 corporate officers was only 15.6 percent, less than in 2005, when the percentage was 16.4 percent. At this rate, women will not achieve parity for forty-seven years (Catalyst, 2007)!

Ironically, the case for hiring and promoting women to a senior rank is strong. A 2004 Catalyst study found that "companies with the highest representation of women on their top management teams experienced 35 percent higher return on equity and 34 percent higher total return to share-holders than companies with the lowest women's representation" (Catalyst, 2004). That is, of 353 Fortune 500 companies, those with the highest percentage of women outperformed those with the lowest percentage.

Women are an important and constantly growing source of talent in the marketplace today. For example, women earned 58 percent of all master's degrees in the United States in 2001. By 2012, they are projected to earn 56.7 percent of all advanced degrees in the United States (NCES, 2002). Representing 46.5 percent of the workforce, they are also diverse within the landscape of gender itself. The Bureau of Labor Statistics tells us that women of color were 13.4 percent of the U.S. labor force in 2002 and are projected to make up 15.2 percent by 2010 (Fullerton and Toosi, 2001).

Looking to the Future

The importance of this emerging female talent pool is augmented by the complex economic and social realities of modern global economies. According to a Center for Creative Leadership survey (Jenkins, 2006), 93 percent of respondents agreed that their organization's challenges are more complex now than they were five years ago. The argument can be made that women are uniquely qualified to meet today's complexities and challenges. Skills such as systems thinking, collaboration, multitasking, and communication are increasingly needed in organizations.

Sally Helgesen, author of *The Female Advantage* and *The Web of Inclusion*, says that "women prepared organizations to begin to move beyond the post-industrial era." In the industrialized world, female-driven change has created more options for work-home balance for both men and women. In the developing world, small enterprise has been championed by women, bringing successes such as the Grameen Bank. In every arena, including corporate social responsibility and the proliferation of nongovernmental organizations, "women have a critical role to play in the creation of sustainable futures," says Helgesen (interview with Jim Wylde, March 20, 2008).

Boris Groysberg (2008) argues that in today's work climate, women, unlike men, maintain and transfer their brilliance successfully from one work climate to another because they "build their success on portable, external relationships—with clients and other outside contacts" and "women considering job changes weigh more factors than men do, especially cultural fit, values and managerial style."

Theresa Wellbourne's research (2007) focuses on the effects of senior women leaders in organizations undergoing initial public offerings. She found that the presence of women on the top management team made a positive difference in both the initial pricing of the offering and long-term firm performance. She attributes this advantage to "better innovation and problem-solving processes in more diverse top management teams" (p. 524). Through their ability to build relationships and operate in a fast-moving and complex environment, women can provide both the dynamism needed to move businesses forward and the strategic thinking to back it up. In this sense, perhaps it will be women who, through their innovation, empathy, and flexibility, will take the blinders off senior management.

Mastering Complexity: A Female Skill?

"Leaders in a Global Economy: A Study of Executive Women and Men" (Galinsky, Kropf, and Harrington, 2003) jointly prepared by the Families and Work Institute, Catalyst, and the Center for Work and Family, affirms, as expected, that men senior executives have higher status than women senior executives, as measured by reporting level, number of direct and indirect reports, and total compensation. Other findings were less predictable. One affirms that women executives are "more likely than men to have made important life decisions in order to manage both their careers and their personal lives." And while men have "higher aspirations" than women at the executive level, affirms another finding, a significant group of senior women executives hopes to join their senior management committee. This supports the notion of women having ambition but in a more collaborative context.

One of the most striking conclusions goes across many of the findings and involves the lack of differences between men and women—or affirms that both men and women face the challenge but respond to it differently. For example, both men and women executives are work-centric in their lives. However, a substantial minority, 32 percent, rates as "dual-centric," placing the same priority on work and family life. The study finds that a strictly work-centric approach is not necessarily beneficial to career development in the long run, and with women at the vanguard, both genders are discovering greater balance in their lives.

Similarly, in interviews, both Tom Vines and Sally Helgesen point to the fact that more than ever before, the line between household issues of men and women is blurring. For example, both men and women have issues of child care, elder care, or partner benefits. It is possible that women may be taking the lead on working effectively within the complexities of work and home life. More female executives than men have found the challenge closer to home and, for better or worse, have had to make sacrifices and payoffs. In the new world of Generations X and Y, where work is not a lifetime commitment and flexibility and meaning are important, this traditionally female perspective will be the foundation for work styles for generations to come.

In sum, investing in women is investing in the productive new multisector, work-life-balanced, fast-moving work world of the future. In regions where management has grasped the value of this investment, the benefits are already clear. Tom Vines believes that the Asia-Pacific region in particular is seeing unprecedented transformation because of the increased influence of women in management. Having grown up in the United States, with experience in both Europe and Asia, he sees in the Asia-Pacific region a "borderless focus on networking and globalizing, very different from the U.S." (interview with Jim Wylde, March 20, 2008) Women in Korea are networking with women in India and China. There is a truly global nature to the collaboration and a web of support across nationality, division, and even generation. To bridge generational differences among women in the region, IBM has used reverse mentoring, a way for more mature executives to learn from "the voice and eyes of Generation X." To see where the gender and generation dialogue is moving, look to IBM and the East.

Women and Brain Science

In her book *The Female Brain* (2006), Louann Brizendine notes that in recent years, scientists have documented "an astonishing array of structural, chemical, genetic, hormonal and functional brain differences between men and women" (p. 4). She sees these discoveries as positive, suggesting that they serve as a launch point for an exciting new era of understanding: "It is my hope that the female brain will be seen and understood as the finely tuned and talented instrument that it actually is." Women commonly develop multitasking skills. Coincidence? Findings point to actual differences in brain chemistry; there are patterns of reasoning unique to the female brain.

In "Women and the Labyrinth of Leadership," Alice Eagly and Linda Carli (2007) ask whether a distinct female leadership style exists and conclude that it does. They point to a recent meta-analysis that integrated the results of forty-five studies addressing this question. The analysis was conducted using a framework introduced by leadership scholar James MacGregor Burns that distinguishes between transformational and transactional leadership. Transformational leaders serve as role models as they gain trust and confidence. They "state future goals, develop plans to achieve those goals, and innovate, even when their organizations are generally successful." One of the key conclusions of the meta-analysis was that "female leaders were somewhat more transformational than male leaders, especially when it came to giving support and encouragement to subordinates" (p. 6).

The Challenges Facing Women Leaders

As the literature demonstrates, the evidence for having women in key leadership roles is indisputable. One key obstacle holding women back is a lack of general management or line experience. In order to gain that experience, they need access to key organizational networks. This issue is important not only to the women who are hoping to advance, but also to the male executives who have the power to promote them. Far too often, the issue is addressed from the point of view of the women, leaving a huge piece of the puzzle unaddressed. Women executives are still often excluded from informal networks, lack mentors and female role models, and have limited opportunity for visibility. This may not be obvious to men inside the organization because they do not experience the same exclusion. The unintended consequence is that male executives may see women leaders as less effective or lacking the requisite skills to reach senior levels.

Particularly challenging is the judgment that male executives sometimes place on women, believing that women's lack of advancement is of their own doing. But leaving women to develop experience on their own, without identifying other sources to do so, is not effective. Access to contacts and exposure to high-profile assignments are difficult to create without the support of key stakeholders inside the organization. Coaching is one of the most powerful tools for providing development and empowerment to capable women leaders. The coach can help a woman find answers to the question, "What kinds of operational skills do I need to get to the top and stay there?" With the coach, the client develops a plan to supplement the experience that might have otherwise been gained by tapping the male network.

Centuries-old patterns in gender culture do not dissipate overnight. Research shows that some women do not favor the word *ambition* because it calls forth negative associations. While men consider ambition a positive quality, even a necessity, the opposite is true for many women. Babcock, Laschever, Gelfand, and Small (2003) reviewed gender differences in negotiating behavior; in one study of recently graduated M.B.A.s, 7 percent of women actively negotiated their salary, while 57 percent of males negotiated for higher wages—eight times as many.

Does this trend affect issues other than salary? Baron (1989) estimates that managers spend as much as 20 percent of their working time in negotiating up, down, and across the organization. Stulmacher and Walters (1999) examined a number of negotiation studies and found a consistent small but significant gender difference in negotiation. They argue that even a small difference favoring males in situations requiring negotiation, when consistent, is enough to create a clear disadvantage to women's advancement. As they point out, although women compose half of the workforce, it is not the top half.

Culturally, women are socialized not to negotiate or promote their own interests. Eagly and Carli (2007) note that women are expected to act in a compassionate, communal manner, while men are expected to assert and control. This has traditionally led to labeling assertive women as "bitchy" or "pushy." Is this experience a thing of the past? No. In a recent study (Brescoll and Uhlmann, 2008), women who expressed anger in a workplace context were overwhelmingly seen as incompetent and out of control by their male counterparts.

Tools for the Internal Practitioner

For women, traditionally rewarded for being caretakers, aggressively pursuing personal wealth and rewards may be seen as unattractive. The trends in gender culture have created an expectation in most organizations that women leave part of themselves—the part of themselves that looks to take care of others or get along—at home. Yet these are the very skills the experts say are necessary for organizations to compete in the future. How can you as an internal practitioner help women bring more of their authentic selves to the office? Affinity groups are one method.

Affinity groups are groups organized by gender, ethnicity, or affinity to provide a social and professional network of like-minded people for personal and professional development. The groups are voluntary and often open to anyone who wants to participate. They meet as often as monthly and as infrequently as yearly. Regardless, they offer a platform of like-minded people to convene and explore issues in a productive way. To be effective, the goals of the group must be aligned with the goals of the organization, and a champion, preferably someone from senior management, should publicly endorse the group.

Far too often what happens with these groups is they meet without guidance or without senior management's sponsorship. They quickly devolve into nothing more than a place to vent about all that is wrong with the organization rather than a constructive platform. This can be extremely damaging to the overall goal of helping women advance.

Cultural conditioning predisposes women toward self-deprecation and self-sacrifice, deflecting attention and credit from themselves and highlighting the accomplishments of others. Research shows that girls and women more openly seek and compete for affirmation when they are with other women. Despite their achievements, women often underestimate what they have done and ascribe much of their advancement to luck, whereas men are more likely to inflate their accomplishments.

A method to help women feel more comfortable distinguishing themselves and their accomplishments is the creation of an internal directory organized by knowledge and expertise rather than title or function. It is a way for organizations to fully leverage employee knowledge and expertise to drive innovation and improve bottom-line performance by collaboration. This approach has the advantage that women do not have to promote themselves. Each person, male or female, is seen by the network for the value of the expertise he or she brings to the table, thus removing the gender bias.

Multinational companies have experienced pressing needs to develop and retain their global workforce, especially in emerging markets such as China and India. Although the current era offers more opportunity than ever before for women, there is an unwritten social norm in many cultures that women must first care for family members. Ambition and competitiveness may be held in even more disdain for women by both women themselves and society at large. Traditional family roles, veneration of the home, and elders all have ancient social roots. Coaches must be knowledgeable and aware of the cultural and social context within which women clients operate and address these issues directly. In addition, globalization requires companies to relocate key employees to other countries to work on short- and long-term global assignments. This has presented great challenges for expatriates, especially women leaders with families.

Kamala, an Indian executive born and raised in Mumbai, faced obstacles related to both gender and culture. After graduating from college in the United States, she found a job at a top firm and within eight years was promoted to management. Although in the United States her bicultural and bilingual foundation was an advantage, when she decided to accept an opportunity to return on assignment to India, she found herself facing unexpected challenges. Her male direct reports and superiors resented her open style of authority, which was well intentioned by U.S. standards, and conflicts arose. Kamala's egalitarian management style ran counter to the Indian management style, which is characterized by male-dominated hierarchy. With the help of a coach, she developed a hybrid method that was respectful of the existing hierarchy, taking the cultural context into account in order to achieve the right balance between directive and collaborative styles. With this approach, she received both the blessing of her leaders and the cooperation of her subordinates. Kamala, like many other women executives, had to learn the gender- and culture-based assumptions that underlay her position title and official responsibilities.

Coaching as Solution: Case Studies and Tools for Development

We have discussed a few methods to deploy inside organizations to advance women. Although each has its merits, it is our belief that coaching is the most effective way to advance women. Coaching uses a targeted, objective approach that most women would not be able to create on their own. Men are socialized to negotiate to achieve what they want. Women, in contrast, are encouraged to focus on the needs of others. One study found that the starting salaries of male M.B.A.s who had recently graduated from Carnegie Mellon were 7.6 percent, or almost $4,000, higher on average than those of female M.B.A.s from the same program. In fact, most of the women had accepted the employer's initial salary offer; only 7 percent had attempted to negotiate. But 57 percent of their male counterparts, or eight times as many men as women, had asked for more. In fact, women may apologize for wanting it all (Babcock and Laschever, 2007).

Although today there is more opportunity than ever before for women, the unwritten social norm is that women must first care for family members. Within Asian and other world cultures, ambition and competitiveness may be held in even more disdain for women. Historical Confucianism, with its emphasis on humility, hard work, and silence, accentuates the value placed on the already subservient cultural position of women. Traditional family roles have ancient social roots. Coaches must be aware of the cultural and social context within which women clients exist and address these issues proactively.

Barriers abound in the workplace. Eagly and Carli (2007) assert that the image of a glass ceiling does not adequately describe the complexity of the situation that women leaders face. In reality, women must navigate in a labyrinth of obstacles. The glass ceiling metaphor, they say, "fails to incorporate the complexity and variety of challenges that women can face in their leadership journeys" (p. 3). Coaching is well positioned to assist women in fine-tuning their skills to meet complex leadership challenges.

Women executives perceive themselves to be excluded from informal organizational networks, mentoring opportunities, and other women who serve as role models. About two-thirds of women and more than half of the CEOs surveyed agree that the failure of senior leadership to assume accountability for women's advancement is a key barrier (Wellington, Kropf, and Gerkovich, 2003). Coaches of women leaders must help them navigate this issue and find formal and informal support for their advancement.

How do executive coaches help women move through the labyrinth of barriers and become more successful? We recommend a specific, scalable behavioral coaching model so that the process is consistently executed with all leaders. Development agendas must be connected with the business results that the leader must achieve, and measurement of success is crucial. The Alexcel model employs the foundations of the behavioral coaching process initially developed by Marshall Goldsmith, coach to top executives in many of the world's leading companies. The positioning of a positive approach focused on helping successful people become more successful as differentiated from a problem-centric approach is a crucial theme of the process. The process steps are shown in Figure 7.1.

FIGURE 7.1. STEPS IN THE BEHAVIORAL COACHING PROCESS

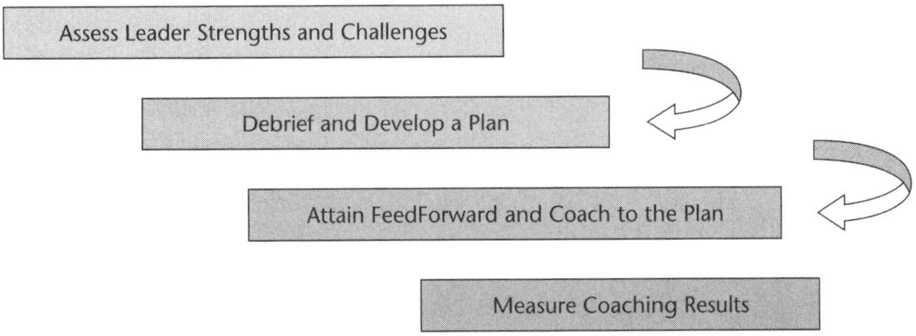

Note: FeedForward, a concept developed by Marshall Goldsmith, is a coaching practice and variation on the term *feedback* that directs advice and insight forward to the future rather than focusing on past behavioral tendencies. More on FeedForward can be seen at Marshall's Web site at www.marshallgoldsmithfeedforward.com.

Assess Leader Strengths and Challenges

The initial step within the Alexcel coaching process is a robust assessment of leaders' strengths and challenges, using a 360-degree assessment focused around organizational values and the competencies and behaviors that drive successful results. For organizations that have not created these tools, there are many that can be purchased and used, including the Leader of the Future assessment designed by Goldsmith. Within the ranks of senior leadership, we use interview-based 360-degree assessments because they gather more precise information about the leadership demands and needs at the highest levels of the organization. In addition, many 360-degree assessments are supplemented by the use of well-normed leadership style assessments to add a self-report of default style and leadership blind spots.

Debrief and Development Planning

After the data are reviewed with the leader, the leader and coach develop a focused action plan with concrete outcomes tied to business context and results, articulating one or two targets for improvement. The leader and her manager review and agree on the plan; the dialogue created at this juncture is often particularly valuable for women leaders, who may hold back on discussing areas for improvement, whether they worry about being seen as too aggressive or think that they should already know how to get better without asking for help.

These ongoing development conversations are positioned so that they create precisely the sort of mentoring opportunity that will not only help the leader around specific action items, but in many cases help her develop a more robust network of support within her organization. In this way, she exercises what Groysberg (2008) calls the "portable skills" unique to women. Figure 7.2 is a development plan model that has proven effective.

With organizational parameters in place, an effective development plan can be established. To ensure success, a development plan should contain these elements:

- The target that the leader will attain, stated clearly and in behavioral terms
- A description of the target in a way that is understandable to stakeholders

FIGURE 7.2. SAMPLE DEVELOPMENT PLAN

Leader: Jane Sample   Date: January 1, 2009

Target: Fully articulate my point of view so that others know the thoughts behind my ideas

Expected Impact/Value: Improved quality of interaction and relationships. Good ideas are more likely to be adopted by others and have positive impact. This action will also help me develop my team.

Actions	Target Date/Frequency
Consciously prepare for conversations that may be complex or controversial. Write down key points that I want to make, and include the thinking behind the points.	Twice weekly
When preparing for a complex conversation, prepare graphics to help illustrate the ideas. If on the fly, try to use graphics/ drawings in the moment to articulate my thoughts.	As needed; practice weekly
Seek FeedForward from my list of key stakeholders.	Two rounds by March 15
Try to, in the moment, take the time to tell people how I came up with a certain idea.	Practice twice weekly
Get in the habit of asking people if they have questions about my thought or idea in the moment.	At least once per meeting

- The return on investment of the target and the reason for choosing this particular action
- Specific steps that the leader will take, with whom, and how often
- Dates by which actions will be completed
- A list of stakeholders for the FeedForward process and the frequency with which each will be contacted
- Obstacles that are likely to arise in the pursuit of this target
- What a successful outcome will look like
- How success will be measured

Attain FeedForward and Coach to the Plan

Coaching is focused on both the individual and the larger organizational context. The coach teaches the leader the FeedForward approach of involving stakeholders to help her. Using the FeedForward approach, the leader identifies a single behavioral characteristic that he or she wishes to work on and seeks unbiased advice that focuses on future solutions, while any feedback or critique on past behaviors is strictly avoided (for more on this model, consult Goldsmith and Morgan, 2004). Aspects of the model speak specifically to the challenges of women leaders. To the degree that many women leaders are reluctant to showcase their achievements, the FeedForward process allows them to showcase their improvement in a nonegotistical manner. If women leaders are to increase their visibility within senior organizational ranks, coaches must be even more proactive in chipping away obstacles. The relationship building that results from the FeedForward process is a powerful tool that can assist women leaders in negotiating relationships, creating internal networks, and developing strategies for effective negotiation.

Measure Coaching Results

At the end of a predetermined time period (generally six to nine months after the development plan is finalized), an outcome measure is executed. Custom online mini-360-degree surveys are created for each leader and distributed to the stakeholders who responded to the original assessment.

The following questions are asked, and responses are given on a five-point scale:

- Did the leader share her development plan with you?
- Did the leader follow up with you through the process?
- To what degree is she a more effective leader at this juncture?
- How well did she execute the specific action items [named in the survey] in her plan?

Positioning Coaching for Success

The internal practitioner/coach plays a particularly important role in connecting individual development with the business strategy of the organization. In the Alexcel model for coaching in general, and with the internal role in particular, it is critical to communicate effectively with senior managers to increase their understanding of the process, its effectiveness, and its contribution to organizational results. Even with the best of internal systems, transformation will not occur overnight; it requires investment over time. Internal resources must frame coaching within business language to gain the buy-in of the CEO. Effective coaching processes must be systemic, long term, strategic, and tactical. When a CEO approaches an internal practitioner and says, "We need more women leaders," the practitioner must provide a reality check. The internal practitioner must manage senior management's expectations regarding the role that coaching plays in helping women achieve their leadership potential. Otherwise, coaching is in danger of becoming a fleeting effort, adding to the cynicism and resignation about women's chances for succeeding at the top.

A successful coaching initiative requires several key steps. The first step is determining whether the organization has a strategic plan for leadership development. Delve into and make links within the current leadership plan, determining if there is a succession plan. In each development plan, the coach must take into account the leader's perspective of herself in the context of the goals of the organization.

Second, before the rollout of an organizationwide coaching process, there must be mechanisms in place that gauge the leadership climate through conversations, polls, or surveys, or some combination of these. Through such inquiry, a practitioner may determine the degree of staff engagement. In this process, it is essential to tap into the full breadth of all demographic groups and truly capture the voice of women.

Once you have collected data on the current status, question whether proposed programs will truly help develop women leaders. Sometimes factors in place hurt women even though the intent is positive. For example, an affinity group formed to advance women in an organization will not fulfill its mission if it has no executive sponsorship. To ensure a successful outcome, the temperature and trends of the organization must be determined. From there, the practitioner can look at the bench of women, see what conspicuous projects or assignments they are on, and determine what more can be done to advance them. ABN AMRO, one of the largest banks in the world, used coaching this way. Its lessons learned echo what the Alexcel data showed.

ABN AMRO's Managing for Value strategy, conceived in 2002 as a fresh approach to the organization's global business management, provides an effective window into how a systemwide initiative builds the leadership bench and brings increased shareholder value. In this initiative, the corporate finance metrics (efficiency in terms of revenue, expenses, and profit) were complemented by a unique leadership component.

Until 2002, the "what" of business results was considered more important than the "how." The Managing for Value approach changed that by altering the way in which leaders approached their business. In order to remain competitive, they had to develop new ways of working together. This required careful consideration of the competitive landscape, a profound understanding of the needs of clients, and, most important, an expansive leadership repertoire. The research on women's leadership style meant that senior women within the organization potentially were well positioned to distinguish their abilities when judged against this new model of leadership.

The executive coaching program stemmed from the need to create a cadre of high-performing leaders. It required a shift in focus from short-term results alone to short-term results coupled with long-term development, a focus generally held more by women than men. This change was particularly challenging since most managers did not have the skills to manage performance against such a framework, assess their own development needs to bridge the gap, or assess the developmental needs of their staff. They began the initiative with an internal competency model used to create a baseline assessment of current leaders' skills.

Analysis revealed a significant gap between existing behaviors and those touted within the Managing for Value structure as necessary for economic return. Executive coaching was viewed as the most effective means by which to give the heads of the lines of business the requisite skills to bridge the skill gap. As we have already noted, often one of the most frustrating aspects of creating change is sometimes that the very people who are committed to removing the barriers are the ones who blindly keep them in place. This was the case with the new model of leadership at the bank. Elizabeth was a senior woman whose style was understated as compared to her peers, male and female. Her business was quite profitable, and Elizabeth was a respected leader. Yet senior management, and in some cases her staff and peers too, spoke about her success as though it was in spite of her leadership style rather than because of it. This is a classic example of someone acting out of the cultural norm.

To set the stage for the coaching rollout, ABN AMRO relied on internal practitioners to help its organizational clients understand the implications of coaching. This had special relevance for the women in the organization. There was a widely held concern that coaching was an exercise one went through as a last attempt to stop a career derailment. The practitioners had to make it clear that executive coaching was considered a developmental activity designed to equip leaders with the proper skills to keep the business competitive. This seemed to make sense to the leaders, and many embraced the concept immediately. However, the practitioners had to help the women see that participating was not an admission of lack of ability. The women in the organization had worked hard to get where they were on their own merits, and they did not want to draw unnecessary attention that they somehow "needed help."

Rather than explaining this to clients, it is better to illustrate how the executive coaching program works. One effective tactic for engaging the client was the use of a process through which the individual client interviewed and selected from a pool of two or three prospective coaches provided by the human resource (HR) or leadership development professional. The client would meet with the coach individually and begin to see how coaching works. This process had a tone of personal choice and provided opportunity for clients to inform themselves and select an individual appropriate to their learning style and developmental needs. As the coach and client begin work together, this synergy contributes to energy and enthusiasm around the development plan. Alternately, if a client has difficulty choosing a coach, this may be a red flag with regard to the client's investment in and understanding of the arrangement. This helped women see for themselves in their conversations with coaches that they were not being marginalized by the process. Rather, it was the opposite: a strong endorsement from senior management that they were worthy of investing in for the future.

Throughout the AMRO initiative, the HR and leadership development professionals worked to develop a uniform message in working with clients. The HR representative brought the day-to-day working knowledge of the client, and the leadership development professional had the overall strategic vision for the coaching process.

As in any other systemwide development initiative, the process was similar to peeling an onion, with business strategy tied to people development, then linked to leadership, getting information, finding out what influences are affecting where, and how women perceive the organization.

This information is important to the coach for two reasons: it brings the reality of the organization and its culture to the coachee and helps the coach understand the environment and give a perspective from which effective coaching can occur. Within these parameters, the coaching is more objective and more clearly linked to performance management.

The Model in Action

A European division of a global Fortune 100 organization employed the Alexcel coaching model in a three-year project to develop the leadership skills of director-level employees. Data from 360-degree assessments were collected in three rounds over a six-year period. The company's stated objectives for the assessment and coaching project were to:

• Improve employee satisfaction
• Optimize the leadership competencies of the organization's managers
• Encourage identification of high-potential leaders

In creating its customized 360-degree evaluation, the company involved three hundred employees in the development of the question-naire and the leadership competencies and behaviors important to cur-rent and future success. Nine high-level leadership competencies were identified, centering around teamwork, business impact, focus, drive for results, developing people, leadership, responsible corporate responsibil-ity, innovation, and customer satisfaction. The instrument was structured around these competencies and behaviors.

The first round of 360-degree feedback and coaching, beginning in 1999 and completed in 2001, consisted of 417 leaders: 388 male and 29 female. The second round began in 2000, and coaching was completed in 2004. This cohort consisted of 379 leaders: 351 male and 28 female. The third round lasted from 2003 until 2005 and consisted of 313 lead-ers: 278 male and 35 female.

Over this time span, female leaders within the top two tiers of this Fortune 100 division went from 6.95 percent to 11.18 percent. While it was not specifically articulated how many female leaders left the com-pany during this time, there is a high degree of retention, and most of the senior female leaders participated in all three rounds of the process.

Within measures of overall leadership competency, results indicated that the company's male and female leaders were roughly equivalent in all measured competencies. The scale's vertical axis measured stake-holder views (deleting the self-rating) of the leader's competency on a 1 to 5 scale, with a 1 indicating a marked deficiency in the competency, 3 indicating moderate or average ability, and 5 indicating outstanding or world-class abilities in the competency.

The trend of the data was examined as the leaders were followed over time, which noted improvements within second-line leaders over three administrations of the 360-degree assessment, and coaching around the development plan shows the expected improvement with execution of the coaching and FeedForward process. Unfortunately, mini-360-degree data were not available for this group to indicate how diligent each leader was in executing the process and following up with stakeholders.

One interesting and consistent difference was noted between the male and female leaders who participated in this coaching process. On each round of the 360-degree surveys, male leaders' self-assessment tended to be slightly higher than the self-assessment of female leaders. While each leader's self-assessment advanced toward the 4 of the 1 to 5 scale, which indicates perception of significant strength in leadership ability, female leaders consistently tended to rate themselves lower overall. This is consistent with the findings of Watson and Hoffman (1996), who studied individuals in a negotiation task. Regardless of their performance, women felt less confident before the task and less satisfied after the task than did men.

FIGURE 7.3.   360-DEGREE DATA ON LEADER SELF-PERCEPTION

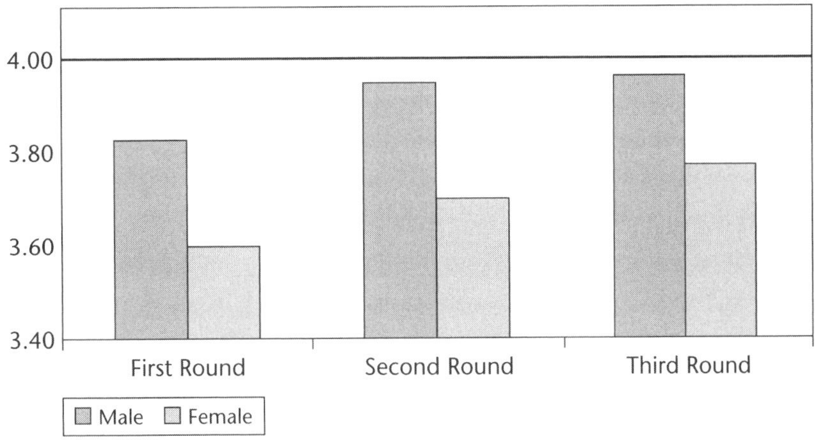

Source: © Alexcel, 2007.

Behind the Scenes: Coaching Women Leaders

Coaching helps leaders decide which actions and changes are most important for short- and long-term success. It is very important for the coach to ask female clients, "Where do you want to be several years down the road?" Taking this strategic perspective with women might lead to thinking through a question like, "If I have children, how can I get all of the parts of my career and home life together? What kind of practices and habits will I need? Are the advantages of advancement worth the trade-offs? What price am I willing to pay?"

Culture comes into play at many levels, and cross-cultural communication can never be seen as a textbook formula. Ximei Liu, a Chinese client from Mars Corporation, recently moved to Nashville, Tennessee, from China with her husband and two young children to take a new position. She adopted what could be perceived as a very Western attitude. Reflecting on the style of Asian women in management, Ximei noted, "We have to work for ourselves. We can't just complain about others or cultural differences. We can always work on our own career path. . . . I'm a very opportunistic person; I don't like to complain. I like to think about the future" (interview with Jim Wylde, March 13, 2008).

Even with this attitude, Ximei pointed to complexities of communication and gender, noting that although the Mars culture itself is relatively uniform in China, Canada, and the United States, these complexities surface regularly. She noted that in her experience, women are often more flexible with respect to schedule and more understanding of adjustments that need to be made (for example, working from home or shifting the hours of a given workday) to adjust to the demands of home and family life. Regarding communication style, she noted that "in America, everyone is so talkative," and in Asia, silence is often revered. In Western culture, however, this behavior is often viewed negatively as shyness, passiveness, and lack of leadership capability. On the flip side, Western women leaders can be viewed as aggressive, arrogant, and even rude when they are using a direct communication style.

Coaching can help break cycles of passivity, instill personal accountability, and empower women to take responsibility for their careers and personal development. Integral to the process of coaching is developing this sense of responsibility and, most important, a woman's sense of responsibility to herself. A coach helps clients decide what to start, stop, and keep doing—to brainstorm, practice, support, and provide resources and perspective. A good coach will do all of these things, incorporating an understanding of both women's issues and women's ways of learning.

Women are concerned with the issue of work-life balance but struggle with giving it meaning, particularly with respect to taking care of themselves. In addition, they do not want to be seen as conflicted or struggling by their peers and superiors. As a change partner, the coach can help a female client make balance workable. For example, one Alexcel coach worked with a very busy executive, Ann, head of R&D for a Fortune 500 high-tech company in the San Francisco Bay Area. With two young children and an executive husband, she has worked with her coach to develop a practical sense of actions to take (and not take) to advance her career and have a happy home life. She is now comfortable with where she is, with no need to prove herself to be an "alpha leader." She proudly displays pictures in her office of her daughter and son, both young teenagers.

One of the secrets of Ann's success is that she has taken to heart the need to take care of herself. She and her coach have developed concrete actions to be inserted into her calendar, and over time she has developed the habits of success. To handle the fast pace of her day, she gets up at 5:00 A.M. to walk with her husband while her children are still asleep. They fast-walk for ½ hour every day, giving priority to their time together. When they return from the walk, the family has breakfast together.

A good coach will always ask a female executive, "What have you done for yourself lately?" Usually self-care is these executives' lowest priority, preceded by business and then family, leaving little time for the woman herself. One client, Diane, said, "I think I would love to try yoga." Her coach suggested that she put that in her development plan, so she did. Diane found a yoga class that energized her and, coincidentally, made a big difference in her ability to get things done. Since then she has become a committed yoga practitioner as well as a more effective leader.

Coaches must assist leaders in becoming aware of gender-related behavior and how it can help or hurt them. Marie, a recently promoted female vice president in a health sciences organization, found herself overwhelmed by her many responsibilities. Her 360-degree feedback and leadership style survey determined that she had difficulty setting boundaries around her tasks and delegating work to her direct reports. A compassionate woman who enjoyed solving problems and hated to say no, Marie exemplified common female negotiation. On reflection, she realized that if she continued in this way, she would burn out, frustrate and underuse her staff, and fail to focus on strategic priorities. Her development plan focused on helping her accept the need to negotiate firmer boundaries with her manager and subordinates and balance her natural collaborative skill with more assertiveness.

Suzanne, a female vice president in a financial services organization, faced a different negotiation challenge. A passionate and assertive driver for results, she was seen by others, particularly her male colleagues, as pushy and aggressive. This behavior led to others' sabotaging her efforts and threatened to derail her career. Her challenge was to learn to balance her competitive spirit with greater cooperation and her forcefulness with more effective listening. Suzanne had to struggle with the knowledge that her drive would likely be more easily tolerated if she were male. Having this conversation with her coach helped move her beyond her disappointment in the existence of a double standard to making decisions about how she could develop leadership behaviors that would drive even more success.

Coaching interventions are also well positioned to help women leaders appreciate their strengths and become more skilled at self-evaluation, particularly women who tend to underestimate their skills and contributions. Linda, a female vice president in the insurance industry, received 360-degree feedback from her manager that she was not assertive enough and needed to develop a stronger executive presence with peers throughout the organization. It became apparent to Linda's coach that she consistently rated herself lower than others on a number of leadership and business-related competencies. The coach used the 360-degree assessment results and the leadership style inventory to describe Linda's strengths as observed by her stakeholders. Initial coaching conversations focused around encouraging her to observe and evaluate her use of these strengths. Over time, Linda was able to understand her strengths and move into a more confident, expressive style, which delighted both herself and her manager.

Good coaching experiences often cascade through their organizations. Jia, an Asian executive, was so inspired by her experience with a leadership development and coaching program that she went back to her office and created an intensive learning initiative for her staff. The standards were as strong as a mini-M.B.A. program. She gave assignments to her teams, and then she and another senior executive would oversee the learning process as it evolved. Every week team members would research and share learnings, providing insights to each other. This constituted an effective way to both accumulate knowledge and share her success with other women leaders.

Conclusion

In this chapter, we have moved from the most global images of women in power to highly localized daily adjustments that a woman must make to achieve success as an executive. In the process, our intent has been to demonstrate that the case for women's advancement is built on both solid business strategy and a leadership development process attuned specifically to the needs and capabilities of women. Investment in women must always ride this middle line. Moving forward requires a clear acknowledgment of the barriers that still exist, despite the successes widely celebrated in the media. Finally, we believe that executive coaching is a practical solution for overcoming obstacles and preparing women for a seat in the boardroom. By making the business case, naming barriers, and focusing on steps to change through coaching, the possibilities for a shift in leadership are significant. Signs of hope are already arising from those who are blazing the trail for sustainable leadership development within organizations and also from courageous women and men who step outside their organizational realm to face complex new global realities.

References

Babcock, L., and Laschever, S. *Women Don't Ask: The High Cost of Avoiding Negotiation—and Positive Strategies for Change.* New York: Bantam, 2007.

Babcock, L., Laschever, S., Gelfand, M., and Small, D. "Nice Girls Don't Ask." *Harvard Business Review,* Oct. 2003, pp. 14–15.

Baron, R. A. "Personality and Organizational Conflict: Effects of Type A Behavior and Self-Monitoring." *Organizational Behavior and Human Decision Processes,* 1989, *44,* 281–296.

Brescoll, V. L., and Uhlmann, E. L. "Status Conferral, Gender, and Expression of Emotion in the Workplace." *Psychological Science,* 2008, *19*(3), 268–275.

Brizendine, L. *The Female Brain.* New York: Broadway Books, 2006.

Catalyst. "The Bottom Line: Connecting Corporate Performance and Gender Diversity." *Catalyst,* 2004.

Catalyst. "Census of Women Corporate Officers and Top Earners of the Fortune 500." *Catalyst,* 2007.

Eagly, A. H., and Carli, L. L. "Women and the Labyrinth of Leadership." *Harvard Business Review,* Sept. 2007, pp. 3, 6, 62–71.

Fullerton Jr., H. J., and Toosi, M. "Labor Force Projections to 2010: Steady Growth and Changing Composition." *Monthly Labor Review,* Nov. 2001, *12.*

Galinsky, E., Kropf, M. B., Harrington, B., and colleagues. *Leaders in a Global Economy: A Study of Executive Women and Men.* Boston: Families and Work Institute, Catalyst, and Boston College Center for Work and Family, 2003.

Goldsmith, M., and Morgan, H. "Leadership Is a Contact Sport: The Follow-Up Factor." *Strategy + Business,* 2004, *36,* 71–79.

Groysberg, B. "How Star Women Build Portable Skills." *Harvard Business Review,* Feb. 2008, pp. 74–81.

Jenkins, J. *LEADAsia.* Singapore: Center for Creative Leadership–Asia, 2006.

National Center for Education Statistics [NCES]. *Digest of Education Statistics.* Washington, D.C.: U.S. Department of Education, 2002.

Stuhlmacher, A., and Walters, A. "Gender Differences in Negotiation Outcome: A Meta-Analysis." *Personnel Psychology,* 1999, *52,* 653–677.

Watson, C., and Hoffman, L. R. "Managers as Negotiators: A Test of Power Versus Gender as Predictors of Feelings, Behavior, and Outcomes." *Leadership Quarterly,* 1996, pp. 63–85.

Wellbourne, T. "Wall Street Reaction to Women in IPOs: An Examination of Gender Diversity in Top Management Teams." *Group and Organization Management,* 2007, *32,* 524.

Wellington, S., Kropf, M. B., and Gerkovich, P. R. "What's Holding Women Back." *Harvard Business Review,* 2003, *81*(6), 18–19.

About the Contributors

Maya Hu-Chan is an international management consultant, executive coach, author, and public speaker, specializing in global leadership, executive coaching, and cross-cultural business skills. Harvard Business

School has chosen her book, *Global Leadership: The Next Generation,* to be one of its Working Knowledge recommended books. She has trained and coached thousands of leaders in Global Fortune 500 companies and worked with major corporations throughout North America, Asia, Europe, South America, and Australia. She is also a contributing author of *Leading the Global Workforce, Best Practices in Leading the Global Workforce, Coaching for Leadership: How the World's Greatest Coaches Help Leaders Learn,* and *Partnering: The New Face of Leadership.*

◆ ◆ ◆

Patricia Wheeler is an expert in leadership development and executive coaching. She works with senior leaders and their teams across industries, from Fortune 500 organizations to small, privately owned companies. She is managing partner of the Levin Group and currently managing director of Alexcel. Holding a Ph.D. in psychology, she guest-lectures at Georgia State University's Robinson College of Business M.B.A. program and Emory Medical School. She publishes the executive resource *Leading News* (LeadingNews.org) with executive coach Marshall Goldsmith.

◆ ◆ ◆

Tracey Wik is vice president of leadership development for a Global Fortune 500 corporation. A trusted advisor, she is adept at building key relationships. She facilitates strategic planning sessions to ensure organizations have the right people in the right roles to compete today and in the future. Her current focus is coaching senior leaders to create an inclusive climate that fosters growth and innovation. Wik speaks on such topics as organizational change, talent management, employee engagement, and executive coaching. She is a faculty advisor in the master's of knowledge management distance learning program at California State University, Northridge.

◆ ◆ ◆

Marta Williams is head of the Washington Quality Group–Spain and an executive coach with Alexcel. She also founded the Institute of

Coaching (Spain) in 2001. As a journalist, she represented ABC News and *U.S. News & World Report* as Spanish correspondent for many years. She was a member of the founding editorial team of *El País*, Spain's most important newspaper, before she began her career as a consultant and coach. She was also a founding member of three women's groups: Madrid Network, The Charter 100 of Madrid, and the International Woman's Forum. In 2001 she received Honourable Mention by the Spanish Federation of Women Entrepreneurs as Business Woman of the Year. She collaborates with Leader to Leader, formerly the Drucker Foundation, and teaches at three of Spain's M.B.A. programs.

PART TWO

BEST PRACTICES IN LEADERSHIP DEVELOPMENT

CHAPTER EIGHT

MCKESSON

Accelerating the Development of High Potentials

Leaders Teaching Leaders

This chapter outlines a simplistic approach to developing leaders that focuses on low-cost, high-impact solutions that are scalable, customizable, and cost-effective.

Although no organization will refute the value of leadership development or its ability to yield results, many find it too expensive to pursue in depth. However, while the size of the investment is nothing to balk at, it is generally overplayed. Most companies cannot afford to invest in all of the best practice leadership development interventions out there, but there is no reason that they cannot design a system that fits their needs at an acceptable cost. Despite being one of the largest companies in the world, McKesson has taken an approach that focuses on choosing only the most simplistic and effective methods based on principles of efficiency and sustainability.

This chapter outlines our leadership development process. And while it may not be perfect for every organization, other organizations can choose individual elements that fit their leadership priorities.

McKesson has found these elements to be effective in designing an ongoing leadership development process:

1. Start with a process to engage executives and supervisors in the learning and developing process.
2. Kick it off with a bang. Engage participants in the development process by beginning with an intervention that gets them together and excited. This will increase the likelihood of their maintaining commitment to their development, both individually and as a team, throughout the process.
3. Combine additional learning events that are easily substituted in or out by the organization based on current leadership strategy and can be easily internalized by participants.
4. Track progress that helps measure return on investment (ROI) and learning while giving participants, supervisors, and business unit leaders a stake in the success of the learning process.
5. Add only the simplest (but still powerful) learning support tools that supplement learning outside the classroom. Anything too complex will be difficult to put into practice by both the organization and participants and may result in excess cost.
6. Be sure to have a senior-level sponsor who is personally committed and pulls in other executive council and board members to become a part of the learning experiences.

Overview of McKesson Corporation

McKesson is ranked eighteenth on the Fortune 500 with more than $88 billion in annual revenue. The company delivers vital medicines, medical supplies, and health information technology solutions that touch patient lives in every health care setting. The depth and breadth of the company's product and service offerings, coupled with the largest customer base in the health care industry, uniquely position McKesson to meet the needs of its customers:

- 200,000 physicians
- 26,000 retail pharmacies
- 10,000 long-term-care sites
- 5,000 hospitals
- 2,000 medical surgical manufacturers
- 750 home care agencies
- 1,800 health care payers
- 450 pharmaceutical manufacturers

Cultural Context for Program Design

McKesson has a highly decentralized operating environment and maintains a delicate balance between individual business unit autonomy and pursuing the "One McKesson" initiatives—that is, combining a unique collection of health care products and services to create unbeatable value and offerings to clients. The culture is highly relationship driven, with the creation of trusting partnerships based on delivering on commitments critical to success in the organization.

Unlike many other companies today, the leadership team is young. The average age of the top two hundred executives is forty-seven. So although the company is not facing large numbers of looming retirements, it does have a critical need to support both organic and acquisitive growth (there have been about thirty acquisitions in the past five years) with a ready supply of talented leaders. McKesson's core business is pharmaceutical distribution, which historically has thin margins but generates tremendous cash flow. Anything it does as a business must be cost-effective and a "salable" to profit-center leaders, who keep a close eye on expenses to remain competitive.

McKesson's vision is to bring together clinical knowledge, process expertise, technology, and the resources of a Fortune 18 company to fundamentally change the cost and quality of health care. With that vision, it needs to be able to continue to execute flawlessly on changing its business internally to shape the cost and quality of health care and be skillful enough to help customers through the change process as well, whether installing a large hospital information technology system or a robot to dispense medications in a pharmacy.

Leadership Development at McKesson Corporation

Historically, McKesson was managed more as independent businesses, but over the past five years, it has been creating shared services and One McKesson processes across all of its businesses. Leadership development has been no exception. Over the past several years, it has designed and implemented human resource (HR) processes and automated systems for performance management, compensation planning, talent acquisition and talent reviews, and succession planning processes.

At the same time it was launching these common practices and end user automation tools, it was also working on workforce development and created a leadership development path for every level of management (see Figure 8.1). It created the McKesson Center for Learning (MCL), which delivers professional management education to first- and second-level managers in the corporation. Next, it created an executive education series to address pressing developmental and business issues for the top two hundred executives. Recently, it designed leadership programs to address the director and vice-president level development needs of leaders in two ways: a three-day leadership development curriculum, Rising Leaders, and a comprehensive nine-month development program for the highest-potential leaders in this target population, called Leaders Teaching Leaders (LTL).

FIGURE 8.1. MCKESSON LEADERSHIP DEVELOPMENT PATH

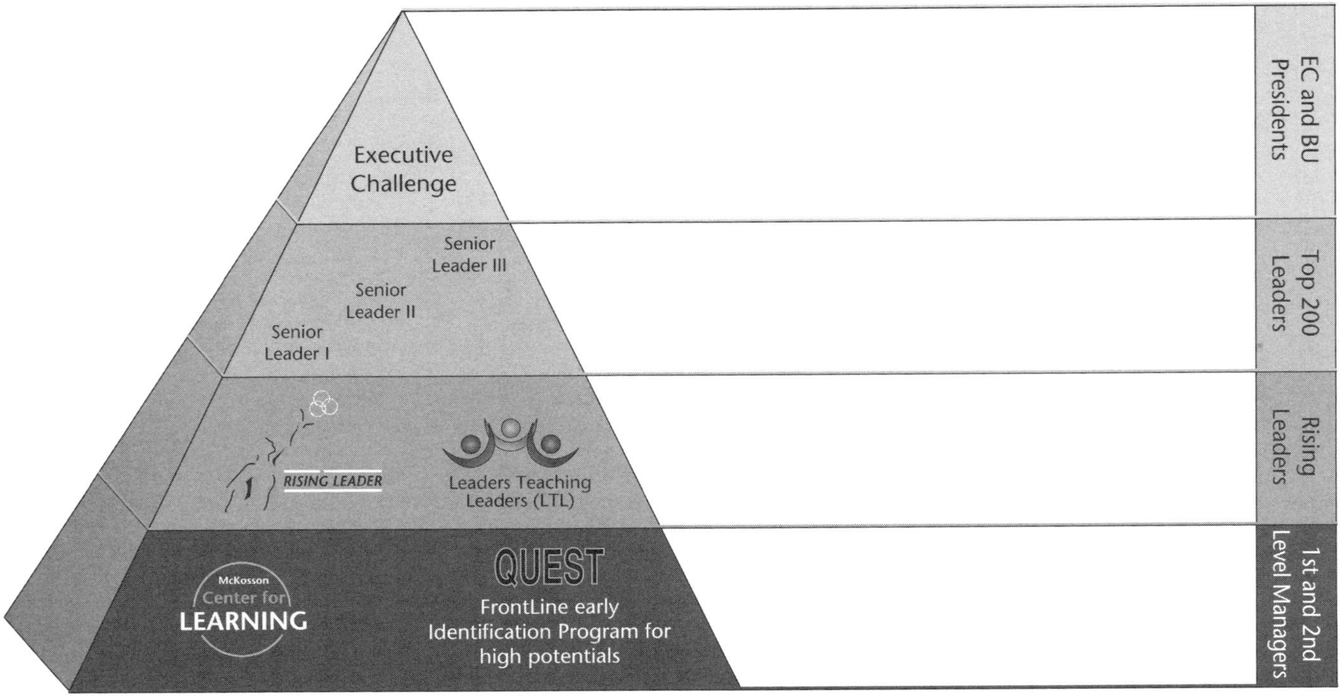

EC and BU Presidents	Top 200 Leaders	Rising Leaders	1st and 2nd Level Managers
Executive Challenge	Senior Leader III / Senior Leader II / Senior Leader I	RISING LEADER / Leaders Teaching Leaders (LTL)	QUEST FrontLine early Identification Program for high potentials

McKesson Center for LEARNING

Source: Scott Boston and Sandy Allred, 2007.

Leaders Teaching Leaders was created with a goal of accelerating the development of high-potential leaders below the top two hundred at the executive level to increase bench depth to support leadership supply needs. The goal was to get the top seventy-five to one hundred highest-potential people through the process within the next three years.

Design Considerations: Why Leadership Development Programs Fail

As the Executive Development and Talent Management team at McKesson began the project plan to design the LTL program, we saw five areas in which leadership development programs fail and wanted to stay clear of them:

- *Too elaborate and try to cover too many areas.* Often designs for leadership programs are too complex, including action learning pieces that require legions of administrative support. These programs try to "fit twenty pounds of stuff in a five pound bag" rather than focusing on a few simple themes and doing them well.
- *Lack of a compelling catalyst to convince participants of the need for change or continued growth.* As managers progress in their careers, they become convinced that they are successful because they have achieved a certain level and often get set in their ways. Leadership development programs tend to work best when people realize that there is room for improvement. This can be accomplished in a number of ways, including 360-degree feedback and assessment instruments.
- *Lack of understanding or involvement of key stakeholders to support learners in the process, yet with an expectation of change and growth.* All too often there is CEO support for programs but little connection to the program from senior line leaders and, most important, participants' supervisors. So while leaders may intellectually understand the importance of programs, they remain at arm's length during the process. This often results in poor support for ongoing budgeting of the program or learner frustration that "they are not doing this too and they need it."

- *Lack of sustainable change.* Even the best among us go to programs and learn about things we need to do more effectively, only to return to a hectic work environment and fall into old patterns. A need for a more prolonged process where learning is applied to actual work experience is necessary and an expectation that "someone is watching progress and actually cares" needs to be maintained.

- *Little demonstration of return on investment for the expense and time away from the job.* Most training departments at some point have pursued the need to conduct training measurement studies to prove the value of their programs. Most often they try to go to Kirkpatrick's level 5 and eventually get frustrated at the complexity of measuring such a process, particularly in the soft skill areas. With leadership development, it is often not necessary to go to such complex analytical lengths, but it is critical that learning and applicability to improvement back on the job are tracked and documented.

Leaders Teaching Leaders Core Components

We designed the LTL program to be a nine-month learning experience—enough time to make something happen in terms of allowing participants time to make meaningful application of the program learnings. The nine-month process consisted of the following components (see Table 8.1 for a time line of events):

1. Nomination process and management expectation-setting Webcasts.
2. Attend Linkage's Global Institute for Leadership Development (GILD). This Institute includes the completion of a 360-degree assessment (to include direct reports, peers, and managers) and three coaching sessions with an executive coach.
3. Identify and execute a project goal (a project that can be applied to the person's business unit that will demonstrate his or her leadership skills and apply course learnings from the program) and two personal targets (areas of improvement) based on 360-degree assessment results.

TABLE 8.1. LTL PROGRAM TIME LINE OF EVENTS, 2007–2008

Date	Action Item
Week of September 16, 2007	Attend the Global Institute for Leadership Development (GILD)
October–November 2007	Executive vice president of HR to call each LTL participant to confirm commitment and participation
November 2007	Executive vice president of HR to host a one-hour Web session for supervisors
November 2007	Complete vetting of project plan and development plan with supervisor
Mid-December 2007	Executive vice president of HR to call participants and review their progress and development plan to date (results compiled from the data in the development engine)
January 2008	Conduct follow-up coaching session with GILD coach (by phone)
January–February 2008	Executive development team will conduct a survey to track feedback and progress on the goals to date
January 14–17, 2008	LTL II: three-day learning event in San Francisco
June 16–20, 2008	LTL III: learning event plus investor day (optional)
August 2008	Compile data and report results

4. Attend two intensive two- to three-day in-house customized learning events, referred to as LTL II and III.

5. Utilize support tools to supplement learning outside the formal classroom environment.

Nomination Process and Management Expectation-Setting Webcasts

The process begins by soliciting business unit presidents to nominate up to twenty-eight high-potential midlevel managers to participate in the program. Great care is taken to ensure that the business unit presidents and executive managers of participants have an understanding of their role in supporting the participants through the process.

To accomplish this, the executive vice president of human resources, Paul Kirincic, and the project team held a mandatory Webcast with the business unit presidents, executives who manage participants, and the most senior HR leader in each business unit to discuss program expectations and roles:

- Coach participants in selection of 360-degree assessors; complete supervisor assessment
- Track participants' progress in the performance management tool
  - Track objectives, competencies, and progress along the participant's Individual Development Plan (IDP)
  - Provide opportunities to demonstrate skills (on projects or various work situations)
- Ensure protection of learning time
- Be an active guide to participants' personal development plan and project goal, and communicate with and provide feedback throughout the project:
  - Use periodic check-ins to gauge progress (learnings) and make adjustments as necessary
  - Provide feedback using the online tracking tool

Participants' managers and business unit presidents are expected to play an active role in the process by discussing their progress on their project, ensuring protection of learning time, and providing feedback on progress periodically using an external online tool, DevelopmentEngine by Fort Hill Company.

This process step is critical because it helps participants get the most out of their experience at GILD, clarifies expectations for the entire process, and sets the stage for helping determine ROI by engaging both the participant's supervisor and the business unit president in the learning and development process. These elements have provided program participants with a much greater degree of executive access and helped build more lasting personal relationships.

Next, we conducted a Webcast with the participants and their supervisors outlining the process and expectations for the participation:

- Full participation (no meetings or conference calls) during the GILD program
- Complete 360-degree assessment prior to attending GILD

- Commitment to a project goal
- Commitment to developing a personal development target (based on 360-degree results)
- Commitment to fully attending two learning events (LTL II and LTL III)

During this session, the HR executive vice president reiterates the intensive time demands of the program to participants in addition to their current workload. (Program commitment is approximately eleven days, with five days at GILD and an additional six days throughout the course of the program, plus any additional time needed to complete project work.) He then extends an invitation for anyone to opt out of the program—no questions asked (with the potential to join next year's LTL program). This offer is extended once more after the first week of the program. Generally there are only one or two participants who recognize that the demands are too great given either work or personal commitments or circumstances and choose not to continue.

Linkage's Global Institute for Leadership Development

Participants begin the process by attending Linkage's Global Institute for Leadership Development (GILD), an intensive week-long learning program where participants are exposed to world-class thought leaders from academic, business, and government circles. Also during the Institute, participants receive 360-degree feedback and two on-site coaching sessions and one additional session thirty to forty-five days after the program. At several points during GILD, learners participate in a McKesson learning team where they:

- Learn more about one another's roles and challenges in the business
- Process key learnings from the GILD sessions
- Develop personal action plans based on their 360-degree feedback and personal project
- Identify leadership challenges they are facing right now
- Set the stage for the learning agenda for the next two LTL learning sessions

There is often a debate about whether participants should mix with other corporations or have their own designated learning teams during GILD week. We tried it both ways and believe that it works better to have intact learning teams since there is a greater need to have managers understand other parts of the business and establish networks to facilitate cross-boundary partnering. For a corporation that has a need to expand mind-sets by exposing managers to those of other corporations, the mixed learning team concepts can be quite effective.

The McKesson learning team environment is led by Chris Cappy, president of Pilot Consulting, who facilitates the learning process and ensures program continuity and customization of each program to ensure that participants' learning needs are met. Cappy brings a broad range of experiences from other landmark leadership development initiatives and also teaches participants the GE Change Acceleration Process (CAP). He also pioneered something we call the oral tradition, where partici-pants are urged to share information. This has elicited some interesting personal leadership stories and related dialogue among participants.

Shortly after attending GILD, program manager Sandy Allred ensures that all participants have an executive coach assigned to them and have scheduled a follow-up appointment to review the progress on their 360-degree assessment within forty-five to sixty days after the GILD session. Allred also ensures they have scheduled a meeting with their manager to discuss their project goal, updated their performance objec-tives to include the LTL program and their selected project goals dur-ing the program, updated their individual development plan to include any personal plans based on their 360-degree assessment results, ensured their talent review process employee profile is current, and have the appropriate information to begin drafting and tracking their project goal and personal targets over the course of the program.

Project Goal and Personal Targets

Prior to attending the first learning activity (LTL II), participants and their supervisors are required to identify a project where participants have an opportunity to lead a change effort within their area of responsibility.

This is not a make-more-work project; rather, it is usually something they are already doing or contemplating doing during the performance period. Projects have these characteristics:

- They are an actual project.
- Results are expected within the nine-month program time frame.
- Participants are required to show leadership and change management skills.
- The project represents a genuine challenge to the leader-learner.
- The project helps drive process improvement, innovation, or double-digit growth.

The project works in conjunction with what we call the 3 P's of the program: the **p**roject to work on, the **p**ersonal action that results from both the 360-degree feedback and coaching process plus other learning from the program, and the **p**laybook, that is, the best practice tools taught for driving growth and innovation and change execution management.

In-House Customized Learning Events: LTL II and LTL III

Three months after participants take part in GILD, they attend LTL II, a two-and-a-half-day session at company headquarters in San Francisco. During this event, participants tour company headquarters and hear from senior company executives on topics such as strategy and financial position. Board members participate as well. They come to the program and discuss what it means to be a board member and share insights from their personal leadership journeys.

This event has three main focus areas. First, participants provide an update on their project goal and personal targets. Second, they participate in a four-hour customized workshop facilitated by Linkage on the topic of growth and innovation, a topic we had identified as critical in our leadership strategy. Focusing on innovation gives us the opportunity to help business leaders understand the disciplines necessary to sustain double-digit growth and assess the growth and innovation potential of participants' action learning projects. The third focus for participants is to learn GE's Change Acceleration Process (CAP), facilitated by Chris Cappy, which gives them over thirty tools to become more adept at change execution management. These tools can be used to help them throughout their nine-month project and beyond.

Leaders Teaching Leaders means three things: (1) external leaders are educating program participants on contemporary leadership topics, internal senior leaders are educating them on the business and their own leadership insights, and participants themselves are teaching one another about the business unit they belong to. This recipe has worked beautifully for us in its diversity of perspectives and simplicity in execution, not to mention the cost savings it yields.

Six months after GILD, participants complete the LTL program by attending the final learning event: LTL III. During this two-day session, participants:

- Deliver their final project update and key lessons learned during the nine-month process (a five- to seven-minute presentation followed by a brief question-and-answer period)
- Have dinner with the executive committee and business unit presidents
- Interact with the CEO, who discusses the business, his leadership insights, and expectations of McKesson leaders
- Hear from other senior executives or board members, or both, regarding their leadership journey and personal leadership insights over the course of their career
- Observe the investor's day event where McKesson officers discuss the business with the investment community (this is an optional half-day)

The final project presentations are videotaped to share with participants after the program and use highlights or clips in presentations that we create for our executives at events such as the senior managers' conference and other events.

Support Tools

To support the learning process, we used five additional tools:

1. *Linkage resources.* Participants had access to eight to ten leadership Web-broadcast sessions showcasing various leadership topics by expert presenters. In addition, the team receives a monthly online follow-up, "The Monthly Leader," which contains tools, articles, and video clips to help them develop in specific competency areas.

2. *Personal learning journals.* Each participant receives a leather-bound personal learning journal to track key learning points during the sessions and back on the job. Most participants found these to be very useful to track their progress and use during their leadership journey.

3. *Abstract executive book summaries.* Each participant receives a year's subscription to an online executive book summary Web site that allows them to pursue summaries on a variety of leadership topics. We also gave each participant an iPod Nano to use in conjunction with many of the summaries that are available to download in audio format in addition to printed media and other formats. getAbstract customized a site specifically geared to McKesson LTL participants in which the executive summary offerings were arranged relative to our nine core leadership competencies, making it easier for participants to search for summaries by specific McKesson competencies. We tracked the use of this resource and found that participants downloaded an average of ninety-five summaries per month and used them to gather data relative to their projects or initiate discussions with their teams.

4. *Internal share point site.* We created an internal site to share all program presentations, resources, and participant-offered resources.

5. *DevelopmentEngine project tracking tool.* This was our first experience using Fort Hill Company's DevelopmentEngine tool. After our first successful wave of using this tool for our LTL program, we integrated it into other leadership development programs.

Tracking Progress and Reporting Results

A key to any successful leadership development program is its ability to follow up and track participants' progress toward their final goals and outcomes and the ability to show the results of the program.

FIGURE 8.2.   ANSWERS TO QUESTIONS ON PROJECT GOAL AND PERSONAL TARGETS

Project Goal One:

In the next 9 months I will:	I will create a new technical leadership team in my business unit. As the new leadership is established, I will take this collection of talent and instill in them a sense of vision.	**Indicate one Goal Category:** ☑ Project Goal
So that:	So that I can align the organization from a technical perspective and drive a level of productivity and synergy that results in efficiencies and cost savings to the organization.	
Indicators of My Progress will include:	• Creation of my new team's organizational model • Selection of the individuals making up the new leadership team • Establishment of an effective meeting and reporting infrastructure • Creation and communication of a common vision and team-building exercises	

Project Goal One:

In the next 9 months I will:	Involve others in decision making. Specifically, involve managers and key team members in establishing and driving the rollout of XXX project	**Indicate one Goal Category:** ○ Strategic Thinking ○ Results Orientated and Energy ○ Leadership ○ Assertiveness and Influence ○ Decisiveness and Judgment ○ Openness and Candor ○ Sensitivity ○ Mature Confidence and Integrity ○ Building Organizational Talent
So that:	Managers and key team members will feel a part of the decision-making process. Involving others in setting the goal and avenues to achieve help ensure adoption and buy-in.	
Indicators of My Progress will include:	• Conduct follow up 360-degree feedback survey to determine progress from previous 360-degree feedback • Conduct Employee Opinion Survey Q1 specific to my department. Baseline survey already conducted. • Conduct a review of project to determine adoption rate.	

To do this for the LTL program, we turned to Fort Hill Company's DevelopmentEngine tool, which (1) ensures that the participants' learning plans are executed, (2) supports participants' growth by offering them the ability to request feedback from the supervisors or coach, (3) minimizes overhead for both participants and administrators (it is a turnkey process), and (4) can be customized to specific program needs and schedules.

We asked participants to answer three questions regarding their project goal and up to two personal targets based on the results of their 360-degree assessment results (see Figure 8.2). Once those had been entered into the tool, we began tracking monthly progress. On the first Friday of each month, the system automatically sent the participants an e-mail reminding them to update their progress. At any time, participants could send an e-mail to their manager requesting their thoughts and comments. At the end of the LTL program, we used the data in the tool to track their goal execution and progress on their goals.

After completing the initial pilot program in 2006 and 2007, we asked participants to complete a survey and provide us with feedback regarding their LTL experience. Here is what they had to say:

"It was awakening, reminding, reinforcing of what I knew, and discovered new things I didn't know."

"The value of protecting some reasonable amount of time to actually think about what I am trying to achieve and the importance of having useful tools to assist in focusing and driving that thinking process."

"My most valuable take away . . . it's all about other people . . . it isn't just one thing . . . but mostly how I leverage my strengths and look for the strengths of my team."

And here are some of the comments in answer to the question of what they would do differently:

"Build better relationships with my peers."

"Do it with more passion and leverage all of my people rather than the privileged few."

"Share more information, improve meeting management, and accelerate change using the CAP tools."

Managers and business unit presidents have also provided feedback to the participants through the DevelopmentEngine tool. This written feedback includes some excellent examples of coaching:

"I have witnessed a dramatic improvement in your second [personal] goal and as a result, I believe your peer relationships have improved and you have further developed the trust/respect of the team. I am also learning by your example and believe it has made you a more effective leader."

"The effort you are making to improve your leadership skills is evident in how you participate in our [leadership] meetings. Since you completed the LTL course, you have increased your communication and input on strategic and operational issues and most recently, in the budget process."

During the initial rollout of the pilot program, of the twenty-six participants, only about one-third of them had individual development plans entered in their performance document. When we began the second year of the program with a new group of high potentials, this number increased to almost three-quarters of the participants having individual development plans in place before attending the program. This is an indicator to us that more and more managers are having these development discussions and are being more effective with planning and tracking of the development of their employees.

In additional, just over 55 percent of the participants in the pilot program had been placed in new roles with greater responsibility within six months of completing the program. One participant reported a savings of $1.8 million on his project by focusing on three leadership behaviors (which were identified based on his 360-degree assessment results, then tracked and developed throughout the program): leading people, leading change using CAP tools, and leading innovation. This participant was promoted to chief financial officer of one of our businesses shortly after this program.

Lessons Learned

We are in our second wave of this program and, based on our experience and the feedback from the learners, have made some modifications to it. The first realization for us was that the degree of McKesson-specific business literacy among the group was lower than we had anticipated. So for wave one, we mixed the team into learning teams at GILD with leaders from other companies. Once we identified the critical need for them to understand the McKesson companies and our products, services, strategies, and other topics, we opted for a McKesson-specific learning team. Results indicate that this was the correct move: participants not only bonded faster but began sharing cross-boundary information and best practices both inside and external to the formal program earlier in the process. Moreover, few business relationships within and between businesses had existed among this group of middle managers prior to the program, so taking greater time for team building yielded great dividends.

Another area of learning for us was that while the business unit presidents and participant supervisors actively supported and engaged in the learning process, the HR community was virtually absent from the process despite being invited to participate. While participants were receiving what was for many of them their first 360-degree feedback from their direct reports and others, questions came up, and many asked, "Where are our HR generalists to help us through these issues?"

A common problem for HR in most organizations tends to be the issue of not having a seat at the table. This is one of many possible strategic entry points to begin that HR business partner relationship and it was missed. For wave II, we have continued to impress on the HR community the importance of their involvement and have seen greater participation, although it has not yet reached ideal levels.

Third, we made some modifications around the individual coaching process. Coaching was incorporated into the overall process through GILD, during which participants received three one-hour sessions. By monitoring their experiences, we were able to identify specific ways that we could get involved to help them prepare for and get the most out of their coaching experience. These lessons are not McKesson specific and apply to any coaching initiative:

◆ ◆ ◆

- *Setting realistic expectations about the purpose and expected outcome of the coaching session.* Participants thought the coach was more of a "life coach" versus providing them with insights for personal development around their 360-degree feedback. To address this, we created a coaching and development guide that speaks to the purpose of the sessions and what to do before, during, and after each one. We then introduced the coaching process using this guide so that participants knew specifically what was expected of them and what process their coaches would be using. This took out some of mystery of what the coach was "going to do to them." We found that made for a more productive experience because participants had to take an active role by providing more rigor to the preparation process before engaging with their coaches.
- *Real-time monitoring of the quality of the coaching experience.* Many participants did not know what to expect from a coaching session. Others were unable to establish rapport with their coaches or felt that their coaches were not particularly helpful at providing insight to assist them in their development planning. To address this, we set a process in place to monitor feedback along the way and selected a smaller group of coaches (based on participant satisfaction) who were able to become more familiar with McKesson and what we expect in the process. From this monitoring process, we learned that the more successful coaches were using a variety of job aids and processes. Based on participant responses about their success with the tools, we began using them consistently across coaches.

◆ ◆ ◆

Finally, in our design we anticipated the three P's as the core framework for the learning process: project, personal action plan, and playbook. We discovered a fourth "P," which we call positive peer performance pressure. Once participants began observing one another, whether in presenting before the group on their individual businesses or in projects they were working on, this contact immediately began to have the effect of raising the bar on the entire group. Participants saw in their peers skills they did not possess and pushed themselves to learn and emulate them throughout the program. They also saw the level and impact of some of the projects and made adjustments to their own accordingly.

In summary, the impact of the LTL initiative has far exceeded our expectations across the board. We have built a highly flexible platform for subsequent action learning work, and there is a high degree of receptivity among leaders to participate and learn more. The quality and value of relationships formed among the future leadership bench of the businesses cannot be overestimated. In terms of cost-benefit, we have kept the learning highly relevant and specific to the needs and realities of our leaders and businesses. By following the design principles of cost-effectiveness, adaptability, and sustainability and using this recipe as a guide, organizations can prepare their own leadership development system that produces the desired results within their budgetary limitations.

About the Contributors

J. Scott Boston is senior vice president of human resources for McKesson Corporation with responsibility for executive development, talent acquisition, organizational capability, diversity and inclusion, and the McKesson Center for Learning. He has over twenty years of experience with Fortune 50 companies leading talent management, HR transformation, and large-scale cultural change initiatives in domestic and international contexts. Prior to McKesson, he worked for seventeen years at BellSouth Corporation in a variety of positions, including chief learning officer, division head HR generalist, and director of executive development. He has an Executive M.B.A. and a B.B.A. from Emory University's Goizueta Business School.

Sandy Allred is the manager of executive development and talent management systems at McKesson. She has managed several cross-functional teams to design, develop, and implement initiatives across the organization. During her ten years with McKesson, she has led several corporatewide initiatives to include performance management, talent review process, and succession planning initiatives. Most recently, she has led two leadership development initiatives: the LTL program and the Rising Leaders Program, both designed to develop high-potential leaders within McKesson. She has traveled internationally to facilitate sessions with McKesson executives, managers, and individual contributors on topics ranging from performance management to ICARE Shared Principles. She is completing her Executive M.B.A. at Georgia State University's J. Mack Robinson School of Business.

◆ ◆ ◆

Christopher Cappy works in the areas of large-scale change management, leadership development, and innovative executive education and coaching. He is founder of Pilot Consulting Corporation, which led IBM's worldwide Accelerate Change Together (ACT) initiative between 1995 and 2000, and he served for eleven years on the faculty of General Electric's Crotonville Leadership Center, which included leading the external consulting team for GE Appliances Workout. Cappy is a founding member of the Learning Network, holds a degree in production management from Rochester Institute of Technology, and is a graduate of Columbia University's Advanced Organization Development Program.

CHAPTER NINE

YAHOO!

This chapter outlines an approach to leadership that focuses on strengths, both at the personal and organizational level, and uses the power of development to reinforce the corporate brand.

There is a well-trodden expression in leadership development circles: "People don't leave companies, they leave managers." The inference is presumably that when the relationship between a manager and his or her direct reports or coworkers breaks down, or the manager acts in a way that is detrimental to the well-being of the individuals around him or her, this can lead to the loss of talent, unanticipated cost in managing or replacing the gap they leave behind, or even sometimes costs resulting from errors and poor performance.

The responsibility for creating an environment where people can give their best and generate outstanding results is shared with all the players in the complex web of relationships, structures, and dependencies that define organizations today. Designing an organization that is aligned and fit for its purpose is every bit as important as the clarity of strategy or the adequacy of information and the extent to which the structure enables people in the system to work together.

Alignment of the organization with the strategy, key processes, structures, and people in the organization is clearly essential, and it is common sense as well. But all too often, common sense is not common practice or easy, and organizations can flounder badly when alignment is lacking. The importance of helping employees in organizations to succeed among this complexity and frequent uncertainty is the central and shared role of the manager and his or her charges. When this fundamental relationship works really well, it can create a unity and engagement that is viral and infectious in nature. I contend that the challenge of building strong, lasting relationships in the matrix of the organization is the most important role and influence managers have, and it is their prime and special responsibility.

If effective relationships between relevant people is the most fundamental means for organizations to react and interact, then interdependency drives effectiveness in decision making, problem solving, communications, creativity, and the other key wealth-generating behaviors inside organizations. Aligning relationships within teams and across the usual matrix structure and groupings is essential. Doing this in a way that is consistent with both the hard measures of success, such as revenue, profitability, and growth, and the softer measures of organizational life is essential because people often value these latter measures just as much and experience a strong emotional resonance with the environment and the culture of the organization they choose to be part of.

The Psychological Contract

Knowledge-based organizations such as Yahoo! know only too well the importance of the softer measures. The concept of the psychological contract—the often unspoken agreement about how economically powerful organizations and the individuals who work in them coexist in a mutually acceptable bargain—is becoming less relevant. The power is shifting, and the so-called digital economy needs the skills and talents of those capable of driving success more than those individuals often need their jobs: demand is outstripping supply. People move constantly, and talent retention and engagement is the name of the game. Certainly great benefits and brand value really help, but newly minted young graduates joining the workforce today understand their value and the options this affords them, and they are seeking powerful experiential development that, coupled with strong market awareness, creates discerning choices. As they move into leadership roles, we have seen compression in the time required to get them ready to lead, as well as the type and length of development intervention needed to make them effective or develop readiness.

At the end of 2003, Yahoo! was at the crest of the wave in recovery of the Internet media sector as the effects of the dot-com crash began to wane, and a resurgence in opportunities for advertising created a powerful platform for growth. Since 2003, Yahoo! has been growing in revenue, market share, users, profitability, and the number of people it employs—up from thirty-five hundred in 2003 to more than thirteen thousand people in early 2008. In a sense, the decimation of the Internet media industry after the end of the first dot-com era in 2001 meant that many organizations were forced back into something akin to start-up mode. Driving this at Yahoo! was a supremely confident and energized executive team, leading a global team of managers from entry-level supervisors, managing upward from one person, to directors and vice presidents running large global businesses and functions.

Part of Yahoo!'s psychological contract was the understanding that a career with the company meant the chance to take on big jobs with heavy responsibility—sometimes very early in one's career or in an untested manner so as to share in the success of the brand and the financial performance of the company. In a sense, this careful management of risk versus opportunity has been very successful: business performance over this period has been strong, and careers have flourished. The strong "relater and achiever" culture at Yahoo!, where bright, socially confident, and ambitious people drove personal success hand in glove with the hours they put into the job, has also created a competitive task-oriented culture. When the competitive landscape changes or growth and size demand increased emphasis on process, planning, and learning to drive scale and success, the behaviors needed have to mature and shift. The emphasis on accountability, communication, and decision making and teamwork became vital.

The Underlying Themes

Yahoo! recognized that the most important component of the success formula was to concentrate on helping leaders at every level throughout the business feel confident and tooled up to manage their people—whether it was understanding the basic principles of being an effective people manager or focusing in a more personal way on how to lead and the extent of the impact of their values and attitudes on their beliefs and actions. In a sense, we were just as interested in tackling the people system as we were the processes and tools needed to create a great product.

The vital underlying theme to our development strategy was to accentuate the positive and the practical. For too long, performance management systems and training interventions have focused on weakness, and we were convinced that this presented only a small portion of the story in understanding what drives high performance and engagement. In partnership with the Marcus Buckingham Company, we drove hard the notion that focusing on strengths and understanding and managing weaknesses will do more than yield better individual performance. It will also:

- Drive engagement whereby individuals feel drawn to work they know they enjoy and can do well
- Drive employee satisfaction, which is delicately linked to how people feel about the work and the meaning it holds for them
- Contribute to team effectiveness because well-rounded teams benefit when they consist of powerful strengths
- Help to drive employee retention and create an environment where diversity can be seen in its broadest sense as the abilities and strengths of all are recognized

Creating a congruent strengths-based strategy is a work-in-progress. It seems that for the most part, people are pretty good at ensuring they operate in a manner that allows them to leverage their strengths. So for some managers, the question is, "How can I understand the strengths and abilities of my team, so I can leverage them and the work more effectively?" For others, the issue is about using this understanding of strengths to know how to build a new team well from the start, or even to know how to tackle perceived poor performance differently. We have taught and discussed these principles through our core curriculum, foundation manager class, executive development program, and team workshops and planning sessions.

The other critical theme to our development strategy was to focus on how managers led and engaged their people—through both the way they helped people perform in the role they had hired them to do and in the way managers engaged their hearts to create a compelling and mutually exciting view of their career with the company. Developing a congruent and effective leadership development strategy was essential for driving employee engagement and company performance.

There was no appetite within the organization for creating a corporate university structure, which was considered inappropriate for the culture and speed of the organization; moreover, providing managers with the tools and resources to focus technical skills development on the job was outside our purview. Our focus instead was to drive awareness of and confidence in managing and nurture the best each individual had to offer in how to inspire and lead.

In tackling this task, we studied and benchmarked the leadership development structure and programming at a number of similar organizations and spent time talking to colleagues in other industries about their best practices and their challenges. We knew we needed to supplement in-class programming with a needs identification process, on-the-job development, coaching, and succession management methodology. Our international staffing team had already established a best-in-class reputation for hiring solid, astute, and culturally aligned leaders, and our colleagues responsible for organizational development had established a broad competency framework and talent identification process as part of the company performance review cycle. The complementary component to this was a strong leadership development program.

We built a simple leadership development strategy complemented by an executive coaching program and support for senior managers to broaden their business acumen. We also used company-sponsored networking events, book talks, "big thinker" industry luminaries, and support to return to business school to acquire new knowledge and qualifications.

Initially this program was focused on the key leaders at the vice president level and at the manager level on a much broader basis of invitation. Participants in the executive program were brought by invitation only to help drive engagement and interest in the program and to begin to build a strong bench of high-potential leaders who could be seen as potential successors to the executive team within a few years.

As the reputation of the programs grew, we opened these up, particularly at the executive level, to all eligible senior leaders in the company. We extended this curriculum to our international business in 2006–2007, running programs around the world for key leaders in major Yahoo! locations. The flagship element at the managerial level was a development program called Leading Big, and at the executive level, a program called Courageous Leadership. Both programs were supported with a curriculum of classes that aligned to the strategic priorities of the business and the competency framework that supported it, including programs on understanding Yahoo! financials, coaching skills, organization awareness, and employee engagement.

The Leadership Curriculum

The leadership curriculum consists of several core and required programs. At the manager level, we developed and offered an intensive two-day program entitled Leading Big, which taught all people managers essential principles of managing at Yahoo!

1. Be accountable.
2. Set goals.
3. Delegate effectively.
4. Engage your team.
5. Develop your people.
6. Coach your people.
7. Recognize their achievements.

This program has been delivered throughout our global business and has recently been revised and delivered to incorporate winning behaviors at Yahoo!—the key attributes we have identified that are seen as the vital cultural component in our continued success. These provided the major emphasis in the program in 2008 and centered on decision making, teamwork, results delivery, and customer satisfaction.

Leading Big has been a spectacularly effective and popular program. The combination of practical tools, discussion, and a focus on strengths as the technology to help get them there has proven popular with leaders. Supplementing this program has been a combination of supporting interventions intended to delve into a small number of the essential elements of managing, a focus on coaching, building financial competence, and setting and managing goals well.

The other key element in this process is recognizing that workshops like Leading Big not only play a part in shaping the culture but also help reflect it back to participants so they can challenge their perceptions about themselves and how effective they are as leaders in creating a great culture. For this reason, we also offered a personal self-assessment for participants in 2008, enabling managers to see how their own perceived style compares to the cultural norms and artifacts of the organization. This is then debriefed inside the workshop, and participants are coached through the conclusions to be aware of and the steps needed to ensure we continue to create a great work experience inside teams. Managers are almost always at the front line of culture, organizational change, and business success, and without personal context setting, which such an assessment helps to provide, we cannot realistically hope or expect them to know how to shift their beliefs and actions or help their team to do the same.

For executives, Yahoo! has partnered with a third-party executive development practice, Axialent, for several years, in the delivery of an intensive leadership program entitled Courageous Leadership. This program is rare in the legion of executive development programs offered in corporate America today, as it deliberately focuses on the heart and consciousness of the individual. It propounds that great leadership starts with a fundamental awareness of self, the core platform that enables these leaders to be seen as compelling and trusting to others, where those within that leader's area of responsibility see meaning in the work and solidarity in the relationships at work.

Much of the focus in business today is on the "it" dimension of life: "What is 'it' that we need?" "What is 'it' that is the problem?" The Yahoo! program moves past this, and considers the "I" and the "we," thereby building on the need for personal integrity and great relationships as the foundation to knowing who I am and what is expected of me as a leader. As the Army Ranger credo states, "Leadership starts with what a leader must be, the values and attributes that shape a leader's character. Leadership is a matter of how to be, not how to do." We have chosen to help participants see the link between their beliefs and values and the kind of organization they lead.

Our vision for preparing and helping leaders to lead is wisely championed by author Mihaly Csikszentmihalyi in *Good Business* (2003):

The search for a life that has relevance or meaning beyond one's material existence is the primary concern of soul. This is the need felt by a person aware of his or her own finitude; the need that motivates us to become part of something greater and more permanent.

If a leader can make a convincing case that working for the organization will provide relevance, that it will take the workers out of the shell of their mortal frame and connect them with something more meaningful, then his vision will generate power, and people will naturally be attracted to become part of such a company.

A leader will find it difficult to articulate a coherent vision unless it expresses his core values, his basic identity. For that reason one must first embark on the formidable journey of self-discovery in order to create a vision with authentic soul.

We chose to invest our resources and the time of our leaders in examining and applying this notion because we knew that these leaders have a hand on the lever that contributes to the experience and enthusiasm that users, customers, and employees feel about Yahoo! The emotional resonance of this brand is felt in the quality of this experience. If Yahoo! is more than just a business that creates or sells widgets, then starting with the heart meant that we needed to start with ourselves and ask how and why we lead—as a company and as individuals.

After all, no one can be forced into being led; we exercise free choice in what we think and feel about the place where we work, the people we work with, and the boss we have. Our premise in Courageous Leadership therefore is to ask, "How do you get someone to give you the gift of their energy? . . . to be led by You?" It's a tough question, partly because the company's culture had never articulated leadership in quite this way before, but also because it strips away the trappings of power and material success that often actualize leaders and forces them to take a look at themselves, and ask. "Where am I today? What do I need to do?"

This popular program, open to all senior leaders across our global business, can be an intensely profound experience for participants. In its first two years, this program was open to participation by invitation only, although we later offered it as a public curriculum event to encourage senior managers to network together and come together in the spirit of "One Yahoo!" to talk about themselves and the business in a way that is rare in such a busy organization.

Courageous Leadership is supplemented with a multirater assessment of personal style that enables the participant to understand his or her perceived work style in relation to the cultural norms Yahoo! has today and is building for tomorrow. It shines a bright light on the delta between where this person currently is and where he or she wishes to be behaviorally. Yahoo! also operates a large and extensive executive coaching program targeted toward its high-performing key players and emerging leaders.

Measuring Value

As with all other such interventions, sometimes it is difficult to assess the return on investment. Matters of the heart and issues of style are sometimes intangible or a little abstract in definition, and not easily measured. However, without clear and unequivocal evidence that these interventions were driving engagement, career development, and ultimately business results, it would be difficult for us to make a case for continued or increased funding and, just as important, the active involvement of senior executives.

To understand value, we commissioned an independent study in mid-2007 from a trusted development partner to answer these key questions. We asked them to survey all managers who had attended the manager-level curriculum classes in the first half of 2007 (at least ninety days out from attending the programs) and to carry out a series of in-depth one-on-one interviews with a number of senior managers who had participated in the executive program. In all, we worked with more than four hundred managers and spoke at length to thirty executives (vice presidents or above).

Until that point, our evaluation had been largely reactive and based on the so-called level 1 Kirkpatrick model (satisfaction after a learning event) after people had attended the class. Although these data were positive in indicating that people were happy with the experience, we wanted to go much further and understand what impacts it had on the performance of the organization and the effectiveness and engagement of the participants.

Our starting point was to conduct a level 2 evaluation and ask, "Has learning taken place?" and then move to level 3 questioning: "Has behavior changed?" When we asked respondents to discuss their learning, the key concepts of both programs continued to resonate strongly, particularly the underlying theme of strengths at work and issues relating to the core principles of managing.

Some 75 percent of all respondents said that they remembered and had internalized the learning from these concepts into their routines at work, particularly in leveraging the strengths of others, setting goals, driving recognition, and engaging their teams. In addition, 97 percent of respondents felt that the programs had made a significant contribution to their ability to be effective at work.

At the executive level, we found that 93 percent of those interviewed believed the programmed content helped them to improve their attitudes and performance at work significantly, and 63 percent also cited significant improvements in their home life. When asked to judge whether they perceived this was a good investment for Yahoo! 91 percent said "yes" or "absolutely." The elements of the program that resonated most strongly with this constituency related to notions of personal humility, accountability, and the importance as a leader of keeping promises. Twenty-five percent of respondents cited a major job change (promotion of increased responsibility) in the months following attendance at the program.

There are obviously significantly more data than presented here. The point is that we were able to demonstrate fairly conclusively that the investment in leaders is a valuable factor in affecting how they show up for work, how they feel they behave with their people, and the impact they have on the culture of the organization. Our next stage is to consider level 4 evaluation: What business impact has occurred and how can it be measured?

How Development Reinforces Brand

Yahoo! is deservedly proud of the brand reputation of its products and services; consumer research has consistently indicated that users see the brand as powerful, fun, engaging, and reliable. Internal brand guidelines at Yahoo! help to reinforce and protect this perception. It is therefore no surprise that internal programs are seen as key not only in the importance they attach to support this perception but also in the way they reinforce a complementary employment brand perception among current and prospective employees.

Research consistently demonstrates that engagement is critical to performance and that employees need to be deeply connected with their job and their employer. The experience of working on a great team and for a great company is important to employees, often to the exclusion of other factors such as location, level, and compensatory elements. In such a fierce employment market, most employees have multiple choices about what they choose to do and for whom, which places great pressure on organizations to offer best-in-class environments, benefits, and opportunities.

Effective and meaningful performance and career development are intrinsic to this. Programs that help people understand how to do their job more effectively and drive their perception that the company is investing in them play a valuable part in their decision to stay and the perception that others have of them. In the study of the senior executives who participated in the Leading Big and Courageous Leadership programs, 25 percent felt that participation in the program had been a factor in positive job change in the months following their attendance. The other element to this is the extent to which effective leadership drives team performance and retention: Yahoo! has historically enjoyed below-industry-average levels of employee turnover.

The Power of Focusing on Strengths

Strengths-based thinking seems obvious when you stop to consider what makes people feel strong at work. Of course, it makes sense that we might focus on the things we do well and perfect them. And yet you would be wrong. For the most part, organizations reference strengths but instinctively talk much more about weaknesses: the things that do not work or the well-trodden euphemism of human resource departments everywhere of "development areas" or "areas of opportunity."

It is no surprise that we think like this. Deficit-based thinking about excellence is everywhere around us: we study divorce to understand happy marriages, provide remedial education time to subjects a child finds hardest at school, and examine sadness to try to define joy. This begins in families and schools and percolates through to companies, creating a performance management disaster in many cases where employees feel misunderstood or neglected or managers feel ill equipped to know how to truly engage their charges.

Creating a more positive strengths-based environment can be tackled by looking at the system or changing the way people and teams think. The former is significantly harder in planning and executing since it is systemwide and requires strategic planning and broad support. Tackling this challenge one piece at a time seemed much easier to us, which is why we implemented strengths-based thinking through all key development programs, including Leading Big and Courageous Leadership.

We also implemented a strengths-based coaching program in partnership with three of the company's most trusted external coaching partners. Our thinking was that in addition to building awareness and confidence in how they manage the strengths of their teams, individual leaders needed help as people themselves to define, enhance, and ultimately draw on their strengths for the benefit of their job and the performance of Yahoo!

The other major element to this work is to see how leveraging strengths can help the team perform more effectively. Research by the Marcus Buckingham Company suggests that the experience of the team trumps that of the company at large. When people work on a great team, they feel energized and insulated from the wider difficulties a company may be experiencing. We saw strengths-based team development as a natural fit to this challenge and created a set of strengths-based team tools to help intact groups figure out what their individual strengths were and how they could leverage them.

The team-based development work was, and continues to be, very different from the public curriculum of classes. This work is exclusive to the individual needs of the team and is 100 percent referral-based work. Several members of the talent development team at Yahoo! spent a large amount of their time on only this kind of work. A lot of team development work is focused on strategic business planning and team formation. Strengths-based activities are highly complementary to these activities and provide a practical foundation of understanding why people perform the way they do. In other circumstances, we were brought to a team for the sole purpose of introducing them to strengths-based thinking.

There are several components to this work. The first step is to build awareness of strengths and facilitate a discussion with team members about performance and contribution. The Clifton StrengthsFinder, an assessment tool developed by Gallup used to measure and apply strengths, is a highly complementary tool to help with this process. This first step helps teams understand what strengths are, differentiate them from the things they might define to be a weakness, and share this awareness with the rest of their team.

The second stage of this process can run concurrently with the first session or as a follow-up stage in the work we did with specific teams. This involved inviting teams to participate in the Simply Strengths program by the Marcus Buckingham Company. Based on Buckingham's best-selling book *Go Put Your Strengths to Work* (2007), this immersion program helps individuals examine their job in the context of day-to-day tasks and activities, understanding the things they "love" and things they "loathe," ultimately as a precursor to setting their strengths free, and focusing on what makes them feel strong. This program operates as both an immersion workshop for intact teams and a virtual classroom for teams or for individuals.

The strengths work proved to be highly popular and was consistently cited by teams across diverse sections of the company as a basis for building understanding of colleagues, greater patience and understanding of their role and contribution, and team morale and effectiveness. This anecdotal feedback was borne out in the study of talent development work at Yahoo! In follow-up evaluations between three and twelve months after completing Yahoo! public curriculum programs or team development programs, the value and practical application of strengths was the most frequently recurring positive feedback that respondents felt had helped them to understand and manage their team more effectively or feel better about how to perform in their role.

Conclusion

Investing in the talent of the organization seems a given as you look from the outside in to a knowledge-based business like Yahoo! with its assets and powerful and successful brand image. The study examined here explains in part some of the steps we took to get the process started. The data suggest that the investment is seen as positive and reinforcing to the culture and performance of the business, and we continue to consider how to augment this with new practices, tools, and interventions.

Leader and manager effectiveness stem from a keen focus on the core things leaders need to know and do. Giving them the time and space to reflect, practice, and improve is equally important. Putting off the investment needed to create great leaders is foolish in our view because leaders play a critical role in the customer value chain; underinvestment will play itself out in poor retention or a restricting or confusing environment for employees.

We also believe that accentuating the positive is important, which is why we have focused on strengths over the past few years and eliminated deficit-based thinking where we can. But if leaders are not held to account for driving the right behaviors in the organization, much of this powerful message could be lost. Ultimately the best learning takes place on the job, not in the classroom, so we have tried to keep class-based learning to a minimum. Although time in class is rare and valuable, the application of this learning back at work is where people get the chance to apply, practice, and grow.

In this sense, the performance strategy of the organization and positive reinforcing behaviors of the most senior leaders to create a model for those beneath them is important if the investments in the classroom are to be nurtured and developed. Like the industry we are a part of, we are probably still at the early stages of a long and interesting journey, but we feel that we have made a solid and interesting start.

References

Buckingham, M. *Go Put Your Strengths to Work*. New York: Free Press, 2007.
Csikszentmihalyi, M. *Good Business*. New York: Viking Press, 2003.

About the Contributor

Stuart Crabb is a human resource leader with twenty years of experience in building high-growth organizations in the United States and Europe. This has included key leadership roles in Yahoo!, HP/Compaq, and Siemens, among others. He has conducted business in more than twenty-five countries and has lived in the United Kingdom, Germany, Australia, and the United States. His most recent corporate role was global head of talent development with Yahoo! Crabb is principal partner and cofounder of Oxegen Consulting, a leadership development and coaching practice based in the San Francisco Bay Area that focuses on strengths-based leadership programming and coaching.

CHAPTER TEN

JOHNSON & JOHNSON

This chapter outlines an effective approach to action-learning, using a cast of deeply engaged internal faculty to create relevant experiential learning across a global organization.

Each May since 2003, twenty-five directors and new vice presidents from all over the globe assemble at the Johnson & Johnson headquarters in New Jersey to begin a year-long experience that will prepare them for executive leadership at one of Johnson & Johnson's two hundred worldwide operating companies.

Participants arrive confident and ready to take on the challenge. Each person has been hand-selected for a high level of technical knowledge in quality and compliance, a demonstrated leadership potential, and an ability to manage teams. As a whole, the group thinks logically and efficiently. They are used to getting things done and are accustomed to being successful. They have no idea that during the year, they will be challenged to act differently, think differently, and "be" in new ways.

Each class goes through a powerful transformation over the course of the year. They shift in the way they think about the business, increase their awareness of themselves as leaders, sharpen their ability to identify business needs, deepen their relationships and expand their global networks, learn how to influence at a board level, learn how to get to the heart of an issue, learn how to work as a global team, and learn how to orient and move forward in the midst of ever-increasing data and continuous change.

All of this learning is experiential; participants learn by doing in a carefully designed action learning program that is both structured and improvisational. This program has produced more than fifteen vice presidents of quality in the past four years and is widely supported by executive staff for its ability to deliver consistent business results.

Lasting Results: Why It Works

The Executive Quality Leadership Development (EQLD) program is widely recognized as a key quality initiative at Johnson & Johnson. The program has grown each year and has survived in the face of organizationwide budget cuts. EQLD remains intact because it produces lasting results, which is a direct reflection of how the program was conceived and how it has matured.

A Burning Platform

EQLD was initiated in response to a specific business need. At the time of the program's inception, more than 90 percent of executive ranks in quality were being filled externally. External recruiting costs were high, wait times for executives were long, learning curves for new executives were steep, and deep company knowledge was being lost each time a high-potential individual left the company to pursue other opportunities. EQLD began as a way to produce a pipeline of "ready-now" quality talent to support the long-term health and viability of J&J. This focus on the business has been at the heart of EQLD from the very beginning, and it is the core of the program.

Business at the Center

At the center of the EQLD curriculum is a complex business challenge that the class must solve by the end of the year-long program. This project is typically an unwieldy, complex issue that the business has not yet addressed. Sample projects from previous years include a due-diligence tool to assess quality risks for mergers and acquisitions, a Web-based tool for creating spinouts (a business with J&J technology at its core but organized with outside capital), and a business development process for new products in medical devices and diagnostics for the European markets.

Each business challenge is purposely broad at the outset. The class is tasked with researching the impact and nuances of the issue to produce a solution that leads to transformational change in the organization. This means researching the issue, soliciting the voice of the customer, producing a variety of solution ideas, vetting these ideas with an executive group, negotiating to solidify scope, developing the actual deliverables, championing and selling the deliverables internally, and implementing the final solution within the organization. This research-based creative process becomes the context of learning for the year. This context offers timely experience in an environment that allows participants to make mistakes, learn, and grow.

The project itself becomes a multilevel win-win for J&J. The business gets a novel solution to a critical problem. Program participants learn how different parts of the organization work and what it means to think and act at the executive level. Executives involved in the program see candidates in action and become acquainted with individuals they might not have known before, and Johnson & Johnson gets a pool of talent that is calibrated on the values and leadership performance expectations that will lead the company into the future.

Executive Involvement

A key structural element of the EQLD success is executive participation. The project for the year is selected by the Global Quality Council (GQC), a collection of vice presidents who oversee quality throughout J&J. Because the GQC wants each class project to happen, it has a vested interest in the class's success from the beginning of the program. This means that GQC members are intrinsically motivated to help, and when there is a difficulty, the class can tap the GQC network to get something done.

Johnson & Johnson quality executives are also involved at a programmatic level. One or two executives are designated each year as project champions, and they become the main executive audience for the class. They are chosen for their subject matter expertise and ability to deliver concise and pointed feedback throughout the year. Five to ten additional executives are designated as project sponsors who make presentations to the class and participate in small-group discussions, subteam activities, and guidance sessions. Project sponsors typically attend the face-to-face class residential sessions three weeks out of the year and provide ongoing support during the virtual work periods. Many sponsors are also members of the GQC.

The rewards of executive involvement are powerful, and there are obvious benefits and more subtle ones. Involving executive talent ensures that the class is mentored by the people they will ultimately work with and that the solution the class creates is relevant and useful to the business. The involvement of executives at these various levels also builds community. To many executives, the activity of bringing up the next generation of leaders is personally rewarding, and executives at the ground level tend to seize the opportunity to shape and guide their successors. Aside from the personal satisfaction inherent in giving back and preparing for the future, executives also tend to enjoy the bonding that occurs with an opportunity to reflect and talk about leadership with their peers. An esprit de corps is built as executives share their personal leadership journeys and give feedback to the class as an executive team.

Learning by Doing

The class project is designed to get program participants talking to people in the business and learning about how J&J works at a global scale. Because each project represents a dilemma that the organization is actually facing, all actions within the program become fodder for learning. Participants learn about the issues confronting the business and what the business needs. They learn about who is where in the organization and how these people think and communicate (in ways that are sometimes very different from the quality viewpoint). They learn how things truly get done and where the opportunities are for new partnerships and collaborations.

This out-and-about approach helps participants build new relationships that break the traditional stereotypes that quality people are the regulation police. Not only does this creative approach break stereotypes, but the people in the organization who are solicited for their thoughts, needs, and opinions also become supporters of the class (and often the project itself).

Focus on Relationships

One of the goals of the EQLD program is to build a network of leaders who can think globally and work on global teams. As such, the class is made up of participants from different J&J businesses throughout the world. The EQLD class of 2008 had participants from seventeen operating companies from North America, Europe, and Asia. With a group this diverse, there is not one method for doing things, and relationship building becomes a key focus of the program. Participants have to focus on listening, asking questions, probing, and exploring to build the understanding that forms solid relationships in such a diverse group. And because so much of the work the class does in the virtual work period is over the telephone, the teamwork and understanding built during the face-to-face residential sessions become even more important.

With an emphasis on relationships and teamwork, the EQLD program gives participants a year-long experience from which to create a powerful personal network of their peers within J&J that crosses company boundaries and franchise organizations. The location of the residency section is selected to expose the participants to the breadth and diversity of J&J companies around the world. This personal network becomes another benefit to the company at large, because the capacity for individuals to get things done within the organization is magnified and expanded on a global scale. This is especially significant in a company like J&J, where the management structure is highly decentralized and the company is divided into many different franchise organizations, each with its own focus, procedures, customers, and concerns. By the end of the year, EQLD participants say that they feel comfortable picking up the phone and calling any one of their classmates for help or advice. The existence of a strong network is cited regularly in retention surveys as one of the important reasons executives stay at J&J, and new J&J recruits say that the presence of programs like EQLD was an important factor in their decision to join the company.

Tied to Measurement

The EQLD program was designed as a promotion and retention initiative, and it has produced results. Thirteen vice presidents have been promoted from the EQLD ranks in the past four years, and now 90 percent of quality vice president positions are being filled within J&J, with a high percentage being EQLD graduates. As a whole, 70 percent of class participants have been promoted or have taken on expanded roles within the organization. These numbers reflect the extended capabilities of the participants and the visibility the program gives to individuals who may not be known in other companies within J&J.

Class participants are also measured at the corporate level according to a global leadership profile, which is administered and monitored by their supervisors. The competencies within the profile are supported by the three large aims of the EQLD program: focusing globally, managing risk, and driving collaboration. These three elements have been combined in a model for quality leadership that includes technical expertise, management ability, and leadership ability, which formalizes a structure for quality leadership at J&J. This model guides the EQLD curriculum and forms the basis of how participants are evaluated for future assignments.

Questions to Consider

Looking back on the vision and design of the EQLD program, one can isolate the factors that contributed to its success, resulting in valuable lessons for future efforts. Following are questions that any internal practitioner must ask when designing or evaluating a leadership development initiative:

- How are you quantifying (and championing) the visible and invisible benefits of your leadership program?
- How are the results of your leadership program made visible to your organization? How are your executive staffs involved in ways that are meaningful to them?
- If your leadership program is not working well, what are the long- and short-term threats to your organization? What is your burning platform, your business case? What do you see as the opportunities?

Approach: The Secret to Making It Work

EQLD has been successful because it reflects business needs and links existing leaders to the next generation. But these structural elements are not the reason the program works. The reason a whole group of people can make dramatic shifts in their thinking, acting, and being has to do with how their experience is being structured and how they are being taught. The secret to making this program work lives in the approach.

Practice, Practice, Practice

Research shows that building an awareness of something takes anywhere from two hours to two days, but genuine mastery takes one to seven years. The path from awareness to mastery relies on simple practice: the act of doing something consciously over and over again. With this in mind, the EQLD faculty approaches its action learning curriculum as an opportunity for participants to incorporate and do—to interact, practice, and reflect.

Reflection Is Key

On the first day of the program, participants are given personal leadership journals and asked to take a moment to reflect on the day's experience. Because the program is designed to build leaders who can orient themselves in the swirl of chaos and ever-changing data, participants are also asked to reflect on awkward situations even as they are happening. Faculty will stop a difficult team interaction to ask, "What's working here?" "What's not working here?" "What can you do differently?" The constant repetition of these three questions teaches participants how to use their own experience to orient themselves in real time and to find new options quickly.

Owning the Experience

Creating opportunities for reflection transfers the learning responsibility from teachers to participants. This transfer of responsibility is another important feature of the EQLD approach. Because program participants are expected to be confident and creative in their future senior executive roles, the EQLD faculty continually prompt participants to use their own experience as a resource and to look at themselves as experts. This removal of an outside authority is a big shift for some participants to make, and very difficult for participants and faculty alike at the beginning of the program.

When the program starts, participants look to the faculty for "the answer" to their business challenge (What should we do here? How should we approach this?), and faculty watch participants struggle as they use old methods of thinking to find "the" answer, assuming that "the right answer" already exists.

At the beginning of the EQLD program, faculty must watch teams be uncomfortable and make mistakes, without giving in to the temptation to step in and give answers. This ability to let participants have their own experience is one element that makes the ultimate learning so profound. Although there may be struggles in the beginning, the stage is set for deep learning, and participants leave the program feeling personal ties to their own experience and their own growth.

This does not mean that faculty remain outside the process. The faculty are intricately involved, guiding the class with questions and teaching tools that will ultimately help participants figure out how to organize themselves, gather information, and come up with a unique solution.

Applying Immediately

The design of the EQLD class challenge has participants in a constant state of interacting and negotiating: How are we going to conduct ourselves as a team? How are we going to negotiate our project scope? How are we going to decide what our subteams should be? How will we present to the champions and sponsors? This interaction is a vital part of the learning process, since negotiating and interacting is a large part of what leaders do.

The need to interact and negotiate also makes participants ripe for learning new skills and tools that they can use immediately. Team dynamics, interviewing approaches, decision-making tools, and meeting facilitation processes are all presented to the class and then applied right away. After each learning module, participants are asked to share with a partner, share with the group, or work as a group to apply the learning to the task at hand. If, for example, a module on interviewing is presented, participants get on the telephone and computer and conduct some best practice research. The knowledge is applied immediately. This application approach coupled with guided reflection (So how did that work? What questions do you have now?) ultimately teaches participants how to build their own skills. The underlying philosophy here is that teaching new skills is good, but the most powerful approach is to teach participants how to build their own skills.

Collaboration and Asking Questions

Knowing how to collaborate is a vital part of leadership, especially true for quality executives who are often in situations of influence where they do not control the resources. By giving participants experiences where they have to be constantly collaborating—with other classmates, with potential partners, with the champions and sponsors—participants who are used to being individual contributors get a full-bore education in teamwork.

Asking powerful questions is the central skill for this leadership area. Participants conduct "Q-storming" exercises, where the objective is not what you know but what questions there are, and they learn to use questions as a way to build understanding and move a group forward. Point of view is crucial here. Questions are not asked from a blaming perspective (Why did this happen?) but from a generative perspective (Who do we need to get on board? What are our gifts here? Who can we invigorate?).

By showing participants how to use questions to get others interested in problem solving and improving, participants learn to engage their peers at higher levels of creativity. This questioning approach also opens the door to participants' getting practice at being curious and open. This is typically where reality starts looking less one-dimensional and more richly multilayered, and participants get to practice dropping their own agendas to listen to what is actually being said.

Improvisation

Being able to improvise is one of the most important leadership skills that faculty can model for participants. Although there are underlying principles to the EQLD curriculum and approach, faculty must be willing to move in the moment based on what a class is experiencing that day. Faculty must be willing to convene ad hoc meetings, rearrange the schedule, and produce teaching experiences on the fly that address a specific group's needs at a given time. These opportunities happen less in the beginning of the program and more in the middle and end of it.

What is important is that faculty are willing to drop their agendas and deal with what is happening in the room. This ensures that the teaching is addressing the needs of the participants and, more important, models skilled leadership for participants.

This approach to modeling improvisation goes hand in hand with providing opportunities for participants to improvise. In the first week of the program, participants interact with senior executives to discuss the business challenge, with the expectation that they will have to jump in without formal preparation. These opportunities to listen attentively and respond to what is happening in the moment occur throughout the program and are an explicit part of the learning.

Personal Support

Throughout the EQLD year, each participant is assigned a professional coach who conducts an individualized leadership profile and supports the participant throughout the year. These coaches are members of the EQLD faculty and attend the residential sessions so they can watch the participants in action. Participants meet with their coaches once or twice during the residential session and discuss what the coach has seen, how the process is going, and options for growth. This just-in-time coaching goes hand-in-hand with the just-in-time training approach.

The EQLD faculty members are cohesive as well, and the support that they get from each other makes the process of running the program collaborative, creative, and fun. Participants sense this cohesion and know that they can go to any one of the staff for insight, support, or assistance.

Dialogue and Feedback

By the end of the EQLD experience, participants are expected to be able to think and act like executives. For many individuals, this means they will need to adjust how they work with others, how they see their role in the organization, how they see themselves, and how they communicate their ideas.

As part of that process, the class gives executive update presentations to project champions and sponsors every three months, and these executives react as a group to how they see the project progressing. In these feedback sessions, executives make challenges and offer suggestions. They respond to the thinking behind the presentation and how ideas are presented.

In the beginning of the program, this feedback can be quite harsh. This feedback is not something the faculty shields participants from, because it communicates something that participants must understand: what is expected of them by a group of their future peers. It also tends to drive home the learning in an unforgettable way.

As the class progresses and begins to make the transformation to more executive thinking and behavior, the relationship with champions and sponsors typically becomes more collegial because the participants have learned how to conduct themselves as colleagues, and these senior executives can see and respect their individual growth. This relationship with champions and sponsors is important for exposing participants to what it is like to be an executive. It also gives them personal experience with a set of people they may work with one day.

Participants get exposure to other leaders in the organization through speakers and presentations. These talks are typically set up as storytelling presentations with a question and dialogue session afterward, so participants can ask questions and interact with company presidents, chief financial officers, and business leaders they would not otherwise meet.

By exposing participants to as many leaders as possible in a format that encourages dialogue and interaction, participants come to understand what kind of people are leading the organization in personally inspiring and memorable ways.

Questions to Consider

A leadership program must be carefully designed to ensure that the right content is being taught to the right individuals and that the impact of the learning is maximized, particularly in the long run. Following are a few questions that internal practitioners may ask themselves when executing a leadership development program:

- What kind of people does your organization need its future leaders to be? How can your leadership program embody this?
- How does your leadership program show people how to continue their own learning? How can you use reflection?
- What are the most important standards your future leaders must meet? How can your leadership program demonstrate those standards?

Program Architecture: Setting It Up

EQLD is a year-long action learning program. Participants come together in early May for their first eight-day residential session. They work after the residential session (virtually) until they meet again for another residential session in late September. The third residential session is in late January, and graduation is May.

In the course of the year, participants must research a challenging business issue, come up with a project or set of projects to address the issue, work together to complete the project, identify an owner of the project, and market as well as implement the project. At the May graduation, the class makes a final presentation to the Global Quality Council about what they have accomplished in the course of the year.

Curriculum for Residential Weeks

The focus of the first residential session is to introduce the business challenge and expose participants to the upcoming leadership journey. The week is characterized by presentations on leadership and tools and activities to begin the research phase. The week culminates with a presentation to the champions and sponsors about how the class intends to structure itself and work together during the virtual period.

Sample First Session Dialogues and Presentations

- Kick-off and welcome
- Project presentation from project champion
- Previous class alumni presentation
- The future of leadership
- Leadership lessons
- Business leader discussion panel

Sample First Session Teaching Modules

- Q-Storming
- Using Questions
- Action Learning Reflections (daily)
- Becoming and Running a Successful Team
- Executive Presentation Skills
- Executive Presence and How to Hold a Room
- Difficult Conversations
- Executive Thinking and Presenting a Business Case

Sample First Session Activities

- Interviews, beginning research
- Large and small group debriefs
- Team-building and communication exercises
- Videotaped presentation and feedback
- Subteam strategy and work sessions
- Circle time

- Mentor selection
- Presentation to champions and sponsors
- Boat tour of New York City harbor and cultural events
- Group dinners with sponsors

The focus of the second residential session is to scope the project and get executive sign-off on the approach. The week is characterized by small-group work sessions, personal presentations by specific executives, and tools for making decisions and dealing with conflict within groups. The week culminates with a presentation to the champions and sponsors about what the class intends to create and the rationale behind it.

Sample Second Session Dialogues and Presentations

- Welcome
- The Leadership Challenge
- Business Leadership
- Integration Research
- The Power of Passion
- Personal Leadership Journeys
- The Importance of Leadership
- Business leader discussion panel

Sample Second Session Teaching Modules

- Authority and Decision Making
- Meeting Facilitation
- Conflict Styles
- Action Learning Reflections (daily)
- Listening Skills
- Creating a Vision and a Value Proposition

Sample Second Session Activities

- Interviews, follow-up research
- Small- and large-group scoping work
- Circle time

- Initial presentation to project champions
- Final presentation to champions and sponsors
- Plant tours of pharmaceutical plants (Rome)
- Group dinners with sponsors

The focus of the third residential session is to market the project and finalize the implementation plans (and get executive sign-off on the approach). The week is characterized by small-group work sessions, large-group discussions, and tools for selling an idea or a strategy within an organization. The week culminates with a presentation to champions and sponsors about the marketing pitch for the project and how the class intends to implement their project.

Sample Third Session Dialogues and Presentations

- Welcome
- Balancing the Work Load
- The Leadership Role in Quality
- Being Bold
- Business leader discussion panel

Sample Third Session Teaching Modules

- The Ten Key Components of Effective Marketing
- Leadership Accountability and Team Performance
- Action Learning Reflections (daily)
- Improv Skills
- Mentoring
- Overcoming Leadership Challenges
- Dealing with Resistance

Sample Third Session Activities

- Small- and large-group scoping work
- Circle time
- Initial presentation to project champions
- Final presentation to champions and sponsors

- Rain forest tour (Puerto Rico)
- Group dinners with sponsors

Virtual Period Activities

Most of the work on the project is completed during the virtual periods. A class typically divides up into subteams, and these subteams meet weekly (or as needed) on the telephone. One faculty member is assigned to sit in on the subteam to monitor progress and provide additional resources as needed. Meeting times are typically a challenge, since subteam members may span several time zones. It is not uncommon for team members to have regular calls at 3:00 A.M. or 11:00 P.M. This is the reality of working on a global team, and it is a factor that team members have to negotiate among themselves.

Most classes also create a project management team, a subteam that has no actual project work responsibilities but manages the logistics of keeping the class well informed and communicating with each other. Often the project management team takes on the more strategic roles of updating sponsors in the virtual period and making large group-related decisions.

Team Structures

How a class divides into subteams is determined by the class. This is one of the first learning activities, and it can be challenging. Very quickly participants discover how difficult it is to make a decision with twenty-five people, and the idea of subteams is proposed. How the class communicates across subteams is also up to them. Some classes figure out a way that works well; others need to try several configurations before they get it right.

Helping participants identify when something is not working is one of the roles faculty plays. Encouraging a team to do something about it is typically a first big "aha!" for a team. As the program progresses, participants develop an understanding of what is working and what is not, and typically they make adjustments on their own.

Graduation and Alumni Network

At the year-end graduation, the class makes a final presentation to the Global Quality Council about what they have accomplished. The feedback on this presentation typically goes well, but participants are responsible for ensuring that their project continues to live in the organization beyond their graduation, and some classes need to do more work to address this requirement adequately. Since the program is now in its fourth year, an alumni network is being established to share information and create work teams as needed.

Faculty Prep

The EQLD faculty meets weekly on a conference call during the virtual periods. Curriculum planning sessions typically happen in a two-day face-to-face on-site meeting, and the rest of the curriculum planning takes place over the phone. The faculty are also involved in the weekly subteam meetings to stay abreast of what is happening in the class. During the residential weeks, faculty are in the classroom and available during the work sessions for the class. They gather one day before a residential session starts and discuss issues. There is typically one faculty meeting in the middle of the session and a meeting after the session is over to debrief and set the calendar for the next phase.

The teaching faculty are supported by two logistics staff members who handle all of the hotel arrangements, transportation, meeting setup, and sponsor arrivals and departures. This staff is on-site during the residential sessions working alongside faculty.

Conclusion

EQLD is a benchmark leadership experience that continues to support Johnson & Johnson well. The program combines good business-centered design, solid adult learning principles, and a faculty who understand that an ability to collaborate and personally inspire is what distinguishes a good executive from a great one.

About the Contributors

Lea Ann Conway is the worldwide vice president of quality and compliance and chief compliance officer for LifeScan, a Johnson & Johnson company. As a member of the Diabetes Franchise Executive Leadership Team, she is responsible for worldwide quality assurance, regulatory compliance, medical and regulatory affairs, health care compliance, government contract compliance, and privacy. She also chairs the Worldwide Council of the Safety, Health and Environmental teams.

Her contributions to quality and operational excellence span a twenty-five-year history with Johnson & Johnson. Her career began with Ethicon and included roles in R&D and worldwide operations. She held positions of increasing responsibility within the quality and regulatory organizations at Ethicon and has significant experience in manufacturing process transfers, new business acquisitions and integrations, and regulatory compliance, interfacing with regulatory authorities and notified bodies worldwide. She was most recently executive director, Medical Device and Diagnostics, and strategic quality leadership at Johnson & Johnson Corporate. During her three years at Corporate, she was recognized as a leader within both Johnson & Johnson and in industry in building the Executive Quality Leadership Development. The program has produced more than fifteen vice presidents of quality for Johnson & Johnson operating companies around the globe. She has worked within a number of franchises within MD&D to improve business results, including the Diabetes Franchise. In addition, she represents quality on the MD&D Vice President of Operations Council; is a member of the Global Quality Council, the Johnson & Johnson Corporate Worldwide Operating Group; and cochairs the MD&D Vice President of Quality Council.

She holds a bachelor's degree in microbiology from Texas Tech University and is a graduate of the Executive Development Program for Senior Regulatory Affairs professionals from the Kellogg School of Management at Northwestern University. She is also a Johnson & Johnson Certified Six Sigma Black Belt and coinventor of the Performance

Indicator tool, a Process Excellence-based risk prioritization tool deployed across Johnson & Johnson, delivering significant results in recall reduction and driving business results.

◆ ◆ ◆

Greg Zlevor specializes in executive development, facilitation, high-performing teams, and executive coaching. He provides consultative assessments, designs and delivers professional education, creates teamwork initiatives, and facilitates leadership improvement for executives and management. He facilitates strategic planning processes and customer focus programs. Zlevor's work has taken him around the world to Europe, Asia, North America, South America, and Australia.

He is the founder and director of Westwood International, a company dedicated to executive education, coaching, consulting, and cultural improvement. He is certified by Interaction Associates in several of its coaching models and performance technologies; a certified trainer for Carlson Learning Products, Inscape; and a sanctioned trainer in Performance Management through Aubry Daniels Associates. Zlevor is a former senior manager and director with Arthur Andersen Business Consulting, where he founded and directed the national team on leadership development. Zlevor is also the founder and past coordinator of the Community in Organizations Conference, an annual event that investigates the knowledge, process, and practice of creating significant, effective, and satisfying relationships within organizations. He has recently published in several books, including *The Change Champion's Field Guide* by Louis Carter, Marshall Goldsmith, Norman Smallwood, and James Bolt.

Zlevor has done postgraduate course work in organizational development. He has a master's degree from Boston College in spirituality and a bachelor's degree from Lawrence University in biology.

◆ ◆ ◆

Taylor Ray has fifteen years of business consulting and management experience serving manufacturing, government services, information technology, enterprise software, education, and nonprofit youth services.

Her work with Westwood International has focused on providing leadership development training, client coaching, and strategic business direction. Prior to joining Westwood, Ray spent eleven years helping organizations in crisis repair relationships, leverage resources, and conduct business more efficiently. Her experience also includes three years with Deloitte & Touche, designing implementations and managing training teams for computer systems administering state and federal programs.

Ray holds a bachelor of science degree in linguistics and neuroscience from Indiana University and a master of science in adult education from the University of Wisconsin–Madison.

CHAPTER ELEVEN

CISCO

Collaborative Leadership

This chapter outlines a collaborative approach to engaging the entire business in the design of a competency model to serve as the foundation for the organization's leadership efforts.

The capability and accessibility of emerging technologies are driving a relentless pace of change in global economic and market trends. At the same time, knowledge, power, and productive capability are more dispersed than at any other time in history.

This complex, decentralized business environment is creating the demand for new operating models and a new approach to leadership. Yesterday's top-down, traditional command-and-control approach is no longer the most effective one, at least not for Cisco Systems.

Cisco Systems is a $37 billion company headquartered in San Jose, California. With over sixty-three thousand employees, the company does business in eighty-three countries across twenty-three time zones. With the boom of Internet 2.0, the organization is experiencing global growth at double-digit rates. With such growth rates, Cisco expects to be a $50 billion company by 2010. Its evolution will largely depend on Cisco 3.0, a global business initiative aimed at bringing Cisco closer to customers. At a time of increased market pressures and fierce competition, Cisco believes the key competitive advantage is a close and solutions-focused relationship with customers.

As Cisco enters new markets and new services, one of the first changes has been to the soft structure of the company. It is the largest functionally organized technology company in existence. To keep the organization agile and close to customers, Cisco operates with six cross-enterprise councils designed to bring leaders and experts from around the globe together on key business initiatives. This soft structure requires leaders to operate collaboratively and in the service of the whole rather than in the service of their respective functions.

Defining Collaborative Leadership

To effectively transform our leadership paradigm, the Cisco talent team, in partnership with the business, needed to define what collaborative leadership was (behaviorally) in a global company and, more important, what collaborative leadership was not.

C-LEAD, a Collaborative Leadership Model

In order to communicate and define expectations around collaborative leadership, the organization needed to construct a competency model. This model, embedded within each of Cisco's leadership efforts, would effectively establish a common understanding and appreciation for the leadership traits associated with success in the company. To stay consistent with the vision, we wanted to demonstrate collaborative leadership in how the model was designed, how our success factors were identified, how the competency model was crafted, and how the model was branded and introduced to the organization. The result was the C-LEAD model, which stands for *collaborate, learn, execute, accelerate, and disrupt.*

We set out with seven operating guidelines:

1. *Focus on differentiators for the future.* The Cisco C-LEAD model needed to create leadership differentiation in the marketplace.
2. *Align Cisco culture and leadership expectations.* The leadership model needed to respect the history of the company and its culture while also being provocative about leadership and innovation needs in the future.
3. *Establish a common language for leadership.* The model, at a minimum, needed to provide a common language for leadership around the globe. Regardless of the function or theater, the core principles of leadership needed to mean the same thing.
4. *Reliably predict success in leadership roles.* The model was created not only to guide how we expect leaders to behave, but also to predict future leadership success.
5. *Develop intelligence about Cisco's leadership pipeline.* The model needed to be leveraged to identify high-potential emerging leaders.
6. *Facilitate internal searches and deployment of talent.* The model needed to assist management with deploying talent, especially in critical or linchpin positions. We wanted future leadership capability aligned to the most critical strategic priorities.
7. *Inform development programs and other investments.* The leadership model would inform and align all training and development activities for managers and leaders.

Using Collaboration to Define Collaborative Leadership

The methodology for developing C-LEAD needed to be robust enough for the business to adopt yet practical enough to develop in a timely fashion. Our primary goal was to leverage the organizational leaders throughout the design phase, so at the end of the process, we could ultimately say that C-LEAD was designed both by and for these leaders.

Step One: Best Practices Review. The C-LEAD process started with a best practices review in the leadership literature for insights that addressed global high-growth industries. We set out to define global leadership for the future, anticipating all of the implications of collaborative technology. To help us arrive at the best definition, we paid special attention to research that applied to leadership trends in high-technology companies. We also looked at common leadership competencies across a variety of industries, leveraging in particular the Corporate Leadership Council's research on executive competencies. Finally, we reviewed the previous two years of *Harvard Business Review* articles to look for patterns and themes related to the evolution of leadership.

Two key competency areas emerged as key differentiators regardless of industry:

- Continuous learning on the fly. This encompassed a leader's ability to take in and integrate new information about self and leadership impact, as well as information about marketplace, technology, and customers.
- Ability to work in an increasingly uncertain, dynamic, and diverse global environment.

Step Two: Senior Leader Interviews. The Talent@Cisco team conducted thirty interviews with senior leaders across Cisco functions and theaters. Leaders were interviewed on their knowledge of Cisco's business, their vision of the future of the organization, and their appreciation of the leadership challenges and capabilities required to lead the company forward.

Two questions were asked of each leader:

- What are the key challenges leaders will face based on current strategy and direction?
- What capabilities will differentiate successful leaders in this context?

Cisco is about to face the most strategic transformation in the history of the company. Leaders recognize the multitude of complexities that this transition creates: the need to grow globally, lead multiple business models simultaneously, and engage managers and employees in new and different ways given the changing demographics of the workforce. In addition, leaders recognized the workforce implications that the success of technology creates regarding workforce experience, workforce collaboration, and workforce productivity.

In an executive staff meeting, John Chambers, Cisco's CEO, reflected what many other leaders had expressed when he said that the executives would all fail as leaders if they were to lead the business in ways that had worked in yesterday's business environment. In order to support significant and rapid business transformation, he offered a call to action to the senior leadership team that became the basis for what we now call Leadership 3.0. C-LEAD was created in part as a response to this call to action.

Step Three: Collaborating with the Organization. Several hundred managers and leaders provided input into the leadership model, leveraging collaborative methods and technologies. Historically, Cisco sent out surveys to solicit feedback. Instead, the C-LEAD design team created a progressive, real-time feedback process that brought together an online community of leaders who used collaboration tools to communicate their ideas and provide ongoing feedback. The model was designed and redesigned iteratively as it moved throughout the organization, benefiting both the design and the adoption of the model.

Step Four: Engaging the Operating Committee. Both the model and the business case for change were taken to the operating committee comprising the most senior decision makers for review, discussion, and adoption. As the executive sponsor of the shift to collaborative leadership, the CEO is the primary sponsor of the C-LEAD model. The executive vice president of business operations, systems, and process has also taken the role of a key driver of the C-LEAD initiative. The overall time to conceptualize, create, and socialize the C-LEAD model with Cisco's top twenty-five hundred leaders was approximately four months, a compelling example of the power of collaboration.

C-LEAD establishes five leadership competencies, each designed to answer an integral question:

- *Collaborate:* Does the leader work across traditional boundaries to achieve success on behalf of the customer and the enterprise?
- *Learn:* Is the leader building individual as well as team skills in order to succeed in a dynamic environment?
- *Execute:* Is the leader engaging others in the work and empowering the team to achieve exceptional results?
- *Accelerate:* Is the leader building bold strategies for the future as well as the capability (talent) needed to achieve those strategies?
- *Disrupt:* Does the leader promote innovation and change in support of Cisco's strategy?

C-LEAD is now being embedded in all of Cisco's leadership and people practices. It creates a common language and a clear definition of what Cisco's leadership expectations and aspirations are. When a leadership paradigm is well articulated, even employees deep within the organization will be better informed regarding the right questions to ask and the best direction to take.

Developing Collaborative Leadership

C-LEAD provides important guidance that informs Cisco's collaborative leadership development approach, but it provides only the foundation.

Experiential programs are necessary for the creative environment for competencies to bloom fully into proven capabilities.

Leveraging Cisco's Executive Action Learning Forum to Build Capability

The Executive Action Learning Forum (E-ALF), launched in fall 2007, is a signature development initiative for Cisco executives. The forum provides high-potential leaders with opportunities to accelerate the development of their general management and collaborative leadership skills by working on projects of high strategic importance to Cisco. E-ALF is the most effective means to develop executives at this level because it combines top-notch business school teaching with hands-on work on actual projects.

Each E-ALF project begins when the business uncovers a significant strategic opportunity that needs to be addressed. E-ALF provides both the methodology and the capability to solve the strategic opportunity by incorporating these elements:

◆ ◆ ◆

- A customized executive assessment and robust development and planning tool, based on the C-LEAD competency model, that identifies key strengths and development needs for the leaders involved.
- Cross-organizational collaborative assignments that bring together senior leaders from around the globe to solve significant strategic problems for the corporation. Rather than being a one-time educational event, E-ALF intends to drive sustainable, transformational change for both the organization and the individual leader.
- Coaching and mentoring support that enables the collaborative leader to tap a broader base of knowledge and expertise regarding strategy and industry trends, operating principles, team and organizational dynamics, and personal leadership effectiveness. An internal coach is assigned to each participant, based on business unit and development need. Coaches play a significant role in three important ways: (1) they

conduct the assessment feedback session and consult with the executive to translate feedback into a robust development plan, (2) they provide ongoing feedback throughout the action learning forum in support of reinforcing the leader's development goals, and (3) they partner with executives after the action learning forum with the goal of sustaining the developmental changes.

- Executive exposure that provides a window into the role and the mindset of a Cisco senior executive. Throughout the forum, senior executives formally engage with participants to provide executive insights regarding industry and technology trends and market transitions. During these sessions, participants are expected to present and test business concepts and product ideas. Executives regularly challenge participants in how they are approaching and leading the project.

Each forum comprises fifteen vice presidents and senior vice presidents who have been identified as leaders with potential to ascend into Cisco's most critical (or linchpin) positions. These participants are divided into two cross-functional global teams that are charged with collaborating with each other to design strategy solutions for "disruptive innovation" business models for Cisco.

To help the participants navigate through the stress and pressure of the experience, an extensive network is put in place to provide support for the project teams. The support team is made up of subject matter experts, executive development coaches, technology advisors, business leaders, and team facilitators. The extensive use of technologies and tools enables the teams to complete projects collaboratively from around the globe and with minimal disruption to their normal business day.

Each E-ALF session extends over twelve to sixteen weeks and has three in-residence phases. Each session has these components:

- *Self-directed learning.* Prior to the in-residence session, participants complete selected readings related to the proposed strategic initiative. Business and industry experts select white papers and business cases to prepare participants for the session.

- *In-residence.* The program begins with a four-day in-residence session designed to develop participants on the topics of business strategy, disruptive innovation, and the disciplines of collaborative leadership. Corporate executives and faculty from Harvard facilitate this in-residence session.
- *Strategy project.* In the six-week period following the in-residence session, participants work in small strategy teams. From the start, participants are expected to demonstrate individual, team, and organizational leadership. As such, they self-govern in every possible way: they set vision and desired outcomes for the forum, they organize and self-govern, they hold each other accountable, and they leverage the capabilities of other strategy teams.
  - Each team is assigned a team facilitator and an internal coach to guide them through the project.
  - Teams have open access to board members and business executives, strategy consultants, technology advisors, and management consultants to help them flesh out their strategy concepts and business models.
- *Project presentation.* E-ALF concludes with another in-residence session where the strategy teams present their business plans to the operating committee.
- *Evaluation.* Each strategy team is evaluated for overall quality of project output and overall leadership. Specifically, strategy teams are evaluated against their ability to set vision and strategy, operationalize strategy, build an organization to execute strategy, communicate the business plan in a disciplined and inspirational manner, and lead collaboratively.

Measuring Impact

The primary measurement of success for E-ALF is twofold:

- Was a business strategy launched by virtue of the rapid prototyping methodology used for new strategies and business models?
- Did leaders elevate their understanding and capability to lead as collaborative leaders?

Several more specific measures are also used to help evaluate how well the actual program was delivered, including tools that measure the quality of the presenters, the quality of the content presented, and the actual administration of program details.

Action Learning in Action: The Case for Mexico

Theory and process are crucial, but results are the reason E-ALF exists. It is Cisco's core methodology for technology innovation and is leveraged twice a year to vet new product and solutions businesses for the company. The most recent session developed two $10 billion business strategies to address the company's targeted entry into software.

Financially, the forum must be measured as a reasonable return on investment. Today, the cost per participant is approximately $10,000, and the total cost of each forum is $160,000. Only when a business idea vetted through E-ALF comes to market is the return of investment literally realized. Obviously each participant's expanded role and capabilities are more broadly leveraged and represent a return as well.

To illustrate how the forum works, I provide some perspectives directly from a team that recently went through an ALF for directors. Both the team coach and the team itself answered core questions to provide a fuller picture of the sum of their experiences.

Based on a previous positive experience with E-ALF, the senior vice president of the software collaboration group wanted a group of emerging executives to look at three countries for complete enterprise transformation: Spain, Germany, and Mexico. The team that shares their story is Team Mexico.

The seven members of the Mexico team were cross-functional and geographically dispersed high-potential emerging executives who had never worked together before. They spent ten weeks identifying the best approach to accelerate growth in a transforming economy. The Mexico market was in a crucial transition, emerging from a developing market into an established market. In addition to being an important market in and of itself, the market condition provided an opportunity to create a case example that could be a model for other emerging markets like China, India, and Russia.

The Mexico team was provided briefing materials from which to formulate a hypothesis and then a set of recommendations. These would be validated and presented to the Enterprise Business Council, one of Cisco's six business councils formed to drive collaboration across the company.

What follows are the verbatim responses from team members and their assigned coach based on a basic set of questions:

❖ ❖ ❖

- What issues did you face?

Team Perspective

It was like a pride of lions that needed to operate with collective leadership, leveraging the strength of the many to be the voice of one. Here we had to accept our peers as equals and develop trust with each other as individuals, and then as members of a team.

While the team had outlined and acknowledged that establishing trust early is critical to building cross-functional, effective teams, this is always easier said than done. It was clear from day one that we weren't short of leaders and everyone seemed to struggle to some extent to subdue our natural tendency to lead from that front. Having our team coach act as our "Jiminy Cricket" was invaluable during those first days. He recognized a little tension in the team dynamic and encouraged us to share our thoughts amongst the team in an open and constructive manner. It took courage to share frustrations and receive feedback, but those first honest exchanges were critical in building the foundations of our ultimate success.

Having cleared the air, we made rapid progress during the first on-site session. However, the introduction of a tight deadline later in the week brought the "Mr. Hyde" out in some of us. Again, honest, open, and genuine feedback brought us back from the brink, ultimately strengthening a mutual respect and regard amongst the team.

❖ ❖ ❖

Team Coach Perspective

Early on there were the issues around defining project scope and deliverables. The project sponsor had set some very broad stretch expectations that the team produce recommendations that were both concrete and out-of-the-box creative. The sponsor was looking for new ways of approaching the challenge of growing the Mexico market both in the short run and over the long term. On the other hand, the sponsor gave little guidance about the way to approach the problem or the range of options that might be considered. Given the execution orientation of many of the team's members, the team was constantly pushed to move beyond their comfort zone around tactical dimensions of the problem, to focus on truly game-changing growth strategies. And the team had to constantly keep a view of how its recommendations might be relevant on a going-forward basis to other countries facing similar transitions to those facing Mexico.

Concerning team dynamics, the Mexico team started as a group of individuals with strong personalities, differing degrees of attention span and patience for discussion, and a penchant for talking over each other rather than building upon each others' ideas and opinions. This mix was a potentially combustible chemistry that could have stopped the team in its tracks, stymied progress, and undermined its capacity to deliver a truly creative and compelling set of recommendations.

Furthermore, most members of the team were used to having the floor as leaders of their respective direct report teams. Here, they were faced with a task where command leadership would not serve them well. The collaborative leadership behaviors and skills of each individual would be chief determinants in the team's success.

• How did this impact your work?

Team Perspective

Ultimately everyone put the team ahead of themselves and gave unselfishly to the common cause. This maturity combined with a rich mix of culture, business style, experience, and a shared passion to do the best we could carried the day.

We created a dynamic that allowed the team to partition work and to leverage the strengths of each individual. We also encouraged team members to take on roles where they did not have total confidence and comfort to support personal development. The feeling of inclusiveness was a key attribute that allowed the team to ensure all members were heard and represented in the process.

Getting to know each other outside of the work environment was key to creating personal bonds. Obstacles were more easily diffused as a result of these improved personal dynamics. Had we not known each other the way we did, I don't believe we would have resolved things as quickly as we did and remained a team as tight as we are. We were able to maintain integrity and respect for each other throughout the process.

◆ ◆ ◆

Team Coach Perspective

To the credit of each member on the team, the team developed a high degree of self-awareness around their mix of individual traits mentioned above, as well as very concrete disciplines for working through and rising above them. Over the course of the experience, the group of individuals transformed themselves into a team committed to each other, and to delivering their absolutely best, most creative effort. As their coach, it was truly a pleasure and a privilege to contribute to and watch this transformation. The Mexico team won top honors in the country project category. They received the highest accolade from one of our most respected senior vice presidents who said that their presentation was emblematic of how all board-level presentations should be made.

There are many reasons why the Mexico team was successful in transcending some potentially limiting traits. The bottom line was that their success was created by (1) the time they took to emotionally bond with each other, (2) their openness to learning and feedback, and (3) their individual and collective commitment to delivering their best.

- How did your work and example impact the organization?

Team Perspective

The team delivered recommendations that have been adopted and implemented by Cisco. However, the team feels that the greatest value of their work came from the insights we gained regarding our own strengths and weaknesses, the friendships we built along the way, and the fact that we can take both the business and life lessons learned and share them with our day-to-day teams.

We became a true team and required the input of every team member in order to be successful. We were able to maximize the strengths of each team member to create the final product, which ultimately created the winning presentation, but more important gave us the opportunity to contribute to a cause we all believe in.

Team Coach Perspective

Executive feedback indicated that the team provided the most balanced mix of concrete, implementable recommendations for the short term with strategic recommendations for changing the game and altering the country business model over the longer term. The CEO and his operating committee acted on one of the team's strategic recommendations within a few weeks. The idea was to appoint a Mexico Board comprised of the most influential Mexican stakeholders from industry and government. The Enterprise Business Council also requested that one or two members of the E-ALF Mexican team be appointed to a key strategic body focused on globalization aspects of its Cisco 3.0 strategy, then an initiative focused on renewing Cisco's customer-driven culture and processes.

From the Foundation to the Top of the Industry

Cisco's C-LEAD competency model provides the framework and a common language for the leadership team. Anchored firmly in the core competencies

C-LEAD articulates, E-ALF provides leaders with the opportunity to apply thought leadership in the pursuit of market leadership.

Rapid growth and technology advancements will continue to push organizations to deploy the best talent from around the globe to accelerate results. Collaborative leaders will be in the best position to leverage these global resources and work across organizational boundaries to create innovative solutions that deliver results. This is why, at least at Cisco, collaborative leadership has been embraced as the best approach for commanding success.

Conclusion

Regardless of the size of a company or the scope of its leadership development program, addressing each of these key steps will provide a sturdy framework for lasting impact. At Cisco, these building blocks created a comprehensive program that is positioning the company for continuous development, success, and innovation:

- *Research.* Gather both industry and insider intelligence. A review of leadership best practices combined with an in-depth assessment of Cisco's specific needs created the basis for a program that provided an ideal combination of the two.
- *Collaborate.* Provide a way for leaders across the company to provide input. This approach improved both the design and the acceptance of Cisco's program.
- *Engage.* The perfect program cannot succeed without executive support. Successfully engaging senior leaders helped create buy-in at Cisco and provided visible executive support at the highest levels.
- *Embed.* Use the language and the competencies in your model across all of your leadership and people practices. Cisco leveraged its program to create a common language and a clear definition that could help inform daily actions at every level.
- *Execute.* Theory is important, but action is what creates business results. Cisco's Executive Action Learning Forum is a signature leadership

and development process that puts competencies fully into practice on actual projects.

- *Measure.* Business impact is the only way to truly measure success. Cisco measured not only understanding and capability in leaders, but also the specific return on investment tied to business ideas that initiated in ALF.

About the Contributor

Annmarie Neal is a talent strategist, executive consultant, and psychologist who designs and develops strategic talent management solutions. She is the founder of Neal & Associates and currently serves as vice president of talent and diversity for Cisco Systems, where she leads global talent management and diversity efforts. She holds a doctorate and master's degree in clinical psychology from the California School of Professional Psychology.

CHAPTER TWELVE

DEPARTMENT OF TREASURY AND FINANCE, VICTORIA, AUSTRALIA

Creating High-Performing Teams

This chapter outlines an executive team development program that leverages 180-degree feedback, action learning, and process consultation to drive leadership effectiveness.

The Department of Treasury and Finance (DTF) is one of ten state government departments in the Victorian Public Service, Australia. DTF provides the Victorian government with economic, financial, and resource management policy advice to assist it in delivering its policy outcomes. DTF has primary responsibility for developing and implementing the government's longer-term economic and budgetary objectives: to achieve economic growth for all regions of the State of Victoria and increase the living standards of Victorians.

DTF's vision is to achieve "a prosperous future for all Victorians" by modeling the values and behaviors published in the DTF Aspiration Statement (see Exhibit 12.1). To achieve this vision, divisions within DTF are empowered to act independently to address their needs and use support from a team of internal organizational development (OD) consultants.

The Case for Executive Team Development at DTF

Like all other organizations, DTF is faced with technological and business challenges and a tightening labor market. Changes in the Australian population, such as aging and a declining birthrate, wage competition from the private sector, and a low unemployment rate are increasing pressure on DTF's ability to attract suitably qualified employees.

The presence of three or four generations in the workforce with differing values and goals is forcing managers to think about the most effective approaches to getting the work done. Better technology has facilitated flexible working arrangements and the ability for employees to work from home. Collaborative leadership teams are required to help DTF cope with skill shortages and support each other to manage in an increasingly diverse and complex working environment.

In the 2006 state election, the government made a commitment to deliver more innovative and efficient services, reduce the regulatory burden, and continue implementing its reform agenda. The senior executive group of DTF identified increased integration of its divisions as a cultural priority to ensure it delivers on these commitments.

Integrated work practices result in collective work products and mutual accountability. Independence and individually produced outcomes are still valued, but only to the extent that they do not contradict or constrain corporate goals and team output. Integration requires "teamwork" and is important in driving excellence in process and outcomes.

Another challenge is the characteristics of the people at DTF, who can be described as predominantly left-brain thinkers who are likely to be analytical, risk averse, and linear. Team and leadership development do not come easily to a highly technical workforce.

Historically, DTF has not developed senior leaders in team or leadership capability; leaders have been rewarded and valued on the basis of technical expertise rather than teamwork and leadership skills. Hence, building team and leadership capability were not a priority for leaders in DTF.

These challenges have clear and important implications for DTF's team and leadership development practices and raise key questions:

- Given that teams are the key mechanisms for how DTF organizes work and that the ability to work within and across teams is critical to organizational success, what is DTF doing to increase team capability and reduce the emergence of silos?
- As DTF continues to confront internal and external challenges, what development strategies are in place to ensure leadership teams are working as teams to meet these challenges?
- What leadership team skills need to be improved immediately to build a culture in which people work together to achieve positive outcomes?

These questions signaled the need to implement an executive team development (ETD) program. Focusing on team development in a leadership team was seen as the best method to confront the challenges and produce a positive culture change, for two reasons. First, behavioral change occurs more readily in a team context. Because of their collective support, teams are not as threatened by change. They also offer more room for growth and change for individual leaders and can energize and focus the efforts of the leadership team to confront these challenges.

The same team dynamics that promote performance also support learning and behavioral change and will do so more effectively than when individuals are left to their own devices.

Second, leadership is the single biggest influencer of the culture of an organization and therefore a pivotal force for bringing about change. The majority of executives in the DTF are leading teams, and their values, preferences, and behaviors have a direct impact on how staff are expected to behave individually and in teams. If executive team performance can be improved, then their way of working will have a cascading effect throughout the DTF.

The study presented in this chapter tells the story of an executive team development program implemented by one of the internal organizational development consultants. This program was conducted over twelve months and focused on building team leadership and executive team capability.

Planning the Team Leadership Development Program

The team leadership development program was first implemented on a divisional executive team with eleven team members. An organization development diagnosis identified that this team needed to improve its leadership capability, align the culture with staff expectations, and deal with labor market challenges. A staff member commented that the executive team was uncoordinated and that "managers are not proactive in engaging with each other. There is not a sense of 'we-ness,' as turf wars are played out to protect ownership of projects. Some managers are unaware of their people issues because they are task obsessive." The team was perceived as a group of executives rather than as an executive team. Some team members believed their role was only to lead their direct reports rather than provide broader divisional leadership.

Staff focus tended to be on the internal unfolding daily dramas or on competition between business output teams, not on working together or identifying new opportunities for DTF. These observations signaled to the head of the division that a better understanding of teamwork was a prerequisite for achieving collaboration between executive team members and would create a more integrated division.

Program Design and Implementation

The executive team development (ETD) program consisted of three main stages over twelve months:

Stage 1: Survey design and gap analysis
Stage 2: Action learning
Stage 3: Evaluation

The program used the principles of action and double-loop learning to develop and reinforce the characteristics of an effective leadership team. An action research approach is a classic organization development choice in which participants learn by doing. Participants worked on team-based projects aimed at building leadership team capability while delivering on the business outcomes. Double-loop learning occurs when participants question and modify the values, assumptions, and norms that led to the actions in the first place. An overview of the program is presented in Figure 12.1.

Designing the Intervention

In this section I will bring you through each of the design processes that contributed to the Executive Team Development Program. During this design process, a number of success factors were identified that are called forth in the text. I find these factors to be universal in the implementation of a leadership development system and have summed them up here:

Survey Design and Gap Analysis
　Success factor 1: Creating involvement and buy-in
　Success factor 2: Setting executive team targets and measures
Action Learning Program: Moving from Awareness to Action
　Success factor 3: Achieving a common team purpose
　Success factor 4: Working with the unconscious system
　Success factor 5: Practicing team process reviews

FIGURE 12.1.   EXECUTIVE TEAM DEVELOPMENT PROGRAM

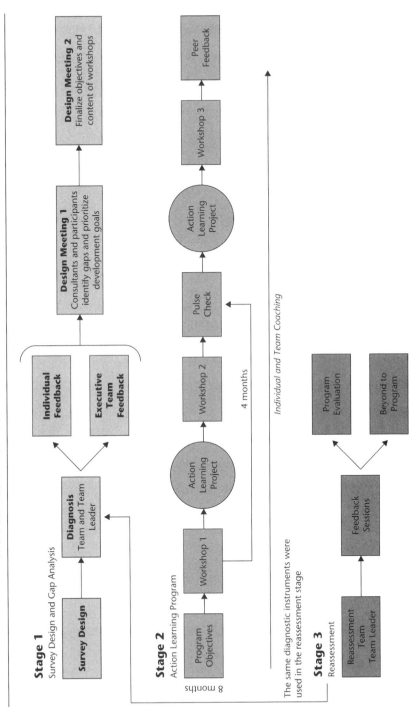

Success factor 6: Incorporating individual coaching
Evaluation
Success factor 7: Working in collaboration with the client

Stage 1: Survey Design and Gap Analysis

The first step was to identify a model of high-performing teams (see Figure 12.2) to guide the development program. Questionnaires were then designed based on five dimensions considered important to creating high-performing teams, based on work by Ancona, Kochan, Scully, Van Maanen, and Westney (1999); Hackman (2002); and Sundstrom (1999); and rated on a six-point rating scale:

- *Team context:* Aspects of the larger organization that influence the team's effectiveness. Elements include the team's mission and vision, environmental influences, broader organizational goals, resources, and customer expectations. Sample question: "To what extent is the team clear about its task and mission?"
- *Team structure:* Relatively stable characteristics of a team, including task, goals, membership, roles, and clarity of task. Sample question: "To what extent do members have clearly defined roles in the team?"

FIGURE 12.2. A MODEL OF HIGH-PERFORMING TEAMS

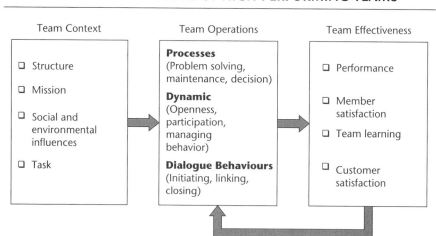

- *Team processes:* How the team goes about its task rather than what is done. Key processes are problem solving, decision making, and conflict management. Sample question: "To what extent does the team explore the problem before proposing solutions?"
- *Team dynamics:* About relationships in the team. They reflect how people feel about each other and the team. The major categories of team dynamics are openness, leadership, evaluation, climate, participation, and emotional issues. Sample question: "To what extent do team members openly share their views?"
- *Team dialogue behaviors:* Core behaviors essential for effective discussion: initiating ideas, building, supporting points of view, and closing the discussion. Sample question: "To what extent do team members build on each others' ideas?"

The reliability and face validity of the survey was established using a small pilot group and expert stakeholders within DTF.

Two questionnaires were used: the team leader questionnaire and the executive team questionnaire. All executive team members completed the executive team questionnaire and self-assessed their own performance as a team leader by completing the team leader questionnaire. The team leader questionnaire was distributed to the leader's direct reports for completion.

The data were analyzed, and two types of reports were produced. The executive team report presented the results of the executive team capabilities as rated by the executive team and their staff. The team leader report was provided to each leader on the assessment of their individual team leadership capabilities.

Group sessions were held to give feedback on the results of the surveys. Team and individual team leadership feedback reports were distributed to the executive team members. Patterns, strengths, and areas for executive team development were presented. Participants were given reflection tasks to help interpret and understand their feedback and personal development planning templates to set their goals for improvement (see Exhibit 12.2).

A gap analysis confirmed the need to develop the executives' capabilities across several areas. Design meetings were held with the participants as a team to explore the findings in greater depth and to prioritize development according to individual needs and business realities. As participants explored gaps and priority areas, they were able to begin opening up difficult issues, and fragile dynamics began to surface in a positive environment that would not have been possible in regular executive team meetings. This formal step allowed participants to develop their own objectives for the ETD program.

The objectives of the executive program were to develop a shared purpose of the executive team, which belonged to team members collectively and individually, and to strengthen team capability in these ways:

- Learn how to intervene effectively in the dynamics of the team
- Improve team processes such as decision making and problem solving
- Develop better skills in closing discussions and taking action
- Work interdependently
- Enhance individual team leadership capability

The first two success factors were identified for this stage:

Success factor 1: Creating involvement and buy-in
Success factor 2: Setting executive team targets and measures

The first challenge was getting the team to agree on the key issues and to begin the development program. The participants spent a lot of time at the start of the program discussing the areas to focus on by exploring the barriers (real or imagined) to higher team performance. The objective was to ensure the program was developed based on their real needs (individual and business), which would improve buy-in and serve as a success factor early on. Other initiatives used to enhance buy-in were ongoing evaluation to examine and evaluate whether the development efforts were in alignment with the program objectives and business needs, emphasizing the practicality and benefits of the program, and continuous active involvement and support from the head of the division. The team's current problems formed the basis of practical work, which helped to achieve skills building and problem solving simultaneously during the development. This contributed strongly to participant buy-in.

Second, the executive team questionnaire was used as a measurement tool to identify gaps between the current and the ideal results. Implementation strategies for each of the three targets were agreed to by the executive team to close the capability gaps. The first set of targets focused on improving a number of team capabilities, the second on developing nonexecutive capability, and the third on improving culture and customer service. Relevant measurement tools and implementation strategies were put in place for these targets.

Stage 2: Action Learning Program: Moving from Awareness to Action

The program was based on the principles of action learning, which can be described as a cyclical process with action and reflection taking place in turn. The program was held as three one-day off-site workshops, separated by six to eight weeks for application of learning. Each reflection was used to review the previous action and plan the next.

In between each workshop, participants worked on real-life problems or projects, such as succession management guidelines, a work prioritization model, a meetings framework, and initiatives to increase integration in the DTF. Participants met in small subgroups to work on the project and apply learnings from the previous workshop. These tasks were not separate from their regular work but were an opportunity to implement the learning as part of a team task. This all helped to ensure that action learning principles were kept at the heart of the process. Activities in the workshops were highly participatory and designed with the belief that learning and change best occur through reflection and experience.

Sessions were organized in five categories: learning contract, information sharing, experiential learning, theory and practice, and skills building. All sessions worked with actual team issues where the group supplied the content, drawing on its real goals, tasks, relationships, processes, and norms.

All experiential activities were followed by a debriefing where participants:

- Reflected on their experience during the exercises
- Received specific behavioral feedback
- Integrated their observations and feedback with theory and models previously discussed
- Identified lessons worth transferring to future situations

The experiential activity generated data and experiences that were used to teach concepts, ideas, and behavioral insights. Each workshop consisted of consultant- and business-led activities. In the consultant-led sessions, the consultant provided a structure and process to help the group work through its activities. Business-led sessions were facilitated by a business representative or a participant.

Consultant-Led Activities. Workshop 1 consisted of four activities. The learning contract exercise established a set of principles that members agreed to adopt for working with one another. These principles were based on values rather than ground rules for meetings (such as "turn the mobile off" and "be on time") and were revisited throughout the program as a reminder or when the principles had been violated. For each of the workshops, the learning objectives were specified, and agreement was made that the learning process would be active rather than passive.

In the second activity, information sharing, the team iceberg metaphor (see Figure 12.3) was used to explain the depth of the program interventions: as you go deeper into the iceberg, the level of risk increases and the emotional work increases.

The third session, on skill building, covered team processes (problem solving, consensus creation) and team discussion behaviors (initiating, linking, supporting, and closing). Participants were encouraged to focus on practicing these skills in subsequent sessions.

The final session was on theory and practice. Aspects of team chartering were facilitated and led by both the consultant and participants, and the consultant facilitated a review of the team mission.

FIGURE 12.3. TEAM ICEBERG

FIGURE 12.4. TEAM PERFORMANCE CURVE

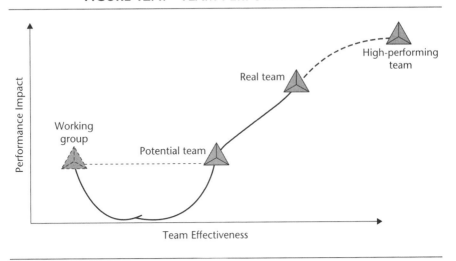

Source: Katzenbach and Smith (1998).

Workshop 2 began with theory and practice. The team performance curve shown in Figure 12.4 was introduced to educate participants on the difference between working groups and real teams and to get agreement on their common purpose. Teams cannot succeed if members remain unclear about what the team wants to accomplish and why. Participants learned guidelines for giving and receiving feedback and then practiced them with their learning buddy. They discussed team dynamics such as behaviors to facilitate openness, interdependency, and trust building and to foster creative tension.

In the experiential learning session, a self-reflection process, "Uncovering Your Big Assumptions," was conducted to foster understanding of what was getting in the way of working together. This process provided participants with valuable insights into their unconscious behaviors and assumptions that were hindering teamwork. Participants were asked to test their assumptions when back at work and commit to correcting them.

Workshop 3 was devoted to theory and practice. The display of competitive behavior in the team continued to be a stumbling block to real teamwork. The session on managing competitive behavior acquainted participants with styles of interaction (see Figure 12.5) and offered them an opportunity to reflect on their own experience and contributions to competitive behavior. Through a facilitated discussion, a set of guidelines for managing competitive behavior was agreed to by the team.

FIGURE 12.5. STYLES OF INTERACTION

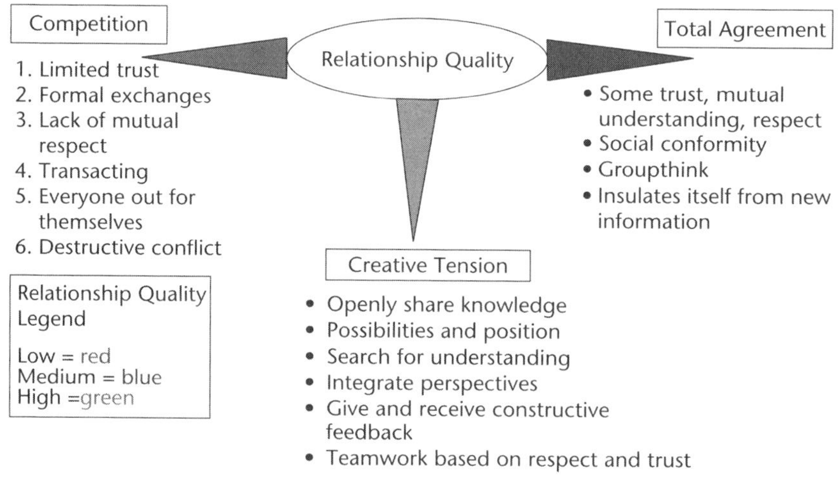

Competition

1. Limited trust
2. Formal exchanges
3. Lack of mutual respect
4. Transacting
5. Everyone out for themselves
6. Destructive conflict

Relationship Quality

Total Agreement

- Some trust, mutual understanding, respect
- Social conformity
- Groupthink
- Insulates itself from new information

Relationship Quality Legend

Low = red
Medium = blue
High = green

Creative Tension

- Openly share knowledge
- Possibilities and position
- Search for understanding
- Integrate perspectives
- Give and receive constructive feedback
- Teamwork based on respect and trust

Two more success factors were addressed here:

Success factor 3: Achieving a common team purpose
Success factor 4: Working with the unconscious system

Many hours in the early stages of the program were spent discussing performance goals and priority areas for development. These discussions surfaced latent tensions, which occasionally brought team progress to a halt. To break the deadlock, executive team members were asked to address the success factor of achieving a common team purpose and reflect on fundamental questions such as, "What should be the role of the executive team?" "Are we a working group or a real team?" Only when there was shared agreement on the leadership role and goals could genuine progress be made on improving the executive team's capability to perform.

During the program, members were distracted by environmental turbulence such as changes to the composition of the team and the sad, and sudden, death of the head of the department and subsequent arrangements and restructuring for the acting leadership. These pressures and distractions often drove team members back to old habits of protecting their patch and focusing on individual accountabilities.

To overcome resistance, the organizational development consultant drew on the relational consultant model (Van Beekum, 2006), which focuses on the unconscious. This is achieved when the consultant shares his or her internal experiences of how the group is functioning, brings the members into the process, and uses experiential activities to unravel the assumptions and belief systems that are driving behavior. This was a powerful exercise and turned out to be a significant success factor for the initiative.

In one session, the consultant pointed out that participants were using external factors to resist change. The consultant held up the mirror to the team, highlighting that they were using external factors to justify their resistance to change rather than focus inwardly on themselves. Once they were conscious of the behaviors, they could manage and address them. This session also increased participants' acceptance and ownership of the resistance. For example, the executive team blamed poor results from a culture survey on external factors rather than on their own leadership. The consultant called the team on their display of resistance, which led to an increase in the team's understanding of the covert dynamics used to avoid behavior change.

During the session, the consultant became part of the process by allowing herself to be affected by the group's behavior and then describing how she felt when specific behaviors occurred. For example, hostile and oppositional behaviors were displayed toward the consultant when she offered perceptions and insights on the dynamics of the team. She shared these feelings with the team in an effort to bring covert behaviors to the surface.

Business-Led Activities. In workshop 1, on experiential learning, participants led a series of discussions about the role and mission of the leadership team. These discussions were used as practice skill-building sessions to hone executive team capability.

The consultant used the model of process consultation (Schein, 1988) to give the team insight into what was going on around them, within them, and between them and to help them figure out how to improve the situation. This team looked at how it functioned as a team. Who took the leadership roles? Did people listen to each other? Were different views encouraged?

The role, mission, and goals of the leadership team were identified and given to participants to refine and bring back for agreement (action learning projects) in one of their fortnightly team meetings.

Workshop 3, also on experiential learning, looked at how executives could change from a tendency to focus on themselves and their tasks and instead concentrate more on the strategic management of the business. The problem of senior management succession was explored and the role that a consistent approach to performance measurement and actions can play to ensure a suitable supply of up-and-coming executives.

In information sharing, a presentation by the head of the division on issues facing the DTF and ministerial expectations provided useful information for the next segment on the strategic plan, output requirements, workload, and budget capacity. This sparked the beginning of an ongoing discussion on priorities and approaches to resource allocations. This was a milestone in the team development journey because the sharing of resources signaled that the working group was becoming a real team.

Pulse Check: Sustaining Momentum. A pulse check with the executive team and their staff was conducted to assess whether improvement strategies implemented in the first four months of the program were translating into more effective executive teamwork and team leadership. The survey is presented in Exhibit 12.3.

The pulse check survey was an interim measure before the formal reassessment of executive team capabilities in December 2006. The results were intended to refocus and reenergize the improvement efforts of the executive team members.

Executive team members and staff reported an increase in teamwork and team effectiveness. The responses indicated immediate improvements, such as improved communication with staff on their development goals, increased effort toward working together, and acting more on staff feedback.

Team leaders who were actively seeking feedback from their staff had the largest reported improvements in their overall team leadership effectiveness. Team leaders who scored low on the feedback had the lowest level of improvement in team leadership. This indicates a positive correlation between seeking feedback from staff and improvement in team leadership effectiveness.

Two more success factors were now identified:

Success factor 5: Team process reviews
Success factor 6: Individual coaching

At the executive team's fortnightly meeting, a team process review was conducted to heighten team members' awareness of both functional and dysfunctional behaviors in the team. A team process review focused on how the group arrived at its decisions, drew conclusions, solved problems, debated issues, and handled conflict. Exhibit 12.4 shows the team process observation guide. The process was critical as it heightened leaders' awareness of team dynamics, which enabled them to intervene effectively in the group. After the consultant demonstrated how to conduct a process review, the task was rotated among the team members.

Coaching and debriefing were provided to leaders who were running workshop sessions and chairing team meetings. Prior to the meeting or workshop, the consultant worked with the leader on the agenda, areas of development for the leader, and advice on managing dysfunctional team behavior.

Debriefing was a review of how the leader managed the session, a focus on process dimensions, and a discussion of conceptual models to explain team phenomena. Leaders found this a valuable exercise because the debriefing experiences crystallized the concepts, insights, and learning. Debriefing was the key to making chairing the meeting or team leadership a meaningful learning experience.

Peer Feedback. A parallel process was conducted to enable participants to gather feedback from their peers to improve leadership performance. The goals of the process were to:

- Increase self-awareness and awareness of strengths and areas for development
- Provide a supportive and safe environment to share concerns that often go unexpressed and help each other's personal growth
- Enable leaders to improve giving and receiving feedback openly and constructively

Sessions were held for groups of six participants and lasted ninety minutes. The facilitator set the scene and the group rules. Participants were allocated fifteen minutes for receiving feedback. Each peer was asked to give feedback to the recipient on two areas: strengths and areas for development. Participants were asked to take ownership of their own feedback time—for example, by recording the feedback, nominating specific areas for feedback, asking for clarification, and sharing responses to the feedback.

During the process, the facilitator provided prompts to ensure the feedback was balanced and all participants had sufficient time. At the subsequent workshop, participants spoke about their personal plan to become more effective in the team. Participants gained a lot from these sessions, and many said that they had grown personally as a result.

Stage 3: Evaluation

Research by Linkage Inc. (Giber, Carter, and Goldsmith, 2000) suggests that it is not enough to just readminister an assessment survey to measure the impact of a development program. The success of a development program depends on how participants have applied their learning to their job performance. Three separate evaluation methods were used to determine if the program objectives had been met.

First, formal reassessments of the original survey were administered to both team members and their direct reports. A substantial improvement was made on all factors (team context, structure, process dynamics, and dialogue behaviors) of team capability as rated by staff and the executive team. The greatest progress was identified in the following areas: better functioning in team meetings; increased sharing of information; better commitment to continuous improvement; and enhanced team skills in decision making, communication, and problem solving. Figure 12.6 shows a comparison of the ratings between executive team members and staff members for the first assessment periods (March 2006) and the reassessment (November 2006).

Second, staff and participants were asked open-ended questions immediately after the program and then six months later. Their responses demonstrated four areas of achievement:

- *The executive team learned the importance of being a team.* "We went from a team who brought our own agendas to meetings, often wouldn't express opinions if we thought they'd be received negatively, and resented others' points of view, to a team who were very open and honest with one another—even when people were poles apart in

FIGURE 12.6.   COMPARISON OF STAFF AND EXECUTIVE TEAM MEMBERS' RATINGS OF TEAM CAPABILITY

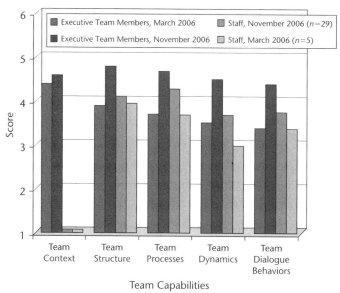

Note: n = number of staff who responded to questionnaires.

their views; there was a time there where that was respected and people could say exactly what they thought."

- *Team meetings were more structured and focused.* "Now we focus on common tasks and goals. . . . We have moved from a collection of competing individuals to a group focused on team objectives."
- *Participants had improved skills in building on others' ideas, closing discussions, and communicating openly.* "We have gotten good at building on ideas and communicating more openly . . . respecting each other's views." "There is a sharper focus in meetings, agenda is stuck to, and it is a true open forum."
- *Staff noticed better communication and delegation.* "Communication of higher-level issues to staff is occurring . . . this gives us a better context for our day-to-day work." "I think the executive team is more open and professional in their activities, e.g., distributing ET [executive team] minutes, . . . sharing ideas, . . . a greater focus and commitment on continuous improvement efforts."

Finally, consultant observation of the executive team found improvements in how the team worked together to achieve the team task and the processes used to do the task. As a method of data collection, this required a significant amount of cooperation and goodwill on the part of the team to allow the consultant access to the team and their work.

A Group Transformed

These evaluation methods present evidence that the development program transformed a group into a team and improved executive team leadership capability.

It is difficult to trace convincing causal links between the team development interventions and business changes because the impact on the business can be due to a variety of factors, such as changes in the composition of the team, other HR or organizational development interventions, or technical or social system influences. While the extent of upstream and downstream benefits flows has not been measured, feedback suggests a growing internal alignment in DTF. That is, behavioral integration has resulted in communication at DTF that is more consistent and more broadly based, reflecting better process.

The commitment and support of senior management for the ETD program sent a positive signal to the direct participants that they are valuable and worth investing in, creating a "feel good" factor. This helped to create an open, trusting, and valuing culture and revitalize DTF's top talent, which the intervention was designed to achieve. It also provided a marker for continuous improvement indicating that this is the beginning of the journey toward achieving the aspired culture.

This illustrates the final success factor:

Success factor 7: Working in collaboration with the client

Collaborating with members of the executive team on the design and delivery of the work was a critical success factor. The consultant met regularly with the executive team leader, acting executive team leader, and another senior member to sound out ideas to ensure that the program reflected the context in which they worked and that it would meet the participant's needs.

Conclusion

During the design, implementation, and evaluation of the executive team program, a number of lessons emerged that may help guide future endeavors.

Lesson 1: Don't expect everyone to buy in into the program. The consultant needs to come with an open mind to seeking engagement to the program and allow a range of responses, typically in these categories: early adapters (20 percent), wait and see (60 percent), and traditionalist (those who say, "We have always done it this way" (20 percent).

Lesson 2: An executive team development program needs to be engaging, participative, challenging, and empowering for those involved. A series of planned interventions combining education, experience, and feedback is required to create a catalytic experience for participants. Having a good balance of workshops, subgroup activities, homework assignments, and readings to fit all learning styles reduces the likelihood of program fatigue.

Lesson 3: The design of the program must incorporate participants' ideas and preferences and accommodate their concerns. Sounding out interventions beforehand with participants helped gain buy-in, as well as gauging if they would be successful. The design also needs to have a strong implementation focus ("What does this mean for me back at work, and what will I do differently?") and support for participants to help them follow through.

Lesson 4: Most participants will not develop a lifelong commitment to behavioral change unless they see compelling evidence of it within twelve months. Without short-term wins, too many participants give up or join the ranks of people who have been resisting change. As predicted, the program peaked, plateaued, and moved into a tailspin halfway through as participants were distracted by urgent cabinet submissions, ministerial briefings, and other DTF deadlines. The pulse survey was used to address development fatigue and reenergize the program. Receiving data on the extent of their progress created a short-term win for participants and moved their development work up as a priority issue. In addition, some participants saw the development as a stand-alone issue and separate from their jobs. The consultant addressed this by providing weekly support and follow-up to keep the process alive, while not transferring ownership of the change.

Lesson 5: The rigor used by organizational psychologists to design surveys is preferable. However, a capability program can still apply general principles of good survey design without having to go into the same depth of validity and reliability testing.

The Journey Continues

The executive team development program had a significant impact on developing team and team leadership capability in a large executive team. The most innovative aspect was the development of leaders through their team social system. The development of leaders in their natural team environment facilitated knowledge transfer in the workshops and also improved the chances of achieving a permanent change in organizational culture.

The achievements of the program and the demonstrable shift in behavior and performance were measures of the success of the intervention. Learning from this program has been leveraged and used in other team and leader development programs at DTF and will continued to be used in the next generation of action learning and team development at DTF.

Working with the Team

Exhibit 12.1. Department of Treasury and Finance Aspiration Statement

This statement describes the organization DTF aspires to be. It provides a framework for DTF standards and expectations for the future.

An organization's vision and aspiration can be articulated and assessed through its behaviors. Behavioral Accountabilities have been set to support these aspirations by defining the behaviors expected of leaders and staff at DTF.

We aspire to our vision, live our mission, and make a difference.

Our customers achieve because we:

Take responsibility for outcomes
Provide innovative and forthright analysis
Are influential and committed to relationship management
Deliver consistently and on time

Our people are challenged to grow personally and professionally because we:

Expect excellence and accountability
Demand and display leadership
Share skills and knowledge
Offer a variety of experience

Our organization is exciting and united because we:

Welcome diversity and creativity
Combine fun and dedication
Are disciplined in applying policies and systems
Celebrate success together

Exhibit 12.2. Reflection and Development Planning Tool

1. Comparison of Self and Direct Reports' Ratings

Examine the capabilities your direct reports rated as your strongest and weakest areas.

- How do your own scores compare with your direct reports' across these key team leadership capabilities?
- On which dimensions of leadership capabilities is there strong agreement between you and other raters? Where are the biggest discrepancies? How do you interpret these areas of agreement and/or divergence?
- Which specific behaviors does your team view as strengths? Which do they view as opportunities for development?
- Is there much variation between the minimum and maximum ratings? What could be the reasons for this?

2. Specific Strengths and Weaknesses

Consider the behaviors that are represented in the top-ranked items and in the lower-ranked items.

- Do any of these results surprise you? Do you recognize known leadership strengths and weaknesses?
- Is there consistency in what you and your direct reports consider to be your key behavioral strengths and your development areas? What do you think is the reason for any inconsistency?

3. Feedback Comments from Your Team

Read the comments carefully—they may contain both honest praise and constructive feedback that respondents may not be prepared to deliver face-to-face.

- What are people in your team trying to tell you?
- Do any of the comments highlight strengths you did not know you had?
- Do any of the comments suggest specific changes that could benefit you and your team?

4. Benchmarking Your Team Leadership Capabilities

Consider how your ratings compare to other team leaders in the executive team. Where are the biggest differences?

   Why do you think that is?

Key Messages from Feedback

Summarize your strengths, areas for clarification, and areas for improvement. Try to frame your areas for improvement as specific positive goals, e.g., "Improve my active listening skills," "Introduce weekly meetings with each team member." For each goal, consider the following questions, and complete the appropriate areas: What will the outcomes be if you achieve this goal? When do you expect this to happen? What can help you achieve these goals? The goals for improvement can be integrated into the action learning project you select from the team development workshops, and in your performance plan.

Exhibit 12.3. Pulse Questionnaire

Assessing the Progress of the X Executive Team's Team Work and Team Leadership Capabilities

Completing the Questionnaire

In March 2006, you completed two questionnaires that measured X Executive Team capabilities and your individual leadership capabilities. Since then we've had several activities focused on building the Executive Team's *team working capabilities*. In addition, you have committed to developing your *team leadership* capabilities. The purpose of this short questionnaire is to measure your progress in these two areas.

This questionnaire is split into two sections.

The first section will address the progress that the Executive Team as a whole has made in their *team working capabilities*. So, when completing this section, you should be thinking about the functioning of the X Executive Team as a whole.

The second section will address the progress of your individual *team leadership* capabilities within the team that you lead. So, when completing Section Two, you should be thinking about your individual team leadership progress. For Section Two you will also be asked to write down your name for feedback purposes.

The objective of this mini-questionnaire is to determine if there is any change in team working and team leadership effectiveness as a result of the first round of questionnaires, the feedback, and ongoing interventions, and to elicit your thoughts on the progress to date.

All X Executive Team members will be requested to complete this questionnaire. The results of the Executive Team capabilities will be aggregated and analyzed at the team level. The Divisional Deputy Secretary and all participants completing this questionnaire will be provided with a summary report of the results. You will also be provided with feedback about your individual leadership capabilities.

Section One: Progress of the Executive Team as a Whole

Instructions: Below are a number of statements assessing the progress of the X Executive Team's *team work* capabilities. Please circle a number that best reflects your perceptions of the Executive Team's *team work* progress. *Remember,* this section is about the X Executive Team as a whole.

1. In the last four months to what extent do you feel the Executive Team now works more effectively as a team?

   Less effective   **No change**   **More effective**
       −3   −2   −1   0   +1   +2   +3

2. To what extent do you feel that the Executive Team has communicated the team development goals with the staff?

   Not at all   **Somewhat**   **Very much**
       0   1   2   3   4   5   6

3. How satisfied are you with the level of effort of the Executive Team toward improving their team work capabilities?

   Not at all   **Moderately**   **Extremely**
       0   1   2   3   4   5   6

4. To what extent do you feel that the Executive Team is on track to meet their team development goals?

Not at all   **Somewhat**   **Very much**
 0 1 2   3   4 5 6

5. What areas do you feel the Executive Team should focus on in the coming months in order to meet their team development goals in December 2006?

Section Two: Progress of Your Individual Team Leadership Capabilities

Instructions: Below are a number of statements assessing the progress of your *team leadership* development. Please circle a number that best reflects your perceptions of your individual *team leadership* progress. Remember, this section is about you and your individual team leadership progress in the team that you lead.

Your Name:

6. In the last *four months,* to what extent do you feel that you have:

	Less Effective	No Change	More Effective
a. Become more effective in your overall team leadership capabilities	23 22 21	0	+1 +2 +3
b. Become more effective in your individual team leadership development goals (i.e. your Individual Team Leadership Development goals*)	23 22 21	0	+1 +2 +3

*Your Individual Team Leadership Development goals refer to the individual goals you agreed to in Workshop One.

7. Have you discussed your Individual Team Leadership Development goals with your staff?

Yes No

8. To what extent have you been seeking feedback from your staff on your areas for improvement?

Not at all   **Somewhat**   **Very much**
 0 1 2   3   4 5 6

9. To what extent have you acted on the feedback you have received from your staff?

Not at all   **Somewhat**   **Very much**
 0 1 2   3   4 5 6

10. How satisfied are you with your level of effort toward improving your team leadership skills?

Not at all			**Moderately**			**Extremely**
0	1	2	3	4	5	6

11. To what extent do you feel that you are on target to achieve your team leadership development goals by December 2006?

Not at all			**Somewhat**			**Very much**
0	1	2	3	4	5	6

12. What assistance, if any, would you like to help you achieve your development goals?

_____

_____

_____

_____

◆ ◆ ◆

Thank you for your participation. Please return the completed questionnaire to the X Team Development Box, located beside X desk.

References

Ancona, D. G., Kochan, T. A., Scully, M., Van Maanen, J., and Westney, D. E. "Making Teams Work." In *Organizational Behavior and Processes*. Cincinnati: South-Western, 1999.

Giber, D., Carter, L., and Goldsmith, M. *Linkage Inc.'s Best Practices in Leadership Development Handbook*. San Francisco: Jossey-Bass/Pfeiffer, 2000.

Hackman, J. R. *Leading Teams: Setting the Stage for Great Performances*. Harvard Business School Press, 2002.

Katzenbach, J. R., and Smith, D. K. *The Wisdom of Teams*. New York: McGraw-Hill, 1993.

Schein, E. H. *Process Consultation*. Reading, Mass.: Addison-Wesley, 1988.

Sundstrom, E. *Supporting Work Team Effectiveness*. San Francisco: Jossey-Bass, 1999.

Van Beekum, S. "The Relational Consultant." *Transactional Analysis Journal*, 2006, *36*(4), 318–329.

About the Contributor

Pauline Lee is a consultant with the Hay Group based in the Melbourne office, Australia. Prior to this, she worked as both a business manager and an organization development consultant

Exhibit 12.4. Team Process Observation Guide

Group process observation guide
Department of Treasury and Finance

Group process analysis on how the group functions and the means of making decisions. It is not concerned with the content of group discussion. It helps to increase awareness of one's own behavior and the behavior of others, and to improve the ability to intervene successfully in the group. Use the following questions to reflect on how the group has worked together:

General
Did you get value from this meeting? Yes/No Why?
How have you behaved in this session—involved/disinterested/committed to the goals?
How would you describe the atmosphere of today's session—cooperative/competitive friendly/hostile?
What was the general feeling of the group?

Group tasks
To what extent were agenda items achieved?
Were participants given time to consider information before the meeting?
Were goals clear or confusing? Did the facilitator focus the group toward the task?
Did the agenda get sidetracked? Were some members jumping from one topic to another?

Participation and communication
Was participation invited from all?
What could have the facilitator/chairperson done to help this meeting?
What processes were used to maximize participation? e.g., asking for information, clarifying
Who were the high/low participators?
Who talked to whom?
How were the silent people treated?
How was their silence interpreted? Consent? Disagreement? Lack of interest? Fear?
Were people listening to one another or talking over each other?

Problem solving and decision making
Were problems analyzed before solutions were generated?
How were decisions made and what were the consequences? e.g., voting, majority rules, "hearing no objectors," full group consensus
How were dissenters treated?
Who was playing "devils advocate"?
Did the decision accurately capture the debate?

Department of Treasury and Finance

Group process observation guide
Department of Treasury and Finance

Conflict
How did members challenge each other in the meeting?
Did anyone take the arguments personally?
Did anyone get angry with another person in the meeting?
Did members feel free to disagree?
Was there any attempt to tiptoe around or ignore tough issues?

Task behaviors
Support: Who supported other members' decisions? How did this affect other group members? Were any ideas ignored?
Initiating: Who suggested ways forward, opened the discussion, got the group started?
Linking: Who built bridges between people's ideas, saw the connections?
Closing: Did the group move on and close a discussion once a clear decision had been made or did the group go around in circles?

Influence
How did the formal leader(s) exert his/her influence? Was there rivalry in the group? What effect did it have? What tactics did members use to influence each other?

Emotional issues
Identity: Who am I in this group? What role should I play?
Goals and needs: What do I want from this group? What do I have to offer?
Power and control: How much influence do I have?
Intimacy: How much trust exists among us?
Dependency: Do I wait passively for the leader to solve the problem or do I resist anyone in the group who represents authority?

Taking action
What improvement could the group make to improve the dynamics and to facilitate better achievement of the tasks?
What will we do differently at the next meeting?

Department of Treasury and Finance

Source: Adapted from Ancona, Kochan, Scully, Van Maanen, and Westney (1999) and Schein (1988).

for three years at the Department of Treasury and Finance in Melbourne. She also worked for GM Holden on developing its knowledge management strategy and building high-performance teams and for Shell as a change manager advisor. She was awarded her doctorate in psychology from the University of Melbourne for her research on the role of leadership and trust in fostering knowledge sharing in teams. She lectures part time on applied organizational psychology and human resource management at the University of Melbourne and has presented at numerous organizational development and psychological conferences in several countries.

CHAPTER THIRTEEN

MACY'S

This chapter outlines a strong approach for building and implementing development programs for leaders at all levels.

Macy's, one of the most successful fashion retailers in the United States, owns and operates more than 850 Macy's and Bloomingdales stores in forty-five states, the District of Columbia, Guam, and Puerto Rico. It also operates macys.com and bloomingdales.com. With 182,000 employees, sales totaled $26.3 billion in 2007.

Despite the organization's powerful brand, department store retailing as a whole is under significant pressure to find its way back into the hearts and wallets of shoppers who now have more choices than ever before regarding where to spend their money. With so many choices for in-store and online shopping, consumers are becoming more and more discerning when they shop. Macy's believes the key to future growth is innovation in product offerings and the customer shopping experience. This is possible only through excellence in leadership.

The Business Case for Leadership

Over the past few years, Macy's has faced a number of fundamental changes that have placed increasing pressure on the company:

- In 2005 the company launched a national branding strategy, changing its own regional nameplates to Macy's.
- With a strategy of growth through acquisition, in 2005 Macy's acquired May Department Stores Company, a large nationwide retailer that came with a very different organizational culture.
- The current down-trending economic cycle has caused decreases in consumer spending.
- The potential talent gap has widened considerably with the impending retirement of baby boomers.
- Recently the company has implemented a large-scale restructuring that has resulted in the deployment of a merchandise planning function to local markets with the goal of getting closer to customers to understand their shopping needs better.

The retail industry is entering a place never before seen, but in spite of this, Macy's enjoys a number of strategic advantages that position it to face these challenges. One of the company's biggest strengths, derived from many years of success, is a clear vision of its positioning in the marketplace. It benefits from well-established brand values that serve as guidelines for how to operate internally. In addition, the organization has a strong focus on well-articulated business priorities:

- Differentiate merchandise tailored to the customer at each location.
- Deliver a shopping experience that ensures that each store is visually appealing, easy to shop, and staffed by knowledgeable associates.
- Simplify pricing to underscore the value delivered to the customer.
- Execute marketing strategies that build the brand and at the same time speak to the local customer.

Finally, the company's history of and strong belief in leadership development as the key to implementing business priorities is a stabilizing factor to be drawn on as Macy's finds ways to generate growth in the new world of retailing.

Addressing the Challenges

In 1999 Macy's, then known as Federated Department Stores, had a record year as measured by the most important financial indicator of success: comparable stores sales growth. It was also in that year that the company launched the Leadership Institute, a facility and a program targeted at the development of the company's top-tier executives. The foundation of the teachings of the Leadership Institute was, and still is, the leadership choice model. This model states that a *great work environment* attracts the *best people* who want to stay and deliver the *best shopping experience* for customers, which produces the *best results* for shareholders (Figure 13.1). The choices that leaders make every day shape the work environment and drive results.

The Leadership Institute and the general imperative of leadership development have continued to grow at Macy's. Today the belief is stronger than ever before among senior management that stepping up to the

FIGURE 13.1.   THE LEADERSHIP CHOICE MODEL

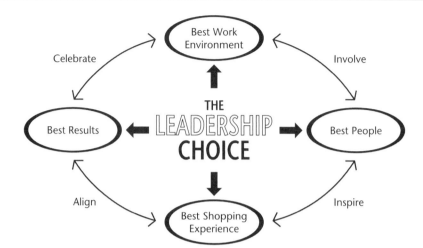

challenges of a changing environment and capitalizing on the company's strengths is dependent on having the right talent and strong leadership at all levels. The leadership choice model has become a well-known icon across the organization and is another stabilizing factor inside the company.

Each of the processes making up Macy's leadership development strategy is derived from the leadership choice model. This decision is reflective of what many consider to be a standard best practice in the field: having uniform language for leadership development. While Macy's employs a variety of developmental experiences at varying levels throughout the organization, the model ensures that the higher vision for each process remains constant.

The Leadership Strategy

Launching the Leadership Institute in 1999 marked a permanent change in Macy's strategy around leadership development. A number of factors influenced the decision to develop a new approach related to business objectives, corporate culture, and market influences. The following questions indicate the strategic concerns in the design of the Leadership Institute:

- In department store retailing, a significant portion of sales revenue is derived from promotional sales, resulting in a culture that is very event based. However, leadership development is a process that must be continuous rather than intermittent. How can leadership development be made into a process rather than a single event? How can leadership development be sustained over time?
- In the retail industry, organizations distinguish themselves by focusing on image, glitz, and glamour. But in leadership development, frills amount to very little without quality of content and genuinely transformational learning. How can a leadership development system be designed that is up to date, exciting, and fun and has depth and meaning?
- Given the immense changes occurring in the retail industry, organizations must be prepared to make necessary changes in corporate culture in order to adapt to the future. How can an overall learning experience be created that works within the existing culture while at the same time encourages the development of something new?

Additional strategic direction was derived from the organization's firm beliefs about effective leadership development:

- The reason for leadership is to deliver on business priorities and brand values. This is how leadership is positioned at all levels of the organization.
- Leadership at all levels is important.
- In order to achieve consistency across the board, the same leadership choice model must be used as the foundation for all leadership development programs from entry level to the most senior executive.
- To establish a common language around leadership, the same coaching model governs communication about performance.

The Leadership Pipeline

At Macy's, developmental processes are executed at all levels, a significant challenge for any organization. Because development often represents a sizable investment, many companies choose to reserve their development dollars for those at the top, focusing on leadership qualities that can be passed down to aspiring individuals at lower levels of the organization. Although this is often effective, it must be considered that development means something entirely different for a high-potential person than it does for someone on a senior leadership team. At Macy's the challenge was to design the best development experiences for leaders at every level of the organization.

Development for senior management (store managers, division merchant managers, support vice presidents) is done through the Leadership Institute. This process for owned, designed, developed, and delivered by the institute itself. Such a centralized process is ideal for targeted groups of leaders because it is typically more coordinated and uses fewer resources than a regionally deployed strategy. It also allows greater quality and consistency in support of the national brand.

High-potential development programs are handled outside the institute. Although they maintain a centralized format for design and development, the delivery is decentralized. This decision was made because of the large numbers and geographical dispersion of the population of entry and midlevel executives in the company. With a decentralized delivery model, learning can be implemented in person in various on-site locations and by distance learning, resulting in greater impact at less cost. The following initiatives represent core leadership curriculum for Macy's. All derive from the leadership choice model.

Foundations for Leadership

The Foundations for Leadership program is an entry-level curriculum that every new executive completes. The curriculum is made of up three programs and is based on the belief that everyone in the organization needs to know the following:

- Macy's organizational structure
- Market positioning for the two nameplates (Macy's and Bloomingdale's) and a knowledge of the competition

- The vision, brand values (internally focused), and image attributes (externally focused)
- The business priorities of the company
- The fundamental merchandising model: lifestyle merchandising
- The importance of inclusion and diversity to the success of the organization
- Customer demographics
- Business acumen (how the company makes money)
- How the individual can contribute in his or her role
- The leadership choice model and how personal leadership is the key to executing the company's vision and business goals
- A set of foundational guidelines for how each individual interacts with another as they work together to achieve organizational goals

At entry and midlevel, leadership development is primarily classroom oriented and delivered by regional training professionals in partnership with line managers who act as subject matter experts.

The first program in Foundations for Leadership is known as Making Choices. This typically occurs within three months on the job for a class of entry-level executives. The focus of this program is to introduce participants to Macy's positioning in the marketplace, the company vision, brand values, image attributes, lifestyle merchandising, and business priorities. This ultimately gives a strong impression for the company and its culture and serves as a powerful case for leadership as a business strategy. A large learning map serves as the foundation of this peer-facilitated program.

Following this program is Retailology 101, which also occurs within the first three months on the job. Using a gamelike approach, this workshop incorporates a simulation to help participants manage a fictional retail operation. Business acumen is built by encouraging leaders to navigate complex factors that influence sales, margin, and profit, as well as to understand how their individual contribution can mean success for the company.

As a follow-up to the Making Choices content, participants take part in two additional workshops during the same first three months: "Principles of Motivation and Respect" and "Valuing Diversity: Our Business, Our

Culture." The first delves into the principles of the leadership choice model and uses interactive exercises to build on the leadership skills that create the kind of work environment where people feel motivated to contribute their best. The second focuses on diversity, its profound impact on the business, and the expectations in managing a diverse workforce.

Through the Foundations for Leadership program, all entry-level executives are introduced to the business case for leadership development to strengthen their commitment to the development process and ultimately improve their engagement in future interventions. The program also introduces them to the key corporate values and strategies articulated by Macy's, thus reinforcing the company's culture among the new class of decision makers. This provides both a strong stabilizing effect and a means of driving culture change through leadership development if needed.

To maximize the effectiveness of the learning, it is essential to look not only at the content itself but at how it is delivered. At the entry level, design approaches must be chosen considering the needs of younger learners. They come from a world of technology, blogs, speed, YouTube, and reality TV. In order to maximize the impact of learning and encourage ongoing engagement, today's learners require the following:

- Creative approaches help to keep the learning interesting and appealing, interactive and concise.
- Use of technology allows a variety of innovative and hands-on approaches, such as simulations, to be practiced either on-site or in remote locations.
- Participants must be exposed to a careful combination of facilitator versus peer learning. While access to facilitators allows the delivery of expert content and advice, peer interaction is important for building networks critical to entry-level executives, as well as support and teamwork.
- Discovery learning is a necessary element in a program-based learning curriculum: unlike lectures, it increases retention through hands-on work and direct application.
- Competitive games are an effective way of tapping into the competitive nature of the participants to drive engagement. They are also

effective in promoting team-based problem solving and incorporating fun and excitement into the learning process.

Performance Through People

Following Foundations for Leadership and within the first six months on the job, executives in supervisory roles take part in the Performance Through People process. This primarily aims at educating supervisors on the most critical leadership functions associated with their role: building connections and a strong sense of followership among direct reports, developing others, building teamwork and motivation among teams of direct reports, and managing change processes within their department or function.

The Performance Through People portion of the model acts as an ideal complement to the Foundations for Leadership process for those who supervise. Whereas Foundations for Leadership focuses on developing leaders' knowledge of the business and basic leadership skills, Performance Through People builds competency around many of the more leadership-oriented areas as a preparation for high roles in the company. Everything that is learned in Foundations for Leadership is now focused on achieving goals through others: on-boarding people to a new team, teaching and coaching individuals to build the skills they need to be successful, developing a united team, and implementing tactical changes in the business. The process itself consists of four instructor-led courses, each ranging from three to four hours in length:

- *Making Connections:* Most new employees decide if they have made the right employment decision during the first days on the job, and turnover is highest in the first few months. This program focuses on how supervisors can provide an effective orientation and build strong connections with their employees.
- *Developing People:* Supervisors learn to identify opportunities for training and coaching their direct reports. Participants practice teaching a new job skill and conducting effective coaching conversations that involve others in their own development. The emphasis is on creating a trusting environment that supports development.

- *Leading Teams:* This program is designed to allow participants to discover the characteristics of effective teams and develop the leadership skills needed to foster trust, support, and high performance in their own teams. This is not about team-building activities, but rather about the day-to-day leadership required to sustain a high-performance team.
- *Leading Change:* As the pace of change continues to accelerate, the need to implement change becomes a critical skill. Supervisors can be implementers of change decisions made at a total company level, as well as initiators of change they would like to make in their own areas. This program examines the dynamics of the change process, the leader's role in paving the way for change, and how to work effectively with those who are affected by change.

The Leadership Institute: Education for Senior Leadership at Macy's

Macy's faces two significant challenges in filling the leadership pipeline: helping leaders make the transition to more significant levels of management and ensuring there are sufficient backups to fill openings of key positions for the future.

The Leadership Institute provides formal education to Macy's top eighteen hundred executives. Programs are designed to build leadership capability while strengthening organizational culture. Two key areas of focus are supporting newly placed vice presidents in their transition to senior-level roles and accelerating the development of high-potential executives.

Developed through a partnership with Linkage, the Accelerated Leadership Development Program (ALDP) is a series of formal learning events and experiential activities to address the skills necessary to meet critical responsibilities identified by Macy's senior executives. Program participants are nominated by their respective divisions or functions and are recognized for their contributions and potential to operate at higher levels. The program is designed to provide personal leadership development, improve business and strategic thinking, and challenge participants' views of retail and Macy's.

The program consists of two sessions, separated by two to three months. The first session prepares participants to address their leadership challenge by assessing and dealing with their skills in such areas as strategy formulation and execution and branding. This session develops the longer-term perspective of these managers, whose demanding jobs often focus them more on short-term conditions. The second session prepares them to influence, coach, and develop others; examine various models of leadership; and apply the best ideas and practices. They also focus on how to ensure that their ideas have impact and how to influence senior leaders across the corporation.

Intensive feedback is part of the program. Participants are given an external coach who interviews the divisional head of human resources (HR), their boss, and the principal for their division about their challenges, successes, and leadership style. This feedback is integrated with their written assessments. All participants receive a mini-survey follow-up and share their results with their direct reports. This mini-survey targets a few key areas of leadership behavior that the participant has chosen to focus on and change over a four-month period. The program content varies each year to address competitive concerns.

Several learning approaches are used:

- Leaders teaching leaders. Top leaders act as facilitators and teachers. These executive committee members become comfortable teaching within their areas of focus or expertise and skilled at facilitating and modeling open dialogues and exchange. They also act as sponsors to the individual action learning projects that participants complete.
- Partnerships with top college faculty and industry experts as needed.
- Use of interactive means to spark creative thinking. This element varies from year to year. It has included a vehicle racing simulation, having actors teach executive presence, and the leadership lessons of Antarctic explorer Sir Ernest Shackleton. The goal is to challenge people's traditional ideas of learning and provide serious business content.
- Hands-on application of tools and practice, which is blended into the design of both formal sessions.

- Leadership stories. Senior executives have shared their leadership stories and use this exercise, based on the work of Noel Tichy, in class.
- In-depth assessment and coaching. This includes the use of the Linkage 360-degree Leadership Assessment Instrument (LAI), a personality assessment (The Hogan), and having participants write an autobiography.
- Business application through use of an on-the-job challenge opportunity. Each participant works with his or her manager and the division principal to define a stretch challenge that they must complete over a six-month period.

Both the assessment and the results of the challenge assignment are connected to the individual's development plan, which is formally reviewed by management. The challenge is a cornerstone of the program. Each year, we increase the learning and business impact of these projects. While many organizations feel that action learning can be done only in groups, this challenge assignment forces participants to stretch and create their own action learning networks as they seek to achieve their tasks.

The projects are reviewed by the institute leaders, divisional HR support, the participants' bosses, and their bosses' boss and senior leaders from other divisions or functions. We use three key criteria: (1) the challenge must push the participant to build a network and influence across functional lines, (2) the challenge can be related to the participant's job but should be an assignment with some risk where success is not guaranteed, and (3) the challenge must prompt new strategic thinking and not have an obvious answer.

During the next six months, there is follow-up on two levels: first in terms of behavioral change and growth in leadership effectiveness, and then tracking the challenge assignments for completion and business impact. Over the years, participants have used projects to test new growth ideas, build new customer services, work on mentoring and diversity initiatives, and expand improved processes in distribution and other areas. There has been a clear, measurable return on investment on many of these initiatives.

We use alumni to teach in the program. The use of in-depth assessment and involvement of senior management signals to participants the interest in them as individuals. The involvement with step-up opportunities and mini-survey follow-up tells participants that this learning is meant to be applied. Finally, the use of various learning approaches helps develop flexibility in learning.

ALDP has become a milestone in the careers of participants and has created an alumni network of more than 150 leaders across the company. This group is a critical part of Macy's future talent pool, and ALDP is only one part of the work to develop leaders as they progress through the company.

Fast Start

Stepping into the role of store manager can be daunting. Store managers are responsible for creating an outstanding shopping experience for customers, executing company strategy, generating millions of dollars in sales, and supervising hundreds of employees. Often they are located in remote markets and may see their bosses only a few times a year. It is critical that they make a successful transition, quickly connecting with their teams, assessing the state of the business, and establishing their vision while building credibility with key stakeholders.

Fast Start, a synchronous distance-learning program, is designed to help store managers make an effective entry and transition to their new roles. Delivered using Centra, a virtual classroom environment provided by the University of North Carolina Charlotte, ten to fifteen store managers meet virtually for two two-hour sessions. Leadership Institute staff and an experienced store manager facilitate each session. These store managers provide wisdom from their own transitions as well as their years of experience in the retail industry. The program helps store managers address issues such as these:

- How do I assess the state of my business and my team?
- How do I understand the culture and the political environment?
- How do I build credibility with my team, boss, and peers?

- How do I avoid typical pitfalls in the transition?
- How do I build a plan to drive the business in both the long and short terms?

At the end of each session, each participant develops a plan to improve performance. Table 13.1 sets out an example of a store manager's plan focused on improving the store's work environment.

The Leadership Choice

Designed for newly placed vice presidents from all job functions, the Leadership Choice program helps executives make a successful transition to more senior levels of management, explore Macy's point of view on leadership, learn about current leadership capabilities, and build a plan to improve business performance and leadership effectiveness.

This four-day program provides 360-degree feedback, explores a variety of leadership topics, and gives participants an opportunity to apply what they have learned in a team-based computerized simulation. Participants learn how to:

- Strategize how to step up to the broader responsibilities of a senior leader
- Identify personal leadership strengths and areas for improvement
- Ensure quality execution, balancing long- and short-term initiatives
- Conduct development conversations that lead to positive outcomes

TABLE 13.1.   A STORE MANAGER'S PLAN FOR IMPROVING THE WORK ENVIRONMENT

Business Goal	Action Plan	Actions Taken	Results
Build morale in sales support areas so that sales and support functions cooperate	Meet with each support group in the store Listen to concerns Develop an action plan to address issues	Include all support associates in meetings, contests, and executive visits	Improved morale Greater cohesiveness between sales and support functions

- Reduce turnover by enhancing the work environment
- Build partnerships and commitment to achieve their plans

During the program, significant time is spent networking with peers and interacting with senior leaders about the challenges facing the business.

In 2007, the Leadership Choice program played a significant role in helping to integrate six hundred senior executives from the newly acquired May Company into the Macy's culture. Because of the importance of this initiative to the future success of the organization, the Leadership Institute, with the assistance of the Advantage Performance Group, conducted a follow-up study to determine program impact. Table 13.2 presents a summary of the study.

TABLE 13.2.   LEADERSHIP CHOICE PROGRAM SUMMARY

Methodology	Data Highlights	Comments by Participants
Sent surveys to ninety-nine participants Received seventy-six responses Conducted twenty in-depth telephone interviews	96 percent of respondents learned something in the program and have used it in their work 60 to 90 percent of respondents are using all targeted behaviors, with many producing positive results	"I recently turned down a job offer from a competitor. I am convinced Macy's has a great future, and I want to be part of it. Many things have contributed to my positive perceptions, with this program being one of those." "I have used the coaching and feedback models to develop my buying team. My leaders are more engaged and aligned and productive." "I was not sure if Macy's was the right fit for me when the acquisition occurred. I have discovered that Macy's orientation to people development, empowering managers with clear accountability, and then investing in people through programs like this have turned my skepticism into positive anticipation. I am in this for the long haul."

Merchant Leadership Development Program

The Merchant Leadership Development Program is designed to accelerate the development of high-potential merchants who are slated for promotion within twelve to eighteen months. Up to this point, these merchants have had minimal supervisory responsibility and one line of business to manage. On promotion, they will manage multiple lines of business with a significant jump in volume responsibility as they supervise a multilevel team.

This program is designed to help executives:

- Think more broadly about the business
- Build credibility with their management and key stakeholders
- Work effectively through others
- Understand the impact of their decisions on the business and people

Through use of a computerized simulation, participants experience what work will be like at the next level. This simulation, along with an individual assessment, helps participants identify the skills they currently have that will benefit them at the next level, as well as their opportunities for improvement. They leave the program with a development plan that they can execute on the job with the support of an HR partner.

The Leadership Institute conducted an impact study in association with the launch of this program in 2004 to determine the degree to which participants were able to apply what they had learned and to measure improvement in skill capability. Table 13.3 summarizes the impact study.

Supporting Key Business Initiatives

In addition to the ongoing leadership development curricula, Macy's learning and development function, including its Leadership Institute, frequently supports significant changes in company strategy. Following the 2005 acquisition of the May Company, the learning and development team led the way in the development and implementation of a plan to help integrate all new employees from the May Company.

TABLE 13.3.   MERCHANT LEADERSHIP DEVELOPMENT PROGRAM
STUDY SUMMARY

Methodology	Data Highlights	Comments by Participants
All participants, supervisors, and HR partners completed presurveys to establish baseline data Same people completed postsurveys six months after the program Structured interviews were conducted with participants and supervisors six months after program	Data showed an increase in the frequency of use and skill capability of four skill objectives taught in the program Majority of participants indicated an increase in confidence. Increased confidence usually translates into greater frequency of use of skills; increased practice potentially translates into increased skill effectiveness	"I've been working on developing the mind-set of the next level and approaching the business from a broader perspective. Since returning from [the program], I've attended more senior meetings and strategy sessions. I've been looking at the entire business for the pyramid and giving recommendations to the team" (participant comment). "I've seen a huge improvement in how she [a participant] looks at the business and develops partnerships. She worked beyond her own area of responsibility and coordinated a plan for the entire division. We saw a 28 percent increase in the business" (supervisor comment).

Through the work of the learning and development function, six hundred senior leaders from May attended leadership conferences, which gave them exposure to Macy's senior leadership, company strategy, and an exploration of cultural differences between the two organizations. Each leader left the conference with a personal leadership transition plan.

Following these conferences, similar events were held in the various divisions and regions of the company for entry- and midlevel leaders. These were followed by role clarification and skill-building sessions designed to help orient all new May employees to the company.

Recognizing that a transition of this magnitude takes significant time, a year later the six hundred senior leaders who joined Macy's as part of the acquisition were invited to the Leadership Institute for additional leadership development. It was their opportunity to learn more about the company's philosophy of the leadership and business model, assess their current leadership capabilities, and build an action plan to ensure their success in the new company.

Future Efforts

For Macy's, as with any other organization, the ongoing practice of leadership development results in natural evolution. As participant feedback is collected and programs are evaluated, new insights emerge for continuous improvement. In addition, the business environment is always changing, resulting in new business strategies, which often call for new leadership development initiatives.

Currently Macy's faces another change. The company has just completed a major restructure in twenty of its markets in support of My Macy's, a new localization effort. The goal is to get closer to customers and more clearly identify customer needs. This will enable each store to provide just the right merchandise and experience for that location. The goal is for every customer to enter a store and feel as if the store is My Macy's.

Again, the learning and development organization has led the way in supporting this strategy. They have been significantly involved in role clarification, development of new business processes, and the design of training to support the restructure.

Conclusion

In many ways, the example of Macy's is unique. First, the retail industry is in a distinct position and comes with natural consumer-driven dynamics not found in other industries. In addition, many smaller companies may not have the budget to support leadership development endeavors of this magnitude. However, there are a number of lessons that any practitioner can take away:

- When designing a leadership development system, give careful consideration to the stabilizing and destabilizing forces that continuously push and pull at the organization. Every company has challenges that must be overcome, and leadership development is a means to that end. Thus, these challenges should be an integral part of the overall leadership development strategy. For example, traditionally high turnover ratios among frontline retail employees prompted Macy's to pursue development interventions that focused on the skills of effective supervising and follower development. In addition to these challenges, stabilizing forces serve as strengths to an organization and contribute to its ongoing success. Macy's has an intimate knowledge of these forces and makes a point of leveraging leadership development as a means of reinforcing these strengths. For example, the company realized that one of its greatest strengths is its firmly grounded and well-articulated set of business values. As a result, the Foundations for Leadership process was designed to offer a curriculum of training around the core values of the business, its customers, and its niche markets. This came in the initial parts of the development process, and thus these values inevitably serve as the backdrop for future development interventions.

- Every leadership development system needs to have a common language to promote consistency and uniformity. Development objectives must remain clear to participants; otherwise, the result will be confusion that will erode commitment and engagement. A clear business case will result from a well-accepted model or strategy that identifies what the organization wishes to accomplish through leadership.

- Solely focusing development on senior leadership teams may be adequate in smaller organizations where learning for those with high potential can take on a less formal approach; however, it is not enough in a large organization. Leadership development initiatives must be conducted among high-potential or entry-level executives not only as a means of improving their best capabilities, but also as a way to reinforce the culture of the organization. To do this, it requires that development processes be molded to align with the needs and priorities of different leadership levels. For high-potential talent, this may mean peer networking and support systems to serve as a resource during an individual's continued growth in the company. Concurrently, senior development efforts may focus more on leading teams or departments, developing others, managing change and transition, or understanding the business scenarios that result in organizational growth.

- Individual leadership development programs must incorporate a number of teaching methods to maximize impact and keep from becoming redundant. Consider the ratios of facilitator versus peer interaction, lecture versus hands-on learning, and technology-enabled approaches versus traditional approaches, for example.

- Success in the retail business is dependent on the organization's ability to understand customers and keep their needs foremost in their day-to-day operations. The same holds true for leadership development. Each initiative must be tailored specifically for the leader to whom developmental resources are intended. For example, the Macy's Fast Start program is built for the store manager, whose role provides very little interaction with a boss or other supervisory figure, requires an ability to quickly read and adapt to business opportunities or challenges, and requires flexibility in the face of transition.

About the Contributors

Debbie Friedman is operating vice president at Macy's, where she heads the Leadership Institute, a training function whose mission is to strengthen the leadership capabilities of the top eighteen hundred executives. Her leadership has helped Macy's reach its place as one of the Top 100 Companies in Training and Development by *Training* magazine two years in a row. She has held other training positions at Macy's, including director of training at Lazarus, a Midwest division, and at AT&T in the sales and marketing education organization.

Friedman holds a master's degree in education from Xavier University, Cincinnati, and a bachelor of arts degree from Stern College for Women, Yeshiva University. She is the author of *Demystifying*

Outsourcing: The Trainer's Guide to Working with Vendors and Consultants (Jossey-Bass/Pfeiffer, 2006).

◆ ◆ ◆

Mary Martin is director of learning and development at Macy's. She is responsible for the training provided in all Macy's stores for sales associates and managers and also for management and leadership development for entry- and midlevel executives.

She began her career at Macy's in 1987 at the Lazarus division of what was then Federated Department Stores. She has also held training positions at AT&T in the sales and marketing education organization and as the community and workplace educator for the AIDS support organization of greater Cincinnati. Other background includes secondary education classroom teaching and genetic counseling.

Martin holds an undergraduate degree in biology/chemistry from the University of Akron and master's degrees in curriculum and instruction and in medical genetics from the University of Cincinnati.

CHAPTER FOURTEEN

BANK OF AMERICA

Executive On-Boarding

This chapter outlines the importance of having a strong executive on-boarding process to reinforce and align with a larger companywide leadership development strategy.

Today more than ever before, qualified leadership is critical to achieving company success in the global market. Not only do uniquely competent individuals produce greater results, but as markets become more competitive, creating a culture of learning and empowerment contributes to lower turnover rates and greater retention of internal knowledge and serves as a powerful competitive advantage. This becomes even more important in the financial services industry, where organizational results are extremely elastic relative to changing economic conditions.

The Business Case

Given its unique history and current position in the financial services industry, Bank of America has experienced rapid changes in a dynamic environment, and as a result has developed its core philosophy around leadership development. Having started as a regional bank in North Carolina, Bank of America has grown dramatically over the past two decades. Since 1990, the company's assets have grown from $61.6 billion to $1.7 trillion in 2007, and revenues have grown from $2.8 billion to $68 billion. During this period of rapid growth, both organic growth and acquisitions, leadership roles have become extremely complex in variety, size, and scope. Talent acquisition and retention have become more critical than ever before. The latest McKinsey War for Talent survey, conducted in 2007, indicated that 89 percent of executives surveyed thought it was more difficult to attract talent than was the case three years back, and 90 percent felt it was more difficult to retain them. Given the bank's exponential growth and increasing complexity of roles, combined with an external environment of global scarcity of leadership talent, the need for effective on-boarding to make executives succeed is even more imperative.

Looking forward, with a priority on organic growth, Bank of America is constantly seeking to strengthen its leadership ranks with smart talent, able to deliver results efficiently and effectively. The bank realizes that a continuous influx of leaders at the senior executive level could create significant obstacles in the pursuit of their growth objectives.

First, individuals hired from the outside or acquired through acquisition may lack knowledge of the company's strategy and culture and require a considerable amount of time to become well versed in their new positions. In addition, frequent promotions from within, which are more frequently stretch assignments, have highlighted the difficulties inherent in individual transitions.

Second, moving to the executive role, whether from the outside or inside, is extremely demanding and provides little time for necessary new learning. During this initial period, most new executives, in a desire to appear in charge right away, pursue little feedback or mentoring from peers and superiors and as a result receive insufficient developmental attention.

Third, one of the essential measures of success in the first few months is the executive's ability to build a solid foundation of healthy business relationships vertically and horizontally. This can prove challenging for even the most competent and experienced of executives.

Well-known research points to the fact that 40 percent of senior managers hired from outside a company fail within their first eighteen months in their new role (Watkins, 2003). In such instances, losing a recently signed executive at the very least will cost the company the direct costs of recruitment and training, which can range from 5 to 21 percent of the employee's annual compensation (Hale, 1998). Given this, Bank of America made a significant commitment to on-boarding interventions focused on the first year of employment, and particularly the first four to five months of moving into the new role.

Purpose of the On-Boarding Initiative

The company found that an ideal on-boarding program should serve three purposes. The first purpose is to accelerate the performance results of the new leader. Research suggests that a senior-level manager requires an average of 6.2 months to reach a break-even point—the moment at which the new leader's contribution to the organization exceeds the costs of bringing him or her on board and developing within this person a critical base of insight into the job (Watkins, 2003). A good on-boarding program should effectively reduce this period by accelerating the building of critical relationships and networks, clarifying leadership and performance expectations, and facilitating the formation of more realistic short- and medium-term performance objectives.

The second purpose is to minimize the possibility of derailment on the job. By providing a clear understanding of the demands and expectations associated with the position and offering abundant support through constructive feedback, coaching, and follow-up, a well-designed program can minimize failures.

The third function of a successful on-boarding initiative is one that particularly serves companies like Bank of America that are experiencing high growth rates or aggressively pursuing acquisitions. The resulting influx of outside managers forces the need to facilitate a far smoother integration experience for these executives than what would be afforded in a typical environment. This is accomplished by helping these leaders rapidly acquire an understanding of the market, socializing them into the organization's culture and politics, building a network of critical relationships, and familiarizing them with the operating dynamics of the executive team.

The on-boarding process at Bank of America has three general phases. The first phase begins the moment the selection decision on a candidate is made. Feedback from the interviews is sent to human resources and leadership development, as well as the hiring manager. Through the collaboration of these groups, a customized plan is developed so that any potential strengths can be leveraged and weaknesses ironed out quickly during the first few months on the job.

The second part of the process extends from the first day in the new position for the next four to five months. During this time, the on-boarding plan guides the leader in relationship building as well as the nuances of the business, the competitive environment, and the culture.

The formal on-boarding process ends with a key stakeholder review, a qualitative 360-degree feedback process conducted for the leader by the leadership development partner. The intent is to provide the new leader with an initial read of his or her performance and make course corrections as necessary.

On-boarding is one component of a suite of leadership development processes embedded in routines of the bank's day-to-day business, all of which continue to develop and support leaders at multiple levels in the organization. The bank's leadership development model guards the process by clearly articulating both the behavioral attributes for success and behaviors that could lead to derailment. Second, talent planning is a formal process where succession plans for critical roles are formalized, so that there is a steady pipeline of talent across the organization. Third, executive leadership programs are in place to both reward leaders identified as a part of the talent planning process and provide them with new skills. Many of the senior executives within the organization have taken active approaches to identifying key leaders and leadership traits that will spell success in the future, thereby assuming accountability for retention of outstanding leadership talent as a critical mandate within the bank. The company's environment is one that encourages candor, trust, teamwork, and risk taking at all levels in the organization. This has led to a culture that served as the ideal environment for a maturing on-boarding initiative.

By developing a robust on-boarding program for senior executives and linking its existing leadership development efforts, the company has been able to achieve its goals of reducing executive derailment, expediting the integration process, and positioning its top leaders for ongoing development throughout their tenure with the company. In addition, the bank realizes significant intangible rewards through reinforcement of the existing culture and strengthening of its image and brand among internal partners.

An Example of the On-Boarding Process

This section uses Bank of America employee testimony to construct the story of Stephanie, a fictional Bank of America executive and beneficiary of the company's on-boarding process, to show not only the effects that on-boarding has had on the company but its impact at the individual level. Although the description is broadly representative of what a typical executive may go through during the on-boarding process, the plan is customized and may look different for different executives depending on their individual needs and situation.

The Selection Process

Stephanie's entry with Bank of America, and her first exposure to her on-boarding experience, begins during the interview and selection phase.

The interview process is deliberately as candid as possible. Stephanie's interviewers waste no time in discussing the unique culture of the company. Questions focus on two areas: behavioral interviewing on her past accomplishments and why she wants to work for Bank of America. Her prospective role is described in terms of both upsides and downsides so that she is given as much insight as possible into not only her potential place within the company but the priorities and expectations of the company.

Following the interview, feedback is collected from all stakeholders, preferably in a team meeting or a telephone call with executives invested in her potential position. This allows them to share their initial impressions and notes from the meeting and solicit feedback from multiple directions with regard to her individual competencies and whether they will enable her to succeed at the bank. Feedback from this interviewing process is captured and used when creating a tailored on-boarding plan for Stephanie.

Entry Phase

For Stephanie, the first few weeks on the job are among the most challenging. During this time, she has the responsibility of adapting her skills to the new role, developing business acumen, becoming deeply acquainted with the organizational culture, mastering the leadership demands associated with her position, and building critical organizational relationships. Bank of America recognizes the last as not only one of the most important but also the most difficult for many executives.

Before she even arrives at the bank, Stephanie is contacted by her manager and her leadership development/HR partner and is given an on-boarding plan with these elements:

- Guidelines for discussion with the manager in terms of clarity of the role and expectations in the first thirty, sixty, and ninety days
- Key stakeholders whom Stephanie needs to interact with to succeed in a highly matrixed environment, critical for her success
- Reports on company history, culture, and financial data
- Organizational charts depicting the company's leadership and departments
- Specific information for her individual unit, including the business plan and financial data
- Key initiatives and assessment of the team's leadership talent

More information on the contents of the typical on-boarding plan can be seen in Exhibit 14.1. What Stephanie finds most interesting is that both she and the manager have a candid discussion around her goals and the most important success factors in the new role. They explore early obstacles during her initial tenure and how her development within the company might help to address these issues. Finally, the manager shares the initial feedback that originated from their first interview, as well as the name of her peer coach who will be her partner and advisor during the on-boarding process.

Providing business coaching resources is a critical part of the on-boarding process at Bank of America. First among them is her peer coach, Pete, an individual at a peer level selected based on common interests, experience, and complementary personality traits. Pete is not only someone with a background in her industry and line of work, but went to the same university for graduate education. He is familiar with the culture of Bank of America and went through an on-boarding plan similar to that of Stephanie. His presence as a peer and his history of similar experiences are a great source of comfort and motivation and help Stephanie navigate through the on-boarding experience while optimizing the value from the experience.

Between her peer coach, manager, and the HR–leadership development (HR/LD) resource, Stephanie is given a great deal of information to help her initiation process. The most important advice is to meticulously go through the list of names and key contacts included in her onboarding plan and take the time to set up appointments with each to meet informally. She quickly realizes that these meetings are not necessarily meant to address specific tasks, but to get to know others through personal conversation and discussion.

Stephanie has a list of thirty names and is strongly encouraged to set up appointments to speak with each person. This may seem like a long list, but in the bank's highly matrixed environment, this list is merely a good start. Before setting up the appointments, she works closely with her manager and the HR/LD support to get to know backgrounds of the executives and two or three key questions around interdependencies and integration so that she is well prepared for her first meeting. Stephanie may be new to these forms of meetings, but most of those who are already in the organization at her level are not. From the top of the company down, individuals are well briefed in the importance of building deep relationships and the value in developing others.

Throughout the first few months, Stephanie spends a good deal of time setting up appointments and interviews with each of the thirty people. Although several run into scheduling concerns, she is quick to note that not a single established meeting is skipped, and not a single person is unwilling to take the time away from the office to meet with her. Each meeting takes roughly one hour and is characterized by candid, informal discussion about matters both business and personal.

Orientation

Apart from her immediate manager and stakeholders, Stephanie is given a broader enterprise view of how the different parts of the business make money and connect with each other through the New Executive Orientation Program. This day-and-a-half session is sponsored directly by the CEO. During this time, Stephanie meets with roughly fifteen to twenty participants from across the organization, as well as the CEO, the executive team, and a panel of other executives previously hired in the Bank of America's on-boarding program.

Prior to coming to the session, Stephanie's peer coach, Pete, gives her insights into the key connect points for her in the bank that she needs to build on during the orientation. On the first day, an informal panel with executives hired into the bank within the past two years share their own on-boarding experiences, and Stephanie learns what to expect and their lessons learned. Following the panel is a series of presentations from the CEO and top executives, who cover topics such as corporate values and culture, risk and compliance expectations, leadership philosophy and expectations, company strategy and financials, key business units, growth strategies, and enterprise initiatives. Also during the program is a social networking event hosted by the CEO and the executive team. Stephanie not only builds cross-functional relationships but also gains new insight into the business, culture, and expectations outlined by the senior team.

•

Integration with the Team

During the next thirty to sixty days, Stephanie goes through a process known as the New Leader–Team Integration Session, which is designed to accelerate the working relationships between the new executive and her direct report team, as well as allow Stephanie to become acquainted with the operating styles and expectations of those with whom she will be working. Prior to this session, her leadership development partner explains what she might expect from this meeting and discusses her goals for the session. Following that, the partner meets with the team without Stephanie to gain a preliminary understanding of the group's issues and concerns. The process takes approximately four hours. During the initial part of the meeting, the leadership development partner shares the questions that were originally outlined with Stephanie, while Stephanie sits in a separate area and reviews the questions and concerns outlined by the team. Later, on arriving at the conference room, she is able to address any questions or concerns of the team in terms of operating style, the way forward as well as the team routines. The intent of this session is to have a candid dialogue between Stephanie and the team on how best to work together to create business results for the bank in the most efficient and effective way. The team also gets to ask questions collectively in a safe environment that fosters trust going forward, an important element of team success.

Feedback and the Path Forward

Stephanie has been working with Bank of America for three to four months. During this time, she has been given a number of resources to help her navigate through her new surroundings and apply her strengths and expertise to the job. Her boss has been instrumental thus far, retaining an open-door policy and in helping her in everything from coaching to working on assignments with her. Her peer coach has been extremely useful as a sounding board and helping her navigate the organization. Nevertheless, her work has been intense and demanding, even more so than she had imagined it would be. Her goals have led her to work on tasks that stretch her out of her comfort zone and allow her to work on diverse teams of members of the organization. Stephanie greatly appreciates the opportunity to prove herself from the start and excels in adding value to her new position.

Stephanie is now invited to take part in a key stakeholder review process, which is a qualitative 360-degree process that gives her a comprehensive view of what is going well, what she needs to improve on, and specifically what her stakeholders need from her. This feedback focuses on her progress through the on-boarding process, operating style, leadership approach, and cultural fit. Through this intervention, Stephanie is given an opportunity not only to understand the motivations and concerns of her stakeholders, but also to learn more about the bank and quickly address some of the areas where she may need improvement.

The timing of this intervention is well planned. At this point in the process, Stephanie has been working long enough not only to display her natural leadership style and means of executing on tasks, but also to work up the confidence to take criticism in stride and act on it to better herself. It is also early enough in the process that by the time of her formal evaluation, she will have had the chance to address and build on the competencies that need emphasis. Finally, by acting on this review earlier rather than later, Stephanie has the chance to improve on her behavior before any particular professional habits become subject to stereotype and association.

To create the review, the leadership development partner conducts anonymous thirty-minute interviews with each of the stakeholders. Once this information has been gathered, the partner reviews it to identify themes and patterns, as well as record specific comments that may be helpful to Stephanie. It is Stephanie's responsibility to work with her boss to identify future objectives and solutions, while the leadership development partner meets with Stephanie to review the report in depth and provide color around the themes.

Overall, this is among the most powerful experiences of Stephanie's on-boarding process. This rare chance provides feedback that is specific and candid and important to ongoing success. It also comes from every direction—peers, direct reports, and superiors, all of whom were part of the on-boarding plan. It shows that all of these individuals are invested in her position and willing to put their own time into guiding her success.

Stephanie internalizes the data from the stakeholder review and makes a plan, taking into the account the salient features of the report and key questions asked by the stakeholders. She discusses the plan with her HR/LD partner and Pete, her peer coach, before talking to the manager for his thoughts and observations. The manager is supportive, and Stephanie has a good sense of what is working, what is not working, and what she needs to do going forward.

A year after the key stakeholder review is delivered, Stephanie goes through a 360-degree assessment that is both an evaluation and developmental tool based on Bank of America's competency model that includes leadership competencies, derailing behaviors, and the bank's core values. This allows Stephanie to track progress against the initial feedback from the stakeholder review and establish an updated developmental plan.

Summary

For Stephanie, the on-boarding process at Bank of America left a strong impression in her mind about the company and her colleagues. This program does not just represent a means of getting the most out of the company's investment in its people during the first year; it is an indicator of the bank's strong adherence to the belief that stronger leaders produce better results. During the many interventions and meetings that took place, Stephanie was able to see the depth of leadership talent at the bank.

With regard to her personal development, Stephanie's on-boarding experience was invaluable in helping her acclimate to her new role. Even an experienced executive generally expects up to six months of initiation before being comfortable in a new role. For a typical senior executive like Stephanie, this all took place in a time frame of three to four months. In her case, as with many others, it is the enhanced ability to establish strong relationships in a short amount of time that made the biggest difference. Within just a few months, Stephanie already felt as if she had a solid network to rely on for candid feedback, assistance, and support in her professional and even personal life. Despite the challenging work that she found herself immersed in from the start, she added value in her own way quickly and has no doubt that the bank is committed to her success.

Conclusion

An effective on-boarding system, when properly linked to other practices of leadership development, is a powerful way to maximize leadership effectiveness not just during the first few months but in the long term as well. One can anticipate a lower frequency of derailment, a shorter initiation process into new and difficult roles, stronger connection to the company among senior executives, and improved performance individually and among teams. The case of Bank of America's on-boarding program leaves a number of lessons to be learned for those in any industry who are interested in any aspect of leadership development:

- An effective leadership development effort requires support not only from the top, but also from all of the stakeholders in each leadership position from the first day in the new role. In addition, the more stakeholders who are involved in the development process, the more connected and invested they will feel in a leader's success.
- Leaders in any role and in any organization are certain to reach an obstacle or stumbling block at some point during their careers. Providing ongoing support and feedback systems will help them not only to overcome these hurdles but also to improve their resiliency in coping with failures.
- As with many other leadership development initiatives, the best approaches are most often those that are incremental. In a challenging work environment, it is too easy for leaders to lose sight of their development interests, and frequent intervention at critical times during their tenure ensures that their focus consistently returns.
- Effective engagement is not just a matter of maximizing touch points, but is highly dependent on open, organized, and candid dialogue.
- When designing an on-boarding initiative, there are a number of questions that must be asked:
  - Does your organization treat on-boarding as a one-time orientation event or as a compressed longitudinal process?
  - What is the breadth of interventions it employs, from integration tools to coaches to formal feedback? Or is it highly reliant on one type of intervention?
  - Does it engage all of the new executive's stakeholders in a candid process that generates constructive feedback and clarifies expectations, or is it focused largely around the executive's superiors?
  - Are interventions delivered in time to get critical and valid feedback to the new executives so that they can constructively respond and maintain their credibility?
  - What programs does the organization provide to new executives to rapidly gain constructive feedback on their leadership approach?
  - What support does the organization provide in helping executives to act on their feedback?

Given the demands on executives today and the need for them to ramp up quickly in their jobs, an on-boarding process is critical for their success in achieving business results. An effective on-boarding process is strongly linked to both top leadership commitment and a support system that allows honest, candid feedback for personal, professional, and business success. Given the rapid growth of Bank of America since 1990 and the greater reliance on external hiring and stretch assignments, successful on-boarding processes as a part of an overall leadership development philosophy are essential to ensure sustainable business success.

The On-Boarding Plan

Exhibit 14.1. Sections of the Written On-Boarding Plan

1. On-boarding objectives
2. On-boarding time line: Expectations for thirty, sixty, and ninety days; key activities to complete
3. On-boarding team roles and responsibilities
4. Questions to consider as you enter the new role: new challenges, optimal time allocation, and issues to tackle
5. Information about Bank of America and its businesses
   a. Key internal Web sites
   b. Key business information in terms of business plans
6. Information about the role
   a. Key management routines
   b. Role description and expectations to deliver business results
   c. Team organization chart
   d. Talent planning information for the organization
   e. Training and development information
7. Leadership model
8. Key stakeholders
   a. Senior leadership team
   b. Internal team
   c. Business partners
9. Check-in meeting discussion points

References

Hale, J. "Strategic Rewards: Keeping Your Best Talent from Walking out the Door." *Compensation & Benefits Management*, 1998, *14*(3), 39–50.

Watkins, M. *The First 90 Days: Critical Success Strategies for New Leaders at All Levels.* Boston: Harvard Business School Press, 2003.

About the Contributors

Mohit Misra is the learning and leadership development executive supporting all leadership development processes across global consumer and small business bank at Bank of America. He joined the bank in 2005 and has held various leadership development positions, specializing in organization design, executive coaching, change management, and talent planning.

Previously he worked as a consultant for Towers Perrin, where he did change management and leadership development work for leading organizations in the Asia Pacific region, including Unilever, Visa, the Prime Minister's Office in Singapore, Singapore Exchange, DBS Bank, and Maxis, the largest telecom provider in Malaysia. He has contributed regularly to business journals on topics around human capital and leadership development.

Misra has a master's degree in human development and psychology from Harvard University and an M.B.A. from the Asian Institute of Management.

◆ ◆ ◆

Roger Cude is responsible for learning and leadership development functions for global consumer and small business banking at the Bank of America, which he joined in 2003. He has held various positions in leadership development and human resources in the global consumer and small business bank and business banking.

Previously Cude was vice president of human resources for McLeodUSA, a leading regional telecommunications provider, where he was responsible for all human resource, safety, and security functions. He has also served as vice president for human resources strategy for Williams, Inc., and was a professor on the faculty of the University of Tulsa. He has more than twenty years of experience in leadership development, personnel, and training.

He received a B.A. in communication from Southern Utah University and an M.A. in organizational communication from Pepperdine University, and he has completed doctoral work in organizational communication at the University of Texas at Austin.

CHAPTER FIFTEEN

HUMANA

Advancing Strategy and Building Culture Through Leadership Development

This chapter outlines the leadership development programs Humana built to advance a new strategic direction and the creation of a networked learning organization that respects its company culture and aligns learning with the business.

Company Background

Humana, headquartered in Louisville, Kentucky, is one of the nation's largest publicly traded health benefits companies, with over 11 million medical members and twenty-five thousand associates. Throughout its forty-seven-year history, Humana has seized opportunities to reinvent itself to meet changing customer needs. Humana was founded by two local entrepreneurs as a nursing home company. Later the company moved into hospitals and integrated health care before its decision to focus solely on health benefits. Humana pioneered the way for a consumer focus in health solutions. The company has experienced rapid growth, doubling in size and revenues over the past few years. Today the company retains the entrepreneurial spirit it has embodied since its beginnings.

The Business Case for Leadership Development

When Michael B. McCallister became chief executive officer in 2000, Humana was facing major challenges. The industry was under pressure as health care costs were rising at a double-digit rate and the cost of insuring the corporation's own associate population was forecast to rise dramatically. McCallister determined that we needed to find a different solution that would serve the company, its associates, and its customers. Humana therefore launched a strategy that would place the consumer at the forefront of health care for the first time. The strategy was designed to empower consumers with the information to make informed decisions about their health care in the same way they make other purchasing decisions.

The company's philosophy is that the consumer is the key to addressing cost, quality, and transparency issues in the industry. This change in strategic direction—a move away from a traditional insurance company to a consumer-focused health solutions enterprise—necessitated a significant shift in the way the company operated and how it acquires and develops talent. To realize the goal of becoming the industry leader in consumerism, the CEO declared his intent for Humana to become a learning organization. That vision led to the creation of the role of chief learning officer whose objective was to advance the company's consumerism strategy through learning, and thereby create a learning organization.

Humana's Learning Consortium: A Networked Organization Model for Learning

The creation of the role of chief learning officer (CLO) in 2002 placed the focus on enterprisewide learning with a single senior leader for the first time. The first priority for the new CLO was to assess the current state of the learning organization: identify individuals performing learning functions across the company, ascertain the scope of ongoing learning activities, identify vendor relationships, and estimate the organization's yearly spending on learning activities. At that time, learning activities were performed by disparate teams throughout the company, with learning leaders reporting to their business units and operating with little to no connectivity to other learning functions in the company.

A small core of corporate learning professionals delivered cultural programs and leadership development. This highly decentralized organizational model ensured that learning had a high degree of business relevance to the various business units. The discovery process, however, also indicated a high degree of duplication in programs, vendor contracts that did not leverage volume, and inefficient use of resources. The compelling business challenge was how to develop and scale a single learning strategy that would complement the company strategy without abandoning client-specific learning expertise and focus.

In determining how to structure the learning function, the CLO's goal was twofold: to build a learning organization that aligned the learning strategy with the business strategy and to create an organizational model that fit the culture and added business value.

The Humana Learning Consortium, a networked operating model for learning, was the result of that thinking. The Consortium represents the collective learning community across the company, including over three hundred learning professionals from key business areas. Figure 15.1 depicts the model and its central elements. It is anchored by a shared services model driven by the corporate learning function, business unit learning teams reporting to their respective business units, and a governance component guided by the corporate learning function and representatives from learning teams.

Shared Services Model

The shared services model represents a portfolio of learning resources that can be leveraged enterprisewide. These include a common leadership development curriculum, common competency curriculum, and common online content. It also includes technology components such as e-learning tools and a learning management system. When these areas were selected as shared services, priority was given to having a common and consistent approach across the enterprise. Shared services are largely managed within the corporate learning functions reporting to the CLO, supported by key partnerships with information technology, finance, and human resources. These functions engage the broader learning consortium to identify and prioritize needs, explore opportunities, and drive shared solutions.

Business Unit Learning Teams

The goal of the business unit (BU) learning teams is to advance the strategies of their respective business units through learning. Business unit learning leaders identify performance gaps in their business units, determine how those needs will be met, and design and manage learning interventions. Often training being conducted within the business units is technical or unique to a particular area. When needs do cross areas, the Learning Consortium provides a vehicle through which activities can be coordinated. Where a shared service or tool does not exist to meet the needs, BU learning leaders initiate and manage the learning process from start to finish. In these situations, the BU leaders may tap into the Learning Consortium to identify a practice or resource that was

FIGURE 15.1. LEARNING CONSORTIUM MODEL: THE NETWORKED ORGANIZATIONAL STRUCTURE

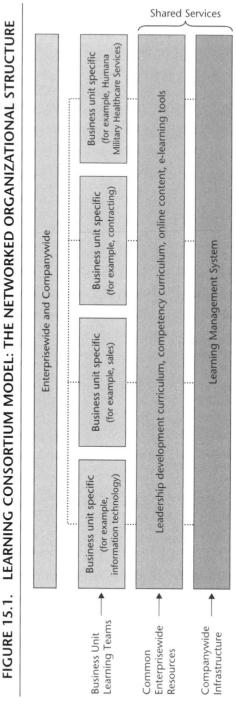

successful in another area, solicit input to increase probability of success, and later share information with other consortium members. In selecting activities to be performed within the business units, priority is given to business relevance and speed of delivery.

Learning Consortium Governance

The role of governance for the Learning Consortium centers primarily on ensuring the continued effectiveness of the consortium. That includes the evaluation and enhancement of the shared services portfolio, alignment and coordination of efforts, and facilitation of information sharing across the consortium. Other active areas of governance are tracking and reporting of learning spending and management of centralized external vendor relationships. The governance function is largely managed within the corporate learning function and supported by partnerships with information technology, human resources (HR), and finance, as well as committees formed around communities of interest.

Rationale for Consortium Approach

The idea of creating an alternative organizational approach for learning emanated from an analysis of decentralized and centralized organizational models. The benefits and drawbacks of centralization and decentralization were thoroughly considered. The consortium model was born out of the realization that while both of these approaches have significant advantages, they also have shortcomings. The goal became to take the best of both approaches and create a new networked operating model— one that would create a unifying framework for learning, leverage scale for efficiency, and keep learning close to the business by maintaining reporting relationships for BU learning teams into the business units.

Launch and Support of the Learning Consortium

Implementing the Learning Consortium began with a communications campaign initiated by the CLO with senior leaders. The goal of those conversations was to engage leaders in dialogue around the business value of the consortium approach and secure buy-in. Leadership support was critical to ensuring participation in the consortium, whose goal is to advance shared objectives through influence leadership and a shared sense of what is best for the enterprise.

Once senior leaders were recruited, the CLO and director of integrated learning held a learning summit to formally launch the Learning Consortium. The goals of the two-day event were to begin building community among learning professionals and establish common goals. Those at the first summit agreed to consolidate vendor contracts and centralize the process for tracking learning expenditures across the company. Subcommittees were established with representatives from across the consortium to drive collaboration on various topic areas. Over the years, communities of practice have also been formed to allow individuals with common interests and disciplines to gather and exchange ideas and best practices. The model is supported by forums such as annual summits, biweekly telephone calls, technology-enabled collaboration forums, and a centralized repository for information sharing.

Successes and Future Focus

The Learning Consortium model, which empowered BU learning teams to focus on their strengths and benefit from shared services, has delivered value in several ways. The model has allowed us to scale learning. Figure 15.2 indicates the extent of increased reach and frequency of learning activities while significantly reducing learning spending. Millions of dollars in cost avoidance have resulted from leveraging volume to negotiate favorable vendor discounts, eliminate duplicate efforts, and increase the use of technology and online learning.

The Learning Consortium has also adapted to other disciplines in the company. Consortium models have been adopted in functional areas, including finance, marketing, and communications, as well as disciplines, including process and business analytics. The model provides a blueprint for how groups can balance the goals of centralization while retaining their unique functional focus. The consortium model provides a network for professionals that enhances peer-to-peer learning, fosters an enterprisewide mind-set, and

FIGURE 15.2. LEADERSHIP DEVELOPMENT COMPASS

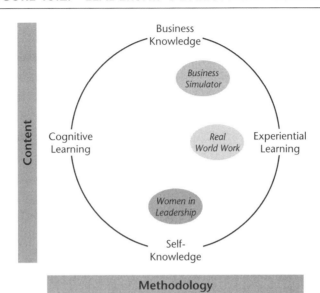

instills a mentality of resource and knowledge sharing. It has also served to raise the profile of talented learning leaders in the broader organization. Learning spending fell 33 percent between 2002 and 2007, while the number of tracked e-learning sessions soared by 5,000 percent and the number of online courses increased by 780 percent in the same time frame.

The Learning Consortium has continued to evolve since its creation. Future areas of focus include building the capability of the learning community through functional and professional development, advancing the talent mind-set of the learning community, and aligning human capital practices to better support networked organizational models across all disciplines.

Lessons Learned

An organizational model that relies on influence leadership and collaboration must seek executive endorsement and identify the benefits for consortium group members and their leaders:

- Find the common value and purpose to keep the group together. Participation will wane without clearly defined reasons to collaborate.

- Instill a mind-set around doing what is right for the business and striking the right balance between individual and group accountabilities.
- Support acceleration though stages of team development using a change management approach. Recognize that it can take time to gain traction.
- Focus on building trust and communication by engaging consortium members in the leadership and process of the consortium. Allow individual voices to be heard.
- Engage consortium members in internal and external professional development opportunities.

The Humana Leadership Institute

Succession management and executive development quickly became the centralized services that complemented the Learning Consortium. The leadership development strategy was created based on early conversations between the CEO and CLO about the company's consumerism strategy and the need for a fresh approach to executive development. Dialogue around the organizational and leadership capabilities required to execute the strategy facilitated the creation of a new set of strategic leadership competencies that included understanding and articulating the business strategy, development of an out-of-industry perspective, collaboration across functional boundaries, and emotional intelligence. The Humana Leadership Institute was created as a forum by which the company could advance the consumerism strategy and develop the competencies needed to take the company in a new direction.

The Leadership Institute focuses development on the company's top 150 leaders and is highly integrated with Humana's succession management program. The integration occurs in two ways: providing an individualized process by which leaders review and select high-potential leaders for personalized development activities and identifying common learning needs, which drive the Leadership Institute's curriculum and system-wide change. This process has provided the ability to tailor individual development plans for high-potential future leaders of the business and look at a variety of leadership development opportunities to support that development.

The leadership development compass illustrated in Figure 15.2 was created to guide choices about methodology and content and blend individual needs with group needs. The content and methodology of each offering in the Leadership Institute can be plotted along two continuums. Content spans from business knowledge on one end and self-knowledge on the other. Similarly, methodology ranges from cognitive understanding to experiential learning. The remainder of this chapter focuses on three key programs within the Humana Leadership Institute that have been particularly effective. Each varies in terms of their placement on the compass.

The Business Simulator

The business simulator was the first major initiative launched through the Leadership Institute. It was an optimal choice for two reasons: first, it engaged business leadership in the process of learning in a way that appealed to their pragmatic nature and technical mind-set. Second, it addressed the strategic competencies of articulating the strategy and working cross-functionally that the CEO had identified as critical.

The business simulator was particularly suited to addressing the issues plaguing health care. It enabled leaders to envision how Humana could drive the shift from a product-focused to a consumer-focused enterprise, now a widespread ideology in the industry. Being at the forefront of this shift, however, presented challenges to Humana's thinking and way of doing business. It became clear that the competencies and thinking of the leaders needed to be augmented in order to move toward the vision. It was also evident that traditional means of training and development would not provide the experience needed to truly internalize and integrate the learning. What was required was a bold learning methodology to complement the consumerism strategy.

Methodology. Partnering with BTS, a world leader in customized business simulations, Humana developed its first simulation in 2003 to address the complexities of its business. The simulation was created with information gleaned from interviews with senior executives and reflected the decisions and dilemmas similar to those that the highest executives wrestle with routinely. Since that time, Humana has developed three additional simulations for the United States with the goal of furthering leaders' knowledge and skills in implementing the company strategy.

Each business simulator is rolled out in two phases: first with the top 150 leaders and subsequently to approximately 300 other senior leaders identified as having high potential. Groups of 40 leaders are invited to participate in two-day Leadership Institute programs that house the simulator. During the selection process, attention is given to ensuring diversity of geographical location, functional area, and gender. That participants receive invitations directly from the CEO underscores the importance of the program.

During the simulation, subteams of five to six individuals run a virtual replica of the company, competing with other teams in the process. Each team member takes on the role of an executive in the mock company, with one individual performing the role of CEO/CFO and others heading up such functions as marketing, HR, sales, information technology, clinical, networks, and legal. The team assumes the helm of the Humana-like company with multiple business models, realistic market situations, competitors, constraints, and external events.

At the start of the process, each team establishes a company strategy, making decisions in areas such as technology investment, sales and service representation, product mix, and associate engagement. Teams are thrown "wobblers": unexpected events that significantly affect their business and require immediate action. In addition to learning from the simulation experience, participants are exposed to "know-how" sessions led by senior executives that cover topics reflecting more subtle ways to drive business success, including consumer and associate engagement. The winning team is the group that has achieved the best results across several key financial and operational metrics.

Successes. Although the primary goal has been to build the business acumen of senior leaders, the purposeful assignment of teams with leaders with different functions, departments, and markets has provided some of the greatest insights. Participants learn the importance of aligning their decisions with a long-term strategy and gain a better understanding of the many factors that affect business decisions. With a more systemic view of the organization, leaders are able to see their place in the end-to-end process and understand the implications of decisions within the company and externally with consumers.

The simulator has been highly successful and has been adapted to build on leaders' knowledge as the business evolves. The methodology has also proven to be applicable within external forums. In the United Kingdom, the simulator is being leveraged to engage health care leaders in dialogue about improving health outcomes in the National Health Service delivery system. Participants in the first session credited the simulation with enabling them to understand the whole system and make better decisions, test ideas in a protected environment, and build stronger team relationships. In addition to being an effective learning tool, this methodology is serving as a differentiator for Humana in the marketplace.

Lessons Learned
- Simulations provide a powerful tool for creating end-to-end systems thinking and reinforcing cross-functional work.
- Simulation taps competitive spirits and provides hands-on learning for busy executives who resist participating in traditional classroom learning experiences.
- Asking participants to assume roles that differ from their functional expertise builds cross-functional understanding and collaboration.

Real World Work

Real World Work is an action learning methodology that brings together a cross-functional cohort of high-potential leaders to examine a business challenge facing Humana. The idea for the program came from the CEO, who acts as sponsor and selects the topics for each group.

Methodology. Each Real World Work cohort comprises eight to ten leaders from across business disciplines. The program begins with a dialogue between the group and the CEO, who provides specific questions for them to explore and answer. Subsequently the group is introduced to an external thought leader who shares subject matter expertise and provides guidance to the group throughout the process. To augment learning, leaders are involved in teaching: each participant is paired with an executive committee member who serves as a mentor during the process.

The Real World Work process is organized into three distinct phases: discover, develop, and deliver. In the discover phase, the cohort agrees on a charter to guide its approach to defining the questions, conducting research, and synthesizing the findings. In the develop phase, the group creates, tests, and develops various solutions. In the deliver phase, the cohort presents recommendations to the executive committee. The average time from cohort formation to presentation of recommendations is about five months.

The Real World Work team focused on perfect service illustrates how the action learning process works. The team was charged by the CEO to articulate what perfect service would look like at Humana with no constraints or limitations. The objective of his question was to drive the creation of a vision for service, and particularly to steer the group away from focusing on perceived organizational barriers or obstacles.

The group began the discovery process by engaging in dialogue about the definition of perfect service, stretching themselves to think beyond standard definitions. They also focused on organizing the team, appointing leaders to manage the process and drive the task to completion. The group formed smaller subteams: one team took responsibility for gathering and analyzing data and another for defining the deliverable for the executive committee and determining how recommendations might be translated into future organizational operations. The second focus for the group was to gather research. An external consultant was invited to share research on best practice with the group. The team conducted its own research internally and externally. Additional benchmarking was completed with on-site visits to a number of companies known for service excellence. Interviews were conducted with Humana leaders to gather internal perspectives on the current state of service and how the company might define and approach perfect service. During the develop phase, the team undertook a comprehensive approach to formulating recommendations, defining the values and principles to support perfect service as well as the cultural impact and change required to achieve it.

The output was a perfect service playbook detailing desired outcomes and enablers across the service organization. This document, coupled with an executive summary, became the basis for the meeting with the executive committee in the final deliver phase.

Successes. This action learning process has achieved success by facilitating resolution of organizational challenges, enabling participants to learn from participating in the process, and disseminating those insights across the organization.

To date, five Real World Work sessions have taken place, and the outcomes compel continued use of this method (Figure 15.3). For example, the session focusing on customer service has produced a number of successes. The perfect service initiative cascaded the message developed by this small group of individuals throughout the enterprise. During perfect service summits, associates engaged in group discussion around improving customer service and operations. Initiatives arising from the summits have significantly reduced administrative costs and greatly improved accuracy rates in claims processing.

In addition to the business benefits, Real World Work has facilitated learning at both the individual and organizational levels. Participants benefit from a process that stretches them to think beyond their functional roles, develop an enterprisewide mind-set, and expand their self-knowledge. By deriving the systemic implications of the multiple processes, they learn to make decisions in accordance. In addition to providing insights for the organization, the process creates new approaches for problem solving. Other benefits of this action learning have included powerful team building, development of leadership competencies, and creating culture change.

FIGURE 15.3.   REAL WORLD WORK SESSIONS TO DATE

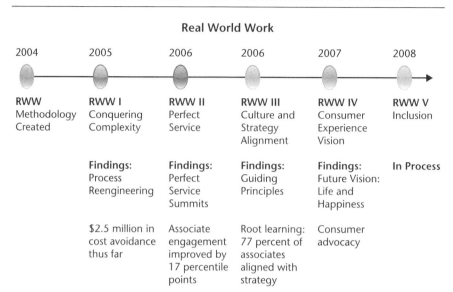

Real World Work

2004	2005	2006	2006	2007	2008
RWW Methodology Created	**RWW I** Conquering Complexity	**RWW II** Perfect Service	**RWW III** Culture and Strategy Alignment	**RWW IV** Consumer Experience Vision	**RWW V** Inclusion
	Findings: Process Reengineering	**Findings:** Perfect Service Summits	**Findings:** Guiding Principles	**Findings:** Future Vision: Life and Happiness	**In Process**
	$2.5 million in cost avoidance thus far	Associate engagement improved by 17 percentile points	Root learning: 77 percent of associates aligned with strategy	Consumer advocacy	

Lessons Learned

- Engage the CEO in selecting the topic.
- Establish mentor relationships between participants and senior leaders: participants will gain perspectives from seasoned executives while leaders gather detailed organizational insights that allow them to own and drive the change process.
- Seek world-class thought leadership on the topic.
- Provide quality facilitation and support for the participants.

Women in Leadership Program

The development of women leaders is a critical imperative to sustaining the growth of all organizations. As in other corporations, women in Humana represent an underused and underdeveloped resource for leadership talent. One factor driving the creation of the company's recent Women in Leadership Program is the desire to increase the internal leadership talent pool significantly to meet the company's future executive leadership needs. By increasing leadership diversity, the company also believes it can bring about greater innovation and better fulfill its core business strategy of

FIGURE 15.4. EXECUTIVE COACHING CYCLE FOR WOMEN IN LEADERSHIP

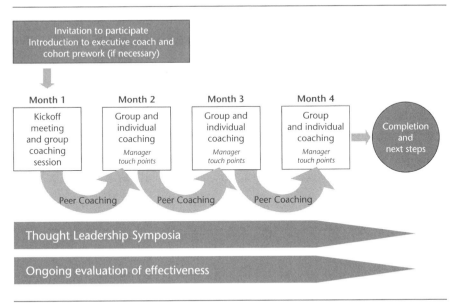

Source: A. Miller & Associates LLC and Humana.

consumerism. Expected outcomes for the Women in Leadership program include improved readiness for succession, enhanced performance and impact, and the capability to encourage an overall coaching culture within the organization, which is critical to creating a learning organization.

Methodology. The Women in Leadership program as outlined in Figure 15.4 targeted the top 150 high-potential women. It has three elements: group and individual coaching sessions with professional executive coaches; peer coaching; and Thought Leadership Symposia, a series of high-impact forums with premier thought leaders. Structured networking opportunities with past and future Women in Leadership program participants augment the experience. The program cycle spans approximately four to five months for each of three groups of twelve to sixteen participants per quarter.

The first element of the program comprises the group and individual coaching sessions conducted by a professional executive coach. The group coaching meetings take place once a month for a half to a full day. During these sessions, participants are exposed to leadership tools and resources and are given an opportunity to apply their learnings to actual work challenges. In addition, senior executives are invited to share insights about their personal leadership journeys. Outside of the group sessions, participants also receive one-on-one coaching sessions, usually conducted by telephone between group meetings. Executive coaches also conduct one-on-one coaching sessions with the participants' direct managers in order to get buy-in and support for the changes the women are making.

The second element of the program, peer coaching, takes place between the group coaching sessions. Subgroups of two to four women leaders convene to provide coaching to one another based on the coaching models they have learned from the group sessions. For the duration of the program, the coach attends some of these meetings with the goal of developing the coaching skills of the participants during the process.

The third element of the Women in Leadership program is Thought Leadership Symposia. The symposia series was developed to provide participants and other Humana leaders with firsthand access to research and expertise from leading academics and business leaders in subject matter areas that connect to organizational development needs and enterprise-wide change initiatives. One past symposium explored the brain's role in decision making and the influence of unconscious bias, a research area that has informed Humana's approach to diversity and inclusion. In addition to the women leaders, attendees include participants' managers and other Humana professionals invited to share the experience. The goal of expanding the audience is to widen the learning across the organization by enabling many leaders to share and reflect on insights from their common experience.

Success Factors. The program is delivering impact in significant ways. First, the combination of having executive coaches on premises and creating peer coaching teams has allowed an expanded segment of the leadership population to benefit from executive coaching in a cost-effective manner. Second, the personal transformations that have occurred with individual leaders are creating a ripple effect within the organization: as the participants gain skill in giving and receiving feedback and trust in their individual approaches to leadership, they are creating the culture around them and replacing the myths about what leadership approaches lead to success. The net result is more open and honest dialogue between the participants and their managers, which leads to authentic feedback and coaching. Third, the networks built inside the program have shown sustainability outside the program, with program alumni organizing formal and informal meetings to support one another. Finally, it is believed that the Women in Leadership program will be a tool by which the company's talented women leaders can better understand and develop their strengths and achieve their career goals. Promotions and role changes that have come about as a result of the program have demonstrated early success in this area.

A few factors differentiate Humana's Women in Leadership program from others and have contributed to its success. The first is its multifaceted approach: several learning methodologies have been incorporated into the program. Each learning experience builds on the others and recognizes that there are various learning styles and preferences. The second is its focus on using a coaching versus a training methodology. This is designed in line with the program objectives of enabling women leaders to be authentic and strengthen their own leadership approaches and away from the notion of fitting into prevailing leadership styles and techniques.

Lessons Learned

- Take the time to set the context for the program with each participant and her manager to ensure everyone fully understands the structure and objectives of the program and their roles. A thorough on-boarding process will increase receptivity to the initiative and the time commitment required.
- Involve senior executives in the kickoff session. Ask them to speak to the importance of the initiative and share their personal leadership journeys with the group.
- When launching an important initiative, refine and define process excellence for internal program managers and external coaches.

Critical Success Factors

Several key factors have contributed to the success of learning and leadership development at Humana. The most important success factor has been to take an approach that respects and works within the company's unique culture. Some organization models and interventions work in some companies where others will not. Finding the approach that best fits a company's unique culture is critical to building and sustaining momentum. What is more important than having a textbook-perfect approach is facilitating the conversations that engage senior leaders and inspire them to take ownership of learning. Executive buy-in and involvement are critical for substantive change to occur. In order to get buy-in, learning leaders must be able to demonstrate an understanding of the business strategy and design a learning strategy that complements the business strategy.

Future Areas of Focus

Over the next couple of years, the intention of the corporate learning function is to build on the successes of the programs and models outlined in this chapter. Further adaptations of the business simulator are taking place to facilitate community dialogue with external stakeholders in the health care system. In addition to creating learning for Humana leaders around the company strategy, the simulator also demonstrates to external stakeholders a new approach to problem solving. A second area of focus is to augment the leadership skill sets that will enable them to build on the networked operating model across the organization. The intent is to increase the use of technology and the Internet to build collaboration and virtual leadership skills in those groups and other teams. Finally, the role of learning will increasingly focus on developing the decision process skills and knowledge of leaders across the enterprise so that they are able to help teams and groups to be more effective.

About the Contributors

Raymond L. Vigil is vice president and chief learning officer at Humana. He is responsible for the Humana Leadership Institute, succession management, organization development, and the Learning Consortium, a networked operating model for learning. Prior to joining Humana, he held senior-level leadership and human resource positions with Lucent Technologies, Jones Intercable, US West, and IBM.

◆ ◆ ◆

Elizabeth H. George is the director of human capital integration at Humana. She is responsible for defining and communicating the company's employment brand. Prior to joining Humana, she was an organizational consultant and headed the learning function for a division of Merrill Lynch Europe.

◆ ◆ ◆

Robin K. Hinkle is a learning consultant at Humana. Her focus is on researching and evaluating the impact of organizational development initiatives on human capital performance. Prior to joining Humana, she held a fellowship at the Army Research Institute at Fort Knox, Kentucky.

CHAPTER SIXTEEN

DELL

This chapter outlines specific best practices for leveraging
executive coaching as an integral part of a comprehensive
leadership development strategy.

As Dell continues to evolve as an organization, so too does its leadership development infrastructure. Today, the company's efforts around leadership provide a model for maintaining leadership development systems that are consistently renewable, sustainable, and relevant.

In this chapter we address two main aspects of Dell's leadership development practices: a review of its leadership development strategy and how this takes place in the global corporation through the success case of its coaching program. Among the many methodologies adopted for Dell's leaders, one of the most significant and mature is its coaching system. We have been using coaching as a key part of leadership development strategy for over ten years. During this time, it has come through the same transformation the business has and is now aligned and centrally coordinated through one global vendor. This chapter provides the background context for this journey and shares how to leverage seamless execution around coaching with an organizational approach to leadership to produce results for any business.

Context

Business sustainability and growth have always been a mix of art and science, a practice that requires leaders to bridge present and future, the aspiration with the possible. One may say that leaders create reality the way artists do: by applying specific techniques to creative work in a way that the outcome, useful and aesthetic, is also unique and powerful.

These are times for leadership artists to become masters of art in order to deal with complexity. In the new millennium, the most limiting factor for growth in global corporations will be a sustained ability to create leaders who respond to challenges in the same way artists approach a masterpiece: with extraordinary proficiency at technique and unique sensibility at adapting and leverage the context.

Therefore, the main issue is how to create the leadership capacity that breaks limitations and takes us to the next level of performance. We believe that the answer lies in the ability to connect the business development agenda and strategy with the people development agenda and strategy.

Like many other global corporations, Dell has gone through a deep examination of its leadership development strategy. Similar to a school of art, this leadership development effort is intended to bring together state-of-the-art technique with practice. The metaphor of art applies in this case because the ways in which every leader will develop those techniques are diverse and unique. Technique has limits; individual imagination does not.

Much has been written about Dell, the company that made the computer a mass market product, the one that became direct in every way possible inside and out, and that is the manifestation of something more lasting and vital than a business model: the business philosophy of customer intimacy and ultimate customer service of Michael Dell. We have had inflexion points and challenges along the way and recently, in changing the executive team, took a hard look at how we are working, what assumptions we are making, and how this translates into a lesson that makes our leadership art school become a competitive differentiator and catalyst for change.

The common concept is that leadership development is related to training, development, selection, and assessment. However, in most durable, successful corporations at the global scale and complexity, this is only half the story. Bob Galvin, former CEO and chairman of Motorola Corporation, wrote many years ago that the most critical competence for a company is its ability to renew itself—not only the ability to address the next big hurdle but to become what it needs to be to stay relevant and vital. In other words, change is not enough; transformation is needed. This is how leadership becomes an art. At Dell we have the aspiration to develop leaders who are change agents and have a blueprint in mind that is unique and responds to a future picture that others cannot see.

That is what Dell considers leadership to be about: a search, a journey, a blueprint, a music score for a grand global orchestra. The unique aspect of this orchestra is the fact that is built not from individual musicians but rather from jazz ensembles with diverse backgrounds and personality.

Priorities

Similar to other global corporations, the priorities for Dell's leadership development strategy are related to developing succession for most senior positions, making sure talent is lined up to cover future critical jobs in new markets and also take care of the basics: solid management across the world and leadership bench strength. What is unique for Dell at this moment is the renovation and reinvention of this corporation. We are changing dramatically in every aspect of the business while running the company at what is commonly known as "the speed of Dell."

This chapter illustrates how Dell is working to produce that leadership capability as a form of art, considering technique and environment. We do not claim we have achieved its potential but believe that sharing the design and its components, as well as the ways in which it is working now, is valuable to readers in search of practices that can work.

Principles

We start with the principles that guided the leadership model.

Clear Mission: Support the Business and Support Its Change

Dell's vision is no different from many others in this function: to make explicit the connection between every aspect of development strategy with critical business priorities. This alone, however, is insufficient. Our experience demonstrates that developing the individual is a great payoff in the mid- or long-term, but dramatic results need something else; we must act at the level of the individual and the level of the organization. This also means supporting the evolving nature of the businesses and recognizing that any truly visionary priority is further ahead than the organization's readiness to act on it effectively. So we do not expect that leadership development translates into organization effectiveness immediately. We chose not to leave that critical translation to chance.

Our distinctive approach to global talent management is rooted in the ability to create the leadership that catalyzes change and increases organizational readiness for that change. That is why our organization development team is part of the talent management team. In other words, we support the business by acting in two dimensions: individuals and organization (teams). We support the development of leaders who are agents of change and at the same time increase the readiness of their organizations to deal with those transformations. Approaching solutions in this two-dimensional approach makes work integrated and collaborative among human resource (HR) professionals and makes it easier for clients to understand. The result is less complication and more impact.

Focus: Differentiated Investment, Meritocracy, and Leadership

This is not a story of the chosen few but rather a story about clarity, focus, and return on investment (ROI). For reasons that are well documented and researched in that literature and also because of pressures to keep the best and the brightest, most companies today have sophisticated processes to rank and differentiate their people. At Dell, we do all the right things most other serious talent-oriented companies are doing, but we chose to differentiate ourselves from others by being strategic at deciding what to do after the differentiation. Beyond the immediate and obvious rewards and recognition, the question is about investment and ROI. How do we allocate resources to keep the leadership development process (our own school of art) relevant for both apprentices and grand masters?

Three levels of solutions address leadership development, and each has specific outcomes and value to the organization (Figure 16.1). First is the solution for all managers: it targets 100 percent of the managerial population, and internally we call it "the many." This is a complete management excellence program whose purpose is to ensure management effectiveness across the organization globally, with common standards and practices. This is the program for *all*, and every manager is part of it. The vision around management effectiveness is based on the notion

FIGURE 16.1. THE THREE LEVELS OF SOLUTIONS
TO LEADERSHIP DEVELOPMENT

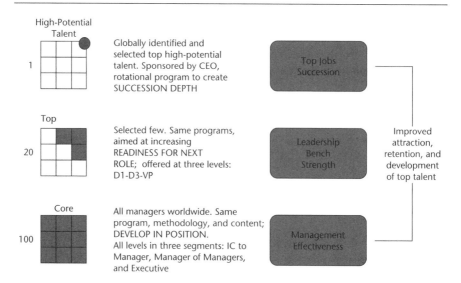

that managers have to be good at all aspects of a well-rounded manager: people, strategy, operation, financial, execution, and global mind-set.

For Dell, this is the foundation and the most critical aspect for ensuring management effectiveness. This will significantly reduce the chances for anyone to experience poor management and thus increase engagement and retention. It sets the bar relatively high for performance with global consistency. This core development responds to a managerial life cycle approach. That is, the courses and tools are built according to our definition of value in the life cycle: a legacy. We frame the stages in terms of getting that legacy defined, initiated, built, and delivered. A life cycle approach to job rotations helps managers understand the importance of developing others, arguably the ultimate legacy for sustained transformation capability. This is our own version of Bob Galvin's renewal mandate. Management effectiveness is, in consequence, the ability of managers to deploy their employees' full potential in alignment with business goals.

But we also wanted to guarantee that being a high-potential employee is not necessary to experience a world-class quality experience and content. We offer courses with extraordinary content, tools, and the usual types of services: assessment, coaching, and mentoring. The vision is to consolidate all management programs across the globe into one Dell courseware and set of tools.

Following in our differentiated investment approach, we have the solution for what we call "top talent": the top 20 percent, whom we call "the few." We have specific solutions for leadership development geared at this select group.

We divide the top 20 percent in three groups: senior managers, directors, and vice presidents. Each level contains a process that includes a thorough identification, assessment, coaching, learning sessions, peer coaching, and action learning. Our goal with this group is to create leadership capability across Dell and therefore add to the leadership bench in the mid- to high-management ranks. The purpose and outcome of having top talent investment is to create something beyond management effectiveness: leadership capability. In other words, the solution for the many is to guarantee that people are being managed by "certified" managers, while the top talent program, also called "leadership acceleration," is to strengthen the bench for the next critical jobs. The value proposition for top talent is transformation capability; it goes back to Galvin's statement that these talented employees will sustain transformation and therefore ensure a solid pipeline at regional levels to support growth.

In the final category are the highest-potential individuals: we call them "the unique." This is the 1 percent highest-potential talent. At the most senior levels, these individuals are the identified successors to the twenty-five to forty highest-level jobs in the corporation. As we move lower in seniority, we will have people who are not strictly attached as successors for specific jobs but represent the caliber of talent wanted for the top one hundred to two hundred jobs worldwide. This is a group of truly exceptional individuals who are game changers by nature. We consider them enterprise property. Unlike the other levels of talent previously identified, individual business units have no discretion to assign critical jobs to this group. For this audience, the executive leadership team decides their next assignments. The proposition is clearly to guarantee succession and should not be confused with readiness only. The idea behind this investment is not to enhance leadership capability alone but to educate, groom, and prepare the next generation of people who will define Dell's transformation.

In the past, Dell spent 80 percent of its budget in the core programs for the many. This was the case in part because each region or business unit had its own leadership academies, accounting for massive duplication and overlap. Today the vision is to even the spending to about one-third on each category: the many, the few, and the unique. We achieve this by having a consolidated core program that is globally consistent and by using alternative learning technologies and providing tools, not just courses.

Accountability: Global Coordination, Ownership, and Sponsorship

We expect regions to have total responsibility for certain grades of talent (midmanagers) and below and to own development decisions in general, providing this service to all business units in those regions; we call these groups *regional leadership pipelines*. We also expect the global businesses (all of them global organizations) to have total responsibility and own the development of the senior managers and above. In this way, they keep track of the senior-most talent globally; we call these groups *global business pipelines*. Both regions and global businesses execute talent management and leadership development processes that are defined centrally by the Global Talent Management center of expertise at the corporate offices.

The rationale for this decentralization of talent management is to focus on connecting the development cycle with the business cycle— that is, to make sure the best talent is assigned to the most important jobs at the right levels. Having regional pipelines will allow regional teams to identify their critical jobs locally and move people across business units, offering a larger array of experiences to more junior talent. As the levels increase and become more global and complex, decisions about assignments are made at global offices of business units, and the talent pools necessarily have to include people from all regions. Nevertheless, the goal is to make sure the best people are in the most critical jobs at the right time.

In addition, we work separately with top executives in a centralized way. We call this group *enterprise talent*. The concept here is that certain individuals belong to the corporation, not to the business units. Therefore, their next career moves, compensation, and all aspects related to development are centrally monitored and decided in concert with business units.

Decentralizing part of this talent management activity is critical for business growth but also for retention of the best and the brightest. These people need to know there is a plan and there is a path, and that they are not confined to a place or a group. This is the one place not best suited for improvisation and is one of the fundamental tenets of talent management for the new generations.

Outcome Orientation: Perform, Develop, Transform, Reinvent

We make decisions about content, processes, and developmental experiences based on our expectations of main accountability and the contribution of each major level in the organization. This is, managers in lower grades are responsible for aspects more related to execution and productivity of the workforce. As we move up in the levels, the accountabilities change from productivity to vitality of the organization; and at the highest levels, vice presidents are responsible for sustainability, long-term vision, and growth (Figure 16.2).

The horizontal arrows, representing the core program for the many, help participants excel at their level and therefore substantially increase their ability to deliver on the contribution, not on the subjects of management disciplines alone, such as strategy, people management, or financial acumen, but in the aggregate, in the emergence of those disciplines to produce what the corporation truly needs: high performance and execution, business and talent development, organization capability and business growth, and the definition of what is next. In order to contribute at this level, managerial skill is not enough; we need managerial art.

Leadership acceleration strategies for the few and unique are intended to help the best talent cross the threshold and start executing at the next level (as suggested by these arrows), therefore being increasingly ready for a next critical assignment.

FIGURE 16.2.   STRATEGIC CONTRIBUTIONS OF DELL LEADERS

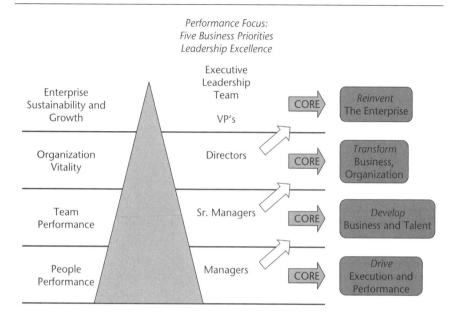

This model has been very useful in producing insights into managers going through the transition between levels and provides common language and direction to coaches, internal and external, during on-boarding and other feedback sessions.

Clear Expectations: Competencies, Accountabilities, and Contribution

Since the beginning of this renewal effort, it was clear that the competency model needed updating because although Dell had changed, the leadership model had not. In five years, Dell had doubled its size and revenue and had gone through significant transformation that redefined the priorities for the entire organization. Major transformation requires new expectations of employees and managers.

The new model is built on a solid foundation. A small team of experts ensured we used thorough data collection, external benchmarking, and interviews with all executives in the executive management team. It was particularly interesting that at least half of these executives had been with Dell less than one year by the time of the study, and their influence was visible as they advocated dropping some technical language in the previous model and adopting a more simplified approach to have fewer competencies that were more focused on a diverse, global audience.

The model consists of three categories or clusters of competencies—engage, execute, and excel—for a total of eight competencies. There is a fourth area we keep separate because we will not develop against those competencies; we will use that cluster mainly as criteria for hiring, or "ticket to entry." This competency model is just being released, and the HR teams are working on the process of aligning the development and talent management tools, promotion criteria, courseware, and assessment to reflect and support those new competencies.

One Dell Curriculum: A Globally Consistent Dell Way for Leaders

To support the vision, we created the new Dell global leadership curriculum, consistent across all businesses and regions and designed to provide solutions for all managers and the top talent eligible for leadership acceleration. This program is a set of stimulating activities that use multiple learning technologies to enhance the learning experience.

Participants interact with peers in face-to-face and virtual networks, gain a better understanding of their leadership style, and gather deep knowledge through leader-led sessions and computer-assisted business simulations. Participants leave with more insight, more leadership tools, and more skills they can use to immediately maximize their potential at Dell.

The vision of this curriculum is to have several key components (Figure 16.3):

- *Process, not programs.* We wanted to eradicate the notion that the development experience is all about the five-day session and the great fun and impact of a masterful team of presenters. Development is a comprehensive process that extends far beyond and begins far before the session.

FIGURE 16.3. GLOBAL LEADERSHIP CURRICULUM

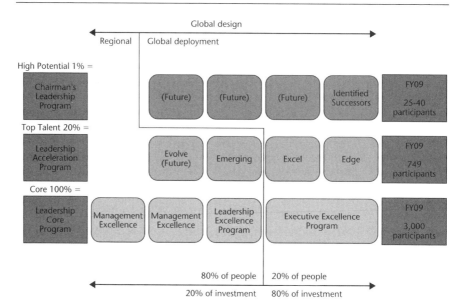

- *Relevant content.* The goal is to ensure a clear understanding of issues, not just an aggregation of themes, and how these build up to create contribution.
- *Varied learning technologies.* We wanted to stay away from lecturing, even if very engaging. We are strongly advocating for simulations, more comprehensive assessments, and the strategic use of coaching.
- *Manager involvement.* We are creating a process that involves the manager as partner for development. The critical aspect of this approach is to keep it very simple or people will not do it. Mainly it is about providing a simplified version of what the program is intending to create at the outcome and behavior level so participants can discuss this with managers and establish commitments against that.
- *Assessment.* We are enlarging assessments to include a larger range: from self-assessments all the way to big investments on assessment centers for the top successors.
- *Have an impact on all participants' development plan.* The goal is to make sure this will stick and have a longer life in people's consciousness than the duration of the program.

- *Coaching and mentoring.* We need to reframe coaching to mean all of the above.

Building Global Platforms Through Strategic Partnerships: A Case Study of Dell's Executive Coaching Program

Dell's approach to leadership at the holistic level is an amalgamation of widely accepted best practices tailored to the needs of the company. This is a task that all leadership development practitioners must face, and one that is considered to be a widely accepted but rarely mastered best practice. Many understand that this critical challenge is dependent on a number of organizational variables—size, industry, global scale, budget, leadership priorities, and others—and cannot be generalized into a universal approach.

The coaching process at Dell has evolved to tackle numerous challenges, some of which are unique to Dell but many of which are universal:

- Should my company use an internal coaching approach or pursue a partnership with an external vendor?
- If we wish to stick with a vendor, how should my company maximize the value of that relationship?
- How do I ensure coaching that is both effective and best exemplifies the goals and priorities of the organization?
- How do I measure the ROI on my organization's coaching efforts?

All of these universal questions are deeply rooted within the design of our coaching system, and the answers can be found in the methodology we use.

Dell is facing the challenge of maintaining relevance and vitality in a coaching process that has been tremendously successful. As a result, we are constantly revisiting and reexamining these questions. We believe that our efforts around coaching provide a great means of answering these critical questions while keeping a strong focus on the future.

Here we examine one aspect of our experience that serves as an example of how the principles come together. This new model is rational, grounded, and supported by mechanisms that keep it flexible. Dell's people are expected to address issues directly, act on them decisively, move to the core, and execute to completion. Perhaps that is the reason that one of our best success stories is our coaching program.

Coaches at Dell are artists too. They help leaders connect the touch points to create contribution and vitality for themselves and others around them. Coaches help leaders effectively "paint" their leadership on to the unique canvas of leading their teams and conducting business.

Coaching is not easy to deploy in a global corporation without quickly going into significant spending or marked inconsistency. A great partnership has allowed us to manage the complexity of providing coaching to executives worldwide, and we believe it deserves to be known for others to replicate.

Since 2003, we have provided a structured and focused executive coaching process for over five hundred executives worldwide in what may be one of the largest coordinated efforts of its kind. It replaced a previously decentralized process that faced differing approaches, instruments, coaches, and pricing. Today the program is consolidated under one vendor, offering a specific methodology, companywide reporting, comprehensive coach screening, and measurable results.

As Dell has grown, so has the use of executive coaches. Executive coaching was embraced early by leadership as an excellent way to meet the growing needs of leaders. But by 2003, coaching had become uncoordinated and difficult to control. Coaches were managed at the business unit level, and differing methodologies, philosophies, and instruments were operating throughout the company. Coaching was not linked to leadership development or talent management strategies. With these countless coaches and coaching firms, we were unable to be consistent in costs and manage spending on coaching. At the same time, we were unable to offer a best practice and consistent approach for all of our leaders.

A team of global learning and development leaders from across the business began to formalize a centralized approach to executive coaching. Standards were devised relating to coaching purpose, assignment lengths, and impact metrics. Agreements on coach qualifications were established, which included formal education, business experience, years of coaching experience, and the extent of senior-level coaching experience.

This effort led to a worldwide search for a single coaching vendor. The vendor would need an action-oriented coaching methodology, worldwide reach, and experience in achieving measurable results. Vendors were interviewed in Austin and their coaches screened, and vendor finalists were invited to a "reverse auction" process, where a negotiated contract rate would be established. We selected a single vendor: CoachSource.

In selecting an external provider for coaching, the following characteristics were key to the decision making:

- Significant experience in coaching at the executive level and demonstrated success in behavior change at the executive level.
- A coaching process that matched Dell's: on-the-job practice, behaviorally focused, measurable outcomes, and adaptable.
- Coach quality. Coaches possess the knowledge, skills, experience, and style that will enable them to be successful in coaching engagements. Coaches possess the required or preferred levels of experience and education.
- Ability to provide a consistent level of coaching globally.
- Vendor possesses strong coaching management capabilities.
- Cost.

The keys to success in building a mutually beneficial relationship with our coaching vendor include:

- *Frequent and regular communications.* This includes not only communications from the vendor to the program manager but the communications between the coach and the stakeholders (coachee, manager, learning and development, and HR). These communications happen in various forms: e-mail, quarterly conference calls, bimonthly progress updates, coach use reports, coach satisfaction reports, and leadership effectiveness mini-surveys for measuring behavior change.

• *Clear accountability.* Having one global coaching provider has made managing an important resource such as coaching easier and more efficient.

• *Common vision/one team.* We view and treat the coaching provider as an extended member of the learning and development team. To accomplish Dell's leadership strategy vision, it is critical for all players to have a common understanding of the mission, vision, goals, and objectives at stake and the critical roles each plays.

Program Structure

The audience for coaching at Dell consists of the top and high-potential vice presidents, directors, and, in limited cases, nonexecutives. Coaching is used to accelerate their development or, for leaders in transitional roles, general leadership performance. Coaching focuses on specific behavioral change: helping good leaders get even better.

Executive coaching is one of the key development efforts used in individual development planning and also optimized as part of our semi-annual organization human resource planning (OHRP) process. The approach is largely aligned with Marshall Goldsmith's methodology: leaders are expected to follow up regularly with their key stakeholders regarding their development objectives, a concept popularly known as feedforward. This approach is action oriented and fits well with Dell's direct culture.

Coordination of coaching and its fit with our development efforts rests with each business unit, while the overall effort is managed at the global level. We work closely with the coaching owners in the businesses, who remain involved in the approval and management of coaching efforts for their leader population.

Coaching is also built into specific global top talent and high-potential programs. Each leader receives a set number of hours of coaching in support of learning in the program, with specialized coaches from the mainline program outfitted in the nuances of these programs. The commitment is not just to offering programs but also to comprehensive development processes by continuing the learning beyond the classroom and integrating learning from the classroom back on the job.

The Process

We often joke about the "speed of Dell" because we move so quickly. People joining Dell comment that a few months elsewhere feels like a few days here. A leader is in a position just eighteen months on average before being rotated.

Because business moves so quickly at Dell, there is an expectation that leader growth and development move quickly as well. Therefore, coaching assignment lengths are quite short compared to other companies. Vice presidents receive four to six months of coaching and directors and nonexecutives two to four months. Very clear and realistic outcomes are outlined with these time frames in mind.

Coaches are expected to hold the executives accountable for these assignment lengths. The coach screening process includes an assessment of a coach's speed and action orientation. Leaders need to justify coaching beyond the set lengths.

Coaching is conducted both face-to-face and by telephone, arranged at the discretion of leader and coach. Coaches also engage the leader's manager and other key stakeholders, such as HR, along the way. Action plans are developed and shared with others. Coaches submit periodic progress reports on their activities to the leader, manager, supporting leadership development, and HR personnel.

Coaches adhere to our competency model and supporting 360-degree instrument. They also examine a leader's performance review, Tell Dell (culture survey) results, and other instruments (we generally prefer the Hogan Assessments and Myers-Briggs). To ensure consistency, we do not endorse the use of other tools in these programs.

Our partnership with the coaching vendor is robust. To support the need for information, the coaching partner has created an online coaching management database. A team of two to four external professionals monitors all activities: new assignments, ongoing progress, billings, and special requests. Monthly utilization reports are run for each business.

Many coaching management processes are automated, greatly reducing administrative challenges. As a result, we are able to get needed data with several hours notice, something we were not able to do internally.

Worldwide Pool

We have a strong worldwide pool of coaches, all of them external independent practitioners. Potential coaches are screened and approved by CoachSource and provided a telephone orientation. We then conduct one to three interviews with our learning development personnel.

We require a minimum of five years as a coach to senior management and ten years in business roles (line or staff or as a consultant to business). We also look for an advanced degree (Ph.D., M.B.A. or M.A. or M.S.) in organizational behavior, organizational psychology, or a related field. We prefer coaches working in large multinational corporations, with a good base of high-technology clients. Because of the nature of executive-level discussions, coaches may not work simultaneously with Dell competitors.

Coaches must be a good fit with Dell's culture. Only three-quarters of the coaches proposed to us by our coaching partner are eventually accepted into the pool. This is due to our tight review of the coach's match to our culture. We seek coaches who are direct, action oriented, and quick on their feet. We have turned down many impressive coaches because we felt they were too wordy or verbose or slow moving for this culture.

Coaches must generally complete several successful director assignments before being assigned to vice presidents. Only the highest-rated coaches and most Dell-experienced coaches work with our top 1 percent of leaders.

The coaching pool now has ninety-one coaches, and they reach around the world, near our major facilities: fifty-three coaches in the Americas; eighteen in Europe, the Middle East, and Africa; and twenty in Asia and the Pacific. We have coaches in sixteen countries. A Web site with information on every Dell coach, divided by region and competency specialties, is an additional resource.

We have had good success matching coaches against our leadership competency model. Coaches indicate two to three competencies that are their particular specialties. Therefore, leaders with development objectives in certain competencies receive coach recommendations most specific for their needs.

Coaching Community

To keep the worldwide pool of coaches updated and connected, calls with coaches are hosted quarterly. Dell news, learning and development updates, and coach feedback are generally included in each.

A first-ever worldwide forum brought a majority of the Dell pool and Dell global learning and development team together in April 2006 to identify ways to continue to increase the effectiveness of coaching. This effort strengthened the partnership between Dell and the coaching network, increased coaches' knowledge about Dell, and encouraged best practice sharing among all. Coaches were also familiarized with assessment tools being introduced in the global leadership development programs.

The response to the invitation to attend was overwhelming. Thirty-seven coaches came from around the world. They were joined by approximately twenty-five learning and development professionals who were "coaching owners" within their respective business units.

The event presented a mix of networking, business, and best practice sharing. Day one included a review of Dell's business results with a senior finance executive, an overview of Dell's new global talent management and leadership development initiatives, and presentations from famed coaches Marshall Goldsmith and Kate Ludeman. Day two focused on best practice sharing, gathering feedback, and exploring merging coaching needs at Dell. Day three included a certification on an instrument that Dell uses frequently in its executive leadership programs. The intention was to help coaches become familiar with this tool because many of their leaders would have this additional source of data. External coaches who attended valued the opportunity to complete the certification as an added benefit of their relationship with Dell.

Outcomes

It is important that Dell is able to measure the effectiveness of this effort. Dell needs to know if we are achieving the desired results to justify our spending. Each assignment has two online metrics: the Coach Satisfaction Survey and the Leadership Effectiveness Survey, both custom designed.

The Coach Satisfaction Survey, generally launched after one to two months of coaching, evaluates the participant's satisfaction with a number of aspects. Results to date have been very impressive: 204 surveys rating forty-two coaches have provided very positive feedback, with average ratings above 4.6 on the 5.0 scale (see Figure 16.4). Written comments are also provided. Coaches with low scores on this survey are informed, and may be removed from the coaching pool if the low ratings persist for more than one or two assignments.

The Leadership Effectiveness Survey is conducted at the conclusion of each assignment. In this mini-survey, key stakeholders (direct reports, peers, boss, and others) are asked about the leader's improvement since coaching began using a seven-point scale.

Figure 16.5 shows the results from raters (23 is less effective, 0 is no change, and +3 is more effective). Fifty percent of raters felt leaders improved at a +2 and +3 level. Eighty-one percent of raters indicated improvement at a +1, +2, and +3 level. The average improvement score was +1.30 (we are generally pleased with anything above +1.0).

The third, and perhaps the most desired, albeit most difficult, way to measure the impact of coaching is business results. We are just

FIGURE 16.4. COACH SATISFACTION SURVEY TO DATE (*N* = 204)

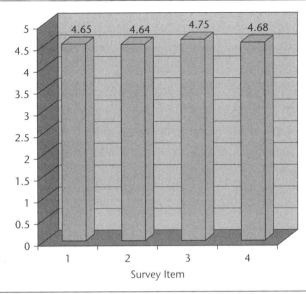

Note: 1 = Clear priorities for growth and development. 2 = Specific, actionable suggestions and advice. 3 = Communicated in a direct and concise manner. 4 = Satisfied with the coaching experience.

beginning to collect data in an attempt to show that those who have had successful coaching experiences tend to perform better along a broad spectrum of personal and business results than those who do not. It will take some time to collect and analyze data for this longitudinal look.

In the interim, we conducted some interviews among leaders who have used coaching as a key part of their professional development over the past two years. Here are some of the results they attribute to an improved leadership capability through coaching:

"While it's hard to isolate, I believe I've had tremendous business impact resulting from coaching. When I took this business over last year, it was a broken business. I had to step it up as a leader to figure out what was broken and lead the team to fix it. In the past year,

FIGURE 16.5. COACH EFFECTIVENESS RATINGS

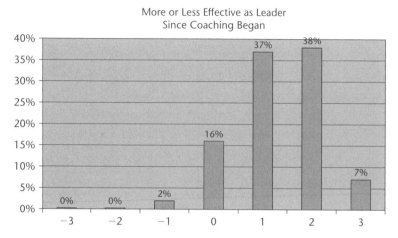

we've gone from a 45 percent attrition rate to 20 percent. We've improved profit by three points. We've gone from single-digit growth to double-digit growth."

"The team did bring in the bottom-line results. They had to implement a number of changes and work better together. Did result in more cost-effective team. Helped me work through a huge recruiting program. OPEX [operating expenses] improved. Asked to take over a very big, complex team across multiple sites with huge growth plans to double in three years. Bottom line? I got promoted!"

"I am now a better manager and can get the best out of my people. I can help them with communications and help the team better. Coaching has also helped me personally to reduce my stress level. It also was a factor in my retention at Dell."

"I had always been able to deliver good results, but I struggled with taking on a challenge where I did not know how to do it: for example, $5 [million] of OPEX [operating expenses], I could see it but not sign up for more, not see the way to $12 [million]. Coaching gave me the confidence to say, 'I will get there.' Bottom line: we signed up for $38 [million] savings. After the first quarter, we are $3 [million] ahead of plan—OPEX plan $10 [million] and $2.2 [million] stretch. We are on track for plan and stretch as well. Customer satisfaction, we targeted to stay at 80 [percent] and no lower; now running at 85 percent."

"Coaching enabled me to enter my new role in another country with a plan. My coach worked with me on a plan that helped me to assimilate into the culture quickly. I gained trust and respect upon arrival. We then focused on our culture. We focused on being a people-oriented culture. We worked on becoming more customer-service oriented. We did lots of things, including launching a big effort to focus on community service. I believe it was the single biggest factor in driving attrition down. We went from a 60 percent attrition rate to a 30 percent attrition rate within six months. We now hover at about 25 percent, which results in a significant cost savings and productivity improvement for the company."

"My team has lower-than-average attrition, high morale, and people want to be a part of this team. This is a tough climate. I don't allow my team to do a lot of non-value-added things. We do high-value-added things and have a positive work environment. My coach helps me by letting me vent and talk through situations so I can drive solutions. She helps me figure out how I can better lead my team and influence the direction of the company."

Some key themes emerged from these interviews:

- Manager engagement is critical. Managers must meet with coaches and be actively involved with development.
- Coaching in executive transitions (to new roles or into the company from acquisition or other, for example) is highly valuable.
- Coaching should be dedicated to high-potential individuals.
- Coach-employee connection is critical.
- The employee level of engagement is also critical. Employees must own and drive to achieve true value from relationship.

- Critical coach skills are being direct and honest, maintaining confidentiality, and demonstrating knowledge of the Dell organization and executives.

Moving Forward

Because this program has been so effective, coaching continues to remain a highly sought after development tool. To help Dell manage processes and coach spending, we continue to look for ways to streamline, create efficiencies, and make sure this program is as effective as possible.

Coaching will be a critical development tool as we continue to evolve and deliver around our leadership development and global talent management strategies. A couple of places we are looking to further integrate or have expanded use for coaching are around our new focus on executive assessments for selection, development, executive promotion, and identification of those with high potential. Some additional strategic uses of coaching we are anticipating and planning for are with executives assigned to lead in emerging markets, high-potential leaders we have placed in large stretch assignments or critical roles, and new leaders from acquisitions. The assignment of a coach will be considered an important support system for these leaders to make the transition, produce results quickly, and prevent derailment.

We will be challenged to meet the coaching needs at the nonexecutive level. We are trying to find ways to provide the same coaching support while continuing to use coaching methodology to build the leadership pipeline.

We are also continuing to find ways to integrate coaching into some other global talent management efforts. We want to use the partnerships with current coaches to bring their skills and Dell experience to other noncoaching needs within the organization.

We are able to pursue these additional efforts due to the close relationship we have with CoachSource. In fact, it is seen and treated as if it were an internal partner, and this is clear from the feedback we receive from our executives who have benefited from coaching.

Conclusion

The story about Dell leadership strategy and its success case around executive coaching illustrate a way in which large companies can deal with the complexities of global deployment, the use of the right concentration of expertise at the point of service, and an enhanced ability to drive and nurture a comprehensive development strategy. For Dell, it is very easy to determine how coaching is performed globally by having a single point of contact to do it. Our energy and time are better spent in ensuring that the right people are receiving this service, that top talent is selected according to the competencies with reliability, and that the future jobs these people hold are connected to those jobs that are most critical for business success.

But this is not a problem unique to very large companies; talent and business connection are just as complex in smaller organizations. We believe that our strategy design principles apply to almost any company that aspires to develop its leaders. Our success case demonstrates a blueprint of a partnership that allows the best concentration of skill at every point in the process. We will continue to foster these kinds of partnerships (external and internal) to build the harmonious leadership required to continuously transform the organization.

We consider the process of leadership development to be a sequence of the right developmental touch points at the right point in people's careers to produce the necessary awareness to enable motion and commitment in the participant. The job of the leadership development strategy is to lay out a road map that facilitates the journey by reassuring employees that there is a plan if they choose to commit and do the necessary work to grow.

In our concept of development, coaching connects all of the development touch points to create a meaningful picture of transformation and self-discipline in the participant's mind and heart.

These key points apply to all types of companies, large and small:

- Change and transformation are the necessary ingredients to develop leaders but also to retain the best and the brightest.
- In order to get the return on investment for development, it is necessary to segment and focus on the many, the few, and the very few or unique, a more rational use of resources and time.
- The main driving force on a successful talent management strategy is the link between its talent development and business development agendas.
- Effectiveness for business transformation requires working with individuals using leadership development and other programs and also working with the organization to ensure that teams are effective and there is receptivity for change. Individual change precedes organizational change.
- Coaching is more than a developmental conversation; it is the glue that helps individuals make sense of the context and information coming their way when they are immersed in comprehensive development efforts.
- Developing partners who can deploy specific capabilities in the development chain is key to program effectiveness. Then everyone engaged will act on the most relevant points of the process with the right skills and expertise.

About the Contributors

Alejandro Reyes is the director of Global Learning and Development for Dell. He joined Dell in October 2006. In his twenty years of professional experience, he worked eight years for Motorola as director of leadership development and executive education, eight years at the

Monterrey Institute of Technology in Mexico as dean of development for Monterrey Tech's Virtual University, business development manager for South America, and head of the quality office. He holds a master of science in manufacturing systems and automation, won the Dana Corporation technology prize in 1992, and is the author of the book *Quality Techniques and Models in the Classroom*, which is being used in Mexico and Latin America for faculty development programs.

◆ ◆ ◆

Ashley Yount is senior manager of global talent development and learning for Dell, responsible for the strategy, development, and deployment of accelerated leadership development and executive coaching. In her sixteen years of experience (the past five with Dell), she has engaged in creating and managing strategies, programs, and processes for executive development, talent management, and organization development. She holds an M.S. in organization development from Johns Hopkins University and a B.S. in psychology from the University of South Carolina. She is the author of "Leaders Teaching Leaders" in *The 2007 Pfeiffer Annual Leadership Development*.

◆ ◆ ◆

Brian Underhill is the author of *Executive Coaching for Results: The Definitive Guide to Developing Organizational Leaders* (2007). He is an industry-recognized expert in the design and management of worldwide executive coaching implementations. His executive coaching work has focused on helping clients achieve positive, measurable, long-term change in leadership behavior. He has also helped pioneer the use of mini-surveys, a measurement tool used to effect behavioral change. He is the founding partner of CoachSource and the Alexcel Group.

◆ ◆ ◆

Steve Sass is the managing partner and chief operating officer of CoachSource and president of Sass & Associates–Performance Consulting. His business career, which spans more than forty years, includes twenty-eight years with IBM in customer service and education executive management, four years as director in charge of the Center for Leadership Development for KPMG, and eleven years as an executive coach and consultant working with individuals and organizations to achieve their true potential. He also facilitates courses in the ASTD Certificate Program in human performance improvement. Sass received an M.S. degree in business policy from Columbia University.

CHAPTER SEVENTEEN

LAND O'LAKES

Leadership Edge Case Study

This chapter outlines a leadership development approach that combines team action learning with innovative strategic games to heighten participant engagement and produce results.

Leadership Edge is a new, ongoing business-based leadership development experience at Land O'Lakes designed especially for high-potential employees at the director level. Leadership Edge, which begins with a robust, three-day learning program, provides these emerging leaders with increased knowledge of the company, customers, and markets; a kit of tools and techniques for developing and implementing strategy; an environment for companywide relationship building with peers and senior leaders; and the opportunity to engage in addressing real-world business challenges through action learning teams.

Setting the Stage for Leadership Edge

Land O'Lakes is a national farmer-owned food and agricultural cooperative with annual sales of nearly $9 billion. A Fortune 300 company, it does business in all fifty states and more than fifty countries. As a leading marketer of dairy-based consumer, food service, and food ingredient products across the United States, it serves international customers with a variety of food and animal feed ingredients and provides farmers and ranchers with an extensive line of agricultural supplies (feed, seed, and crop protection products) and services. Land O'Lakes also provides agricultural assistance and technical training in more than twenty-five developing nations.

Land O'Lakes's vision is to be one of the best food and agricultural companies in the world. To help achieve this vision, CEO Chris Policinski has identified four strategic imperatives for the company and its employees:

- Best cost
- Best people
- Superior insight
- Superior portfolio

Policinski is transforming the Land O'Lakes business structure from its current holding company model, in which business units are more autonomous, to more of an operating company, in which the parent company plays a greater central role, particularly in relation to functions common across diverse business units, such as accounting, information systems, and human resources. Land O'Lakes's modified operating company approach calls for business activities, particularly those that most directly touch the customer or affect the business unit's bottom line, to remain directly under business unit direction and control. As Policinski has stated, "A significant focus in our journey toward more of an operating-company culture has been to bring increased standardization, collaboration, and discipline to all of our processes—including leadership development and succession planning."

Together, the superior insight strategic imperative and move to an operating company culture provided the impetus, inspiration, and foundation for Leadership Edge and an opportunity to drive business change through leadership development.

Green Light for High-Level Development

With a CEO championing renewed focus on leadership development and strong support from the twelve-member senior strategy team that reports to the CEO, the human resource (HR) division moved forward to strengthen the development of higher-level leaders at Land O'Lakes, including officers and directors. Basic leadership training already was in place, but as HR evaluated its programs, it found that director-level development needed attention, especially for high-potential directors, defined as directors who have the desire and potential to be promoted at least two levels and could become officers of the company. These are the emerging leaders and an integral part of the company's succession plan.

As a first step toward developing a program for these high-potential directors, HR examined the annual individual development plans of each of the 215 directors in the company to find what they needed to take them to that next level. Across the board, improved strategic thinking was the most striking need, and that finding would become the foundation for Leadership Edge. The stage now was set for developing the program itself.

Creating a Customized, Business-Focused Development Program

Human resources wanted a multidimensional approach to leadership development that would involve external thought leaders, top-level management, lots of dialogue, relationship building, collective learning, and an environment that encouraged thinking differently about Land O'Lakes and its businesses. The team also wanted to communicate to high-potential directors how valuable they are to the company and that Land O'Lakes is investing significantly in their future.

Leadership Edge Design Team

Human resources began working with the senior strategy team (SST) to identify broad themes for the program. The superior insight strategic imperative was a natural fit, given the company's focus and the development needs of the possible participants. To help design the program, Land O'Lakes brought in MDA Leadership Consulting, a Minneapolis-based leadership development firm.

The SST was given the ultimate responsibility for selecting forty participants from a pool of directors initially identified by officers in each business unit. The company's succession plan was a key factor in the process as SST members evaluated the depth of backup within Land O'Lakes.

To take the program from concept to completion, HR enlisted the SST to invite eight company officers at the vice president level or higher to form a steering committee and represent their businesses and functions. No SST members were part of the committee because they were the final arbiters of the committee's recommendations. The steering committee met for only one hour every two weeks over the course of several months. Once a month, the steering committee provided a program update to the SST.

Developing Program Objectives

One of the first assignments for the Leadership Edge team and steering committee was to develop objectives for this learning experience. From a company standpoint, the objectives were to:

- Promote better understanding of an operating company business model
- Provide leadership development tied to business needs and goals
- Provide information about our industries, customers, and markets
- Introduce common models, tools, and techniques to drive superior insight
- Attract and retain high-potential employees

The program's objectives for the participants included:

- Enhanced strategic thinking skills and the opportunity to use them
- Improved understanding of the environment in which Land O'Lakes does business and of business units other than their own
- Introduction to and hands-on experience with common models, tools, and techniques for developing and executing strategy, including customer segmentation and competitive analysis
- Exposure to the SST and other selected officers through presentations, informal gatherings, and action learning teams
- Stronger and closer relationships with peers across the company
- Recognition of their contributions and value to the company
- Increased commitment to the company's direction and their future with Land O'Lakes; and
- Having fun

To achieve these objectives, the Leadership Edge development team designed a multiyear experience with a number of activities and events, including assessment, a three-day event, and action learning teams

(Figure 17.1). The experience began with a learning event held at a resort and conference center in northern Minnesota.

Shaping Business-Relevant Content

The cross-functional group of officers on the steering committee brought their perspectives to content development but with one universal goal: the content had to be relevant to Land O'Lakes. Rather than being a silent partner, the committee was integral in shaping the Leadership Edge experience. Not only did members suggest topics and speakers, they also challenged proposed design elements such as breakout sessions that would have divided the group into Dairy Foods and Ag Services segments. The committee vetoed those kinds of exercises because they did not support the operating company model.

The final topics for Leadership Edge coalesced around the building blocks of strategic thinking:

- Gathering information
- Formulating information into a strategy
- Competitive analysis and market segmentation
- Implementing the strategy

The agenda for the three-day event was built around these four topics (see Table 17.1).

The Leadership Edge development team drew on steering committee recommendations for presenters from within and outside Land O'Lakes. They wanted the information to be challenging academically and up to date so that participants would experience the type and level of information that more senior leaders in the company use when formulating strategies. For example, Land O'Lakes had commissioned a customer-segmentation study for its Ag Services businesses. The release of those results coincided with the Leadership Edge event, so participants had a preview of the findings. In addition, presenters were coached to break the information into digestible segments interspersed with exercises that allowed the participants to put a concept or theory to use or practice a related skill.

FIGURE 17.1. THE HIGH POTENTIAL LEADERSHIP DEVELOPMENT ACTION LEARNING PROCESS

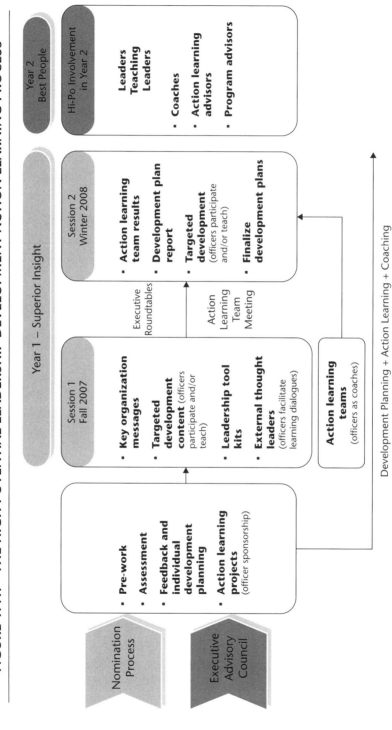

Nomination Process

Executive Advisory Council

- **Pre-work**
- **Assessment**
- **Feedback and individual development planning**
- **Action learning projects** (officer sponsorship)

Year 1 – Superior Insight

Session 1 Fall 2007

- **Key organization messages**
- **Targeted development content** (officers participate and/or teach)
- **Leadership tool kits**
- **External thought leaders** (officers facilitate learning dialogues)

Action learning teams (officers as coaches)

Executive Roundtables

Action Learning Team Meeting

Session 2 Winter 2008

- **Action learning team results**
- **Development plan report**
- **Targeted development** (officers participate and/or teach)
- **Finalize development plans**

Year 2 Best People

Hi-Po Involvement in Year 2

Leaders Teaching Leaders

- **Coaches**
- **Action learning advisors**
- **Program advisors**

Development Planning + Action Learning + Coaching

TABLE 17.1. LEADERSHIP EDGE AGENDA

Timing	Day 1: External Insights	Day 2: Customer Insights	Day 3: Direction and Commitment
Morning	1. Travel time	1. Review/preview	1. Review/preview
	2. Opening/welcome Opening by CEO Program and participant introductions	2. Customer and market segmentation Models Simulation (external consultant)	2. Competitive positioning Generic positioning and tactics Market entry and exit tactics (business school professor)
	3. Future of agribusiness and cooperatives (external consultant)		
Lunch			
Afternoon	1. Consumer trends (external speaker)	1. Voice of the customer	1. Executing strategy (external consultant)
	2. Implications of external insights	2. Amazing Race	
	3. Competitive analysis Models Simulation (business school professor)		2. Program close (CEO)
Dinner	Participants plus all SST members	Plus awards ceremony	
Evening	1. Fireside/bonfire chat (three to four SST members)	1. Action learning teams (SST and officer sponsors)	
	2. Networking	2. Networking	

Exercises 1 and 2 focused on market entry and exit tactics. In exercise 1, across-business groups were asked to determine the best market entry tactics for specific products or services that Land O'Lakes might consider, such as biofuels and organic feed. In the next exercise, cross-business groups were asked to look at products and services in different businesses to identify their place in the product life cycle and determine appropriate exit tactics for them near the end of the life cycle. The third exercise addressed cross-business groups and developed a SWOT (Strengths, Weaknesses, Opportunities, and Threats) analysis for a specific Land O'Lakes business based on information provided by participants from that business unit plus additional information regarding key customers and competitors.

More Than One Way to Learn

Hands-on exercises were just one way to enhance the leadership development and learning experience of participants. Time was set aside each day for journaling about leadership—what participants were learning and their thoughts about their own career and life goals. The first evening, participants were invited to a "bonfire chat" with several SST members who shared their own leadership journeys, the most important lessons they learned in their careers, and one piece of advice for the participants about their own careers.

Presentations, exercises, journaling, and chats with senior executives all helped Leadership Edge meet key objectives. But it was the Land O'Lakes Amazing Race that was designed to build across-the-company relationships in ways that are not possible in a conference room or even sitting by a bonfire.

The Amazing Race

Participants were carefully placed on teams to maximize networking opportunities and achieve a diverse mix of skills on each team. Each team chose a name and colors and then, sporting their colors, the teams were set loose to accomplish a schedule of activities from blindfolded putting to paddleboat races. Not all the activities were physical; some involved mental challenges like brainteasers and Sudoku.

Each race takes roughly three hours, followed by a final challenge. During the race, teams are expected to participate in a certain number of physical or outdoor activities and problem-solving activities. Following the race, teams make brief presentations, finally ending in an awards ceremony to recognize the victors.

Each activity was intentionally designed to highlight a particular aspect of leadership or team building. The teams most successful at these challenges were those that developed a strategy before jumping in to perform the task, consciously considered the skills of their team members, and exhibited a combination of steadfastness and flexibility in implementing their strategy.

CEO Policinski had this to say about the program:

It has been our experience that leadership development is most effective when you combine theory with practical application, when you take
learning beyond the classroom and into the workplace. Leadership Edge
takes that very straightforward, action-oriented approach to learning.
The curriculum and the exercises are driven by real-time organizational
goals, strategies, issues, and needs. Participants learn by applying key
principles to genuine organizational issues. Ultimately, since the issues
are real and the results are real, the learning experience becomes more
real and more effective.

Making Learning Relevant

The first part of the program focused on these elements:

- Providing information and insights about the environment in which
  Land O'Lakes does business: trends, competitors, markets, and cus-
  tomers
- Introducing common models, tools, and techniques for analyzing a
  business and its competitive position
- Developing robust strategies based on that analysis

After each major project, cross-business groups discussed how the information or tools could be leveraged in specific businesses and across Land
O'Lakes as a whole.

The last part of the program was devoted to tactics and tools for
effectively implementing strategies. Participants were introduced to the
alignment model (Figure 17.2), which brings the company's mission,
vision, values, customers, needs, strategies, and action plans into alignment and provides a system for identifying systems, structures, leadership, staff, and skills needed to achieve the business's goals and then
measure and evaluate progress and success. Participants then had the
opportunity to pull together everything they learned in their action
learning teams.

FIGURE 17.2. THE ALIGNMENT MODEL

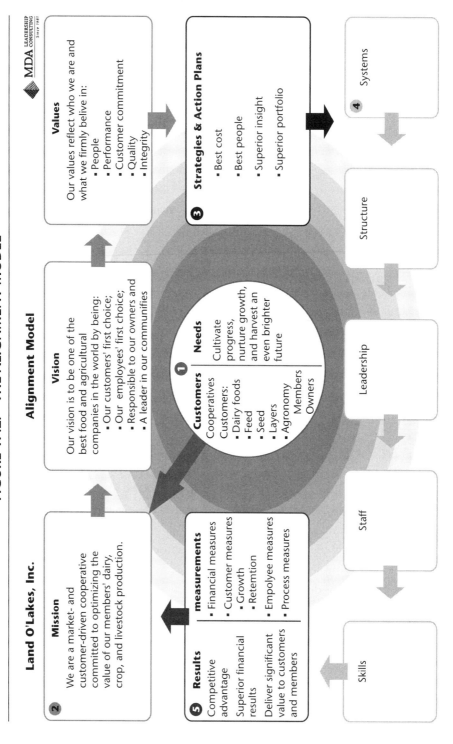

Land O'Lakes, Inc.

Alignment Model

MDA LEADERSHIP CONSULTING
Since 1981

Vision

Our vision is to be one of the best food and agricultural companies in the world by being:
- Our customers' first choice;
- Our employees' first choice;
- Responsible to our owners and
- A leader in our communities

Values

Our values reflect who we are and what we firmly belive in:
- People
- Performance
- Customer commitment
- Quality
- Integrity

③ Strategies & Action Plans
- Best cost
- Best people
- Superior insight
- Superior portfolio

② Mission

We are a market- and customer-driven cooperative committed to optimizing the value of our members' dairy, crop, and livestock production.

① Customers

Cooperatives
Customers:
- Dairy foods
- Feed
- Seed
- Layers
- Agronomy
  Members
  Owners

Needs

Cultivate progress, nurture growth, and harvest an even brighter future

measurements
- Financial measures
- Customer measures
  - Growth
  - Retemtion
- Empolyee measures
- Process measures

⑤ Results

Competitive advantage

Superior financial results

Deliver significant value to customers and members

④ Systems

Structure

Leadership

Staff

Skills

Action Learning Teams: Putting Strategic Thinking into Practice

Following many development programs, the reaction of participants is, "Well, that was interesting, but how am I going to put it to work?" The Leadership Edge development team found a unique answer to that question: action learning teams. Each team was given a strategic challenge related to Land O'Lakes business and three months to develop recommendations for meeting that challenge. Not only did the action learning team concept allow participants to practice their strategic-thinking skills, it also secured critical buy-in from the SST, whose members played key roles in mentoring and coaching the teams (Table 17.2).

To ensure that participants were learning and leveraging their new skills, each was required to create an individual development plan that applied to his or her action learning team project and corresponded with its goals.

The Strategic Challenges. The SST strategic challenges were presented to the action learning teams. With input from their officers, the SST members drew up an initial list of topics they knew needed more scrutiny and wanted to unleash some fresh, energetic talent against. All of the topics had an immediate application to Land O'Lakes business. Some were universal to all business units of the company, and others were more specific. In the end, the final list was a mix of both and included such challenges as sustainability, innovation, and diversity.

The Structure. The forty Leadership Edge participants were divided into action learning teams of six to seven members. Teams were organized to represent a cross-section of the company and a blend of skills, strengths, and weaknesses.

An SST member or officer was assigned to each team as a sponsor, coach, mentor, and resource. In addition, MDA Leadership provided external coaching to bring outside perspective to the process. The sponsors helped the teams frame their strategic challenge. For instance, the team assigned the topic of sustainability first had to determine what sustainability meant in terms of Land O'Lakes and then focus on a particular set of issues. The sponsors also served as sounding boards for the teams, helped keep them on track, pointed them in the direction of other

TABLE 17.2.   ACTION LEARNING TEAM CHARTER EXAMPLE

Action learning team members Sponsor	Names, titles, contact information
Team purposes • Task purpose • Learning purpose	Task Purpose: Brief description of the purpose of the action learning project; the result Learning purpose: Brief statement of what the team and individual members expect to learn as a result of participating in the action learning project (for example, new competencies, enhancing existing skills and abilities, expanding internal network)
Links to Land O'Lakes's organization context	How the purpose of the action learning project contributes to specific organization strategies and objectives, addresses gaps in organization performance, or addresses specific customer needs
Boundaries of the project	Issues outside the scope of the action learning project, beginning and ending points of a process to be improved (if applicable), decision-making authority
Key milestones	Formal reviews, deliverable dates, final deadline
Measures • Progress measures • Success measures	Progress measures: interim task and learning measures Success measures: measures of task outcome and learning outcomes
Team processes	Specific problem-solving and decision-making methodologies, conflict resolution techniques, communication protocols
Resource availability and constraints	Budget, internal experts, equipment, support staff
Team member time commitments	Meeting schedule; full team and subteams (if appropriate)
Sponsor time commitments	Meetings that will include team sponsor
Learning coach time commitments	Meetings that will include team learning coach

resources such as people or experts they may not have been familiar with, provided perspective, and reacted to and challenged their findings. For example, a sponsor might ask the team about the ideas they discarded to further the participants' understanding of the strategic thinking process.

But the sponsors did not do the work. As one SST sponsor said, "My team did all the heavy lifting. I was there as a resource for them." The sponsors also scheduled regular and informal check-ins with the teams and individuals, increasing the participants' exposure to and interaction with these seasoned leaders.

FIGURE 17.3. LAND O' LAKES HIGH POTENTIAL LEADERSHIP DEVELOPMENT ACTION LEARNING PROCESS

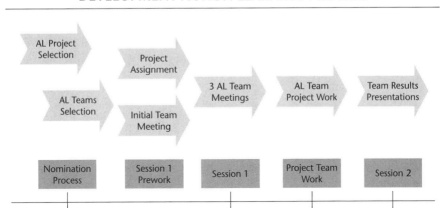

The Action and Learning. The action learning teams were given three months to prepare their presentations. The time frame initially was considered too short by the Leadership Edge development team, but in the end, the participants preferred the compressed period. Figure 17.3 shows the entire time line from nomination of the team members to program completion and results presentation. The action learning teams were not allowed to hire consultants, but they could bring in experts from around the company and tap into information already being gathered for Land O'Lakes such as surveys and market research.

Each team's first step was to develop a charter that defined the scope of its project, set out its mission and goals, outlined the team's work process, and served as a work contract between the team and its sponsor (Table 17.2).

The teams had to live and breathe what they learned during the formal Leadership Edge event while they worked on these high-profile challenges with high business stakes. And they had to do this on top of their regular workload, an intentional decision by the Leadership Edge development team. The development team did not want participants to become focused solely on one project, which is unrealistic in the real world. While much of the work was done independently, team meetings were also set up. The action learning teams discovered that despite the challenges of remote team members, meetings were most effective when they were face to face and lasted longer than one hour.

The Presentations. Each action learning team presented its findings to the entire senior strategy team. This gave the groups practice conveying results to these high-level executives—something that is not typical for employees at the director level. SST members asked questions and took the teams' recommendations under consideration. The SST has implemented at least one recommendation from each action learning team and all of the recommendations from several teams. Although their work was officially concluded with the presentations, some ALT members were asked to work on the projects through implementation.

Measuring the Program's Success

At the end of the Leadership Edge program, participants completed an evaluation that asked them to rate the various aspects of the program and provide comments and suggestions. On a scale of 1 to 4, with 4 meaning "excellent," the program overall scored 3.92. No segment rated less than 3.31. Not surprising, the Amazing Race scored 3.79 and received rave reviews as a networking and team-building exercise that was fun. One participant recommended that a rematch be scheduled in six months to bring the Leadership Edge participants together again. The segment on executing strategy also scored high, 3.69, which pleased the development team since this was the crux of the program (Table 17.3).

The official survey was one way of rating the program's value, effectiveness, and success. The group also conducted informal interviews to determine how the experience measured up to the objectives. Here is a sampling of what a cross-section of respondents said:

Objective: Promote Better Understanding of an Operating Company Business Model

"The concept of an operating company became more than words. We were putting it into practice and living Chris's [Chris Policinski, CEO]

TABLE 17.3.   LEADERSHIP EDGE EVALUATION RESULTS
(NUMBER OF RESPONSES)

Program Element	4: Excellent	3: Good	2: Adequate	1: Poor	Total Number	Average Rating
Agribusiness insights	26	11	2		39	3.62
Competitive analysis	20	15	4		39	3.41
Fireside chat	18	17	4		39	3.36
Customer/ market segmentation	23	13	3		39	3.51
Voice of the customer	29	11			40	3.73
Amazing Race	31	8			39	3.79
Introduction to action learning teams	14	18	3		35	3.31
Anticipating reactions of customers	16	20	2		38	3.37
Executing strategy	28	10	1		39	3.69
Overall program	34	3			37	3.92

vision for the company. You could feel the cultural shift as we better understood our roles as members of an operating company."

"In an operating company, there's more emphasis on strategically moving talent around. I've been fairly siloed within my division, but now I've been exposed to the potential in other groups. If I had the opportunity to move, I would know so much more about the company than I did before."

Objective: Provide Leadership Development Tied to Business Needs and Goals

"What we learned feels sustainable because, through the action learning teams, we were able to create a strong deliverable related to a real strategic challenge for the company."

Objective: Encourage Collaboration Across the Company

"I don't have a lot of touch points with Dairy Foods, but I learned that we face many of the same issues; just the business units are different. My ability to collaborate across the organization was greatly enhanced by the program. I have new resources as I go through the decision-making process and can seek opinions beyond those I'm familiar with."

"There's amazing talent in the company, and now these people are resources that I can turn to."

"Not only is there a whole new group of people to reach out to when I'm working on a problem, but I can coach others to reach out to some resources they probably didn't know about before."

Objective: Enhanced Strategic Thinking Skills and the Opportunity to Use Them

"I believe I'm thinking more strategically now. Our group has been very tactical, but I think my perspective is broader and that I'm more aware of anticipating changes in the business and thinking about how to manage through them."

"It reinforced the decision-making process for me and let me apply what we were learning to something that's really happening, something that really matters to the company, not just made-up scenarios or exercises."

"This was real-world information. We learned about the segmentation model, and right after the program, I was able to use it two or three times."

Objective: Enhanced Relationships with Peers Throughout the Company

"As a director, I have sixty reports but kind of work in a bubble. Whatever my thoughts are, that's the good idea—no one challenges me, even though I encourage them to. So it was a good experience being exposed to such a talented group of peers who had no problem challenging me! I was a little intimidated, but that's a good thing. We challenged each other, and that made us go back and think things through again. It was the best leadership experience of my career."

"We were learning to work together on the go, to collaborate with others and reach a goal. It really opened up the world of cross-collaboration for me."

Objective: Feeling Valued by the Company and Increased Commitment to the Company's Direction and Their Future with Land O'Lakes

"I was impressed that the company took the time and energy and made the financial investment in us. I feel that Land O'Lakes cares about our futures and that we're part of the company. It makes me feel more loyal, more committed to the company."

"I feel more positive about the company, and from a business standpoint, I'm more informed and more optimistic about where Land O'Lakes is going."

Leadership Edge Impact, Next Steps, and Lessons Learned

Five months after the Leadership Edge learning event, the final action learning team presentations had been made to the SST, and the Leadership Edge development team began to see the impact of the program on the company:

- The action learning teams stretched the participants and provided fresh, insightful recommendations for strategic business challenges. As one SST member said, "We learned a great deal more about the subject and can now make better-informed recommendations and decisions."
- The action learning teams exposed SST members to the talents of individuals at the director level, providing them insights into this group of emerging leaders.
- Leadership Edge and the action learning teams accelerated the process of cross-pollination of ideas and cross-collaboration on strategic issues around the company.
- Through a common experience, a common learning environment, and a common language and tools, this group of high-potential directors is now more aligned with the company's journey toward becoming an operating company and with Land O'Lakes strategic business direction.

The development team is aware that challenges exist for "keeping the pilot light on" for this group of Leadership Edge leaders. Participants have said, "Don't forget us; keep us in the loop. We want to keep getting opportunities like this."

Leadership Edge has become a key element of Land O'Lakes's leadership development and will alternate with an officers' conference so that each year, high-potential employees will have access to unique, customized development opportunities. The company also is exploring other avenues for bringing more people into this development experience to broaden the group, which will cascade learnings through the company.

Lessons Learned

Leadership Edge provided a learning experience for Land O'Lakes high-potential, director-level employees and the team that developed it. Key among the lessons learned were these:

- *The model needs to be sustainable.* Leadership Edge is unique, and it was designed to be sustainable and provide an ongoing learning experience and jumping-off point for further leadership development.
- *Buy-in by senior executives is critical.* The CEO and his twelve-member senior strategy team were instrumental in making the program a success. Not only did they help select the participants; they also weighed in on the program's design and content, participated in the event itself, selected the topics for the action learning teams, and served as sponsors and coaches for the teams.
- *Exposure to senior executives is a learning opportunity.* Three of the twelve senior strategy team members (including the CEO) participated in the entire three-day event, while the others were in and out for various portions of the program. The participants had the opportunity to learn from them, and the executives also became better acquainted with these emerging leaders.
- *Multiple design perspectives build a stronger experience.* Land O'Lakes drew on its internal resources—human resources staff, the SST, the steering committee—as well as an external consultant, MDA Leadership Consulting, to develop Leadership Edge. During the process, all brought their own perspectives to the design and challenged each other as well.

- *Focus on the elements that meet the most needs.* Winnowing topics to a select few was a challenge. The Leadership Edge development team used the program's objectives as guidelines for shaping content.

- *"Talking heads" alone don't cut it.* With high-potential participants, the learning has to be high level as well. The Leadership Edge developers strove to balance academic learning and internal and external presenters with other techniques, including leaders teaching leaders, dialogues, journaling, hands-on exercises, and activities to create an experience that was varied, challenging, engaging, and fun despite the intense environment and long days.

- *Networking does not happen spontaneously.* Networking was a formal component of Leadership Edge to meet the program's objective of building relationships and collaboration across the company. The development team carefully chose groups, teams, and seating arrangements to maximize networking opportunities.

- *Not everyone can participate.* The Leadership Edge experience was developed for just 40 high-potential directors out of a pool of 215. The development team provided supervisors with detailed scripts for those who were invited and those who were not, but learned they often were not used. Going forward, the team realized it will need to manage this aspect of the experience better by encouraging supervisors to use this opportunity to coach directors about their development and their aspirations within the company—and then follow up to ensure these conversations take place.

Conclusion

Leadership Edge, a leadership development experience for forty high-potential, director-level employees of Land O'Lakes was designed to provide a business-based learning opportunity for these emerging leaders that combined insights plus application plus action to equal success:

- Content was relevant, real-world, and integrally tied to Land O'Lakes businesses and the environment in which they operate.

- Action learning teams provided participants with the opportunity to put their newly learned strategic thinking skills to immediate work as they spent three months preparing recommendations for addressing a strategic challenge that the company faced.
- Participants formed a better understanding of Land O'Lakes's movement toward an operating company model and became acquainted with resources and peers across the company, which is key to the success of an operating company.
- Both participants and senior executives learned from their experience together.
- The groundwork has been laid for the continuation of Leadership Edge, as well as additional high-level leadership development for groups such as the senior strategy team and company officers.

In the end, Leadership Edge met all its objectives and was deemed by all measures a resounding success by the CEO, SST, the development team, and the participants themselves. As the CEO has stated: "We have found that we can generate increased energy and passion for leadership by bringing high-potential employees together to develop leadership skills and capabilities. There seems to be a compelling drive among participants to not only meet their personal expectations, but also those of their high-potential peers. In essence, working together, Leadership Edge participants raise the bar when it comes to the definition of exceptional leadership."

About the Contributors

Karen Grabow is vice president of human resources for Land O'Lakes. She has been with Land O'Lakes since 2001 and has experience in corporate human resources and consulting, with major emphasis on strategic human resource leadership and organizational effectiveness. Prior to Land O'Lakes, she worked at Target Stores for seventeen years where she also was vice president of human resources. Grabow has a B.A. from the University of Illinois, Champaign, and a Ph.D. in industrial/organizational and counseling psychology from the University of Minnesota.

Grabow is a licensed psychologist in the State of Minnesota. She has been a lecturer at the University of Minnesota, University of St. Thomas, Macalester College, the Society of Industrial/Organizational Psychology Annual Conference, and the American Psychological Association conferences.

◆ ◆ ◆

Deb Suhadolnik is director of organizational and leadership development for Land O'Lakes. In this role, she is responsible for corporate training and development, online learning, and critical companywide processes, including leadership development, performance management, and succession planning. Suhadolnik joined Land O'Lakes in 2002 after many years as a human resource consultant specializing in organizational effectiveness and leadership development. Her clients included 3M, Cargill, Prudential Insurance, DTE Energy, Xerox, the Coca-Cola Company, AT&T, British Air, and Target.

◆ ◆ ◆

Scott E. Nelson is a partner and vice president of leadership development for MDA Leadership Consulting, a Minneapolis-based firm specializing in selection assessment, succession planning, executive coaching, leadership development programs, team development, and change management consulting. Nelson has more than twenty years' experience building talent management and leadership consulting programs for the City of Tulsa, Personnel Decisions, Hay Management Consultants, and Linkage Inc. In 2005, Nelson began at MDA as vice president of leadership development and in 2007 became one of the owners. He has worked with a wide range of companies to develop selection systems, competency models, and succession systems, but his real passion is in building leadership capacity through large-scale, customized development programs and executive coaching.

Nelson holds a B.A. in psychology from Luther College and an M.A. in industrial/organizational psychology from the University of Tulsa.

❖ ❖ ❖

Susan Zemke is a senior consultant and executive coach with MDA Leadership Consulting. Her work in developing strong, engaging leaders has benefited clients in a broad range of industries, from health care to quick-service restaurants, to automobile manufacturers. Clients have included Resurrection Health Care, Allergan, Fairview Health Services, Land O'Lakes, Payless ShoeSource, McDonalds, Federated Department Stores, Sallie Mae, and DaimlerChrysler. Prior to joining MDA, she worked as a senior consultant for Linkage Inc., organization effectiveness manager at the St. Paul Companies, and vice president of training at First Bank System.

Zemke earned her B.A. in history and secondary education from Trinity College, Vermont, and her M.S. in reading and reading administration from the University of Bridgeport, Connecticut.

CHAPTER EIGHTEEN

PRICEWATERHOUSECOOPERS

A Global Leadership Development Program for High-Potential Staff

This chapter outlines an approach to designing a leadership development off-site that draws resources internally and creates buy-in for participants and faculty alike.

PricewaterhouseCoopers (PwC) provides industry-focused assurance, tax, and advisory services to build public trust and enhance value for its clients and their stakeholders. More than 155,000 people in 153 countries across the network share their thinking, experience, and solutions to develop fresh perspectives and practical advice. The PwC network has member firms in 153 countries, with 155,000 people and $28.2 billion in revenue.

Genesis Park, PwC's global leadership program for high-potential staff, is a critical element of the organization's global talent management strategy. Genesis Park has a global focus, targeting PwC professionals from more than forty-five countries and across all business lines. High-potential individuals who are approaching the partner level represent ideal candidates. The program is structured as a four-month, full-time residential experience with three cohorts per year running concurrently on each campus. Each cohort is culturally diverse, with a minimum of ten countries represented at any one time.

One of a suite of programs, the focus of Genesis Park is to promote:

- Business leaders capable of driving value
- Global networks that deliver a distinctive service experience to clients
- Personal transformation that supports and accelerates PwC strategy

This focus reflects the challenges of a changing business environment in which the quality and depth of PwC's leadership have become increasingly vital determinants of success. Genesis Park was PwC's response to this challenge. The program was established in 2000, and our commitment to and investment in it has deepened over time. Genesis Park's annual enrollment has grown from twenty-four people to more than one hundred. And from its original site in Washington, D.C., Genesis Park has expanded to a second site in Berlin, with a third site in Asia under consideration.

Genesis Park emphasizes business leadership and people leadership and uses multicultural immersion, extensive professional coaching, and a balanced and intensive curriculum as its methods of leadership development. Business leaders drive value when they have strategic vision, executive insight, and relationship skills to develop their organizations and the self-awareness, authenticity, and confidence to lead and develop others. Because of the nature of our network, PwC depends on strong relationships among its leaders around the world. Consequently, Genesis Park also emphasizes the importance of multicultural understanding and commitment to building personal bonds across national boundaries.

When individuals are immersed in an intensive experience in which trust, support, and challenge are coupled with feedback, learning, and insight, a personal transformation can result, and the qualities essential to leadership can be developed. This is the core aim of Genesis Park. In creating Genesis Park, our intent was to build a program that would fundamentally alter the fabric of the organization, and we are well on our way to accomplishing that goal. We estimate that by 2021, more than a thousand partners across member firms will be alumni of Genesis Park. And in demonstrating strong business leadership and people leadership skills, they will be fulfilling the promise of the program and shaping the strategy of our organization.

PricewaterhouseCoopers and Leadership Development

PricewaterhouseCoopers is a leader in its profession. Like other businesses that operate globally and are committed to maintaining their competitive edge, we must manage the rapid and often volatile changes occurring within our own business and across the broader market environment. Ultimately we are a people and knowledge business; the skills, knowledge, and experience of our people are what our clients value.

PwC's business model creates some unique challenges in terms of talent management and development. In most countries, PwC is organized as a partnership. Individuals join PwC at a relatively young age and work, on average, more than twelve years before reaching the partnership level, at which time, as owners of the business, they acquire an equity stake. Given the average length of time necessary to complete the partnership track, coupled with the importance we place on long-term succession planning, it is essential that we engage our people throughout their careers so that we are assured a sufficient number of highly qualified candidates for consideration as PwC leaders.

PwC has traditionally struggled with the problem of retention. In part, this is a consequence of our own success. In most markets we continue to be the most attractive employer in our profession according to a variety of sources. As a consequence, we are able to recruit highly capable people, to the degree that other organizations frequently target our people right at the point in their careers at which we might begin to take full advantage of their learning and experience. While some turnover is desirable, we must work hard to keep our turnover rates below 20 percent annually. Across the globe in 2007, PwC firms hired more than thirty thousand professionals and had annual turnover rates of 18 percent.

Clearly, in order to retain the best people and maintain a full pipeline of future leaders, PwC must pay careful attention to what they expect from us as an employer. Through surveys and focus groups, it is plain to us what they want and expect:

- Development experiences that help them grow personally and professionally
- International experiences that expand their range of skills and personal networks
- Opportunities to advance quickly if they demonstrate sufficient aptitude

Our talent management and development approaches are also shaped by what clients want and expect of us. Our clients operate in an increasingly complex and interdependent marketplace. In 2007, PwC provided services to 368 of the companies in the Fortune 500 and 422 companies in the Fortune Global 500. These are companies with global reach and global needs. Through surveys, conversations, and careful analysis of market trends, we have found that our clients expect PwC to:

- Respond to their needs with strategic perspective and innovative thinking
- Assemble client service teams that respect and reflect the diversity of our clients' own organizations
- Bring our best people to bear on client issues regardless of national boundaries

Our people and our clients are our most important stakeholders. PwC has listened carefully to them and committed itself to some key talent strategy objectives over the next five years:

- Strategic insight and leadership capability, with a particular emphasis on emerging markets and innovation
- Diversity within client teams so that they may more effectively serve a diverse client base
- The means to provide all client service professionals with a wide array of enriching work experiences
- A cadre of key talent who can move fluidly across geographical boundaries and are comfortable living and working in other cultures

Key to delivering on these commitments is the ability to provide leadership development opportunities for PwC's high-potential staff. Genesis Park is the oldest, largest, and most intensive of PwC's programs to do that. The program grew out of a collaborative effort between a PwC global business leader and a PwC senior consultant. The goal was to create an experience for high-potential staff that would accelerate their development as leaders, expose them to PwC's global strategy and business challenges, and equip them with the skills, at an earlier time in their careers than had been traditionally the case, to shape the future of our organization.

Guiding Design Principles

Genesis Park's design has evolved over the past eight years. The current design principles reflect lessons learned and are helpful reference points for other programs still on the drawing board or in an early delivery phase.

Get the Right Participants into the Program

The importance of a selection process that results in recruiting the right participants cannot be overstated. When they return to their home countries, Genesis Park alumni become, in a sense, the Genesis Park "brand." So if members of the program are not capable of extracting sufficient learning from the Genesis Park experience and therefore do not demonstrate the value of the program through their actions when they return to their home countries, support for the program will wane.

Consequently, leadership development programs must understand exactly whom they are targeting. PwC, for example, has a range of leadership development programs designed for staff at different points in their career, from new managers to new partners and beyond. Genesis Park's target population is high-potential professionals who have demonstrated exceptional technical competence and are clearly recognized for their promise as leaders. At PwC a high-potential employee is defined as someone who demonstrates an exceptional ability to move to a position two levels above his or her current level. Genesis Park targets those who are at the top 1 to 5 percent of their staff class, have eight to twelve years of professional experience, and are within five or six years of partnership. Candidates are generally at the experienced manager through director levels.

At these levels, candidates have generally acquired professional maturity. They have had rich and diverse professional experiences that have given them the perspective and context for understanding their own capabilities and potential. They are also in a position where they can put what they learn into practice immediately on returning to their teams. They have demonstrated, by their career progression and success, a level of alignment and engagement with PwC that bodes well for their long-term commitment to the organization. At the same time, because they are not yet partners, it is feasible, albeit still expensive, to absent them from client service for the full four months required by Genesis Park. At the partner level, that much time spent away from client service would be much more difficult to justify.

After articulating the type of person to recruit comes the process of identifying and selecting people who fit the profile. For Genesis Park, identification and selection are done by local territory and business unit leadership with the support of Genesis Park faculty. But for Genesis Park, the selection of participants requires more than just looking at performance ratings or a recommendation from a partner or business leader. The best process is one where potential candidates surface during the annual review process. Ideally, they then enter a competitive process where they are evaluated relative to one another, an application and interview process that addresses behavioral attitudes and capacity for change, and probing one-on-one conversations with the sponsors putting candidates forward.

Getting the right people into the program does not end with setting criteria and establishing a rigorous selection process. It is also about effectively managing the recruitment pipeline. Participants need to be identified far enough in advance to allow sufficient planning, from managing client service obligations to obtaining visas. At the same time, the assessment process needs to consider relevant performance and development data. We generally find that candidate identification is best done six to nine months prior to their prospective starting date in the program.

Be Integrated and Aligned with the Business and Flexible in Response to Its Needs

Alignment with the business is a critical success factor for leadership development programs. In our experience, ownership by the business line and a high level of passion and commitment from one or more key business leaders are key to Genesis Park's success. Initially Genesis Park met resistance because business leaders were asked to commit very talented staff on a full-time basis for more than four months. So in addition to the expenses associated with a four-month residential program, the opportunity costs of pulling revenue-producing professionals off-line were also substantial. In addition, the level of investment required by Genesis Park in the development of nonpartners was unprecedented for PwC. No one argued against the need for leadership development, global networks, and high-impact personal transformation, but there was a high level of skepticism concerning the program's return on investment. Getting business leaders to buy in required a personal campaign led by a tenacious few who spent much of their personal capital targeting and persuading skeptical business leaders.

Genesis Park's short-term value proposition was to use the program to help deliver think-tank-style innovation and strategic insights to PwC. The longer-term value proposition was the quality of leadership and networks that would emerge from the program. This seemed compelling to sufficient numbers of PwC management so as to enable Genesis Park to enroll eight people from around the world in its first class. Relatively quickly, as they began to see fundamental differences in the behavior of Genesis Park alumni and the added value they brought to the business, PwC's business leaders sent more people and advocated the expansion and continued investment in the program. Ownership of the program in terms of faculty, curriculum, design, and selection process was always firmly in the hands of PwC's business leaders. Although human resources (HR) has played an important role in supporting Genesis Park, management's ongoing proprietary interest in the program protected against any perception that Genesis Park was simply an HR "flavor of the month."

Approaches to ensuring continuing leadership support of Genesis Park take several forms. First, it involves maintaining the sponsorship of the individual members of PwC's global management team—primarily its human capital and global business line leaders. These sponsors play an important role in terms of governance, strategy, and advocacy for the program and play a critical role in the life of Genesis Park. The sponsors meet and get to know program participants and serve them as mentors and resources long after participants have completed the residential component of the program. The sponsors' role is very hands-on and critical to the Genesis Park experience.

Genesis Park is also in vertical alignment with business unit leaders in the individual countries in which PwC operates. This is important for us.

Without a direct connection to leaders at every level of PwC's complex management matrix, Genesis Park might easily be viewed as a program that was being forced on local country firms from outside. Consequently, on a regular basis, we reach out to the sponsor of each Genesis Park participant to discuss the participant's progress and performance and to share with the sponsors some aspects of the program and invite their engagement in program activities. Indeed, we regularly invite a broad spectrum of PwC people who have distinguished themselves in some way—as business leaders, subject matter experts, or excellent mentors—to participate in the program as speakers or project sponsors. They give their time to Genesis Park because they value the ideas, insights, and perspectives that participants provide. For example, a PwC leader working on a global strategic initiative might want to spend time at Genesis Park in order to use a culturally and professionally diverse group of accomplished high-potential staff as a sounding board for ideas.

Genesis Park's recruiting approaches reflect the markets, geographies, and industry segments in which PwC is currently investing. For example, as China and India have become more important to PwC's business, we have increased the percentage of program participants from those two countries. On a selective basis, we have also recruited PwC people who work in strategically important support roles rather than in client-facing roles.

Genesis Park operates three classes annually at each of its two campuses. There are multiple classes each year in part to accommodate the business cycles inherent in our diverse businesses and to allow larger and smaller classes based on the resource needs of PwC's business. This kind of flexibility has served us well.

We are also opportunistic in terms of taking on cutting-edge projects for PwC's business leaders. We arrange schedules and project plans to accommodate these projects and update or revise our core curriculum in order to accommodate sudden shifts in PwC's business.

Deliver on a Unique Value Proposition

A leadership development experience has to have a compelling value proposition for both the participant and the participant's sponsor. Both stakeholders must make a decision that requires difficult trade-offs and a commitment of substantial resources. Fundamentally, leadership development should be viewed as a long-term play; however, there must also be some short- and medium-term benefits for the stakeholders. At Genesis Park, the value proposition is to deliver:

- Business leaders who drive value
- Global networks that deliver on PwC's promise of distinctive client service
- Personal transformation that supports and accelerates PwC strategy

Business leaders drive value when they demonstrate strategic vision, executive insight, excellent relationship skills, and the ability to develop others. These qualities require self-awareness, authenticity, and self-confidence. At Genesis Park, we focus attention equally on the development of business leadership and people leadership.

Global networks deliver on PwC's promise of distinctive client service when those networks are based on people with a deep level of multicultural understanding and a passion and commitment for building relationships across national boundaries. Genesis Park's emphasis on relationship building and cross-cultural understanding is one of its most distinctive aspects. It is defined in part by the diverse mix of participants targeted for each class. There is always representation from each of our business lines, and in classes of twenty-five participants, often more than fifteen countries are represented. While many PwC people have the opportunity to gain international experience, nowhere else in the organization are such deep and intense bonds being formed among people of such diverse cultural backgrounds. Adding to the international flavor of the experience is the current faculty of seven who come from six different countries. In addition, the curriculum and the strategic projects that the participants take on address globally focused business issues.

The other notable aspect of Genesis Park is that it is transformative: participants experience a developmental shift. The personal and professional development that occurs is sufficiently significant that when participants finish the program, they can be said to be operating at a higher level. Their relationship to PwC shifts as well in that they view themselves as owners with a personal stake in the business. This sense of ownership makes the shift sustainable.

Two key elements of the Genesis Park experience account for its transformative effects. The first is intensity. From one perspective, Genesis Park provides participants with a break from the intensity that is typical in providing professional services to clients. In reality, Genesis Park introduces a new sort of intensity to its participants. For a period of four months, participants are focused daily on their own capabilities, potential, and development. Coupled with the high expectations of PwC's senior leadership, as evidenced by the time they spend at Genesis Park and the scale of PwC's investment in the program, this intensity makes it clear that "to whom much is given, much is expected." The bar is set high.

The second element is support and challenge. The Genesis Park culture is one where support and challenge are present in equal measure because both are vital in creating an effective learning and development environment. Support is provided through the relationships with the coaches, fellow classmates, and alumni and the inclusion of family in elements of the experience. Challenge is provided through open and direct feedback, difficult assignments, and a high level of accountability. Support and challenge encourage trust and openness, providing participants with space to learn.

Development Focus

Genesis Park is closely aligned with PwC's business strategy. But as well as instilling core business skills and acumen, Genesis Park is also premised on the idea that leadership development must foster self-understanding and good people skills. Focusing on one without the other is incomplete and ineffective. Striking a balance between them ensures accelerated development. This balance is part of the philosophy of Genesis Park and is reflected in all aspects of the program.

The learning objectives of the program encompass each ring of the diagram in Figure 18.1 with self-development at its core and a balanced approach to learning about business leadership and people leadership.

FIGURE 18.1. PROGRAM LEARNING OBJECTIVES

Target candidates are generally at a point in their careers where they have focused their energies primarily on developing technical expertise and delivering solutions to clients. Now, as they begin to think about themselves as leaders, they must step beyond the realm of the technical and raise their game both as businesspeople and as mentors to others. Many leadership programs struggle with finding a balance between the development of hard skills and soft skills. If a program focuses too much on personal growth and development, the experience runs the risk of being disconnected from the business and confusing to participants because the learning does not tie closely enough to their career progression. If a program focuses too much in the other direction, the experience runs the risk of lacking meaning and depth—of simply being a training experience focused on skill building. Our model reflects a balance of self-reflection, analytical rigor, and challenge and with strong links to the business. In other words, the experience is about the whole person because it is only at that level that true transformation can occur.

Underlying our development focus is an emphasis on four behaviors that are key to PwC's culture and help drive the learning objectives at Genesis Park:

- Invest in relationships
- Share and collaborate

- Put ourselves in each other's shoes
- Enhance value through quality

Faculty Model

The Genesis Park experience is facilitated by a full-time in-house faculty of senior PwC professionals with a passion for developing people. We employ a rotational model where faculty members join Genesis Park for eighteen months to two years and then return to their business unit. The rotational model has the advantage of embedding people with the developmental expertise they have acquired at Genesis Park back into the business as developmental practitioners.

Faculty members are predominantly from the client-facing side of the business and have some experience with strategy, teaching, and facilitation. We also recruit specialized practitioners with expertise in coaching and training design and delivery. While most faculty members are at PwC's director level, one of the more distinctive elements of the program is our use of retired and second-career partners who serve as site leaders. Genesis Park participants benefit from gaining the perspective and expertise of a highly experienced partner, and those partners in turn are able to have a positive impact on the future of the firm by helping to create PwC's future leaders.

While the faculty deliver the program under the guidance of the two site leaders, the program's managing director together with the program sponsors provide the overall strategic guidance and direction and ensure our alignment with the business.

Curriculum

Genesis Park focuses heavily on experiential learning: participants learn by doing. We also employ a blend of structured assignments, self-directed learning, case studies, simulations, and sessions with internal or external thought leaders. This blend of approaches is reflective of the best thinking in adult learning and leadership development and is common to leadership development programs across our organization. Employing a range of methods is a way of keeping the experience fresh and ensuring that different learning styles are accommodated. We also believe that one effective approach to development is to create challenging situations that force people outside their comfort zones. We believe that development occurs in the space between what the development experience demands and what a participant does not yet know how to do.

We group the curriculum into three distinct categories:

- Leader forums
- Learning modules
- Strategic projects

Leader Forums

Participants regularly engage PwC leaders in candid discussions about clients, strategy, and emerging issues shaping business today. Leaders present business cases during which competing views are shared and debated, and the importance of examining issues from multiple perspectives is stressed. These exchanges are meant to simulate C-suite-level strategic discussions. The participants play a critical role in managing these forums. They not only facilitate the conversations as a team, but they also play a role in identifying and inviting forum speakers. These forums provide Genesis Park participants with an opportunity to practice their executive communication and facilitation skills and offer a good balance of information sharing about all aspects of PwC. We establish a safe but challenging space for discussions with ground rules that ensure confidentiality, thereby encouraging unusual candor on the part of forum speakers.

What Works

- Speaker sessions involving a case study, either client related or firm related, but always globally relevant

- Ensuring participants are exposed to leaders at every level of the organization and from different countries and different market segments
- Pairing the speaker sessions with smaller group lunches, receptions, or dinners that provide an opportunity for a more informal exchange

Learning Modules

Participants experience a range of learning modules that build capabilities and deepen understanding around a variety of topics. The modules employ a blend of structured assignments, self-directed learning, case studies, simulations, and sessions with external thought leaders. The content is introduced by program faculty with support from external contractors. The modules include:

- Understanding PwC's Business—looking beyond your business unit
- Strategic Thinking and Problem Solving—your business, your client's business
- Executive Communication—think on your feet
- Authentic Leadership—vision, values, action

This list is adjusted over time as situations demand and opportunities arise. Although we use a blend of faculty and external contractors to deliver this content, we get the best results when we have in-house faculty involved in the delivery, often by cofacilitating.

Strategic Projects

During the second half of the Genesis Park experience, the participants break up into small groups and take on a strategic project. The projects address high-priority strategic issues currently facing PwC. Project teams must demonstrate a strong commercial sense, work cross-functionally, and take into account the global implications of their recommendations. Given that each team's output is expected to be of substantive use to the projects' sponsors, the stakes surrounding these projects are quite high. The projects serve as a platform for additional learning and put into play the new insights the participants have gained about themselves and about strategy, leadership, and teaming. The substance of the projects can range widely, from issues regarding internal PwC strategy, to building business plans for new markets, to thought leadership. Past projects have included:

- Developing a framework for structuring potential outsourcing opportunities for PwC
- Designing change management for the introduction of a new global competency model
- Contributing content to the book *Building Public Trust*, in which PwC provides its vision of corporate transparency as a means of restoring investor confidence

While the projects are diverse in nature, they must all meet certain criteria. Projects must:

- Be strategic and globally relevant
- Have a sponsor who is committed to working closely with the project team
- Challenge participants to stretch their minds and widen their perspectives

What Works

- Sourcing projects that deal with PwC's most pressing business issues. This allows Genesis Park faculty and participants to stay abreast of these issues and connect with issue thought leaders.
- Spending sufficient time at the start setting expectations with project sponsors. This will ensure alignment between the sponsor's needs and the project's deliverables.
- Avoiding projects that are heavily research dependent or overly technical. These kinds of projects are difficult for a cross-functional group to tackle in a short period of time and are often not as rewarding for the team's members.

Focusing the Learning and Making It Stick

Some of the biggest challenges facing leadership development programs are making sure that their focus is effective and that the developmental gains participants hope to achieve are sustained when they are back in the normal ebb and flow of their jobs. At Genesis Park, we have developed a three-pronged approach for making sure that learning is occurring and is lasting:

- Feedback: Understanding what needs to change
- Coaching: Learning how to change
- Sponsor engagement: Keeping it up

Feedback

The feedback process is critical to helping participants zero in on their development objectives and monitor and adjust their behavior throughout the program. At the beginning of their stay at Genesis Park, each participant undergoes a 360-degree feedback process through an online software program that solicits feedback from their direct reports, their peers, and various PwC leaders. In this way, participants begin their Genesis Park experience with valuable insights about how they are perceived by others, and a case is made for changing their behaviors in more positive directions.

With the help of a coach, participants use this feedback, together with their own self-reflections, to narrow in on two to four development priorities for themselves. During their four months in the program, they undergo two additional formal feedback events during which they hear from their peers and the Genesis Park faculty. Additional informal feedback sessions occur frequently during the course of the program. At the end of the program, participants close out their development plans by completing a self-assessment that is paired with a faculty assessment and shared with their sponsors in their home business unit.

Coaching

Many leadership programs use coaches in order to reinforce a participant's experience of the program. But at Genesis Park, our approach to coaching is unique. All coaches are members of our full-time faculty. Consequently, they are able to observe the participants in action on a continuous basis and use their observations to deepen the coaching experience. In addition, as skilled businesspeople, Genesis Park coaches are able to help participants improve their business skills, as well as increase their leadership effectiveness. Every participant is assigned a coach with whom they meet biweekly for the duration of the program. At the outset, the coach works with the participant to help process the feedback the participant has received and define development goals. During coaching sessions, the coach makes observations, suggests practices, and assigns readings that support the participant's developmental objectives. As needed, coaches provide career counseling and mentoring. In addition to the participant's coach, each project team has a coach who works directly with the team on issues related to sponsor engagement, project approach and deliverables, and team performance.

Sponsor Engagement

Genesis Park participants must be sponsored by a senior PwC partner who, in practice, is often a PwC business unit leader or country leader. The role of the sponsor in the participant's experience of Genesis Park cannot be overstated. There is a clear correlation between the extent to which a participant fully uses what he or she has learned at Genesis Park and the level of the sponsoring partner's engagement with Genesis Park. Engagement is promoted through a combination of e-mails, Webcasts, and individual telephone calls between members of the Genesis Park faculty and the sponsor. Candid conversations ensure that everyone—faculty, sponsor, and participant—shares an understanding of what is working, what is not, and what is next. On completion of the program, a specific conversation helps the sponsor prepare for the participant's return and find a role for the participant that makes the most of what he or she has learned.

Evaluating Effectiveness

We use a number of measures to track the effectiveness of Genesis Park. These measures indicate that Genesis Park provides tangible benefits to PwC, the most important of which are these:

◆ ◆ ◆

- *We are keeping our best people longer and deploying them more effectively.* The retention rate for Genesis Park participants is atypical for PwC as a whole. Since the program's inception eight years ago, the retention rate of alumni has been in the mid- to high 90 percent range in comparison to an annual attrition rate of 15 to 20 percent among the broader PwC population. We attribute this in part to the level of commitment to PwC that is created as a result of the Genesis Park experience. We also have evidence that Genesis Park improves PwC's use of talent. Genesis Park faculty and sponsoring partners are able to use the participants' time in the program to clarify the highest and best use of their skills and experiences. As a result, after completing the Genesis Park program, many participants go on to international assignments or other rotational work at rates far greater than their peers do. They may also be shifted to different business units, client portfolios, or other areas of responsibility.
- *Business leaders want to send more people to Genesis Park.* The best testament to our success is the rate of expansion of the Genesis Park program. The sponsors who send their staff to Genesis Park see value in what they get in return and want to send more people to us.
- *Our network is flourishing.* Our 350 alumni live and work in forty-five countries, and their shared experience of Genesis Park helps connect the PwC organization, break down organizational silos, and improve communication and execution of key PwC strategies. Looking ahead, we expect that over the next twelve years, more than a thousand partners will have attended Genesis Park. This will be one of their career-defining experiences, and their connection to one another will provide a deep level of professional support.

- *PwC is getting better at talent management and leadership development.* Genesis Park has been a conduit for engaging PwC's business units in a forward-thinking conversation on issues related to talent, succession planning, and leadership development. Across PwC, we have been able to help improve the approach and consistency of programs for managing high-potential staff.
- *Participants are progressing more quickly than their peers.* Because of the multitude of factors that influence progression, this measure is difficult to quantify. That being said, we have strong qualitative evidence from business and country leaders that many of participants achieve partnership or otherwise advance more quickly than their peers do. We believe this occurs because of the qualities they demonstrate after completing Genesis Park, as well as the visibility and support they receive as a result of the program. Of equal significance is that participants who have been admitted to the partnership following their Genesis Park experience typically demonstrate a broader business acumen than their peers and take a nonhierarchical approach to team leadership, which is reflective of the program's approaches and methods.

The Future for Genesis Park

Genesis Park has grown and expanded substantially over its eight years. While we continue to deliver a high-impact global leadership program for PwC, we are also working on a redesign of the alumni program. During the early years of Genesis Park, we hosted an annual meeting of all alumni, bringing them together to connect with new graduates, learn about new PwC initiatives, and recharge and refocus their continuing development. But as the program grew, all-alumni meetings became impractical. Currently on the drawing board are smaller, targeted programs that bring groups of alumni together for learning experiences in different countries with an emphasis on PwC clients.

The second priority for Genesis Park is to explore ways to establish a physical presence in Asia through an additional campus or the alumni program. Asia continues to be a strategic market for PwC and is strategically important to Genesis Park's future.

Lessons Learned

Following are some of the key highlights covered in this chapter as well as a few additional insights:

- To be successful in the short term, leadership development programs must engage leadership at multiple levels of the organization, get the right staff into the program, and create a development experience that simultaneously addresses the needs of the business and the needs of the individual participants. To be sustainable, programs have to reflect shifts in the organization's culture and strategy and nurture a network of leaders who will champion the program.
- Leadership development is the responsibility of the business and should be owned by the business. Find the most vocal and effective business leaders, and give them the support they need to champion the cause and influence critics and detractors.
- Successful programs consider the needs of the business in real time. The participant selection process must respect the business cycle, and the curriculum must reflect the dynamics of the marketplace.
- Business unit heads must promote the program to their executive leadership and demonstrate their commitment to participants and alumni.
- Leadership development has to focus on hard skills (business skills and business acumen) and soft skills (self-understanding and people skills). Focusing on one without the other is incomplete and ineffective. Striking a balance between them ensures accelerated development.
- Employing a range of curriculum delivery methods makes the learning experience more interesting and is an excellent way to accommodate different learning styles.

- A model that includes feedback, coaching, and sponsor engagement helps ensure that learning occurs and developmental gains are sustainable.
- Multicultural teams do not gel simply by virtue of their members working together. Cultural biases exist and must be removed by means of coaching and intervention.
- Finding the right faculty members may be more critical than selecting the right participants. Dealing with strong-willed, ambitious personalities who nevertheless have not had much experience being introspective or receiving candid feedback requires faculty who are both flexible and confident in themselves.
- After a successful developmental experience, program participants often want to evangelize the world. A key part of the coaching model should help participants understand that attempts at mass conversion are usually ineffective. Instead, influencing the behaviors of others is best achieved by setting a personal example.

About the Contributors

Rich Baird is PwC's global managing partner–people and serves on the Global PwC Leadership Team, Gender Advisory Council, and Global Operations Group. He has been a primary sponsor of Genesis Park since its inception and works closely with the program coaches and site leaders, participant teams, and Genesis Park alumni. Baird was project leader for the book *Building Public Trust: The Future of Corporate Reporting* (2002) and is coauthor of *Inside the Minds: Updating Your Company's HR Strategy* (2008). He currently serves as chairman of the board of trustees at Albion College in Michigan. He has been an instructor at INSEAD's Executive M.B.A. program in Fountainebleu, France. In December 2007, he was awarded an honorary doctorate for his work in education and community service from Eastern Michigan University.

❖ ❖ ❖

Bethann Brault is the cofounder and managing director of Genesis Park, PwC's Global Leadership Development Programme. In 2007, she was named one of the World Economic Forum's 250 Young Global Leaders, a group selected for their professional accomplishments, commitment to society, and potential to contribute to shaping the future. Brault has a background in strategy consulting.

Amber Romine is an experienced leadership development consultant and executive coach. She is a director in PwC's Global Human Capital unit, where she helps to drive global leadership development strategy. Previously she was program director for Genesis Park and worked as a management consultant in PwC's advisory business. Romine serves on the faculty of Georgetown University's Leadership Coaching Program. She earned her undergraduate degree from Rutgers University and her graduate degree from the Harvard Kennedy School.

APPENDIX: GLOBAL SURVEY—HOW ORGANIZATIONS PRACTICE LEADERSHIP

In 2000, the Linkage research team conducted a survey of leadership development practitioners to understand the top priorities they set in their respective organizations and the most pressing challenges they see in their work every day. To follow up on this and provide context for the theories and best practices in this book, the team once again conducted a formal survey among our contributors and database of leadership development practitioners. The results were divided into several key areas: (1) organizational overview of leadership development, (2) leadership competencies, (3) selection, assessment, and development, (4) most impactful key features of leadership training, and (5) future leadership development improvement.

Organizational Overview of Leadership Development

How effective is your organization at executing leadership development?

FIGURE A.1.   EFFECTIVENESS OF ORGANIZATIONAL LEADERSHIP DEVELOPMENT EFFORTS

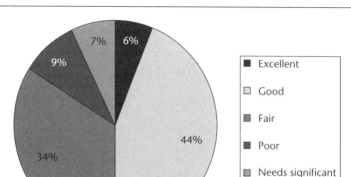

Every organization will undoubtedly rate its leadership development efforts by different criteria, and what means success to one company may have little or no impact on another. Still, it is doubtful that a company would have a positive outlook on its efforts unless focused and deliberate efforts are being made. More than anything else, it is interesting to see that companies now take great pride in the investment they are making in leadership development and that these investments consistently produce results.

Historical context: Fifty percent of all companies surveyed rated the effectiveness of their leadership development efforts as either "excellent" or "good," compared to 32 percent in 2000 (Figure A.1). This shows a general increase in activity around leadership, as well as more effective execution on leadership investment over the past eight years.

◆ ◆ ◆

How many years has your leadership development program been in place?

The majority of organizations surveyed indicated that their formal leadership development systems have been in place for somewhere between one and three years, while the next highest percentage of

FIGURE A.2. AGE OF ORGANIZATIONAL LEADERSHIP
DEVELOPMENT SYSTEMS

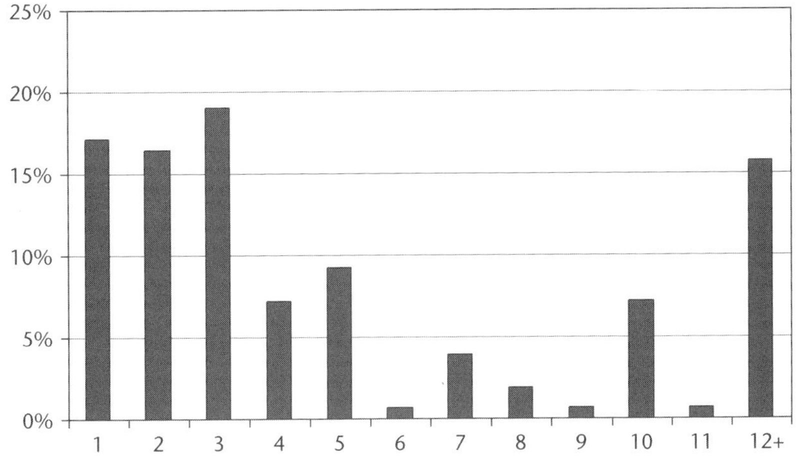

respondents indicated having practiced leadership development for twelve or more years (Figure A.2). Overall, the average age of a formal leadership development infrastructure is roughly five years.

Leadership development is a critical function to any organization, and one that has become increasingly accepted in the past decade. Although many companies have historically operated ahead of the curve and have led the way, this seems to be a newer practice for most. Relating back to the previous question, a trend can be seen in that many companies that have been practicing leadership development only within the past three years have already achieved a level of confidence in the effectiveness of their efforts, showing that results, whether formal or informal, have been seen relatively quickly.

How involved is the CEO in leadership development throughout the entire process?

It is largely recognized that CEO support and direct involvement are critical success factors in leadership development. Having clear buy-in

FIGURE A.3.   CEO INVOLVEMENT IN LEADERSHIP DEVELOPMENT

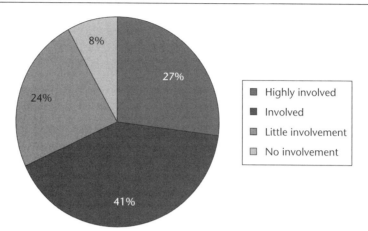

from the top has an invigorating effect on leadership. Not only are practitioners typically given more leeway and more budget allocation with which to design leadership development systems, but engagement among selected leaders and managers is visibly higher when encouragement comes directly from the uppermost slats on the ladder. These data suggest that leadership development is a considerable priority among CEOs today.

Historical context: In 2008, 68 percent of companies recorded their CEOs had at least moderate involvement as compared to 53 percent in 2000 (Figure A.3). While leadership development was still a priority eight years ago, this trend has increased by a statistically significant amount in the past several years.

◆ ◆ ◆

What is your 2008 budget (estimated or actual) for leadership development (includes training, coaching, and assessments)?

The results here are quite split. While many organizations recorded spending within $50,000 on leadership development, a close number also recorded spending over $500,000 each year (Figure A.4). Together these two groups represent the majority of companies surveyed.

FIGURE A.4.   BUDGET ALLOCATED TOWARD
LEADERSHIP DEVELOPMENT

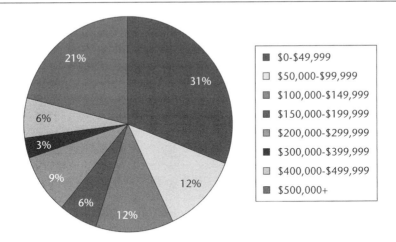

■	$0-$49,999
☐	$50,000-$99,999
■	$100,000-$149,999
■	$150,000-$199,999
■	$200,000-$299,999
■	$300,000-$399,999
☐	$400,000-$499,999
■	$500,000+

◆ ◆ ◆

What are the populations targeted for leadership development within your organization?

Much of our research, through surveying and direct conversations with leadership development practitioners, suggests that one of the highest priorities, and greatest challenges, for organizations is the development of senior leaders (Figure A.5). Success in this objective is dependent on multiple actions: identifying the competencies that differentiate top leaders in a company, finding the right combination of adult learning methodologies to maximize retention, eliciting engagement from high-level employees, and instilling a culture of teaching and knowledge transfer from senior leadership positions down throughout the company.

Historical context: The data from this survey vary little from the data collected in 2000. Although the proportionality among which leaders are targeted remains the same, it has been noted that the percentage of companies that focus on executives and middle managers has increased slightly since 2000.

FIGURE A.5.   POPULATIONS TARGETED BY LEADERSHIP
DEVELOPMENT

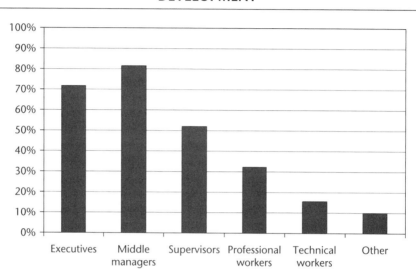

◆ ◆ ◆

Which components of leadership development represent the areas where you believe your company has its strongest practices?

An effective leadership development system is based on a long list of success factors. Often the greatest challenges lie not only in identifying and developing leaders, but in facilitating a smooth integration between leadership development (LD) efforts and other functions of the business (Figure A.6). This is critical to the success of an LD system as business success relies on the ability to develop the right leaders to execute on the right strategies and corporate initiatives.

Historical context: In 2008, the majority of companies expressed four key areas where they felt their leadership development systems were the strongest: helping participants meet the challenges of a changing work environment, developing leaders, identifying potential, and building ongoing commitment to leadership development. In 2000, many of these top factors were the same; however, overall effectiveness of each individual factor was significantly lower. In addition, individuals polled in 2000

FIGURE A.6.   AREAS OF GREATEST PROFICIENCY

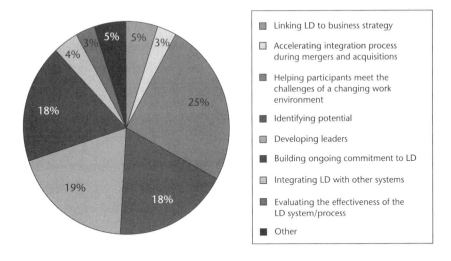

- Linking LD to business strategy
- Accelerating integration process during mergers and acquisitions
- Helping participants meet the challenges of a changing work environment
- Identifying potential
- Developing leaders
- Building ongoing commitment to LD
- Integrating LD with other systems
- Evaluating the effectiveness of the LD system/process
- Other

FIGURE A.7.   AREAS REQUIRING THE MOST SIGNIFICANT IMPROVEMENT

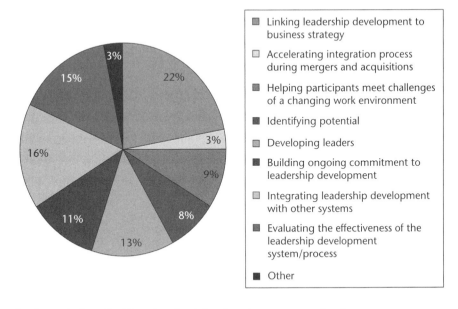

- Linking leadership development to business strategy
- Accelerating integration process during mergers and acquisitions
- Helping participants meet challenges of a changing work environment
- Identifying potential
- Developing leaders
- Building ongoing commitment to leadership development
- Integrating leadership development with other systems
- Evaluating the effectiveness of the leadership development system/process
- Other

indicated that linking leadership development to business strategy was one of their most proficient areas. This was the exact opposite in 2008, with strategic alignment identified as one of the most critical challenges: 22 percent of all organizations list it as a noteworthy issue (Figure A.7).

This is most likely due to several factors. Organizational strategy has become more complex as globalization, improved technology, increased competition, and values-based or ethical business play a greater factor. In addition, the emphasis placed on linking development efforts with corporate strategy has increased, making it more of a priority among practitioners who wish to see improved results.

◆ ◆ ◆

Do leaders in your organization attend external leadership development programs?

While many organizations have extremely robust and effective internal leadership development systems, even the most renowned learning companies often rely on external services or vendors to assist in some aspect of their leadership training. Among the most common external services practitioners use are leadership development programs, which include off-site conferences, executive education programs, training workshops, and institutes. Among the various reasons for using external development programs, many practitioners agree that putting on a leadership development program can be very expensive if handled internally and sometimes is not justifiable under budgetary limitations. Vendors that specialize in such services are able to allocate greater resources to design and execution, while spreading costs over a larger pool of participants so as to keep prices down.

Historical context: Our 2008 results show that 73 percent of organizations polled send leaders to external leadership development programs (Figure A.8), while in 2000 only 61 percent reported doing so. This change is likely due to several factors. First, internal leadership development efforts have become more complex and more long term, while offering a greater range of learning methods and resources. The increased use of varying methodologies such as business simulations, action learning teams, coaching and mentoring, multirater assessments, and job rotation have decreased the amount of resources spent on internal programs. At the same time, the market for leadership development has increased, leading to a greater supply of renowned programs spanning private, academic, and nonprofit sectors.

FIGURE A.8.   PARTICIPATION IN EXTERNAL LEADERSHIP DEVELOPMENT PROGRAMS

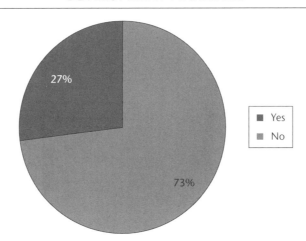

Leadership Competencies

What key characteristics/skills are you trying to develop in your leaders?

One of the first steps in designing a leadership development system is to identify the variables that make up the ideal leader—the competencies that are most critical to success in the organization. Because every organization is different, each one rates leaders by different criteria. Based on our polling, the clear top priorities among practitioners were strategic thinking, communication, relationship building, and talent development, with strategic thinking being the most prioritized competency by a wide margin (Figure A.9). This coincides with the previous findings suggesting that aligning leadership development with organizational strategy remains one of the biggest challenges for practitioners. Beyond strategic thinking, the emphasis rests on some of the softer aspects of leadership such as communication, inspiring trust, and building relationships. This shows an increasing level of value placed on the aspects of charismatic leadership and illustrates that many organizations have a need for more leaders with the emotional perception and maturity to lead successfully.

FIGURE A.9.   MOST WIDELY RECOGNIZED LEADERSHIP
COMPETENCIES

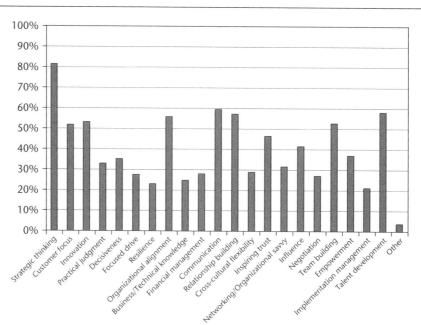

The lack of emphasis placed on some of the more role- or context-specific competencies such as financial management, business/technical knowledge, or networking/organizational savvy is an interesting trend. It makes sense, though, when compared to previous findings on the populations targeted for leadership development. Most organizations polled had a focus on senior leaders, whose responsibilities are traditionally less geared toward task management and more toward strategic design, vision, and organizational leadership qualities.

Selection, Assessment, and Development

Does your organization have a formal process for selecting high-potentials for leadership development?

Formal selection processes for high-potential employees are a staple of a robust succession plan. While many of the organizations polled

FIGURE A.10. FREQUENCY OF FORMAL HIGH-POTENTIAL SELECTION SYSTEMS

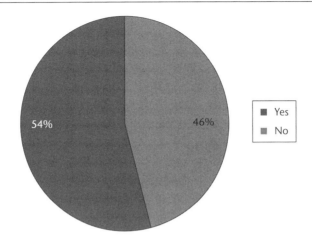

54% 46%

■ Yes
■ No

showed confidence in the effectiveness of their development efforts, only 46 percent reported formal processes for selecting those with high potential (Figure A.10). One possible explanation is that the majority of populations targeted for leadership development are senior leaders within their respective companies. Many organizations that do not have tremendous budgets for leadership development find effective ways of preparing their senior leadership teams, but do not get the chance to expand their efforts to less tenured populations within the company.

Historical context: Since 2000, the percentage of organizations that invest in formal high-potential selection processes has increased by a significant amount: from 34 percent to 46 percent.

Is information on an individual's status as a high-potential person shared openly with the company?

This is one of the more highly contested subjects in leadership development, as it is unclear which practice is considered to be best practice. Many organizations believe that sharing information on an employee's high-potential status as a leader will likely increase that person's engagement

FIGURE A.11.   RATE OF STATUS DISCLOSURE AMONG HIGH-POTENTIAL POPULATIONS

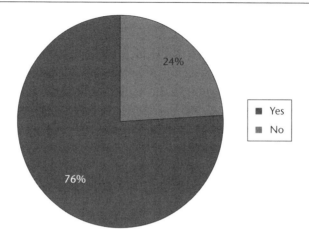

in development efforts and improve commitment to the organization. However, other practitioners attest to the notion that employees who are informed of high-potential status will be more likely to become complacent, demand greater compensation, or brag to colleagues. The reality is that the effectiveness of this approach is dependent on the organization itself and its unique culture.

Historical context: Although the percentage of those who do not inform individuals of their high-potential status is quite high in 2008, at 76 percent (Figure A.11), the rate was even higher in 2000, at 81 percent. Not only have organizations become more liberated in their leadership development practices over the years, but development efforts geared toward those with high potential are becoming increasingly common. It is likely that the frequency at which high-potential people are selected and informed of their status will increase in the future.

◆ ◆ ◆

FIGURE A.12. IMPORTANCE OF 360-DEGREE FEEDBACK IN TRAINING INITIATIVES

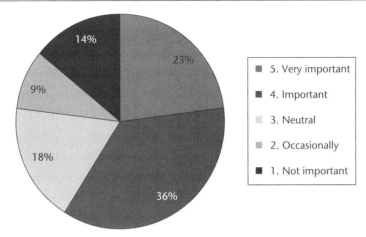

- 5. Very important
- 4. Important
- 3. Neutral
- 2. Occasionally
- 1. Not important

How important is feedback from 360-degree assessments in the design and delivery of your training programs?

Often 360-degree assessments are considered to be the most comprehensive and accurate form of assessment, factoring in multiple raters including peers, managers, and direct reports. These results can be tied directly into another aspect of leadership development by contributing to the formation of an individual development plan and serving as the foundation for one-on-one coaching efforts.

Historical context: Since 2000, the practice of 360-degree assessment has become much more central to the leadership development process. Our earlier survey showed 34 percent of participants rated 360-degree feedback as important or very important, compared to 59 percent in 2008 (Figure A.12). This is closely related to the increasing popularity of one-on-one executive coaching, which has fast become a staple in many leadership development systems.

◆ ◆ ◆

Most Impactful Key Features of Leadership Development Training

Which of the following methodologies do you currently employ in your leadership development initiative?

One of the most challenging tasks in designing a leadership development system is choosing the best suite of adult learning methods. A number of methodologies are considered to be best practice, but designing a system is much more than throwing together a hodgepodge of best practices. Practitioners must design their leadership development efforts around the unique aspects of their organizations, such as their mission and values, employee demographics, short- and long-term strategies, and budget. Not only that, but in a system that incorporates multiple methodologies, each has to complement the others so as to create a seamless and consistent system.

Among the most widely leveraged development formats, participants in 2008 identified 360-degree feedback, leadership development programs, facilitated discussion, individual development plans, and team building (Figure A.13). This shows a general leaning toward more hands-on methods (360-degree assessments, facilitated discussion, team building) and customized solutions (individual development plans). Certainly over the past few years, organizations have taken part in a general shift away from well-worn approaches such as executive M.B.A. programs and accelerated promotion in a move to stay on top of the innovation curve. Meanwhile, leadership development programs remain a high priority for their variety and relative cost-effectiveness.

Historical context: The most significant change that can be seen from 2000 is in the use of two methodologies: coaching and distance learning. First, the use of internal and external formal coaching efforts has increased by 7 and 18 percent, respectively, while the use of internal and external informal coaching efforts has increased by 10 and 14 percent, respectively. On average, internal coaching efforts are more widely used in 2008; however, we see a larger incremental increase in the use of external coaching as more and more companies are becoming well known for their success in aligning with external coaching vendors in a

FIGURE A.13. MOST WIDELY USED LEADERSHIP DEVELOPMENT METHODOLOGIES

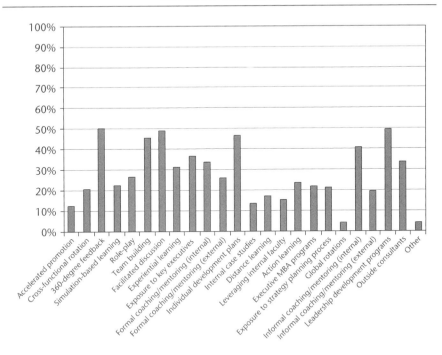

way that complements their individual strategies. Meanwhile, internal coach training methods have become more effective and more accepted, yielding increases across the board. Fueling the flames of coaching are new and innovative methods such as Marshall Goldsmith's FeedForward approach, which has seen enormous acceptance among internal and external coaches.

Like coaching, distance learning use has increased over the years— this one more dramatically. In 2000, our surveys showed that none of the companies polled were formally engaging in distance learning compared to 18 percent in 2008. First and foremost, we see a wide acceptance of technology-enabled blended learning methods over the years. In addition, our conversations with various leaders and organizations show that distance learning broadcasts can be an effective foundation for facilitated team-building interventions. Finally, the spreading global distribution of many companies demands the use of remote or virtual learning methods in lieu of face-to-face team interaction. It would not be surprising to see a further increase in the use of remote or technology-enabled learning methods in the future.

Future Leadership Development Improvement

Which of the following methodologies do you think your leadership development initiative would benefit most from?

The results in this case are fairly consistent across the board. Among the methodologies most frequently selected, most represent best practices that have been widely accepted but remain difficult to execute (Figure A.14). Cross-functional rotation is a frequent challenge for practitioners who have

FIGURE A.14.   MOST UNDERUSED LEADERSHIP DEVELOPMENT METHODOLOGIES

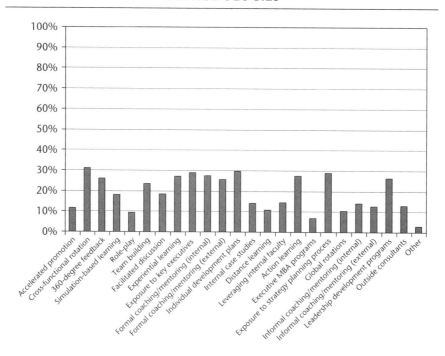

difficulty extracting their leaders from existing roles in which responsibilities and demands are high. Exposure to the strategy planning process is a development tool widely heralded, but generally possible only with high levels of commitment from the top. Exposure to key executives can be a challenge as long as these key executives remain inaccessible.

However, when comparing results from 2000 to 2008 in all aspects of the survey, one overwhelming trend is that leadership development continues to become a high priority for organizations in all industries around the world. Senior commitment continues to increase, as well as engagement among target leaders. The sacrifice of committing one's time to personal development and the development of others becomes less and less unbearable, and it is safe to say that the hump that stands in the way of incorporating many of these growing methodologies will shrink.

Conclusion

When comparing 2008 survey data with data from eight years ago, promising trends emerge. First and foremost, it becomes clear that leadership development is gaining traction in the business world. CEOs and top executive teams dedicate more of their time to selecting and developing their best successors and high-potential populations; technology continues to become more accessible, allowing formal development to take place among virtual teams and throughout remote locations around the globe; vendors are becoming more competent and specialized, offering more solutions with greater customization at lower prices; and thought leaders continue to flood the leadership development space with new and innovative approaches that can easily be executed.

At the same time, practitioners are getting better at what they do. It can be seen from the data that they are becoming more selective of traditionally used models such as executive M.B.A. programs and accelerated promotion, and instead are focusing on tailored development methods that fit carefully selected competencies for their business and their leaders such as one-on-one coaching and individual development plans.

Among leadership competencies in the workplace, two categories stand out: strategic alignment and emotional intelligence. The corporate scandals of the late 1990s have had a great effect on the business world, causing companies to become more attuned with their unique and uncompromised value systems. Concurrently increasing competition has forced organizations to adopt carefully crafted strategies and focus on niche markets. Together these factors encourage leadership development to move in a direction that focuses on alignment and strategic capability: building the next generation of leaders with those who are home grown, devoted to the culture and values of their respective companies, and who have the broad strategic focus to lead their organizations toward new market opportunities.

At the same time, the focus on softer skills such as communication and relationship building shows a new perspective on leadership development. Practitioners have a clear line of sight to results that are less tangible and less measurable, such as improvements in charisma and emotional perception. Many see the leader of the future as the person who can craft a vision, communicate it effectively, and exude the trust and authenticity necessary to rally others to become invested in its completion.

Over the next decade, we anticipate a further rise in leadership development budgets. Much of this will undoubtedly be spent on technology, particularly given the rate at which organizations are switching their focus to the globally dispersed playing field. Use of 360-degree assessments and feedback will also continue to rise as younger generations of leadership talent come in with a greater desire to learn and develop themselves. Coaching efforts will see an increase. Vendors and global coaching networks will continue to expand and improve their offerings to provide the best partnership possible to their clients. Meanwhile, companies such as PepsiCo and HP lead the way in leaders-teaching-leaders approaches: maximizing the teaching capability of internal executives to create a sustainable and completely internal cycle of learning from one generation of leaders to the next. This will continue to evolve, and with it will be a further increase in the use of formal internal coaching efforts.

Finally, we anticipate a greater rise in the development of leaders at all levels, from senior leaders down to high-potential people, with unique attention given to the development of women and global leaders.

We have seen leadership development rise consistently over the years. New generations of employees come to work expecting their organizations to invest in their development, and at the same time organizations place more emphasis on the capability of high-performing leaders and leadership teams to stimulate growth. As the need for talent becomes greater and global competition becomes tighter, organizations will respond. We have already seen companies like General Electric and Procter & Gamble lead the way. More organizations will follow suit by developing efficient and sustainable systems for leadership development.

SOURCES

Ancona, D. G., Kochan, T. A., Scully, M., Van Maanen, J., and Westney, D. E. "Making Teams Work." In *Organizational Behavior and Processes.* Cincinnati: South-Western, 1999.

Anthony, S. D., Johnson, M. W., Sinfield, J. V., and Altman, E. J. *The Innovator's Guide to Growth: Putting Disruptive Innovation to Work.* Boston: Harvard Business School Press, 2008.

Babcock, L., and Laschever, S. *Women Don't Ask: The High Cost of Avoiding Negotiation—and Positive Strategies for Change.* New York: Bantam, 2007.

Babcock, L., Laschever, S., Gelfand, M., and Small, D. "Nice Girls Don't Ask." *Harvard Business Review,* Oct. 2003, pp. 14–15.

Barnard, C. *Functions of the Executive.* Cambridge, Mass.: Harvard Business School Press, 1935.

Baron, R. A. "Personality and Organizational Conflict: Effects of Type A Behavior and Self-Monitoring." *Organizational Behavior and Human Decision Processes,* 1989, *44,* 281–296.

Bennett, N., and Miles, S. *Riding Shotgun: The Role of the COO.* Stanford: Stanford University Press, 2006.

Bennis, W. *On Becoming a Leader.* London: Arrow, 1989.

Bernthal, P., and Wellins, R. S. *Leadership Forecast: 2003–2004.* Bridgeville, Pa.: Development Dimensions International, 2004.

Blanchard, K., and Hersey, P. *Management of Organizational Behavior: Utilizing Human Resources.* Upper Saddle River, N.J.: Prentice Hall, 1969.

Bolt, J. *Executive Development Trends 2000.* Kansas City, Mo.: Executive Development Associates, 2000.

Bolt, J. *Executive Development Trends 2004: Filling the Talent Gap.* Kansas City, Mo.: Executive Development Associates, 2004.

Bower, J. *The CEO Within: Why Inside Outsiders Are the Key to Succession Planning.* Boston: Harvard Business School Press, 2007.

Brescoll, V. L., and Uhlmann, E. L. "Status Conferral, Gender, and Expression of Emotion in the Workplace." *Psychological Science*, 2008, *19*(3), 268–275.

Brizendine, L. *The Female Brain*. New York: Broadway Books, 2006.

Buckingham, M. *Go Put Your Strengths to Work*. New York: Free Press, 2007.

Burns, J. M. *Leadership*. New York: HarperCollins, 1978.

Catalyst. "The Bottom Line: Connecting Corporate Performance and Gender Diversity." Catalyst, 2004.

Catalyst. "Census of Women Corporate Officers and Top Earners of the Fortune 500." Catalyst, 2007.

Charan, R., Drotter, S., and Noel, J. *The Leadership Pipeline: How to Build the Leadership Powered Company*. San Francisco: Jossey-Bass, 2001.

Chesbrough, H. *Open Innovation*. Boston: Harvard Business School Press, 2003.

Christensen, C. *The Innovator's Dilemma*. Boston.: Harvard Business School Press, 1997.

Collins, J. *Good to Great: Why Some Companies Make the Leap and Others Don't*. New York: HarperCollins, 2001.

Council, C. L. *Driving Performance and Retention Through Employee Engagement*. Washington, D.C.: Corporate Leadership Council/Corporate Executive Board, 2004.

Csikszentmihalyi, M. *Good Business*. New York: Viking Press, 2003.

Dodds, P., Muhamed, R., and Watts, D. "An Experimental Study of Search in Global Social Networks." *Science Magazine*, 2003, *301*, 827–829.

Dotlich, D., and Cairo, P. *Why CEOs Fail: The Eleven Behaviors That Can Derail Your Climb to the Top—and How to Manage Them*. San Francisco: Jossey-Bass, 2003.

Dotlich, D., Cairo, P., and Rhinesmith, S. *Head, Heart, and Guts: How the World's Best Companies Develop Complete Leaders*. San Francisco: Jossey-Bass, 2006.

Drath, W., and Palus, C. *Making Common Sense: Leadership as Meaning-Making in a Community of Practice*. Greensboro, N.C.: Center for Creative Leadership, 1994.

Eagly, A. H., and Carli, L. L. "Women and the Labyrinth of Leadership." *Harvard Business Review*, Sept. 2007, pp. 62–71.

Fiedler, F. E. *A Theory of Leadership Effectiveness*. New York: McGraw-Hill, 1967.

Fullerton Jr., H. J., and Toosi, M. "Labor Force Projections to 2010: Steady Growth and Changing Composition." *Monthly Labor Review*, Nov. 2001, *12*.

Fulmer, R. M. *Next Generation HR Practices*. Houston, Tex.: APQC, 2005.

Fulmer, R. M., and Conger, J. A. *Growing Your Company's Leaders: How Great Organizations Use Succession Management to Sustain Competitive Advantage*. New York: AMACOM, 2004.

Galinsky, E., Kropf, M. B., Harrington, B., and colleagues. *Leaders in a Global Economy: A Study of Executive Women and Men*. Boston: Families and Work Institute, Catalyst, and Boston College Center for Work and Family, 2003.

Gandossy, R., and Effron, M. *Leading the Way*. Hoboken, N.J.: John Wiley, 2003.

Gardner, J. W. *On Leadership*. New York: Free Press, 1990.

Gibb, C. A. "Leadership." In G. Lindzey (Ed.), *Handbook of Social Psychology*. Reading, Mass.: Addison-Wesley, 1954, pp. 877–917.

Giber, D., Carter, L., and Goldsmith, M. *Linkage Inc.'s Best Practices in Leadership Development Handbook*. San Francisco: Jossey-Bass/Pfeiffer, 2000.

Goldsmith, M., and Lyons, L. *Coaching for Leadership: The Practices of Leadership Coaching from the World's Greatest Coaches*. San Francisco: Jossey-Bass, 2006.

Goldsmith, M., and Morgan, H. "Leadership Is a Contact Sport: The Follow-Up Factor." *Strategy + Business*, 2004, *36*, 71–79.

Goleman, D. *Working with Emotional Intelligence*. New York: Bantam Books, 1998.

Gort, M., and Klepper, S. "Time Paths in the Diffusion of Product Innovations." *Economic Journal*, 1982, *92*, 630–653.

Granovetter, M. "The Strength of Weak Ties." *American Journal of Sociology*, 1973, *78*, 1360–1380.

Grint, K. *Leadership: Classical, Contemporary and Critical Approaches*. New York: Oxford University Press, 1997.

Gronn, P. "Distributed Leadership as a Unit of Analysis." *Leadership Quarterly*, 2002, *17*, 681.

Groysberg, B. "How Star Women Build Portable Skills." *Harvard Business Review*, Feb. 2008, pp. 74–81.

Hackman, J. R. *Leading Teams: Setting the Stage for Great Performances:* Harvard Business School Press, 2002.

Hale, J. "Strategic Rewards: Keeping Your Best Talent from Walking out the Door." *Compensation & Benefits Management*, 1998, *14*(3), 39–50.

Hanna, D. *Designing Organizations for High Performance*. Reading, Mass.: Addison-Wesley, 1992.

Heifetz, R. *Leadership Without Easy Answers*. Cambridge, Mass.: Belknap Press of Harvard University Press, 1994.

Heifetz, R. *Leadership Without Easy Answers*. Boston: Harvard University Press, 1998.

Held, D., and McGrew, A. *Globalization/Anti-Globalization*. Cambridge, Mass.: Polity Press, 2002.

Hofstede, G. *Culture's Consequences: International Differences in Work-Related Values*. Thousand Oaks, Calif.: Sage, 1980.

Hosking, D. M., and Morley, I. E. *The Skills of Leadership*. In J. G. Hunt, R. Baliga, P. Dachler, and C. Schriesheim (Eds.), *Emerging Leadership Vistas*. Lexington, Mass.: Lexington Press, 1988.

Huston, L., and Sakkab, N. "Connect and Develop: Inside Procter & Gamble's New Model for Innovation." *Harvard Business Review*, 2006, *84*, 58–66.

Innosight, LLC. *Mastering Transformation*. January 2008.

Jaques, E. *Requisite Organization: The CEO's Guide*. London: Cason and Hall, 1986.

Jaques, E., and Clement, S. *Executive Leadership*. London: Cason and Hall, 1991.

Jaques, E., and Clement, S. D. *Executive Leadership: A Practical Guide to Managing Complexity*. Oxford, U.K.: Wiley-Blackwell, 1994.

Jenkins, J. *LEADAsia*. Singapore: Center for Creative Leadership–Asia, 2006.

Katzenbach, J. R., and Smith, D. K. *The Wisdom of Teams*. New York: McGraw-Hill, 1993.

Kegan, R., and Lahey, L. "Adult Leadership and Adult Development: A Constructivist View." In B. Kellerman (ed.), *Leadership: Multidisciplinary Perspectives*. Upper Saddle River, N.J.: Prentice Hall, 1983.

Kirkpatrick, D. L. *Evaluating Training Programs: The Four Levels*. (3rd ed.) San Francisco: Berrett-Koehler, 2005.

Klepper, S., and Grady, E. "The Evolution of New Industries and the Determinants of Market Structure." *Rand Journal of Economics*, 1990, *21*(1), 27–44.

Kotter, J. *Leading Change*. Boston: Harvard Business School Press, 1996.

Kouzes, J., and Posner, B. *The Leadership Challenge*. San Francisco: Jossey-Bass, 2002.

Lencioni, P. *The Five Temptations of a CEO*. San Francisco: Jossey-Bass, 1998.

McGahan, A. M., and Silverman, B. S. "How Does Innovative Activity Change as Industries Mature?" *International Journal of Industrial Organization*, 2001, *19*(7), 1141–1160.

Menkes, J. *Executive Intelligence: What All Great Leaders Have*. New York: HarperCollins, 2005.

National Center for Education Statistics [NCES]. *Digest of Education Statistics.* Washington, D.C.: U.S. Department of Education, 2002.

Ortiz, A. "Executive Assessment for Succession Planning and Development: A Sequenced Process and a Few Helpful Hints." In J. Noel and D. Dotlich (Eds.), *The 2008 Pfeiffer Annual Leadership Development.* San Francisco: Jossey-Bass/Pfeiffer, 2008.

Palus, C., and Drath, W. *Making Common Sense: Leadership as Meaning-Making in a Community of Practice.* Greensboro, N.C.: Center for Creative Leadership, 1994.

Phillips, J. J. *Return on Investment in Training and Performance Improvement Programs.* (2nd ed.) Burlington, Mass.: Butterworth-Heinemann, 2003.

Rioux, S. M., and Bernthal, P. *Succession Management Practices.* Bridgeville, Pa.: Development Dimensions International, 2006.

Roberts, M. J., and Tempest, N. "ONSET Ventures." *Harvard Business School Case* 9–898–154, 1998.

Rooke, D., and Torbert, W. "Seven Transformations of Leadership." *Harvard Business Review,* Apr. 2005, pp. 1–11.

Salob, M., and Greenslade, S. *How the Top Twenty Companies Grow Great Leaders.* Lincolnshire, Ill.: Hewitt Associates, 2005.

Saslow, S. *Current Challenges in Leadership Development.* Palo Alto, Calif.: Institute of Executive Development, 2004a.

Saslow, S. *Leadership Development in European Organisations: Challenges and Best Practices.* Palo Alto, Calif.: Danish Leadership Institute and Institute of Executive Development, 2004b.

Schein, E. H. *Process Consultation.* Reading, Mass.: Addison-Wesley, 1988.

Shaw, R. *Trust in the Balance.* San Francisco: Jossey-Bass, 1997.

Smart, B. *Topgrading: How Leading Companies Win by Hiring, Coaching, and Keeping the Best People.* New York: Penguin Group, 2005.

Sobol, M., Harkins, P., and Conley, T. *Linkage Inc.'s Best Practices in Succession Planning: Case Studies, Research, Models, Tools.* San Francisco: Jossey-Bass, 2007.

Stacey, R. *Complex Responsive Processes on Organizations.* London: Routledge, 2001.

Stephenson, K. "What Knowledge Tears Apart, Networks Make Whole." *Internal Communication Focus,* 1998, *36.*

Stogdill, R. M. "Personal Factors Associated with Leadership: Survey of Literature." *Journal of Psychology,* 1948, *25,* 35–71.

Stuhlmacher, A., and Walters, A. "Gender Differences in Negotiation Outcome: A Meta-Analysis." *Personnel Psychology,* 1999, *52,* 653–677.

Sundstrom, E. *Supporting Work Team Effectiveness.* San Francisco: Jossey-Bass, 1999.

Trompenaars, F. *Riding the Waves of Culture.* London: Nicholas Brealey, 1993.

Trompenaars, F., and Hampden-Turner, C. *Managing People Across Cultures.* Chichester, U.K.: Capstone, 2004.

Van Beekum, S. "The Relational Consultant." *Transactional Analysis Journal,* 2006, *36*(4), 318–329.

Vancil, R. *Passing the Baton: Managing the Process of CEO Succession.* Boston: Harvard Business School Press, 1987.

Watkins, M. *The First 90 Days: Critical Success Strategies for New Leaders at All Levels.* Boston: Harvard Business School Press, 2003.

Watson, C., and Hofffman, L. R. "Managers as Negotiators: A Test of Power Versus Gender as Predictors of Feelings, Behavior, and Outcomes." *Leadership Quarterly,* 1996, pp. 63–85.

Watts, D. *Six Degrees: The Science of a Connected Age.* New York: Vintage, 2004.

Wellbourne, T. "Wall Street Reaction to Women in IPOs: An Examination of Gender Diversity in Top Management Teams." *Group and Organization Management,* 2007, *32,* 524.

Wellington, S., Kropf, M. B., and Gerkovich, P. R. "What's Holding Women Back." *Harvard Business Review,* 2003, *81*(6), 18–19.

Yates, M. *The 4E's Leadership Framework (MSc).* Paris: HEC, 2004.

INDEX

ABOUT THE EDITORS

David Giber is a senior vice president in charge of leadership development and consulting at Linkage Inc. with over twenty-five years of experience in organizational development, human resource management, leadership development, and executive coaching. Nationally known as a leader in his field, Giber helps transform companies into high-performing organizations by creating integrated human resource and leadership systems with measurable business impact. He has consulted with leaders from a wide variety of international corporations, universities, and other organizations on such issues as succession planning, management development, action learning, executive coaching, workforce assessment, and developing performance and selection systems. An experienced executive coach, he helps leaders achieve professional and personal success by focusing on both the hard business skills they need and personal development and leadership qualities. He has also used his expertise as a facilitator at many senior executive meetings and retreats, as well as international conferences. He helped design many of the Macy's leadership programs described in Chapter Thirteen in this book.

Giber has served in director-level positions in human resource management and leadership development for leading companies in the high-tech, financial services, and travel industries. He is an industrial/ organizational psychologist and received his B.A. degree from Stanford University and his Ph.D. from Duke University. He is the editor of two top-selling books in the field: *The Leadership Development Handbook and Best Practices in Organization* and *Human Resources Handbook*.

Giber's clients include Allergan, Brigham and Women's Hospital, LEGO, Levi Strauss, Macy's, Principal Financial Group, Sallie Mae, Schering Plough, Toyota, Varian Semiconductor, and Wyeth.

◆ ◆ ◆

Sam Lam is the president of Linkage Asia and one of Asia's top practitioners in the field of leadership development. His work focuses on the development of leadership competency models to support business growth and innovation, culture change, and top team effectiveness. In addition, he serves as executive coach and advisor to a number of notable CEOs and senior government officials in Singapore, Europe, and Asia.

Prior to his appointment at Linkage Asia, Lam was the managing consultant for Towers Perrin Singapore, where he led an office of top human resource practitioners in performance leadership, executive compensation, sales incentive design, and compensation, benefits, and talent management. Previously he was director of the HayGroup, where he spent five years leading major projects in leadership development, organizational improvement, and performance management.

His major clients include GlaxoSmithKline, Unilever, Prudential, CIMB Bank, and various branches of the Singapore government.

Lam graduated with a B.A. from the University of Southern California and has an M.A. from the National University of Singapore.

◆ ◆ ◆

Marshall Goldsmith is a coach to top executives in many of the world's leading companies, a prominent speaker and educator, and the well-known author of many books and articles on leadership. He is one of the foremost authorities on how to help leaders achieve positive, measurable changes in their own behavior and in the behavior of their people and teams. Goldsmith cofounded Marshall Goldsmith Partners, a network of top-level executive coaches.

Recently the American Management Association named Goldsmith one of fifty great thinkers and leaders who have influenced the field of management over the past eighty years, and *BusinessWeek* listed him as one of the most influential practitioners in the history of leadership development. He is a Fellow of the National Academy of Human Resources, America's top human resource honor. His work has been featured in a *New Yorker* profile, a *Harvard Business Review* interview, and a *Business Strategy Review* (London Business School) cover story. Major business press acknowledgments include *Wall Street Journal* ("one of the top ten executive educators"), *Forbes* ("one of five most-respected executive coaches"), *Economic Times* (India; "one of five *rajgurus* of America"); *Economist* (UK; "one of three most credible executive advisors in the new era of business), and *Fast Company* ("America's preeminent executive coach").

Goldsmith's Ph.D. is from the University of California, Los Angeles. He teaches executive education at Dartmouth's Tuck School and frequently speaks at leading business schools. His work has been recognized by almost every professional organization in his field. In 2006 Alliant International University honored him by naming its school of business and organizational studies the Marshall Goldsmith School of Management.

◆ ◆ ◆

Justin Bourke is a program manager at Linkage. In this role, he assumes design and delivery responsibility for two of Linkage's flagship leadership development programs, the Global Institute for Leadership Development and the Best Practices in Leadership Development Summit. During his tenure with Linkage, he has served in key leadership roles in the production of a number of recent publications, first as production head for *Linkage's Best Practices in Succession Planning* and later working with John Hammergren and Phil Harkins as research head and coauthor of *Skin in the Game: How Putting Yourself First Today Will Revolutionize Healthcare Tomorrow.*

Bourke graduated with a B.S. from the University of New Hampshire.

ABOUT LINKAGE INC.

Linkage Inc. is a global organizational development company that specializes in leadership development. We provide clients around the globe with integrated solutions that include strategic consulting services, customized leadership development and training experiences, tailored assessment services, and benchmark research. Linkage's mission is to connect high-performing leaders and organizations to the futures they want to create. With a relentless commitment to learning, Linkage offers conferences, learning summits, open-enrollment workshops, and distance learning programs on leading-edge topics in leadership, management, human resources, and organizational development. More than two hundred thousand leaders and managers have attended Linkage programs since 1988.

Linkage (http://www.linkageinc.com) is headquartered in Burlington, Massachusetts, with operations in Atlanta, Minneapolis, New York, San Francisco, and outside the United States in Athens, Brussels, Bucharest, Istanbul, Johannesburg, Seoul, Singapore, and Tokyo.